Midlothian Libraries

901207746   0

This book is to be returned on or before
the last date stamped below

2 4 SEP 1992

- 8 OCT 1992

D0835779

Crossing the Border:
Essays in Scottish Literature

Also by Edwin Morgan from Carcanet

Collected Poems
Poems of Thirty Years
Selected Poems
Themes on a Variation

EDWIN MORGAN

Crossing the Border

Essays on Scottish Literature

238873/820.809411

CARCANET

First published in Great Britain in 1990 by
Carcanet Press Limited
208–212 Corn Exchange Buildings
Manchester
M4 3BQ

Copyright © Edwin Morgan 1990
All rights reserved

British Library Cataloguing in Publication Data

Morgan, Edwin, *1920-*
  Crossing the border: essays in Scottish literature
  1. General essays in English
  I. Title
  082

  ISBN 0-85635-897-5

The publisher acknowledges financial assistance
from the Arts Council of Great Britain

Set in 10½ pt Bembo by Bryan Williamson, Darwen
Printed and bound in England by SRP Ltd, Exeter

Contents

Preface

This book contains twenty-two uncollected or unpublished essays on Scottish literary subjects, together with five reprinted from the out-of-print *Essays* of 1974 ('The Resources of Scotland', 'Dunbar and the Language of Poetry', 'The Poetry of Robert Louis Stevenson', 'MacDiarmid at Seventy-five', 'Edwin Muir'). I have resisted the temptation to rewrite, but have left the dates of the essays, as at least a pointer to the fact that interests, opinions, and styles can change. I have also not attempted to smooth out obvious differences of register between essays intended for formal publication and those delivered as talks.

Although this is a collection of occasional pieces and does not tell a continuous story, it seemed a good time to bring these writings together. Scottish literature is in a fairly vigorous state at the moment, and its concerns are so diverse, so little reducible to formula, that any attempt to backbone it with a tight concatenation of traditions would do it no service. A number of histories of Scottish literature such as were adumbrated in the essay 'Towards a Literary History of Scotland', written twenty years ago, have duly appeared, and have their obvious uses. It may also be useful to make a case for considered, though not for vacuous, heterogeneity.

To save space and leave a clean-cut text, quotations in Scots have not usually been glossed, but readers may be directed to the handy *Concise Scots Dictionary* (ed. Mairi Robinson, Aberdeen University Press), or of course to the richer resources of the *Scottish National Dictionary* and the *Dictionary of the Older Scottish Tongue*.

E.M.
May 1990

Towards a Literary History of Scotland

'The book is not addressed to those who have arrived at full knowledge of the subject without knowing the facts.' Ezra Pound's sardonic little prefatory note to *ABC of Reading* might serve as a good motto for a good history of literature, though it could also be used to bolster up a dull one. Whatever literary history is, it must on one level be concerned to find out and record the facts of the case. When Burns, in his long autobiographical letter to Dr Moore, tells how 'meeting with Fergusson's Scotch Poems, I strung anew my wildly-sounding, rustic lyre with emulating vigour', he is giving us a morsel of literary history which lets us know, if we did not know from internal evidence in the poetry, that 'Fergusson's Scotch Poems' burst crucially on him (crucially because emotionally, because urging him towards 'emulation') at a time when the main poetic influences in his reading (despite his knowledge of Allan Ramsay and other Scottish writers) had been the English-language poets from Shakespeare to Pope, Thomson, and Shenstone. From this, the literary historian goes on to trace the exact influence of Fergusson on Burns and tries to establish the literary relationship between the two. This in turn may suggest wider reflections on Burns's 'rustic lyre' and Fergusson's mainly urban one, or between the west and the east of Lowland Scotland (R.L. Stevenson, one remembers, loved the Edinburgh poet but always felt the Ayrshire poet to be a bit of an alien). Into all this, the literary historian's sensibility and judgement will of course have to enter, but on the back of the facts.

A less obvious reference by a more allusive author still has to be followed up in much the same way. When Milton at the beginning of *Paradise Lost* tells us that he means to pursue, and with no mediocre flight either, 'things unattempted yet in Prose or Rhime', he is throwing out the bait of an in-joke for literary historians and multilingual aficionados of epic who will recognize the line as a translation from *Orlando Furioso*, where Ariosto had made the same boast before him. So Milton is really saying (a) I have read my Ariosto, but (b) I am a better poet than Ariosto, but (c) you, dear reader, will not understand my aims unless you too know something about Ariosto and about the whole chain of epic tradition in which I am the latest link. This means that the literary historian has to work out not only what the 'things unattempted' are (and this is not so straightforward as it might seem) but also what exactly Milton's position is in the centuries-old international genre of epic. But suppose we say – despite the grandeur of the theme and the fame of the author – that this is unimportant, that literary history has better things to do than to establish facts about the priority and development of ideas about epic? In the book by Ezra Pound already referred to, which could be described as an attempt to rewrite the literary history of English poetry, Milton does not even appear at all in the new sequence of recommended and significant poets. Neither does Spenser, Wordsworth, or Tennyson. But we do find Chaucer, Gavin Douglas, Rochester, Crabbe, and Browning. And however eccentric the result may seem, Pound presents a coherent and pithy case for the new set of co-ordinates he intends to lay on the history of poetry. Facts are still important, but it is as if he was trying to discover an entirely fresh clutch of facts, and casting out, in the process, a huge burden of existing facts which he saw as irrelevant or even harmful. But if facts can be harmful, are we then in a post-literary-history era?

Much evidence suggests that we are. F.R. Leavis would scarcely consider himself to be anti-historical, but he followed Pound in insisting on the importance of 'revaluation', and revaluation in practice involved a ruthless relegating of all writers not considered central to a defined tradition. A didactic and proselytizing passion in men like Pound and Leavis simply had no time for the faceless blandness of belletristic pieties and open-arms policies, and Leavis's scornful parenthesis '(Are not they all in the literary histories?)' when he is dismissing such minor Victorian novelists as 'Trollope, Charlotte Yonge, Mrs Gaskell, Wilkie Collins, Charles Reade, Charles and Henry Kingsley, Marryat, Shorthouse' from serious consideration in *The Great Tradition*, shows the typical downgrading of literary history which a trenchantly revived modern literary criticism has forced us to take note of. The result of this is that if you have D.H. Lawrence, you don't speak about Wells and Bennett and Galsworthy at all. If you absolutely cannot avoid including Spenser or Shelley, you hold him up with pained tongs. If this strenuous, bracing field of operations is regarded as complementary – '(Are not they all in the literary histories?)' – then all is well, or at least could be argued to be well, but if, as in Scotland, the basic literary history in any full contemporary scholarly sense is just not there, then we are caught in an unhappy dilemma. However unfashionable it may be, we have to write our literary history first. But being aware of the objections that have been raised to histories of literature, and knowing that most so-called histories of literature today are merely loose collections of essays by divers hands (for instance the *Sphere History of Literature in the English Language*, which for all its proposed eleven volumes can nonchalantly omit, in the twentieth-century volume, the key-name of F.S. Flint from its historical account of Imagism, and have no reference at all to distinctive but offbeat writers like Charles Doughty, Robert Tressell, Mary Webb, Lewis Grassic Gibbon, Mervyn Peake, Olaf Stapledon, and Henry Williamson), we may be encouraged to feel a double inhibition – not wanting to inflict our own fushionless shoal of minor names on a world grown impatient of nimiety, yet sensing that to write literary history at all it will be necessary to swim against the strong current represented by the *Sphere History* and the *Pelican Guide*. To do a 'J.H. Millar Seventy Years After' would clearly not meet the case. Remarkable though *A Literary History of Scotland* was when it appeared in 1903, we need something on a larger scale, and something which will take into much greater account the social and historical background of the different periods. Kurt Wittig's *The Scottish Tradition in Literature* is, as its title suggests, not comprehensive enough to be a literary history, and although lucid and amiable, is too much concerned to force a pattern of national characteristics rather than to let the varied evidence speak. The *Scrutiny*-inspired insights (and corresponding limitations) of John Speirs' *The Scots Literary Tradition* are well-known, but the scope of these essays leaves them as no more than useful exploratory diggings into their subject. Useful also, but of course dealing with only one of the literary forms, is the *Scottish Poetry: A Critical Survey* edited by James Kinsley. Another partial covering of the ground is David Craig's refreshingly non-parochial, well-documented, yet at times rather wilfully unsympathetic *Scottish Literature and the Scottish People 1680-1830*, where a mixture of Leavis and Marx that might seem to be unholy has worked in fact surprisingly well to produce a serious study of an important period in Scottish life and writing.

All things considered, a literary history of Scotland on a reasonably generous scale seems called for. Without subscribing, I hope,
to a multitudinously name-dropping, Concord-and-Walden-
haunted Van-Wyck-Brooksism, we have the duty to ourselves
to do what the Americans have done: to map out, as part of their
own nationhood, what their literary history means to them, even
at the risk of boring sophisticates with over-enthusiastic esti-
mates of Fenimore Cooper or Cotton Mather. In the present
climate of revived interest in Scottish literary studies, it seems
more than ever necessary that we should look freshly at minor
as well as major figures, from whatever period, as well as fill in
the gaps we are painfully aware of in periods of literary history
such as the seventeenth and nineteenth centuries where topics
and individuals equally clamour for scholarly, but imaginatively
scholarly, attention. I say 'imaginatively' because value-judgements
and rescue-operations are just as necessary as investigation of
influences or establishment of texts. It is no use shying off from
Macpherson's Ossian and Henry Mackenzie as if they were
beneath serious concern. The history of drama in Scotland may
be the blank it seems to be, and then again it may not; the fact
is that until a complete history of it is written we are talking
about it from insufficient knowledge. Does the vigorous Scotch
dialogue of Joanna Baillie's *Witchcraft* redeem its melodramatic
mechanics? Is Archibald Pitcairne's *The Assembly* too narrowly
sectarian in its satire or does it lift into true comedy? Do poems
like 'Helenore', 'The Siller Gun', and 'The Luggie' thoroughly
deserve the oblivion that has overtaken them? Perhaps they do;
but again, we want to know more about them, about their place
in literary history, about their authors, about any relevance they
may have gained to balance what they have lost. So much of
Scottish literature exists in a ghostly limbo of non-discussion
that we must surely consider ourselves to be ready to take the
various risks associated with an overhaul. D.M. Moir in his
Sketches of the Poetical Literature of the Past Half-Century (1851)
said of religious poetry:

> The most sublime poetry, by far, to which the world has ever
> listened, is that of the Hebrew... All is simply grand, nakedly
> sublime; and man before his Maker, even in the act of adora-
> tion, is there made to put his lips in the dust. So have done
> the great bards of succeeding times, Milton, and Young, and
> Thomson, and Cowper, and Pollok.

'And Pollok.' And Ozymandias, King of Kings. It is hard to imagine any revolution in taste which would reinstate the author of *The Course of Time*, renowned though he was, and well beyond Ballagioch. Yet Moir's four pages on Pollok tell us something about the temper of the times which is no longer accessible to J.H. Millar writing his history fifty years later, and still less to us. Conversely, J.H. Millar was able to express a contemptuous attitude to kailyard, as a recent phenomenon of excess, but the passage of time has now made his contempt seem excessive, and any dismissal of kailyard in need of qualification from a number of important points of view. Hazards abound, but each generation should have the courage to stamp its judgements and speculations on the age as well as its creative achievements. The case for a history of Scottish literature may have to be made with an air of being out of phase with critical developments against such histories, and be hedged round with warning notices of every description, to say nothing of snide remarks about the brontosaurus stirring again, but provided the project is not allowed to develop such overbearing proportions that it topples into absurdity, it seems an idea that has much to be said for it at this time.

Scottish Literary News, vol.1 no.2, January 1971.

Scottish Poetry in English

Scottish poetry may be thought to be particularly lucky, or particularly unlucky, according to the point of view, in that it presents its riches to the reader in three languages, Gaelic, Scots and English – and if one wants to be thoroughly historical, in Latin and Welsh as well, to say nothing of such reminders of the Auld Alliance as the sixteenth-century William Fowler's

> Prest pour m'eloigner from this monde, madame,
> I leave my sins to it, to heavens mon ame,
> my sight aux vents, mes pleurs unto the seas,
> my flames to feu, mes gazings unto your ees,
> mon cœur to yours, avec his chaud affections,
> both bred and buried be your rare perfections.

Although the question of a national language cannot be brushed aside, and there are still recurrent language riots in many parts of the world to drive home the point, each country has its own situation and true parallels are hard to draw. If Gaelic, Scots, and English had all continued, under a different set of historical circumstances, to grow and develop side by side in Scotland, as French, German, and Italian have done in Switzerland, this would seem on the face of it to be a healthier fate than what we have actually undergone, with our dislocated, atrophied, rejuvenated and endlessly tinkered-with language-systems; yet for all the linguistic untidiness we inherit, we cannot sense any literary inferiority to Switzerland – rather the reverse, indeed. It may be that an awareness of the continuously shifting potentialities and admixtures of a varied and unsettled language situation can stimulate the art of writing in individual cases, even while at the same time it makes steady development within any literary genre more difficult than it ought to be. A fair corollary of finding some virtue in the ramshackle tabernacle of our language-systems would be that we should burnish the several treasures kept therein and exert ourselves to make sure they are in good order. If Gaelic is dying, people are still writing very good poetry in it; therefore they must continue to write poetry in it, including poetry which will stretch and test the language. If Scots is a case of arrested development, yet still alive and kicking in its own (sometimes misunderstood) ways, in both speech and writing, then poets are not going to stop trying to find out what it can still be used to express, including things it might not seem able to express. If English came last on the scene and was often poorly used in the past, there is absolutely no reason for poets now, in the twentieth century, not to employ and extend its resources with confidence and flair. From Edwin Muir to W.S. Graham, and including MacDiarmid himself, the evidence this century became clear that a Scottish poet could produce work of quality in English.

It was not always so. In the period just before and after the Union of the Crowns in 1603, when Scots poets were faced with the invidious trauma of anglicizing the language of their poetry, whether or not they followed the Court from Edinburgh to London, every kind of Scots, Anglo-Scots, Scoto-English, and English makes its appearance. In so far as this weakened the use of Scots for serious or elevated poetry, it was a thoroughly bad situation, from which it took the remnants of the Scottish language a long time to recover; yet this period also marks, for the Scottish writer, the beginning of the new expressive possibilities of English, which were to prove eventually, even to the most nationalist-minded and sceptical, a source of power not divorced from national aspiration. William Fowler, whom I quoted earlier, wrote in everything from a very pure Scots to a shaky but determined near-English, with macaronic verse in at least seven languages thrown in by the way. His more distinguished nephew, William Drummond of Hawthornden, was the first Scottish poet who can be said to have mastered a convincing and pleasing English style. Does the strain show? Ben Jonson thought it did, when he said Drummond's poems were 'all good... save that they smelled too much of the Schools'. What Jonson did not perhaps realize is how Scottish Drummond still was. In the manuscripts of his poems the old Scots words lurk unchanged: *thole* and *syne*, *lauch* and *tane*, *sal* and *suld*, *brocht* and *nocht*, *brunt* and *hereefter*.

One of Fowler's sonnets begins 'I pistomrise he is sogonimate...' which would have appealed to Hugh MacDiarmid, and also, I suspect, to the James Thomson of *The Seasons*, to the

Robert Fergusson who wrote 'To Dr Samuel Johnson: Food for a new Edition of his Dictionary' (a poem relishing what it ostensibly satirizes), to the word-collecting John Davidson of the 'Testaments and Tragedies' – and not least to the Sir James Murray who, as a Scottish lexicographer, enjoyed the irony of editing the *Oxford English Dictionary*. If an interest in language itself is, as I have suggested, no surprising part of the Scottish poet's makeup, whether it shows as the aureate diction or 'fouth of language' of the medieval makars or (later) as an excited discovery of the vast resources of English or (at all periods) in a fondness for translating poets from other tongues, it is something which may have both encouraged and held back the emergence of a good English poetry in Scotland. Such poetry no doubt had to flex its muscles in a number of ways – had to prove it *had* muscles! – and a salient, interesting, but at times pedantic or prideful English lexis was down payment for what might become a more natural or easygoing occupation of the language as it was used more often and by more poets. The modester touches of a Stevenson, an Andrew Young, a Norman Cameron, a Hamish Maclaren, clearly had their place. If poetry in English has now established itself in a wide range of poets – and in the MacCaig/Scott *Contemporary Scottish Voice* anthology, which is generally representative and includes Gaelic poetry too, well over half the contributors are mainly English-writing – and if the Calvinist conscience does not make one too wary of assuming that anything under the sun will last, it looks as if more attention than has so far been paid should be directed into the problems, hopes, aims, and fears of this poetry. There is no history of it; there is no anthology of it; yet it is what most people write. We have justifiably, in the recent past, laid stress on those writers who have concentrated on the revival and expansion of Scots, and perhaps we now look round, with some uneasiness, at a large, different, more elusive territory, where we rub shoulders with Americans, and Australians, and West Indians, and Irishmen – the 'English' language(s).

Books in Scotland no.3, Winter 1978-79.

The Resources of Scotland

An old pot seething with dissatisfaction which fortunately can be relied on never to come to the boil might be the English politician's view of Scotland. Something of the same irritability, allied to a similar short-circuiting of full power, has often been felt in the past to characterize the Scottish literary scene. The egg cracks, and out steps Vociferous Fissiparous, son of Antisyzygy. The Pictish succession is assured. But there are signs of change, signs of a dissolving of this stereotype, which have been emerging gradually in the past three or four years.

No one could say that a spirit of sweet cooperation has descended on Scotland, but there is evidence that the old polarities do not command the devotion they did. Many writers (and educators and others) have clearly decided that some approach to a concerted effort is both possible and opportune, not only as a rescue operation for Scottish writing of the past (including the recent past) which is neglected or out of print but also as a positive encouragement of contemporary writing through information and discussion. The Association for Scottish Literary Studies, the Lallans Society, Comunn na Cànain Albannaich (the Scottish Language Society), and Club Leabhar (the Highland Book Club) are all recently formed organizations which may have a diversity of aim but which taken together are beginning to plot out, show, recommend and develop the whole literary culture of Scotland.

'Literary culture of Scotland' is a desperately plastic phrase for what people actually feel, write, read, speak, sing, and act, and obviously the literature of any place will remain to some extent as unamenable to encouragement as to polemic or apathy. You can't help Sholokhov; you can't hinder Solzhenitsyn. Yet the bristly, defensive divisiveness of so much Scottish culture, however well-rooted it has been in real differences and real difficulties, has had a long innings and not always a very productive one, and we might well give its opposite a chance.

The feeling that accompanies these remarks – and I know that others share it – is rather like the end of Philip Larkin's 'The Whitsun Weddings', a sense of disparate things coming together and (because they are brought together) being released towards a destination. Those who share the feeling would not always agree as to whether the destination is the recovery of a national self-respect (a *natural* self-respect – a national self-*credibility*, for God's sake!) or something that in the end can only be political, whether devolution or independence. Political in the widest sense it already is, if anything that earnestly concerns the cultural health of a nation is political – and Tom Scott's long, gritty social meditation 'Auld Sanct-Aundraeans: Brand Soliloquises' is neither more nor less so concerned than Ian Hamilton Finlay's 'The Olsen Excerpts' with its punning double tribute to the Scottish fishing industry and to Charles Olson and the genius loci. Between two such extremes of literary expression (and Tom Scott would no doubt deny that 'The Olsen Excerpts' is even literary) there is scant hobnobbing, yet someone like Ezra Pound would understand both, and how both can be related to the needs of a time and a place.

But the pressure towards something that would be political in the narrower sense is also undeniably present in the general movement I have been outlining. There is not only a very widespread feeling that some sort of devolution is necessary, but there is also, now, the awareness that the constitutional changes which must take place in Ireland, and even in the United Kingdom itself as a result of entry into the Common Market, give the first opportunity for hundreds of years of rethinking the whole constitutional situation. It is significant that when *Lines Review* 37 (June 1971) was given over completely to an anti-nationalist essay, 'The Knitted Claymore', by the poet Alan Jackson, this proved to be rather a damp squib. Those who were attacked replied; but there was no great debate, as there would have been ten years ago. This is not to say that the essay was not useful in launching a few sprightly darts at the uglier, knuckle-rapping, xenophobic side of nationalism (which of course is not peculiar to Scotland), but Alan Jackson pushed his case too far until it began to topple over, and it was indeed virtually contradicted by some of his own passing parentheses (since he is an honest man). The main effect revealed by the essay, however, was that writers as a whole were no longer eager to join in the false fray of a flyting since flyting is an art form and not a true agent of change, for all its appearance of violent involvement.

So although it would obviously be untrue to say that 'we are all nationalists now', there is nevertheless something approaching a consensus among Scottish writers that what is being produced here – forgetting all the older and perhaps threadbare definitions of 'Scottish' – has some value and is worth encouraging, especially by writers being willing to stay and work in their own country. But what guarantee have we got that what we are doing is distinctive and could not have been produced anywhere else?

The mature answer would be that there is no such guarantee and that it does not matter: Scottish writers must simply write as well as they can, and leave it to others to decide whether their provenance stands out, and what value it infuses into their work. Unfortunately Scotland is not in a mature state, and that mature answer would still be something of a luxury. So long as the political situation remains unhappy, the economic situation unhappier, and the language situation as complex and confused as it is, a Scottish writer will tend to be tugged, kicking against the pricks as hard as he likes, into at least the but if not the ben of involvement with the whole north-of-the-border ethos problem. Here, bad vibrations abound for many. What – do your own thing, in Scotland?

> inner attractional
> somebody says death
> and they all come rushing
> home to agree and look stern and solemn:
> enter fourteen editors with analysis kits.

(Tom McGrath, 'Nicotine Withdrawal' Psychotic Rage Poem)

And how to relate yourself to traditions that may seem more like locks than keys?

> let us exorcise
> the old god of Scotland
> with his knotted brain and jellyfish eyes
> who has tormented his children
> from generation unto generation

> (Tom Buchan, 'Exorcism')

And history? What use is history? Is history not the opium of the imagination?

(Eastward
Culloden
where the sun shone
on the feeding raven.
Let it be forgotten!)
(Iain Crichton Smith, 'The White Air of March')

These quotations may suggest that the contemporary Scottish writer often finds himself saying: Redefine my task; redefine my field of operations; redefine my country.

To a Highlander like Iain Crichton Smith, bilingual in Gaelic and English, and prolific in poetry, novels, short stories, plays, essays and reviews, the problem of definition must always be particularly acute because the national aspirations of (mainly) Lowland Scotland can scarcely be his, because his 'country' is not only Oban and Lewis but a country of the mind that stretches from Robert Lowell to Kafka and Dostoevsky, and because his first language, Gaelic, is so obviously in a state of decline that to attempt to extend and modernize its expressive potential (as he has done – and been blamed for it by conservative Gaels) can only seem a paradoxical activity. In one of his Gaelic poems he speaks of himself in the image of a court jester, dressed in motley – 'Beurl' is Gàidhlig, dubh is dearg' (English and Gaelic, black and red) – and fears that in the rainstorms of his anxiety the two colours will run into one and become indistinct and muddy. Yet, although his Gaelic is freely peppered with English words, both in order to produce special effects and also (as he admits) for experiment's sake, he is clear in his mind that such things have to be done and tried, whatever hope or lack of hope there may be for the future of the tongue. As he points out, Gaelic and English are in entirely dissimilar situations, each of which offers its special challenge to a creative writer: 'So much has *not* been done in Gaelic that confronted by such a huge uncharted waste one is tempted to spread one's energies, and to try new things. So much in English has already been done that the situation is different.'

Gaelic poetry, then, not only survives but survives strongly, in the work of Iain Crichton Smith, Derick Thomson, George Campbell Hay, Donald MacAulay, and above all, Sorley Maclean. But as Colm Brogan has remarked, 'It is no good trying to be the Proust of the Hebrides.' The Gaels have never taken to the novel as a literary form and there are few serious examples of it. Nor is there any Gaelic professional theatre, though many plays have been written for the amateur stage, and Gaelic drama has been produced on television, played somewhat stiltedly by amateur actors. Poetry and song can be trusted to survive under the most adverse conditions, and it is the meagre development of the other forms that shows the relative weakness of the Gaelic cultural position on any over-all view.

Gaelic writers themselves are not given to making optimistic pronouncements about the future of the language, and the prospect of its ever becoming the national tongue of Scotland is even more remote than that of its sister-languages in Ireland and Wales. Comunn na Cànain Albannaich, founded in 1969, is devoted precisely to the implementation of that remote end, and this organization has the brave slogan 'Tìr gun chànain, tìr gun anam' (The country without a language is a country without a soul). But what is Scotland's language? Most people would regard the Society's title, Scottish Language Society, as a somewhat high-handed appropriation, since Gaelic looms less large in the Scottish consciousness than Welsh does in Wales. The 'Scottish Language', for most Scots who think about the matter, is primarily Lowland Scots, or Scots, or Lallans – it is best called Scots. The Lallans Society, established in 1972, would have called itself the Scots Language Society but for the naughty pre-emption of Comunn na Cànain Albannaich. There is obviously a place for both groups, however, and they could even draw together in a growing climate of opinion that favours de-Londonization as a general aim.

One of the chief objects of the Lallans Society is 'to foster and promote the emergence of Lallans as a language'. This'll no gang faur furrit till mair an mair fowk – educatit fowk anaa – kin be persuadit tae *yaise* the leid an no fin it lauchable tae dae sae. Gin ye're lauchin owre whit's prentit here thenoo, I'se tak ye tae the Race Relations Board, ma mannie, an nae boather. The trouble is that 'Scots' is itself a far from monolithic term, ranging in applicability from the Scotch English that is mainly a matter of accent plus the occasional 'scunner' or 'outwith', to the varieties of urban and rural Scots which at their raciest (Glasgow, say, or Aberdeenshire) depend on quite a thick complex of non-English speech-habits.

All of these are available to, though underexploited by, the Scottish writer, for both verse and prose. The Scottish writer's dilemma today is that while he might want to keep helping a

general literary Scots to develop, whether in the eclectic or
'Synthetic Scots' tradition of Hugh MacDiarmid or in some other
way, he is on the other hand strongly urged, by the movement
towards not only a spoken poetry (if he happens to be a poet or
perhaps a playwright) but also a 'sincerity' theory of artistic
expression (whether in verse or prose), to write on a basis of the
actual language of men. On the whole, the second alternative is
in the ascendant among younger poets using Scots (e.g., Donald
Campbell and Duncan Glen) or more specifically an urban dialect
(Stephen Mulrine, Tom Leonard). Novelists, possibly frustrated
by their London publishers who are afraid that glo'al stopes, or
even bus-stopes, might reduce sales, are disappointingly smooth
and untruthful in their dialogue these days, with very few excep-
tions; it is high time they reasserted the ear and the tongue. The
Glasgow speech in short stories by Alan Spence shows a nice
awareness of what is wanted.

There is also a great deadlock to be broken in the theatre,
where directors and managements seem to be hypnotized rigid
by the polarity of Received Standard versus Costume Scots –
neither of which any Scotsman actually speaks. Only rarely do
Scottish theatre audiences hear that modest and unforced reflection of their own living speech-habits which an English or American audience takes for granted. Revivals of Bridie; C.P. Taylor's
Bread and Butter; Stewart Conn's *I Didn't Always Live Here*; Bill
Bryden's *Willie Rough*; recent plays by Joan Ure and Alasdair
Gray; and that's about the list. The small and still struggling
Stage Company (Scotland) has been formed to encourage the
writing and performing of such plays, and this is a hopeful sign,
though it remains to be seen what real impact the company will
make. Naturalism is no panacea, and in any case television to
some extent takes care of it, but it would be good to have at least
one theatre which was devoted to exhibiting and exploring the
actual state of life in Scotland. At the same time, an honest
observer has to admit that such an alien and unScottish theatre
as the Glasgow Citizens' has become under Giles Havergal also
has a useful function, a function recognized by its enthusiastic
and often young audience, despite unrelenting rifle-fire from
Scottish critics. What could be more incongruous than a company
who eschew Scottish plays and Scottish actors developing a stun-
ningly physical, spectacular, antiverbocentric, and markedly
transvestite theatre on an island of the crumbling half-demolished
Gorbals? Stuffy old uptight heterosexual Scotland may not take

kindly yet to the gestures of a male Cleopatra, riggish as they come, but disguise and transformation and the use of the body are what theatre is about, and the Scots have been apt to forget this, in their strongly literalized and often literal-minded ways of thinking. The very incongruity of the Citizens' is dialectically productive – and highly suited to Glasgow, that incongruous place.

But suppose we strip away the props, the local speech, the language societies, the desideria. What minimum exists that would make us say, This is a Scottish, and not an English or 'British' writer? Subject-matter or thematic interest would give us an answer in many cases: George Mackay Brown's Orkney, though stylized, is still Orkney: the Edinburgh of Sydney Goodsir Smith and Robert Garioch, and the Aberdeen of Alexander Scott, come through strongly as places, even if satirized or fantasticated; the Glasgow of Archie Hind or of Cliff Hanley has not been imagined or got up; the brooding intensity with which 'the matter of Scotland' is treated in Fionn MacColla could only come from a ruthless identification with one place, one country. But is Norman MacCaig's 'Culag Pier' really about Culag Pier? Is the sharp-clawed creator of Miss Jean Brodie, a writer quoted as claiming that she must remain an expatriate Scot since she 'could not hope to be understood' in Edinburgh, a Scottish novelist? Is Sheila MacLeod (ex-Stornoway) or Campbell Black (ex-Glasgow) a Scottish novelist? The strict answer to these questions can only be an unsatisfactory 'yes and no', since life and the pursuit of literature are not tidy and docketable.

But it is a matter of contexts. Within Scotland at the present time, with the desire to gather together rather than to disperse, and with the consciousness of a common effort being at last not utterly inconceivable, the inclusiveness of 'yes' – whatever the risk of accusations of chauvinism – would be preferred to the pedantry of 'no'. The ongoing bibliography of current Scottish writing published in the extremely useful and (one is ashamed to say it) pioneering *Scottish Literary News* (the newsletter of the Association for Scottish Literary Studies) makes no apology for including all items emanating from Scottish hands, so that Chaim Bermant and Flashman rub shoulders with Helen Cruickshank's *Collected Poems* and Sorley Maclean's *Poems to Eimhir*.

And this is as it should be, it is impossible not to add. There comes a time when out of respect for itself a country must collect its resources, and look at its assets and shortcomings with an eye that is both sharp and warm: see what is there, what is not there, what could be there. Perilously, without any political underpinning yet, Scotland is now consciously at that stage, and that is mainly what I as both observer and participator have wanted to write about here, rather than draw out a painful and familiar filigree of the 'Scottish qualities' of X's novel or Y's poem or Z's play. We can hope that, having taken certain almost tacit decisions with Scotland, we are now getting on with the job.

The Times Literary Supplement, 28 July 1972.

Flyting

Flyting is a curious subject, with a long history, still going on, but there's quite a lot we don't know about it, so we shall have to indulge in some speculation as well as give facts and examples. *The Concise Scots Dictionary* provides at least a nice concise definition of flyting: 'a contest between poets in mutual abuse'. Nothing about humour, you will notice (the subject of today's conference); but we shall see. Well, that's a literary definition, but the words *flyte* and *flyting* are used in a much wider context than the literary. To flyte with someone or to have a flyting with someone is to engage in some kind of dispute or row, preferably in public, so that everyone can enjoy it. Not that it is or was always enjoyable. In medieval Scotland there were laws against public flyting or scolding, especially if defamation of character was involved, and lots of women had the nasty punishment of being put in the branks (an iron bridle and gag) or the jougs (an iron collar attached to a post) to keep them quiet. So flyting, in the sense of a public altercation, had its perils. We may note, in passing, that there are surviving relics of this public flyting, or were until very recently, in rituals like the Glasgow sherricking, where (in the proper use of the term, i.e. not merely in a domestic 'scene') one character publicly taunts and challenges and shows up another, with an audience gathered round, usually in the street. A famous example occurs in Alexander McArthur's novel *No Mean City*, in the chapter called 'The Sherricking of the King', where the hero Johnnie Stark, the Razor King, is sherricked by Mary Hay, the girl he's made pregnant but refuses to have anything more to do with – it's both serious and yet ritualistic – the girl puts on her best clothes, even though it's going to involve physical violence as well as verbal abuse – and the audience make it into a kind of street theatre, they're described as 'waiting for the sherricking, thrilled, curious, eager, callous, not caring what came of it, greedy of sensation for its own sake' – she butts him, he punches and kicks her, he wins the encounter, but her honour is satisfied.

But going back to the literary associations of flyte and flyting: the word flyting comes from the Anglo-Saxon verb *flitan*, to dispute, to contend, to quarrel. It had lots of derivatives, and two of these are of particular interest to us: *flitcraeft* meant dialectics, the craft of disputing or arguing. And *flitgliw* meant mockery, literally the glee of flyting, the game or sport of disputing with someone. Hence (1) an intellectual connection and (2) an entertainment connection. So the Anglo-Saxons knew about flyting, and there's an instance in the epic poem *Beowulf*. When Beowulf, the hero of the poem, arrives at the court of the Danes to help the Danish king to get rid of the monstrous enemy Grendel, he is taunted and challenged by Unferth, the king's spokesman, a witty, satirical man who is a sort of court poet and who is jealous of the incomer Beowulf: Beowulf answers him, equally sharply, tells him he's been drinking too much beer, defends himself and attacks Unferth in turn (not much of a fighter, though 'you did kill your own brother' – ouch). So flyting, if we want to trace it back, is Anglo-Saxon (or Germanic), but it's also, and even more so, Celtic and Old Norse. People have tried to find influences from French and Provençal and Italian poetry – perhaps so – but I think in the main it's a northern thing, north European rather than south. The medieval Welsh and Irish poets loved nothing better than a good flyting, and were experts in satire, so it wouldn't be surprising if the Scottish writers learned something from these Gaelic and Welsh traditions. Kenneth Jackson's *A Celtic Miscellany* (1971) quotes a fifteenth-century Scottish-Irish poem, 'Maguire and MacDermot':

> There are two chiefs in the land of Ireland, the one mere dregs, the other a choice man of slender fingers; an old outlandish starveling cripple and a bountiful man of noble lineage.

> It is not wrong to compare them, a rod of alder and a rod of yew, a stick of twisted alder wood and my many very generous timber.

> The beggarly tainted chief of Ulster and the brave king of Connaught, the bright liberal merry lad and the stingy grudging man.

> MacDermot of Moylurg and Maguire the refractory; it is justice gone askew to compare them, meagre rye beside wheat.

Tomaltach deals in pure feats of valour, Tomás in vice and arrogance; his paws are always in the scales, so that half my poems have rotted away.

It is not right to set side by side the warrior and the refuse of the hosting; the stinking-gummed half-blind oaf, ah me! and the warrior of the strong sword-blade and the many retainers . . .

That poem was written in Scotland in Irish Gaelic. The Irish in particular were thought to have an almost magical power in their command of satire and invective, and the professional poets, or bards, were feared because of this. This was an understandable fear, since the bards were historians as well as entertainers, their words would last long after they were dead, a generous brave prince or king would have a good reputation, a stingy cowardly one would also not be forgotten. It was widely believed that there was a mysterious power in the words of a poet, that it was not advisable to get on the wrong side of one. You could suffer physically, just as if someone were sticking pins in an image of you. There's an example of this belief, the belief that in fact you could be 'rhymed to death', in Ben Jonson's play *The Poetaster*, where the 'Author', speaking in blank verse near the end, wonders if he should try to get the better of his critics by lampooning them:

> They know I dare
> To spurn or baffle them, or squirt their eyes
> With ink or urine; or I could do worse,
> Armed with Archilochus' fury, write iambics,
> Should make the desperate lashers hang themselves,
> Rhyme 'em to death, as they do Irish rats
> In drumming tunes.

(The point about the ancient Greek satirist Archilochus is that he is said to have taken revenge on his girl-friend's father when he refused permission to marry, by writing such a fierce satire on him that both father and daughter hanged themselves.)

If the Irish had this reputation, the Old Norse poets were not far behind. Let me just mention the curious fact that the word *scold* – and to scold is to flyte, a scold is a flyter – is the same as the Old Norse word *skáld*, which means poet but also satirist or lampooner; and the word *skáldskapr* means poetry but also libel, as if there was some basic connection between poetry and satire. It may seem strange to us, and indeed there are those who would regard satire and invective as one of the lower kinds of poetry. But if you think about it, it wouldn't have been a strange view to the Romans, or to Pope and Dryden and Swift, or to Burns and Dunbar, or certainly to Hugh MacDiarmid. MacDiarmid was a scold, a flyter, but he was also a skald, a bard, and knew he was, writing a short poem called 'Skald's Death':

> I have known all the storms that roll.
> I have been a singer after the fashion
> Of my people – a poet of passion.
> > All that is past.
> Quiet has come into my soul.
> > Life's tempest is done.
> > I lie at last
> A bird cliff under the midnight sun.

That poem, published in *Stony Limits* (1934) belongs to the period when he was living on the Shetland island of Whalsay, well on the way to that 'northern' Old Norse midnight sun.

Scotland then seems to be a part of this northern European leaning towards satire and mockery; but in Scotland the flyting, as a particular and rather specialized kind of satire, came to be developed in a more determined and sophisticated way than anywhere else. We have examples from the 1480s to the 1980s – perhaps even from the 580s, if we believe (and why not) the story that when Columba was trying to convert the Picts under King Brude at Inverness, there was a singing-contest between the Christian monks of Columba and the pagan druids of the Picts. At any rate, we know that when King James VI wrote his essay on Scottish poetry (1584), *Ane Schort Treatise, conteining some Reulis and Cautelis to be Observit and Eschewit in Scottis Poesie*, he included 'Flyting' and 'Invective' among the other kinds of poetry and obviously didn't see any need to defend the genre, and from the rules he gave he clearly knew what he was talking about, for example flytings should be written 'hurland ouer heuch', rushing over the cliff, in 'tumbling verse', with alliteration; and he gives examples, from what was then contemporary poetry.

There are three main medieval flytings in Scotland: between William Dunbar and Walter Kennedy, between Sir David Lyndsay and King James V, and between Alexander Montgomerie and Sir Patrick Hume of Polwart(h). The first and last of these are complete, the middle one is only a fragment.

We know more about the Montgomerie-Polwart flyting (c.1580) than about the others. You'll remember the definition of the flyting from *The Concise Scots Dictionary*, 'a contest between poets in mutual abuse'. This poem of some thousand lines is certainly that, and the abuse is such that when J.H. Millar was writing his *A Literary History of Scotland* in 1903 he said: 'I have sought through the poem in vain for an extract suitable for presentation in these pages; but there is scarcely a single characteristic stanza, however promising, which is not rendered unfit for the purpose by the presence of some word or image that would not be tolerated in print at the present day.' I don't think we need to find ourselves so inhibited eighty years later. But the abuse does not mean that the two writers were enemies – far from it. This is made clear from a prefatory poem 'To the Reader' (we don't know who wrote it), which says in part:

> No cankring envy, malice, nor despite
> Stirred up these men so eagerly to flyte;
> But generous emulation: so in playes
> Best actors flyte and raile, and thousand wayes
> Delight the itching eare...
> Anger to asswage, make melancholy lesse,
> This Flyting first was wrote – now tholes the presse.
> 　　Who will not rest content with this epistle,
> 　　Let him sit down and flyte, or stand and whistle.

There are two points of interest here. As the phrase 'generous emulation' shows, the element of competition, of contending, is obviously present, but it's within a spirit of give-and-take, of generosity of feeling. And secondly, the reference to plays and actors reminds us that the flyting between Montgomerie and Polwart was performed before an audience at the Scottish court, like a two-man play, meant to give delight to a live audience ('make melancholy lesse'), and the audience were asked to judge at the end who had won: Montgomerie, but only just. As the poet puts it himself in 'Sonnet 27': 'Love whome they lyk; for me, I love the King, / Whose Highnes laughed som tym for to look / Hou I chaist Polwart from the chimney-neuk.' (In a draughty medieval palace the chimney-neuk was a highly desirable place, kept for the king and his most favoured friends.)

So – entertainment as part of the flyting, and humour as part of the entertainment. You cast wide and terrible aspersions on your opponent's parentage, you describe his physical appearance and habits in the most bizarre and revolting manner possible, but you don't want to go too far into the surrealistic or incredible, otherwise the appeal for the contemporary audience would be less – they know both characters and they want to see a *basis* of truth in the attacks. If Kennedy keeps calling Dunbar a dwarf in his flyting, you can take it that Dunbar probably was of small stature – either that, or six feet six! – but not a man of average height. But although there's this small core of truth, the judgement of who is the better flyter takes into account the force of his imagination and inventiveness, and also the command he has of all the technical resources of language: metre and rhyme, alliteration, vocabulary, imagery and comparison. The poet has to prove himself, show he is a master of his craft. Usually the two poets work up to an exciting climax in their last sections, pull out all the stops towards the end; this again is clearly designed for an audience – perhaps indeed the one who got the greater applause was the winner.

The opening section of the poem, the first 'Montgomerie to Polwart', shows already the interest in form and technique, with its curious metre and repetitions, rather like a spell:

Polwart, ye peip like a mouse amongst thornes;
Na cunning ye keip; Polwart, ye peip;
Ye luik lyk a sheipe and ye had twa hornes:
Polwart, ye peip like a mouse amongst thornes.

Bewar what thow spekes, litle foull earthe taid,
With thy Canigait breikes, bewar what thow speiks,
Or ther sall be weit cheikes for the last that thow made:
Bewar what thow speikes, litle foull earth taid.

Foull mismaid miting, born in the Merss,
Be word and by writting, foull mismaid miting,
Leiv off thy flyting, come kis my ersse,
Foull mismaid miting, born in the Merss.

And we mell thow sall yell, litle cultron cuist;
Thow sall tell even thy sel, and we mell thow sall yell;
Thy smell was so fell, and stronger nor must;
And we mell thow sall yell, litle cultron cuist.

Thou art doand and dridland like ane foull beist;
Fykand and fidland, thow art doand and dridland,
Strydand and striddland like Robin redbreist:
Thou art doand and dridland like ane foull beist.

But that is still quite polite, Montgomerie hasn't really got going
yet. Probably the best part of the flyting is a later passage called
'The Secund Invective', which purports to tell how Polwart was
born, begotten between an elf and an ape, found in a bush by
witches on Halloween, so ugly that they curse it and instead of
giving it blessings wish on it a long list of all diseases known to
man, christening it (if that is the word) by a dedication to Satan,
and finally fondling it and joining with it in a sort of screaming-
match: the whole section very imaginative, nightmarish, and
vivid. Here is a part of the baptism:

'Be the moving of the mone, mapamone, and the Kingis Ell,
Be Phlegitoun, the Sevin Starnis, and the Chairlwane,
Be the hicht of the heavin, and lawnes of hell,
Be all the brether of Belliallis buird in ane band,
Be the pollis, the planeittis, and singis all tuell,
Be the michtis of the moone – lat mirknes remane –
Be the elements all that our craft can compell,
Be the floodis infernall, and furies of pane,
Be all the ghaistis of our gang, that dwellis thair doun,
   In signe of Stikis, that stinking strand,
   And Pluto, that our court command,
   Resave this harlot of our hand,
      In name of Mahoun.

If you want to compare Polwart, here is a passage from his last
flyting:

Mad manter, vain vanter, and hanter of sclaverie,
Kaily lippis, kis my hippis, in grippis thow's behint.
Pudding prikker, bang the bicker, nane quiker in knaverie.
Bale brewer, poyson spewer, mony trewer hes bene tint.
   Swyne keiper, dirt dreiper, throt steiper fra the drowth!
   Leeand lymmer, mony trimmer, I maun skymmer in thy
      mowth.

Fleyit fuill, mad mule, dee in dule on ane aik.
Knave kend, Christ send evil on that mow!

Pudding wricht, out of sicht thow'se be dicht lyk a draik.
Jock Blunt, thrawin frunt, kis the cunt of ane kow.
  Purspeiller, hen steiller, cat keiller, now I knaw thee.
  Rubiatour, fornicatour by natour, foul fa thee!...

Blind brok, kis dok, boird bloik, banischt townes!
Allace! theifis face, na grace for that grunyie!
Beld bissat, marmissat, lance-pissat to the lownes!
Deid dring, dryd sting, thow will hing but a sunyie.
  Lik-butter, throt-cutter, fisch-gutter, fyll the fetter!
  Cum bleitand, and greitand, and eitand thy letter.

The flyting ends, then, in pure but ingenious abuse, and a final
appeal to Montgomerie to admit defeat, to bleat and greet and
'eat his letter'. The three internal rhymes in each line, as well as
end-rhyme, make a classic flyting-type appeal to the audience
through technical display, verse prowess, even if the audience
on this occasion preferred Montgomerie's more imaginative
approach.

'The Flyting of Dunbar and Kennedy' (c.1500) is an earlier
poem in similar style, about half the length, showing similar
brilliance and ingenuity on both sides. In real life, Dunbar
respected and admired Kennedy, just as Montgomerie respected
Polwart. In his 'Lament for the Makaris', in fact, Kennedy's is
the last name he mentions; among the roll-call of dead poets,
only Kennedy and Dunbar himself survive: 'Gud Maister Walter
Kennedy / In poynt of dede lyis veraly – / Gret reuth it wer that
so suld be: / *Timor mortis conturbat me.*' So the flyting with Kennedy is only a dramatic court entertainment, a test of skills, a
wildly humorous poetic contest. There is one recurring feature:
Dunbar makes a great deal of the fact that Kennedy is a Gaelic
or Highland or (as he says) 'Ersche' bard ('Highland' but coming
from Carrick in Ayrshire, which was still Gaelic-speaking at that
time) and as everyone knows, Dunbar the Lowlander says, barbarous Highlanders have no culture – Kennedy retorting the same
charge, that it's the Highlanders or Erschmen who are the true
and ancient representatives of the culture of Scotland. Yet we
have to remember that it is only a flyting, and that as two people
who respect each other they are really making fun of the popular
stereotype of teuchter and lowlander. This is how Dunbar makes
his attack:

Iersche brybour baird, vyle beggar with thy brattis,
Cuntbittin crawdoun Kennedy, coward of kynd;
Evill farit and dryit as Denseman on the rattis,
Lyk as the gleddis had on thy gulesnowt dynd;
Mismaid monstour, ilk mone owt of thy mynd,
Renunce, rebald, thy rymyng; thow bot royis;
Thy trechour tung hes tane ane heland strynd –
Ane lawland ers wald mak a bettir noyis.

And Kennedy replies:

Thou lufis nane Irische, elf, I understand,
Bot it suld be all trew Scottis mennis lede;
It was the gud langage of this land,
And Scots it causit to multiply and sprede
Quhill Corspatrick, that we of tresoun rede,
Thy fore fader, maid Irisch and Irisch men thin,
Throu his tresoun broght Inglis rumplis in:
Sa wald thy self, mycht thou to him succeede.

Sir David Lyndsay's 'The Answer to the Kingis Flyting'
(*c.*1535) is a seventy-line fragment, James V's part not having
come down to us – or indeed the rest of his poems. The king,
who was half Lyndsay's age at the time, had evidently been
taunting Lyndsay that he was getting past it as far as acts of love
were concerned; Lyndsay admits this is true, but attacks the king
for his amorous exploits and loose living:

For, lyke ane boisteous bull, ye rin and ryde
Ryatouslie lyke ane rude rubeatour
Ay fukkand lyke ane furious fornicatour.

Quite strong words to address to your king; and Lyndsay may
have felt he had gone too far, ending the piece shortly thereafter,
and saying: 'Now schir, fairweill, because I can nocht flyte'. This
is really very interesting, because it shows that a flyting contest
should be between equals, each must feel totally free to be as
outrageous as he wants, and a ruler and his subject are not in that
position.

The examples given so far belong to the heyday of flyting,
down to the Union of the Crowns in 1603 and the move of the
court from Edinburgh to London. Flyting still survived, but in
a desultory sort of way, appearing now and again, and it lost its

status, lost its rules, lost its cultured audience. In the seventeenth century there was plenty of satire around, relating to the religious wars and disputes of that time, and some of it is vigorous enough, but mostly pretty ephemeral, requiring a lot of explanation about day-to-day events before readers in later centuries could make much of it. Also, although it's savage and hard-hitting, it isn't often very funny. This is because the authors were not greatly concerned to give pleasure, they were fighting for theological and political points. Just before the Union of 1707 there was a flyting between Lord Belhaven, a strong anti-Union man, and Daniel Defoe, the English agent who was sent up to Scotland to find out what we were all thinking. Unfortunately neither of the two was much of a poet, and the result is a sort of doggerel which is hardly worth quoting. In fact it bears out the point that the best flyting comes from people who actually respect each other, which Defoe and Belhaven didn't.

Jumping to the twentieth century, we must not forget Hugh MacDiarmid who was very much a flyting-type person, and his work in both prose and verse is scattered through with little or even big flytings of every kind. It's a pity that these flytings are usually one-sided; for a number of reasons, there's no direct engaging with the opponent who keeps the attack going and who is clearly identified. For example, MacDiarmid wrote a book-length flyting poem called *The Battle Continues* against the South African poet Roy Campbell, in 1940, after Campbell had published a book-length poem called *Flowering Rifle*, in 1939. Campbell's poem was about Spain and the Spanish Civil War, and took up an extreme right-wing position, defending the Fascist dictatorship and its close alliance with the Catholic Church, attacking everything on the left from the most mildly pink poets to hard-line Communists, and throwing in plenty of highly offensive references to Jews, blacks, and gays. It was a virulent book, and MacDiarmid was so enraged that he wrote *The Battle Continues* in answer to it. Only parts of this were published at the time, because of the war and for other reasons, and it didn't come out as a whole until 1957. Just as it was being printed, Roy Campbell died – perhaps a nice instance of being rhymed to death, as the old Irish bards would claim. But we must regret that this is a one-sided flyting: there's no doubt that Campbell would have given as good as he got. MacDiarmid sets out to demolish both Campbell's poetry and his prowess as a soldier when he fought on the Fascist side in Spain:

And all the Spanish War newspaper clippings
Dried out like the lives of so many of my friends?
Forgotten – that's the way you would like it,
Calf-fighter Campbell, I have no doubt,
But there's an operation to do first
– To remove the haemorrhoids you call your poems
With a white-hot poker for cautery,
Shoved right up through to your tonsils!

Campbell, they call him – 'crooked mouth', that is –
But even Clan Campbell's records show no previous case
Of such extreme distortion, of a mouth like this
Slewed round to a man's bottom from his face
And speaking with a voice not only banal
                                    But absolutely anal.
Franco has made no more horrible shambles
Than this poem of Campbell's,
The foulest outrage his breed has to show
Since the massacre of Glencoe!...

The 'old soldier', Skunk, unconsciously transposes
The properties of Poetry and of Mars,
Giving his gun a wreath of paper roses...
Was even a worse dud, incredible though it be,
                        Than in the lists of poesy.
Witness the honours Franco showers upon him,
The general admission of the Rebel leaders
That but for this bogus Byron, this great Reichs-Marksman,
Moscow had won!
Single-handed almost, . . .
This Gun-Smoke McGonigle, this vest-
Pocket edition of *The Decline of the Wild West*,
Eddie Cantor Campbell in *The Kid from Spain*,
– Maximum of smoke & minimum of fire! –
Routed the Bolshevik hordes & saved Civilisation!
This Sydney Horler of the English Muse
In Franco's wayzgoose is himself the goose,
Or bustard rather, that, when its foe comes nigh,
Cocks up its shitepoke & with that lets fly
– A better shot with that
                Than with a gat!

Passages like that have some of the old flyting extravagance, and there is humour as well as an object of derision.

Lastly I'd like to refer to one more recent example. In 1985 a joint book of poems called *Sterts & Stobies* was published by two young Scots poets, Robert Crawford and W.N. Herbert. It has sections of poems by each of them, but also, in the middle, it has 'The Flyting of Crawford and Herbert', which is written quite consciously in the flyting tradition, in Scots. Crawford mocks Herbert's habit of writing very long poems:

> 'He wiz aye at sea
>
> In aw he wrote – sae R.I.P.' – or's near
> Tae P. as aebody expecks wha kens
> Yon foul stramash yir vast mou generates;
> That muckil bus-park o a mou, wi hens
> Peckin roon molars, an spittil-wattir-rates
>
> Jist astronomick! Mou an mou an mou!
> Ther's nae a LITRY GUIDE fur years tae cum
> Will miss yon Fingal's Cave-*manqué* – yir mou
> ('A true Blak Hale.' 'A daurk titanic lum...') –
>
> Makin thi puir Scoats launscape aw aroon
> Ae dumpin-groon fur thi warld's B.O.'drous skip
> Tae disgoarge tripe an swell yon garbage foon!
> I'yir pit-mirk mou Ah christen HERBERT'S TIP!

Herbert defends the freedom of his long and apparently random poems as against the more tightly controlled stanzas of Crawford:

> Ah, therr's yir West-coast cant,
> yi Frasir-in-Graham's pants,
> yi Muir-in-MacDiarmid's socks;
> therr's yir nidus o Glescae cock!
>
> Yi waant yir ane Criterionic case
> o draw-latch stealth fae raw-datchied makars
> aa guizerd in thon nebulon o noth,
> *Thi Concise Warld o Craford*;
> reality rabbd o health an scouth –
> an since yi cannae afford

tae plaister the haill place wi yir haimald fiss,
yi've sent aa rufflirs aff ti thi knackirs.
But whit's Limbo fur you Glescae bimbos is
a leal-leid-lubbirs' (seal an cypher-sirens') Libertad
o googy wurds in freedom;
a mair-nor-moisty Easterly you caa bad
becoz yi ken ut's yir freedom –

So two young contemporary poets, one from Glasgow and one from Dundee, go back full circle as it were, and still find stimulus in the old flyting tradition: something comic, something satirical, and something friendly too. Like Montgomerie and Polwart, they have read their flyting in public, together, and have kept something of the sense of performance. Flyting lives!

My conclusion would be, in relation to the title of the conference, 'Quite Without Humour...?', that for all the strangeness and extravagance of the flyting tradition, the Scots are definitely not quite without.

Lecture to the Association for Scottish Literary Studies, University of Glasgow, November 1987.

Dunbar and the Language of Poetry

'Of what we call genius', wrote Matthew Arnold, 'energy is the most essential part.' Energy in poetry, however, is compelled to manifest itself through form, not simply or necessarily metrical structure but a continuous inevitability of movement from word to word ('continuous' ideally, or only in the greatest poetry, but the sense of control of direction must be interrupted as little as possible), startling the reader's mind into considering something which the poem follows to the end of consideration and closes with a satisfaction. If poetry is the manifestation of energy in order, Arnold's statement is still the backbone of the argument; we are dealing with ordered energy, not with energetic orderliness. The final reflection we make on a great passage of Shakespeare is that his feeling for control and pattern has been *adequate* to the demands so peremptorily made on it by the majesty of his energy. Energy without order usually gives us the feeling that we are in touch with a poet but not with a poem: the forges clang, the air is thick with the spark and fume of production, but in the end nothing is made, no object is presented to us that we can grasp and appraise. Such is Whitman's 'Song of Myself'. Order without energy is exemplified by the poet whose inspiration is fitful and less than a match for his knowledge of what effects poetry can produce – as in Robert Bridges's sonnet-sequence *The Growth of Love*. Of the two imperfections, the first takes us nearer the fountainhead, and no amount of that virtuosity which may be the complement of the second's deficiency will atone for the lack of Arnold's 'most essential part'. But there is a complication, which Arnold did not consider. Energy may be felt by the poet primarily *as order*. A poet with a strong sensuous and linguistic tone to his imagination can find himself inspired within his own concern with words, with rhythm, with shape, with concatenations that are audible as well as thematic: elements which would normally be a hazard, a mere snare of formalism. Verbal energy of this kind is well exemplified in Hopkins, and it occurs to an important extent in the poet about to be considered here as well as in some of the poetry which influenced him. Where a major writer like Shakespeare will most commonly keep his sound-effects mysterious, contributory to a more salient preoccupation –

> Ensear thy fertile and conceptious womb,
> Let it no more bring out ingrateful man*

– the poets who are attracted by the 'energy as order' mode try to make of such half-felt and unanalysed word-linkages something concrete, basic, and sustaining, by opening up the way to them more externally and consciously; and they are helped by our stubborn alliterative tradition, in Middle English a dying alternative to the imported syllabic verse of France, and later absorbed by it, though breaking out periodically from it. This tradition, which influenced Dunbar, must now be looked at more closely.

II

It is well known that Dunbar and his fellow-poets in fifteenth-century Scotland wished to repay their literary debt to Chaucer. Chaucer was the 'rose of rethoris all', the 'horleige and reguleir' for the future movements of poetry. But their references to Chaucer's 'sugurit lippis', 'aureate termis', and 'eloquence ornate' rather than to his pathos, his simplicity, or his narrative gift help to betray the background of their eulogies, where Chaucer is set as an inescapable yet partly alien figure. The poets did not refer to the northern alliterative poetry as they referred to Chaucer – with the respect and enthusiasm of the disciple and imitator; but their practice proves that the older tradition was very pervasive and very congenial to the Scottish spirit, and they pay it that debt of exemplification which is often more revealing than their addresses to Chaucer. We do not find acknowledgements of the great alliterative poems which have been preserved from the North Midlands and the North-West of England, of *Pearl* or of *Sir Gawain and the Green Knight*; instead we have passing references to the more popular developments of this way of writing, especially to the romances and the farcical or fantastic alliterative and semi-alliterative poems composed in Scotland as the influence

---

* *Timon of Athens*, IV, iii, 188-9.

spread north and received its disequilibrating infusion of forth-right zestful topsyturvydom. We may take a glance at some of these once widely-known and still interesting productions. The following stanza (LII) from an anonymous poem mentioned by both Dunbar and Gavin Douglas, *Rauf Coilyear*, shows the more serious use of alliteration in romantic description, partly brilliant and pictorial, partly an eking out of narrative with conventional alliterative phrases. The uncouth hero of the romance, Ralph the Collier, enters the great hall of Charlemagne in Paris, and is dazzled by its array:

> Thocht he had socht sic ane sicht all this sevin yeir,
> Sa solempnit ane semblie had he not sene;
> The hall was properly apperrellit and paintit but peir,
> Dyamountis full dently dentit betwene;
> It was semely set on ilk syde seir,
> Gowlis glitterand full gay, glemand in grene,
> Flowris with flourdelycis formest in feir,
> With mony flamand ferly, ma than fyftene;
> The rufe reulit about in reuall of reid,
> Rois reulit ryally,
> Columbyn and lely,
> Thair was ane hailsum harbery,
> Into riche steid.

Apart from the alliteration, this stanza-form, with its closing 'wheel' of short lines which comes in with a light dancing rhythm and ends on a little eddy or turn back into the state of rest, had a special attraction for the Scottish poets; Henryson, Dunbar, Douglas, and Lyndsay all have their examples of it.

Rauf Coilyear combines the alliterative rhythm with regular rhyme. In other poems we have, as a further stage, a fairly regular syllabic verse with rhyme and irregular alliteration: the poet has perhaps half an intention of trochaic tetrameters or trimeters rhyming in pairs, but any excitement in the writing breaks the structure down into a loose alliterative swing, and usually where this is allowed to happen and the older non-syllabic rhythms prevail, the verse takes on a flailing verve and momentum, and if it is satirical or fantastic, as it often is, an effect is produced which is a notable Scottish characteristic of the period – wild, flamboyant, ludicrous, and 'fouthy' with words. Here are some lines from *The Cursing of Sir John Rowll* (33-50), one of the most popular of those poems, which was referred to by Lyndsay and probably by Dunbar. Sir John calls down anathema on certain persons unknown, 'resettaris and preve steilaris', who have pilfered from his yard 'fyve fat geiss' and many another bird of his owning.

> Now cursit and wareit be thair werd
> Quhill thay be levand on this erd,
> Hungir, sturt, and tribulatioun,
> And nevir to be without vexatioun,
> Of vengance, sorrow, sturt, and cair,
> Graceless, thriftles, and threidbair;
> All tymes in thair legasie
> Fyre, sword, watter, and woddie,
> Or any of thir infirmeteis
> Off warldly scherp adverseteis,
> Povertie, pestilence, or poplecy,
> Dum, deif, or edroposy,
> Maigram, madness, or missilry,
> Appostrum or the perlocy,
> Ffluxis, hyvis, or huttit ill,
> Hoist, heidwark, or fawin ill,
> Kald, kanker, feistir, or feveris,
> Brukis, bylis, blobbis, and bleistiris...

It is said that fashions change preferences beyond recognition, but the modern reader who may be dismayed by Rowll's *Cursing* should compare the kind of gusto which blows through it, and the cataloguings and word-linkages that its gusto takes, with similar outbursts in Rabelais, Skelton, Urquhart, or James Joyce – passages of

> such a climacterical and mercurially digested method, that when the fancy of the hearers was tickled with any rare conceit, and that the jovial blood was moved, he held it going with another new device upon the back of the first, and another, yet another, and another againe, succeeding one another for the promoval of what is a-stirring into a higher agitation; till in the closure of the luxuriant period, the decumanal wave of the oddest whimzy of all, enforced the charmed spirits of the auditory, for affording room to its apprehension, suddenly to burst forth into a laughter.*

* Sir Thomas Urquhart, *ΕΚΣΚΥΒΑΛΑΥΡΟΝ*, Maitland Club edn., p.229.

Another very popular poem, *Colkelbie Sow*, mentioned as a famous anonymous romance by Douglas, is referred to more than once by Dunbar, who was greatly taken by the highlight passage of its first 'fitt', the hilarious and satirical feast where the 'merry man' Colkelbie's pig is to be served. Dunbar likens the fools and rogues who gain preferment at Court to the select list of invited guests at this banquet. The list is in what James VI would have called 'tumbling verse'; it tumbles at its best, and stumbles at its worst. Dunbar would see the ideal form or latent possibility of a poem relatively without art but containing this appealing virtue of rhythmically underlined verbal proliferation in the easy pell-mell helter-skelter of its 'tumble' down the page.

Finally, Dunbar was familiar with the last stage of the absorption of alliterative writing by syllabic and rhyming modes as exemplified in some of the best passages of Henryson. Here there is nothing to distinguish the structure of the verse from that of Southern Chaucerian poetry except the frequency and the heightening descriptive use of alliteration (as, for example, in *The Testament of Cresseid* or *The Garmont of Gud Ladies*).

The poet of *Sir Gawain and the Green Knight* told his readers that he was going to give them the romance

> As hit is stad and stoken
> In stori stif and stronge,
> With lel letteres loken,
> In londe as hatz ben longe.

– 'as it is firmly set down in story, bound together with true letters, the ancient practice of this land'. Here is the Old English tradition, struggling to maintain itself against changes in the language, yet admired and used by a master who is invoking the past at a time when Chaucer was already writing his *Canterbury Tales*. And this is the tradition which forms the basis of alliterative writing in Scotland. But the 'locking of true letters', the far-off 'word gebunden' of the Anglo-Saxon *scop*, must be seen as supplemented in Scotland by other influences, and it is these in combination that would perhaps yield, if fully investigated, some of the secrets of the sudden superiority of Scots verse at this time as well as a description of its characteristics. Alliteration on the 'popular' side of poetry recommended itself to the Scots because it was an apt medium for racy narrative, because it established an immediate link between verse and the fund of alliteration in common proverbs, tags of speech and phrases from ballad and songs, and because it encouraged the peculiar Scots leaning towards the wild and the outspoken, the vituperative and the incongruous. Alliteration on the 'art' side of poetry is one aspect of a larger movement which affected all the poets of the time: the wakening consciousness of language as a ground open to deliberate enrichment and of literature as a growth springing from that prepared soil. We find in Scotland at the end of the fifteenth century a brilliant, optimistic, zealous, unhappy, and premature attempt to produce what England successfully developed later in the next century – an instrument of expression that would fuse what was most valued and accessible in popular speech with an immense body of reference-extending terms built up mainly from Latin and Greek. Douglas tells us in his Prologue to Book I of Virgil's *Aeneid* how hard it had been to translate the classical Latin into a worthy modern utterance:

> Besyde Latyne our langage is imperfite,
> Quhilk in sum part is the caus and the wite
> Quhy that of Virgillis vers the ornate bewtie
> Intill our toung may nocht observit be.

He complains bitterly of his 'bad harsk speche', his 'lewit barbour tong', his 'rurall vulgar gros', and his 'corruppit cadens imperfyte'. He warns the reader that his Scots has been abundantly fortified and broadened from Latin, French, and Southern English –

> Nocht for our toung is in the selfin scant,
> Bot for that I the foutht of langage want.

'Fouth' is to Douglas what 'copie' – *copia verborum* – became to the Elizabethans, the quality of meaningful variety, and with variety subtlety, both intellectual and musical, such as classical poetry was felt to possess. Liberty of experiment, importation, invention, and revival were wanted to widen the range of expression and to increase the possibility of those striking original collocations of words where poetry begins to jet out of the melting-pot, with new life whirling in the very materials it springs from. It can easily be seen what latent power there would be in the adding of this specific linguistic ferment and expansion of vocabulary to a writing tradition derived from both alliterative and Chaucerian sources, the alliterative source being itself both 'popular' and elaborately artistic. Some of the distinctive resulting forms may be noted and illustrated.

First there is the simple 'aureate' style, Latin-influenced but not extravagantly or emptily, the faint sense of formalism giving a stateliness and assurance to the verse, the suggestion of consonantal pattern inclining description towards a very makar-like onomatopoeia. So Douglas in his 'lusty crafty preambill' to Book XII of the *Aeneid*:

> For to behald it was a gloire to se
> The stabillit wyndis and the cawmyt see,
> The soft sessoun, the firmament serene,
> The lowne illumynat air and fyrth amene...

Douglas will also supply an example of the second important development, which might be called the 'anti-aureate' style. Here the lesson of latinism was shown to have been learned: the effect of culture, of authority, of the hieratic, of clarity and resonance, which a due latinizing supplied in descriptive passages where beauty, brilliance, splendour, and pleasure were involved, gave place at other points to an equally typical effect of deliberate harshness, apparent uncouthness, surface obscurity, and greater onomatopoeic emphasis, and for this the poets had recourse to Anglo-Saxon and Scandinavian rather than to Latin and French components, to the tough, concrete, and actively sensuous rather than to the tranquilly majestic, however gleaming and marmoreal. This experimental differentiation of vocabulary is striking and original, but not unexpected at that period of linguistic awareness. It is only in part a conscious artistic device; it is just as much a natural turning to the older Germanic in dealing with the physical, and especially the disagreeable-physical, where its words retain great force and have powerful non-literary associations, the Romance elements having on the whole weaker physical associations and a more literary and cultivated field of reference. This is how the Scottish winter sets in in Douglas's 7th Prologue, the *tristis prologus*:

> Dym skyis oft furth warpit feirfull levyne,
> Flaggis of fyir and mony felloun flawe,

Scharp soppis of sleit and of the snypand snawe.
The dowy dichis war all donk and wait,
The law vaille flodderit all wyth spait,
The plane stretis and every hie way
Full of fluschis, doubbis, myre, and clay;
Laggerit leys wallowit farnys schewe,
Broune muris kithit thair wysnit mossy hewe,
Bank, bra, and boddum blanschit wolx and bair;
For gurll weddir growyt bestis haire;
The wynd maid wayfe the reid weyd on the dyk;
Bedovin in donkis deyp was every syk,
Our craggis and the front of rochis seyre
Hang gret isch-schoklis lang as ony spere...

A third characteristic of much of the makars' poetry is a lyrical run or lilt of a peculiar kind which comes from a nice fusion of native alliteration and French-based verse-form. The fact that the alliteration does not always coincide with the syllabic accent but leads the reader on with a sinuous stress of its own gives the writing a chatoyant and dance-like quality which is very attractive. A good example is the anonymous *Peblis to the Play*, or *Tayis Bank*, or the lyric *My heart is heich above*. In the last stanza of *Tayis Bank* the alliteration binds the lines in couplets, while the repeated rhyme draws on the couplets to the end of the verse, the whole being alive with movement and lightness:

The rever throw the ryse cowth rowt
And roseris raiss on raw;
The schene birdis full schill cowth schowt
Into that semly schaw:
Joy wes within and joy without
Under that wlonkest waw,
Quhair Tay ran down with stremis stout
Full strecht under Stobschaw.

Lastly, there should be mentioned the chief Scots development of the alliterative habit – satirical invective and 'flyting', with many variants from the norm of harmless 'aesthetic' *tour de force* improvising to the two extremes of serious denunciation and outspoken bawdiness. The force here is in the combining of the alliteration of old verse-forms with the alliterative tendencies in vehement and vulgar speech; rhyme, often internal as well as final, is a spice in a total flavour which will not be to everyone's taste. The form, however, is both interesting and important in Scots writing, and particularly in Dunbar, as will be seen later.

III
Than cam in Dunbar the mackar,
On all the flure thair was nane frackar...

These lines from Dunbar's *Dance in the Quenis Chalmer* might well describe his equally nimble and lively entry into poetry. What is immediately noticeable in his work is the *display* of *poetic energy* in forms that have considerable technical and craftsmanly interest, rather than the *distillation* of *poetic situation*, in personal emotional encounters. His first mark is a certain effectual brilliance that may commend him more keenly to the practising poet than to the ordinary reader – an agility, a virtuosity in tempo and momentum, a command of rhythm. His poems were produced by cooperating with and transforming the linguistic trends of his age rather than by relying (as Henryson did) on the ancient common fund of human situation and story from which poetic feeling can be summoned with less expenditure of the specifically poetic verbal gift. If Dunbar has at times 'words with no matter', Chaucer and Henryson in their less satisfactory passages have matter (the story) and form (the careful metre) but no word-energy. These are complementary wants; and if we sometimes sigh for a Henryson-leavened Dunbar we can also wish, more heretically perhaps, for a Langland-leavened Chaucer. The fusion of the two elements had to wait for Shakespeare. Dunbar's character as a poet – his wild imagination, his quickness of response to particular situations in a humorous and mocking spirit and to general ideas in a serious spirit, his evident delight in gesture, in presentation, in fanfare and march and rout and climax – fitted hand-in-glove with all those tendencies which in Scotland supplemented the influence of Chaucerian poetry. His work shows how far a writer could go at that time whose poetic energies could be released so largely by formal preoccupations.

The most general effect of the various echoic combinations of alliteration and rhyme Dunbar used (with internal rhyme often acting as an additional vocalic alliteration) was to accentuate the movement and increase the speed of the verse. Like sounds draw the ear forward, sometimes before it has assimilated the sense, and encourage it to participate in the poet's glancing and headlong jugglery as a delight in itself, and not only that, but to see how from this delight he was more able to work up the fiery poetic object. Not only does the verse dance, but in many of the best poems this rhythmic success bears its fruits within the subject-matter, where either dancing or some other vivid movement is described, and the approach towards such a scene is one of Dunbar's greatest pleasures.* Thus we have the free and hilarious *Dance in the Quenis Chalmer*; the *Dance of the Sevin Deidly Sinnis* with its sombre nightmare processional of the involuntary revellers of Hell and its sweep-the-board ludicrous catastrophe in the 'Highland pageant' called up and dissipated by Satan; the strange tale of the *Fenyeit Freir of Tungland*, which can hardly wait to describe the charlatan aeronaut's 'flight' from Stirling Castle, pursued and mobbed by all the birds of the air, attacking and crying alliteratively and cumulatively according to their characters; or the concluding blow struck in the *Flyting* with Kennedy, where he conjures up a vision of Kennedy the 'Carrick cateran' entering Edinburgh, fleeing through the streets with dogs at his heels, boys and old women shouting after him, fishwives throwing their baskets, horses running away with their carts – and a valedictory word-drubbing in the clattering last two stanzas when even the preceding movement is speeded up by the device of three internal rhymes to each line in addition to the normal end-rhyme and alliteration:

> Loun lyk Mahoun, be boun me till obey,
> Theif, or in greif mischeif sall the betyd;
> Cry grace, tykis face, or I the chece and sley;
> Oule, rare and yowle, I sall defowll thy pryd;
> Peilit gled, baith fed and bred of bichis syd,
> And lyk ane tyk, purspyk, quhat man settis by the!
> Forflittin, countbittin, beschittin, barkit hyd,
> Clym-ledder, fyle-tedder, foule edder, I defy the.
>
> Mauch-muttoun, byt-buttoun, peilit gluttoun, air to
>   Hilhous;
> Rank beggar, ostir-dregar, foule fleggar in the flet;
> Chittirlilling, ruch-rilling, lik-schilling in the milhous;
> Baird rehator, theif of natour, fals tratour, feyindis gett;

---

* A recurrent pleasure in Scots verse, as witness *Colkelbie Sow*, *Tam o' Santer*, and *The Witch's Ballad*.

> Filling of tauch, rak–sauch, cry crauch, thow art oursett;
> Muttoun–dryver, girnall–ryver, yadswyvar, fowll fell the:
> Herretyk, lunatyk, purspyk, carlingis pet,
> Rottin crok, dirtin dok, cry cok, or I sall quell the.

Next we may notice how Dunbar was able to use and improve on the effects of the semi-alliterative 'popular' verse like Rowll's *Cursing* and *Colkelbie Sow*. The subject-matter of such poems was congenial to him, and the form was one which particularly suited his combination of word-linkage and rhythmic liveliness. Here again his poetic feeling is stirred up by the movement of the verse; cataloguing becomes denunciation, reporting becomes satire. But he ends more seriously than jocularly, applying the lesson in presentation he gained from the 'popular' verse to a different purpose. The motley swarm of adventurers and climbers Dunbar watched at James IV's court through the eyes of slighted merit might have been dealt with in the uproarious mode of the *Flyting*, but this time, when he came to write his *Remonstrance* and his *Complaint* to the King, the poetry raised through the rushing form took on a harshness and gravity which may be felt to reach nearer the personal than the quite spiteless dismissal of Kennedy. In the *Remonstrance* these are his enemies:

> Fenyeouris, fleichouris, and flatteraris;
> Cryaris, craikaris, and clatteraris;
> Soukaris, groukaris, gledaris, gunnaris;
> Monsouris of France, gud clarat-cunnaris...

And this is his conclusion:

> My mind so fer is set to flyt
> That of nocht ellis I can endyt;
> For owther man my hart to breik
> Or with my pen I man me wreik;
> And sen the tane most nedis be
> In to malancolie to de
> Or lat the vennim ische all out
> Be war anone, for it will spout,
> Gif that the tryackill cum nocht tyt
> To swage the swalme of my dispyt!

The piling up of defamatory variants is of course an ancient method of satire, based on the invective of vulgar speech; its tendency is towards humour, in literature as in life, because of the element of fantasy or incongruity which increases the longer the variation is kept up. Here we have rather the semi-realistic catalogue than the list of variants, and the choice of tone is more at the will of the artist. He describes actual groups of people in a way which shows his contempt for them; they come tumbling out into the metre, flung together unceremoniously in the levelling process of sound-echo, *soukaris* with *groukaris*, *gunnaris* with *clarat-cunnaris*, and they are left to stand long enough for the writer to knock them down with his comment. The theme of broad inclusive denunciation by an onlooker whose attitude sways between simple scorn and the epideictic, half-ethical, half-aesthetic, was one Dunbar liked and returned to; it gave him the double opportunity he desired to exploit vocabulary on the technical level and to ride on Urquhart's 'decumanal wave' on the emotional level, the emotion coming largely from and through the technique.

Another of Dunbar's methods of raising pleasure and excitement formally may be seen in his uses of Latin, as in the *Testament of Andro Kennedy* and the *Dregy of Dunbar*. Macaronic intermingling of English and Latin was an old tradition, going back through Middle English to Anglo-Saxon times, and it was extended greatly during the fourteenth and fifteenth centuries, often admitting French as a third language. It was naturally associated with the ritual and especially with the hymns of the Church; many religious poems in English had a Latin refrain which gave the recurrent gesture of authority and devotional remembrancing; *Piers Plowman* has much Latin interpolation, often within a half-line of verse; and it was obviously a usage which would offer itself to the consideration of a formal artist like Dunbar for purposes of unexpected contrast, the ancient religious echoes being made to apply to things the most profane and reprobate. To weave Latin, not tags but original phrases, into a body of rhyming verse was a challenge to his dexterity; in the feat itself was pleasure, and in the result humour. So he sets off in his *Testament of Andro Kennedy*:

> I, Maister Andro Kennedy,
> Curro quando sum vocatus,
> Gottin with sum incuby,
> Or with sum freir infatuatus;
> In faith I can nought tell redly

> Unde aut ubi fui natus,
> Bot in treuth I trow trewly
> Quod sum dyabolus incarnatus.

The extreme improbability of the statement's ever being made, coupled with the neat light assurance of its utterance, produces an attractive ludicrous effect which is kept up for fourteen stanzas, the half-Latin and half-Scots terms of his legacy bolstering up a continual expectation and quasi-secretive unfolding of the testamentary revelations. In the *Dregy* Dunbar enjoys himself even more. This parodies the 'dirge' or office for the Dead, and is ritually arranged with readings, responses, and final prayer. It is for the soul of the King, 'exiled' in the purgatory of Stirling from the heaven of Edinburgh, and all the saints and fathers are invoked to permit his quick release and return with his company: 'Requiem Edinburgi dona eis, Domine'. Here, in a parody of the liturgical form, Dunbar has found his aesthetic form ready to hand. The humour of this cleverness, this adaptiveness of his in the sudden taking up of an unusual structure, begets an enthusiasm which explodes all its force within a relatively narrow compass, so that the feeling for form has little chance of being dispersed, and the joke retains its point along with the poetry. Dunbar also made a more serious use of Latin, however, in the refrain-lines of his religious poems, in his *Lament for the Makaris*, and in such a poem as 'Into this warld may none assure'. In this poem the same use of close contrast is made as had appeared in the *Testament*, but with exactly opposite effect. Now the Latin offers no element of surprise, brings in no ridiculous finishings of the sense of the Scots, but strengthens, emphasizes, continues, and sharpens the already serious meaning, and gives it an impressive background or harmony of old non-poetic admonitory reference. Here the Latin breaks in at the end, as the poem's formal climax. It had been preceded by a growing amount of alliteration with the measured return of a refrain-line bringing each stanza nearer the concluding burst of energy. The verses mount towards a scene of breaking and loosening commotion, not (this time) a dance or a flight or a chase, but the tumult of the Judgement. Form pounds on till imagination rises and sees its object, and, with its warning Latin voice, the poem rings out and subsides:

> O quho sall weild the wrang possessioun,
> Or the gold gadderit with oppressioun,

Quhone the angell blawis his bugill sture,
Quhilk onrestorit helpis no confessioun?
Into this warld may none assure.

Quhat help is thair in lordschips sevin
Quhone na hous is bot hell and hevin,
Palice of lycht or pit obscure
Quhair yowlis ar with horrible stevin?
Into this warld may none assure.

Ubi ardentes animae
Semper dicentes sunt Vae! Vae!
Sall cry Allace! that women thame bure,
O quantae sunt istae tenebrae!
Into this warld may none assure.

Than quho sall wirk for warldis wrak,
Quhone flude and fyre sall our it frak,
And frelie frustir feild and fure,
With tempest keyne and thundir-crak?
Into this warld may none assure...

Something like the obverse of Dunbar's vituperative legacy
may be examined in the formal usages of his religious poems,
notably the *Nativitie*, the *Resurrection*, and the *Ballat of Our Lady*.
The force of exultation which distinguishes these poems from
the rest of his religious work matches exactly the decrying and
demolishing gusto of the *Flyting* and the *Fenyeit Freir*. The utterance is high-pitched; there is an accumulation of similar views
or variants of an idea, giving the reader no breathing-space and
gathering him up with its momentum (and, in the last of the
poems at least, almost dazzling him with sparks in a pyrotechnic
ascent); and we have a brief refutation of Dr Johnson's dictum
that 'the topicks of devotion... can receive no grace from novelty
of sentiment, and very little from novelty of expression'.* The
all-importance of the formal foundations is strikingly confirmed
if these three successful religious poems are compared with Dunbar's other attempts – the *Passioun*, the *Table of Confession*, and
the *Maner of Passing to Confession*. In each of the first three there
is a most distinctive use of several kinds of pattern (cataloguings

---

* *Life of Waller.*

and collections of variants, alliteration and assonance, extensive and often significant or stressing rhyme, Latin liturgical lines), and in the other three the absence of such components accompanies and accounts for their lack of expressive vehemence.

Finally, for the combining of many of these formal usages to produce effect in a relatively long and ambitious poem, there is the excellent and remarkable *Tretis of the Tua Mariit Wemen and the Wedo*. The workmanship of this poem, which is in rhymeless alliterative lines, is pleasant and easy, and shows that this experiment in structural archaism was congenial, a narrative medium loose and smooth enough to keep the story moving for several hundred lines and yet interesting enough formally to hold him always on the threshold of poetry. Chaucerian couplets would have told the story for him, but failed to draw fire; rhyme added to alliteration in syllabic verse would have served his poetry, but failed to keep the narrative on its necessarily low level of general intensity. The metre was therefore convenient; it was also a source of pleasure, along different lines. It is a late-flowering growth of a very old tradition, which pleases by showing what it sprang from – and its author's awareness of this: the ghostly prevalence of Anglo-Saxon rhythmical types, seen through the lighter and longer Middle English line, links it with the medieval alliterative romances and behind them with the more heroic poetry of Old English – not in any more than a suggestive way, but with recurring hints and recollections in the fall of the words and in the use of old alliterative phrases, sometimes transformed, sometimes consciously taken over. It gave scope for that lavish and glittering scenic description Dunbar required as a contrast to his ladies' revelations when they spoke up and 'sparit no matiris':

> Quhyt, seimlie, and soft, as the sweit lillies
> New upspred upon spray, as new spynist rose;
> Arrayit ryallie about with mony rich vardour,
> That nature full nobillie annamalit with flouris
> Off alkin hewis under hevin, that ony heynd knew,
> Fragrant, all full of fresche odour fynest of smell.

What has its basis in the conventional May-morning vision of the romances becomes with Dunbar an instrument of sharp descriptive clarity and ringing verbal beauty. The care with which he has composed is reflected in a passage like the following, where the repeated alliteration clings to the sense-division of the lines into pairs:

> Thus draif thai our that deir nyght with danceis full noble,
> Quhill that the day did up daw, and dew donkit flouris;
> The morrow myld wes and meik, the mavis did sing,
> And all remuffit the myst, and the meid smellit;
> Silver schouris doune schuke as the schene cristall,
> And berdis schoutit in schaw with thair schill notis;
> The goldin glitterand gleme so gladit ther hertis
> Thai maid a glorius gle amang the grene bewis.
> The soft sowch of the swyr and soune of the stremys,
> The sueit savour of the sward and singing of foulis,
> Myght confort ony creatur of the kyn of Adam,
> And kindill agane his curage, thocht it wer cald sloknyt.

Thirdly, and as the converse of this, it suited equally well Dunbar's purpose in the loose-tongued satirical part of the narrative where something of the spirit of the flytings was needed. When the first wife says of her husband,

> I have ane wallidrag, ane worme, ane auld wobat carle,
> A waistit wolroun, na worth bot wourdis to clatter;

or when the widow tells of her aged first husband how she would

> kemm his cowit noddill,
> And with a bukky in my cheik bo on him behind,
> And with a bek gang about and bler his ald e;

or says softly of herself

> I wes dissymblit suttelly in a sanctis liknes:
> I semyt sober, and sueit, and sempill without fraud,
> Bot I couth sexty dissaif that suttillar wer haldin:

we can see that the alliterative form of writing was no strain on the range and measure of Dunbar, nor on the other hand was it an excuse for mere wordy excess, with epithets empty of everything except the requisite sound. Both the artistic control and the eager verbal impetus are present, as they are in the descriptive passages at the beginning and end.

The dance and lightness of the verse, typical of most of Dunbar's best poems, need little emphasis here. These lines, however, might be quoted to show the variety and surefootedness of rhythm obtained. The widow, in mourning 'as foxe in a lambis fleise', goes to church:

> Full oft I blenk by my buke, and blynis of devotioun,
> To se quhat berne is best brand or bredest in schulderis,
> Or forgeit is maist forcely to furnyse a bancat
> In Venus chalmer, valyeandly, withoutin vane ruse:
> And, as the new mone all pale, oppressit with change,
> Kythis quhilis her cleir face through cluddis of sable,
> So keik I through my clokis, and castis kynd lukis
> To knychtis, and to cleirkis, and cortly personis.

She concludes her long discourse with a joyous recollection of the gatherings of young gallants at her house, a lodging amorously hospitable, situated apparently on the Venusberg,

> quhen baronis and knychtis,
> And othir bachilleris, blith blumyng in youth,
> And all my luffaris lele, my lugeing persewis,
> And fyllis me wyne wantonly with weilfair and joy...

After which the medieval Anna Livia Plurabelle rests her defence – 'I am so mercifull in mynd, and menys all wichtis' – and the three ladies join in laughter and concord and pass the cup round 'with comfortable drinks' until dawn. The festive scene at the widow's lodging melts into the summer night fantasy-scene of the ladies in their own festive arbour, and these figures themselves are then melted into the gradually lightening real landscape of the May morning, their laughter becoming birdsong, their voices the 'soft sowch of the swyr', and the gold and green and silver of their garments and goblets the dewy glitter of wood, field and burn in the first sunlight. These are masterly transitions, and nowhere in Dunbar is stylized language so keenly felt to be appropriate – for the return to that almost onomatopoeic descriptive reality the setting demanded, and for the conveying of this curious poet's word-conducted energy to its earth, safely reached after the long stretch (for him) of over five hundred lines.

Dunbar's restless and nervous force and his darting quick-silver personality almost invite the impatience with his writing he so often receives. It is only when his limitations are realized, when we no longer look in him for the particular kind of great poetry we have become over-accustomed to by Burns's lyrics and songs, when we make the effort to find his own individual value, that we can see him undistorted by not a little irrelevant prejudice. As has been indicated, his is not the singing voice which celebrates the perennial relations of the sexes in heartfelt immediacy and simplicity. Lacking this gift, he disturbs us by a startling indifference to theme in poetry; we are uneasy as we watch him turn from the Rabelaisian endearments of 'In secreit place' to a religious *Nativitie* or *Resurrection*, from a mocking address to a Negro lady to his 'Quhat is this lyfe bot ane straucht way to deid', from fantasy to ethics, from ethics to satire, and from satire to stately elegy and eulogy, with no category botched, no nonchalance of treatment, however he may have alighted on his subject. The answer to such half-formulated queries of his 'sincerity' or his 'seriousness' is that Dunbar's main interest in poetry was a formal one, that he succeeded in writing poems of great worth *because* his energies as well as his literary preferences were canalized verbally. In saying this the distinction must be repeated – with its bearing on Dunbar's real limitation as a poet – between the stylized language that carries its own evidence in alliteration or anaphora or rhetorical cataloguing or any other device and the more usual language of the greatest poets where created meaning rises out of the relations between words *unlikely* from the immediately rhetorical or resonant point of view to be fruitful. Here Dunbar does not escape from the still primitive, however struggling, example and conception of his period's poetry, and it is the pity or tragedy of his achievement, if I may speak for Scotland, that his genius had to write under dawn's left hand. But with a little adjustment on our part, a tackling of the vocabulary, a tolerance of tastes and pleasures which much of the poetry we know best has not shared, and a realization of how frequently the effects in Dunbar belong to something permanent in the spirit of the language, manifesting itself at different times in different disguises, he can be appreciated for the fine energy issuing through all his works in forms as dexterously wrought as they may be superficially extravagant.

Essays in Criticism, vol. II no. 2, April 1952.

How Good a Poet is Drummond?

(A paper read at the Quatercentenary Conference on William Drummond of Hawthornden held in Edinburgh under the auspices of the Scottish Branch of the Society for Renaissance Studies and Edinburgh University Library on 11 December 1985; it was intended as a general survey, introductory to more specialized papers by other speakers.)

I have posed a question which it would be very hard for any one person to answer, since a poet's reputation depends on many factors in society and is always in a state of flux and change. All I want to do is to try to clear the air sufficiently to offer some kind of overall picture as I see it at the moment, and I think this is worth doing because Drummond is for a number of reasons a difficult poet to get into focus. He has suffered at various times from different prejudices, both literary and political, and of course one is not saying that he himself is not to blame for encouraging some of these prejudices in the first place, but there is all the more reason for having another look at the range of his work.

We can identify two main problem areas: his Scottishness (or lack of it), and his plagiarism. He was a Scottish poet, born in Scotland and living most of his life there, who had to learn his craft at the very time when the Union of the Crowns and the departure of James VI and I and his court, and many court poets, to London gave a new meaning to the term 'Scottish poet' which no one had yet come to grips with. A poet who went to London would have given up the fight. Could a poet who stayed in and around Edinburgh continue the fight, and if so, how? Drummond certainly spoke some kind of Scots, and his early poetry was more Scots than English. But he followed the general drift of his contemporaries towards English, and eventually wrote an English verse that was acceptable in England. Yet his manuscript poems remained much more Scottish than those he published or than the versions of the manuscript poems he published, and even in his latest work there are still many Scottish forms lurking around which must have given a flavour, or possibly a sense of awkwardness, to the English reader. Now Drummond was trying very hard to write English! – so do we give him the benefit of the doubt and praise him for what he accomplished – he was, after all, historically speaking, the first Scottish poet to write successfully in English, though others may have shown the way – or do we dig about in his work for relics of the auld leid which might allow Scottish critics to take him to their very suspicious bosom? The fact that Drummond was one of the stars of Palgrave's *Golden Treasury* did not help him one bit in our twentieth century, in either England or Scotland. But it is interesting to consider that as late as 1911 he was still a star in Sir George Douglas's *Book of Scottish Poetry*, where he was given thirty pages; however, in Tom Scott's *Penguin Book of Scottish Verse* of 1970 he does not appear at all, and the editor in his introduction says merely that he 'belongs to the English tradition of poetry'. In between these two dates, of course, the whole modern Scottish Renaissance movement had taken place, and in Tom Scott's very committed view the emphasis on Scottishness should be as overt as possible, and Drummond did not pass this test. What has happened since then, in the last fifteen years, is the gradual emergence of an attitude that is not in any way unScottish but sits more easily and readily to the whole variety of manifestations of writing in Scotland. It is possible to deplore the fact that Drummond's native tongue shows itself only in the odd *thocht* and *brocht*, *lauch* and *thole*, *sal* and *suld*, *syne* and *hereefter*, *threeds* and *sterve* and *tane*, and various recurring grammatical forms. But we are surely at liberty to make what we can of what is there. I don't find myself agreeing with Robert McDonald in his excellent book on Drummond's library (*The Library of Drummond of Hawthornden*, 1971) when he says (p.22): 'We must read Drummond as he wished to be read, as an English poet, and resist judging him by the mass of private verse he suppressed, which has only been added to his canon by diligent editors.' Ironically, he himself became one of these diligent editors five years later, when he printed hitherto unpublished poetry in his Drummond selection (*William Drummond of Hawthornden: Poems and Prose*) of 1976; rightly so, even if he had changed his mind.

On the question of plagiarism, attitudes have altered there too, more than once and in several directions. The first revelation of the extent of Drummond's imitations, from French, Italian, Spanish, English, and Scottish poets, though he said relatively little about the last of these, came in L.E. Kastner's Scottish Text Society edition of 1913. Kastner comes over as being a little flushed with the delight of having tracked down so many originals of Drummond's poems, and so he overstates the case against him. In the introduction he says (Vol. I, pp. xliii–xliv): 'A full third of Drummond's compositions are translations or close paraphrases, and betray in no uncertain manner the imitative temper of his Muse. The rest are best described as adaptations from foreign models... All claim to originality he must forgo... [E]ven as an imitative poet, he cannot pretend to the highest rank; for that, his range is too limited, confined as it is to some hundred and thirty sonnets, about the same number of madrigals and epigrams, and less than a score of longer pieces.' We are now, seventy years later, a little less blunt and cocksure about the use of sources in poetry (and indeed in prose too), partly because we have become more aware of the complexity and subtlety of the Renascence doctrine of imitation, and partly because modernist writing, from Eliot and MacDiarmid to Lowell and Burroughs, has forced us to reconsider the whole question of plagiarism or (a rose by any other name?) intertextuality. There is a nice irony in the fact that plagiarism in a legal sense, relating to laws of copyright, is today far more tightly and severely considered, and is therefore more dangerous, than it was in the days of either Drummond or Kastner, while at the same time it has gained a new aesthetic acceptability both among critics and (it seems to me) with the wider public. So does this mean that Ronsard and Marino can birl in their graves as much as they like, but our withers are unwrung? The answer is probably yes, unless we are French or Italian, when we may find ourselves saying, Have I not heard this before? National priority is not entirely a dead body. But with Drummond we have a man who is aware of these problems; he is not a novice; he knows the languages he uses; he tries everything from close translation to the working up of mere hints and lines; and when we make studied comparisons with the originals (as Dr R.D.S. Jack has done in his books and articles) we can admire the kinds of transformation Drummond achieves. I'm sure this is a matter which another speaker at today's conference will be taking up when he talks about the sonnets, so I won't go into it further myself, beyond pointing to one example of where a small deliberate change has interesting consequences. Drummond's madrigal 'To the delightfull Greene / Of you fair radiant Eine' is based on a madrigal of Tasso's which begins 'Al vostro dolce azurro'. The altered colour of the lady's eyes from blue to green is unusual in itself, but it also leads to a very different poem, where conventional blue eyes and blue sky are replaced by not only green eyes but a green heaven which reflects the green of the sea:

> The Heavens (if we their Glasse
> The Sea beleeve) bee greene, not perfect blew.
> They all make faire what ever faire yet was,
> And they bee faire because they looke like you.

And not only that, but the poem links back and forward to its neighbours, which are sonnets, and where a theme of colours, both real and symbolic, is seen to emerge, and this spread of imagery beyond the boundary of the single poem is something we often find in Drummond. In the sonnet preceding the madrigal ('When Nature now had wonderfully wrought'), Nature considers what colour the lady's eyes are to be: black like the night-sky, an azure blue, or (the final choice, pointing forward to the madrigal) 'a Paradise of Greene'. Three colours again appear in the sonnet following the madrigal ('In vaine I haunt the colde and silver Springs'), where the unhappy lover, feverish in the lady's absence, receives no solace from the silver of water, the gold of an eastern sun, or the red of a western sunset. This sonnet also locks itself back onto the madrigal through the near-echo of two rare colour words (it is almost like a coded message, or even a misprint): Cynoper (= red) in the sonnet, Sinople (= green) in the madrigal. So imitation is only part of a larger story which is going on in Drummond's mind and is his own.

Looking into the general qualities and values of his poetry: perhaps what would strike us most today is that the earlier emphasis on the lyric poet, refined, often melancholy, craftsman-like, 'enamellit' as the medieval Scots would say, is in need of some shift, some dislocation: not that we would want to remove or undervalue his lyricism but that we want to bring forward other aspects of his work which have been neglected, perhaps because they failed to appeal at certain periods, perhaps because the material was simply not published, not known, perhaps because of doubtful attribution in some cases. (And one might add, in passing, that we still lack a proper edition of the poet's works, so that in a sense we are still making interim judgements.) The short poems, the sonnets and madrigals, will probably always be the centre of his work, and the best of these stand rereading, stand analysis, stand up well even under a different aegis of poetic theory – sonnets like 'Sleep, Silence Child, sweet Father of soft Rest', 'Slide soft faire Forth, and make a cristall Plaine', 'My Lute, bee as thou wast when thou didst grow', 'Triumphant Arches, Statues crown'd with Bayes', 'Of this faire Volume which wee World doe name', 'The last and greatest Herauld of Heavens King', and madrigals like 'This world a Hunting is', 'A Dedale of my Death', 'This Life which seemes so faire', 'My Thoughts hold mortall Strife'. All these, and others, are masterly pieces, and have their own subtle music. The madrigals are particularly fine, and if Drummond learned something of the art of compression from Tasso and Marino, he evidently had the tact of meaningful brevity in himself, and it is not surprising that he also tried his hand at epigrams and epitaphs and iconic and figurative poems. The madrigals have been thought of as the 'English' heart of his poetry, even if neither 'Elizabethan' nor 'Metaphysical' seems the right adjective to apply to them. Yet sometimes they seem very Scottish. As an experiment, let me read the madrigal 'Astrea in this Time' first of all as it stands in English:

> Astrea in this Time
> Now doth not live, but is fled up to Heaven;
> Or if shee live, it is not without Crime
> That shee doth use her Power,
> And shee is no more Virgine, but a Whoure,
> Whoure prostitute for Gold:
> For shee doth never holde her Ballance even,
> And when her Sword is roll'd,
>> The Bad, Injurious, False, shee not o'rethrowes,
>> But on the innocent lets fall her Blowes.

With just a few changes, one can begin to sense a grimmer Scottish poem beneath the English overlay:

> Astrea in thir Times
> Noo disna leeve, but has flee'd aff tae Heeven;
> Or gin she leeve, it isna athoot Crimes
> That she does yaise her Pooer,
> And she is nae mair Virgin, but a Hoor,
> Hoor prostitute fur Gowd:
> Fur she does niver haud her Balance even,

And yince her Swird is row'd,
    The Bad, the Fause, the Skaithfu she nocht owrethraws,
    But on the Ill-less she lats faw her Blaws.

Perhaps because of the impressiveness of the shorter poems, Drummond's longer pieces have received less critical attention, yet the poet obviously did feel the pull of more extended, or more ambitious, or sometimes more public work. The longest of these poems, the unfinished 450-line 'The Shadow of the Judgement', is the least successful; although it has one or two strong passages, the whole apocalyptic conception seems to have weighed Drummond down and led him into some rather forced and makeshift writing, as for example:

Where shee doeth roame in Aire faint doe the Birdes,
Yawne doe Earths ruthless brood & harmlesse Heards,
The Woods wilde Forragers doe howle and roare,
The humid Swimmers dye along the shoare;
In Townes, the living doe the dead up-eate...   (ll. 243-47)

(When Drummond is bad he really *is* bad!). Much more interesting, and more attuned to the poet's Christian–Platonic idealism and characteristic sense of space, colour, distance, and light, is 'An Hymne of the Fairest Faire', subtitled 'An Hymne of the Nature, Atributes, and Workes of God'. This poem has recently been singled out by John MacQueen, in his book *Numerology* (1985), as an example of how Drummond, like Spenser and Milton before and after him, can be placed in a numerological tradition, where hidden structures, to say nothing of hidden meanings, may be teased out by a diligent enquirer. His main argument (though it becomes complex as it goes along) is that the poem deals with the weight or weightiness of the great engine of the universe powered by the Trinity, the Fairest Fair of the title. Therefore its 336 lines, divided by the 3 of the Trinity, give us three parts of 112 lines, the numerical equivalent of a hundred-weight, or 112 lb. It would perhaps be a good medieval disputation to decide whether the Trinity weighs three-hundredweights. But I would not be disposed to write off this approach to Drummond, even if in this instance I think the 112-line division is open to some question: it works all right at line 112, but not at 224, which ends with a comma and is part of a continuing sentence and argument. I suspect that other Drummond poems might well

yield new information from a numerological analysis: I am thinking especially of the madrigals, where the interweaving of double
and triple rhymes, in threes and twos, seems possibly relatable
to varying numbers of feet and syllables and to the total number
of lines. The more public poems, *Forth Feasting* and *The Entertainment* [of the High and Mighty Monarch, Prince Charles, King
of great Brittaine, France and Ireland, into his ancient and Royall
Citie of Edenbourgh, the 15. of June. 1633] show an altogether
different aspect of the supposedly retiring and solitary laird of
Hawthornden. In fact as a man he was rather like Yeats, and
showed some envy of those who were active and even violent
in public, social, political, or military affairs; Hawthornden was
his Thoor Ballylee from which he watched *his* civil war raging
back and forth. One remembers also the patents Drummond
took out in 1627 for new and fearsome weapons and other military devices; even if these never got beyond the drawing-board,
the mere fact that he had thought them up, apparently with some
care, presents an extraordinary contrast to any view of him as a
delicate lyricist and nothing more. Anyhow, I shall not say anything further about these poems, since another speaker will be
dealing with *Forth Feasting*, beyond making the point that to see
Drummond fairly, we have to be willing to register his surprising
scope, and in these pieces we see a certain eloquence in praise of
Scotland which we might not suspect from the short poems, and
a particular kind of two-edged patriotism very characteristic of
a poet caught in Drummond's time-warp, having to, or feeling
he has to, praise or welcome absent and merely visiting kings
who from one point of view have deserted their country, and
even Drummond as a convinced monarchist did sometimes see
it that way.

One other long poem, *Polemo-Middinia*, usually escapes critical
comment or evaluation because its authorship is not certain. Having looked fairly closely at the evidence, I am persuaded it must
be by Drummond. The poet had personal and family connections
with both places involved in the mock battle near Crail in Fife;
when the poem was published in 1684 his eldest son was still
alive and accepted the poem as his father's, as indeed did all
Drummond's surviving friends; Drummond's interest in languages, and the fact that his library contained similar macaronic
writings by the Italian poet Folingo, seem to fit in; and finally,
as Drummond's early biographer Bishop Sage remarked, and he
never doubted the authorship, the poem 'suits exactly with the

humour and genius of the nation' and is in a tradition of Scottish burlesque which Drummond knew about. If we can accept it as part of the canon, it takes us even further away from Palgrave's lyricist, since it is a racy, rich, outspoken, coarse, very physical and very funny mock-epic incident, in a mixture of Latin and Scots, describing an attempt by the folk belonging to Scot of Scotstarvet to establish a right-of-way through the domains of Cunningham of Newbarns by driving muck-carts across the enemy territory: they don't quite succeed, and a truce is called at the end: '*Barlafumle* clamat, & dixit, *O Deus, O God!*' What is notable about the poem is the contrast between the down-to-earth knockabout burlesque of the action and the ingenuity of the Scoto-Latin hexameters, the delight the author takes in using the everyday Scots words which perhaps he was otherwise inhibited from drawing on. This list of local worthies would have pleased William Dunbar, and yet is already abutting on the world of the Sempills of Beltrees:

> Hic aderant *Geordie Akinhedius*, & little *Johnus*,
> Et *Jamie Richaeus*, & stout *Michael Hendersonus*,
> Qui jolly tryppas ante alios dansare solebat,
> Et bobbare bene, & lassas kissare bonaeas;
> *Duncan Oliphantus* valde staluartus, & eius
> Filius eldestus joly boyus, atque *Oldmoudus*,
> Qui pleugham longo gaddo dryvare solebat,
> Et *Rob Gib* wantonus homo, atque *Oliver Hutchin*,
> Et plouky-fac'd *Wattie Strang*, atque inkne'd *Alshinder Atkin*,
> Et *Willie Dick* heavi-arstus homo, pigerrimus omnium...

Neberna, the virago commanding the Newbarns defenders, harangues the invaders like some Dulle Griet in Bruegel (and indeed one of the cannons of which Mad Meg was the patron anti-saint, Mons Meg, appears elsewhere in the poem); her language has a controlled wildness that is all the more effective as humour because a drop of the horrific is still left hanging there:

> Ite, ait, uglei felloës, si quis modo posthac
> Muckifer has nostras tentet crossare fenestras,
> Juro ego quod eius longum extrahabo thrapellum,
> Et totam rivabo faciem, luggasque gulaeo hoc
> Ex capite cuttabo ferox, totumque videbo
> Heart-blooddum fluere in terram.

No heart-blood flows, however. The intruders give up when their leading fighter, Geordie the grieve, is painfully *stobbatus* by a Newbarns seamstress's needle driven into his *privatas partes*. *Sic fraya fuit*, the poet says, *sic guisa peracta est*. Almost like a piece of street theatre, the guising, the masque, has been acted out.

If we were absolutely sure that *Polemo-Middinia* is Drummond's, it would not only extend his range of effects but would also link up with some of his later satirical verse, of which there is a great deal, some of it beginning to be better known at long last, not all of it first-rate but the best of it very sharp and surprising, sometimes politically bitter or angry, sometimes scurrilously erotic, sometimes merely amusing in a relaxed manner. In what is probably the best known of his political satires, 'A Character of the Anti-Covenanter, or Malignant', he makes a clever, ironic, Swiftian mock-attack on his own royalist position. But this is very different from the direct, desperately angry approach of the untitled poem 'Against the king, sir, now why would yee fight', written at the time when he at last gave in and signed the Covenant in 1639. Here is a roused, cornered Drummond, striking out like a scorpion:

> Give me a thousand covenants, I'll subscrive
> Them all, and more, if more yee can contrive
> Of rage and malice; and let evrye one
> Blake treason bare, not bare Rebellione.
> I'll not be mockt, hist, plunder'd, banisht hence
> For more yeeres standing for a ———— prince.
> The castells all are taken, and his crown,
> The sword and sceptre, ensignes of Renown,
> With the lieutenant fame did so extoll,
> And all led captives to the Capitoll;
> I'll not die Martire for any mortall thing,
> It's enough to be confessour for a king.
> Will this you give contentment, honest Men?
> I have written Rebelles, pox upon the pen!

His short occasional poems in the satirical mode – epigrams, epitaphs, and what he himself called 'Skeltonicall verses' made '*a las roguerias de ses amicos*' – might be called anti-madrigals, the avocation of a madrigalist. Four lines dispose of the great parliamentarian, John Pym, who died in 1643:

When Pime last night descended into Hell,
Ere hee his coupes of Lethe did carouse,
What place is this (said hee) I pray mee tell?
To whom a Divell: This is the lower howse.

('On Pime')

Both scolds and skalds receive a nip in these untitled lines:

Flyting no reason hath, for at this tyme,
It doth stand with reason, but in ryme.
That none save thus should flyte, had wee a law,
What rest had wee? how would wyves stand in aw,
And learne the art of rhyming! Then how well
Would this and all good flyting pamphlets sell!

The Petrarch of the North takes a fine anti-Petrarchan shot at his contemporary Alexander Craig (helping to remind us, incidentally, that the 'solitary and retired' Drummond fathered at least twelve children):

With elegies, sad songs, and murning layes,
Quhill Craig his Kala wald to pitie move,
Poore braine-sicke man! he spends his dearest dayes;
Such sillie rime can not make women love.
    Morice quho sight of never saw a booke
    With a rude stanza this faire Virgine tooke.

('Sextain')

The epitaphs often display an odd, sidelong humour that is again very different from the stuffiness of the image Drummond has been – I think he would like the word-play – saddled with:

Here lye the Bones of a gentle horse
Who living used to carrye the corse
Of an insolent preacher. O had the asse
Of Balaam him carryed, he had told what hee was!
Now courteous readeres tell so, if yee can,
Is the Epitaph of the horse or of the Man?

Humour gives way to savagery in the longer, 60-line poem 'For a Ladyes Summonds of Nonentree', a diatribe against Kite, a woman the speaker had been with eight years ago and whom he now refuses when she offers to re-open the relationship; he is disgusted by her years of nymphomaniac promiscuousness and expresses his regret and revulsion in Donne-like couplets:

> Kite.
> Summond not mee to enter, there's no doubt
> These twice foure yeeres and more I have been out,
> And I it not denie, I did you wrong
> At first, but since could not come in for throng.
> Counts, knights, and Gentilles so hanted your Roome
> Then your kinsmen, yeomen, and evrye Groome.
> Why should I press'd? What? should I been there
> Where Brother Nepheu were so familiare?
> And that with his French page sore-galled lord
> Whom our east-Neighboures brought unto accord?
> When all are gone and desolate's the place
> Yee will mee enter, altred is your case;
> Now it no more is like that thing
> That earst it was then a gate is like a Ring...
> Let your geometrike foot-man serve your turne
> Or the porter whom last yeere yee did burne
> Or your learned childrens Tutor, who well can
> Teach any Woman to decline to man,
> That will himself a diphthongue turne with you
> Pox on them if they tell what e're yee doe...

With such samples of his varied powers in mind, it seems important that we find some way of accepting a more complete portrait of Drummond than we had in the past; the satirical, the public, the angry, and the humorous Drummond are all truly there, and eventually we must sort out the weight we would give to aspects of his work which appear to be at war with others. A revaluation in the direction of inclusiveness seems to be what we want, and we shall find ourselves with a more credible and indeed more interesting figure, and one we certainly need not reject from the Scottish pantheon.

Scottish Literary Journal, vol.15 no.1, May 1988.

Gavin Douglas and William Drummond as Translators

My aim in this paper is to take up the point which seems to me to be of the greatest interest in any comparison between Douglas and Drummond and that is the different times at which they wrote, the gap of a hundred years that in this case can make it seem as if the early sixteenth and the early seventeenth centuries were worlds apart. Although Gavin Douglas has been described as an early humanist, looking forward to the English Elizabethan translators, and although William Drummond has been described as an old-fashioned and indeed reactionary figure still in thrall to a rather passé and unadventurous brand of humanism, this (even if we assume it's true) does not help to make the two poets meet on common ground somewhere about (say) 1560. They remain obstinately and significantly distinct in their aims and practice.

When Douglas began translating Virgil he knew that he was in a pioneering situation. He had no models, in the sense that his would be the first attempt to translate one of the major classical poems into English or Scots, and his long Prologue to Book I, where he discusses the problems of the translator, shows in its self-consciousness, its mixture of pride and humility, its con-
tradictions, even in its length, that Douglas was well aware of the pioneer's varied and difficult responsibilities. The motive for undertaking a translation can affect the way in which the translation is carried out, and although Douglas tells us his task was taken up at the request of 'my speciall gud Lord Henry, Lord Sanct Clair', there were no doubt deeper motives at work, literary, didactic, and political or national. If we look at one very obvious characteristic of Douglas's *Aeneid*, that it is much longer than the original, and ask why it is longer, the reasons throw some light, though not an entirely clear light, on Douglas's motives. The expansions may be examples of the translator's delight in elaborating something with greater physical detail, where Douglas is carried away by an almost dramatic, identificatory

enthusiasm (not unlike his fondness for accumulating details in the original Prologues and in *The Palice of Honour*). Or they may come from a desire to be extremely explicit, like someone incorporating footnotes into a text, to make quite sure that every reader of the translation will know not only what Virgil said but also what his commentators – and especially the diligent Ascenius, whom Douglas made continuous use of – thought it wise to explain. In the first sort of expansion, Douglas writes as a man in love with language, aware both of the underdeveloped state of Scots and of its potentialities; in the Prologue to Book I he swithers between conventional depreciation – his 'bad harsk speech and lewit barbour tong' – and a sense of the dignity of what that barbarous tongue has enabled him to achieve:

> ... this buke I dedicait,
> Writtin in the langage of Scottis natioun.
> (Prol. I., ll. 102-3)

Here, we can see Douglas as indeed an exemplar of Renaissance vernacular revival, when country after country in Europe seized on translation of established classics as an act of linguistic independence and maturity, implying at the same time a culturo-national independence and maturity.

If we glance at the other aspect I mentioned, the explicitness of the translation, its incorporation of elucidatory notes and phrases, we might see this as confirming a motive to produce a 'mirror for princes' as some critics have suggested – a mirror for princes on the eve of Flodden! This view of the poem would certainly square with his praise of Aeneas in the first Prologue, where he argues that Virgil is not concerned with Aeneas as an individual but as a type or an emblematic figure:

> Not forto say sikane Eneas was,
> Yit than by hym perfytely blasons he
> All wirschip, manhed and nobilite,
> With every bonte belangand a gentill wycht,
> Ane prynce, ane conquerour or a valyeand knycht.
> (ll. 328-32)

But Douglas seems unwilling to restrict the impact of his poem to princes and nobles. He says different things about this at different times, and perhaps never did decide what audience he was writing for. But he does give some strong indications that he hoped he might have eventually a wide audience, including the illiterate to whom the poem could be read aloud (interesting, in view of the rhythmical freedom of his metric, as well as the frequently homely vocabulary) –

> And to onletterit folk be red on hight
> That erst was bot with clerkis comprehend.
>
> ('Ane exclamatioun', ll. 44-5)

– and including also, for their sins, children in school who are learning Virgil:

> Thank me tharfor, masteris of grammar sculys,
> Quhar ye syt techand on your benkis and stulys.
>
> ('Direction', ll. 47-8)

This second group of motives, then, would encourage Douglas to make his translation, as he says, 'braid and plane', so that his readers from princes to schoolboys would understand it and imbibe its message of high duty and heroic action. It follows, I would suggest, that there was a tension, but a profitable tension, between the didactic and the enthusiastic aspects of Douglas's conception of his task. The poem spreads itself, but never gets out of hand; the language is full of vivid detail and is much more concrete than Virgil's, but it doesn't lose the ongoing sense of a great enterprise. There are things in Virgil that Douglas never quite reaches: ambiguities, dying falls, the *lacrimae rerum*. He knew he was dealing with a poet of elusive depth, but the busy, concrete vocabulary he builds up, for all its vitality, tends to act as a barrier to the mysterious and the profound – which is of course why Ezra Pound liked it, since he regarded Virgil as somewhat effete. Douglas's own comment on the unplumbable depths he sensed in his author is worth quoting:

> So profund was this wark at I have said,
> Me semyt oft throw the deip sey to waid;
> And sa mysty umquhile this poecy,
> My spreit was reft half deill in extasy.
>
> ('Direction', ll. 103-6)

(I like that 'half deill': there's something very Scottish about his reluctant ecstasy.) However, even these limitations, which most critics except Ezra Pound have assumed, are not as damaging as one might think, and there are many good passages of the original poem where Douglas in his rendering seems thoroughly on top of his task. I'd like to refer briefly to one moment in the epic where the translator shows his mettle in ways that are different from those he most commonly gets credit for (e.g. dealing with sea and ships, fights, descriptions of place and weather).

The end of Book I is a fine passage in Virgil. Dido has set up a great banquet for Aeneas and his men, and as she drinks she finds herself more and more deeply in love with her guest, the poem already calling her 'infelix Dido' though her tragedy is still far away. Like Desdemona with Othello, she is fascinated by his exotic wanderings and misfortunes, and ends Book I by pleading with Aeneas to tell his story:

> Onhappy Dido alsso set all hir mycht
> With sermondis seir forto prolong the nycht,
> The langsum lufe drynkard inwart ful cald.
> Full mony demand of Priam speir scho wald
> And questionys seir twichyng Hector alswa;
> Now with quhais armour the son of Aurora
> Come to the sege, and now inquir wald sche
> Quhat kynd horss Diomede had in the melle,
> Quhou large of statur was ferss Achillis.
> 'Have done, my gentill gest, sone tell ws this
> Per ordour,' says scho, 'fra the begynnyng, all
> The dissait of the Grekis and the fall
> Of your pepill and of Troy the rewyne;
> Thi wandring be the way thou schaw ws syne,
> For now the sevynt symmyr hyddir careis the,
> Wilsum and errant, throu every land and see.'
>
> (I. xi. ll. 109-24)

The differences are small but telling. Douglas gives Dido her many speeches, her 'sermondis seir', '*forto* prolong the nycht', whereas Virgil simply says 'noctem trahebat', 'she wore out, spun out the night'. Douglas makes her more conscious of time, more anxious ('set all hir mycht'), more open to tragedy. And in the next line 'The langsum lufe drynkand inwart ful cald' he has added the 'ful cald' (Virgil has 'longumque bibebat amorem'), which is perfectly in the spirit of the text, since the wine she was drinking would be cold, but it adds a most expressive proleptic shiver at that point. And in her direct speech, it seems to me that Douglas with his very free rhythm and enjambment, despite the rhyme, has given an excellent impression of Dido's eager, agitated soul. The last two lines also enact, in their sound-echoes as well as their long hypermetrical movement, the many years of wandering and voyaging. This is not a 'lewit barbour tong' but a skilled deployment of resources to match a character's inward feeling and outward speech.

On the whole, Douglas's pioneering work meets the challenge remarkably well – the challenge of translating a major poem into Scots from a language of very different construction. He extends the range of Scots, and his translation ought to have been one more landmark in the development of a Scottish language. That it was not such a landmark, that it came at the end of a phase of Scottish cultural growth rather than the beginning, was hardly Douglas's fault. The national or patriotic implications of what Douglas had achieved (despite his being in his own life a renegade from Scotland who died in exile – never trust the teller, trust the tale!) had to wait till the eighteenth-century revival, and Thomas Ruddiman's edition of the poem in 1710. Ironies abound in this whole situation, particularly when we bring in William Drummond, whose *Works* Ruddiman also published, a year later in 1711, as part of his patriotic programme. We have Douglas making his enormous effort to 'prove' the potential of vernacular Scots when it was too late to have any immediate or widespread effect in his own country; and then a century later we have Drummond, who unlike Douglas remains in Scotland when so many of his literary contemporaries go south and yet who makes *his* enormous effort to prove that Scottish poets could write well in English. And just as Douglas never did entirely without English forms (even in his day), so Drummond never entirely swept his cupboard bare of Scots. But it was the near-medieval Douglas who was in some ways in advance of his time, writing long before the great Elizabethan translators; and it was Drummond, the first Scottish poet to write continuously and well in English, who was the real conservative, and whose works as Ben Jonson rightly if unkindly said 'smelled too much of the Schools, and were not after the fancy of the time'.

In this tragi-comedy of ironies, it is Drummond rather than Douglas who stands in need of defence, and it is good to see that interest in Drummond has been growing. Drummond is like

Shelley: people mock at 'Hail to thee, blithe Spirit!' and forget
The Mask of Anarchy. Drummond is first and foremost a meditative lyric poet, but he also wrote satirical, political, scabrous,
and bawdy verse (some of which, as we now know, was silently
omitted by the prudish Kastner from his Scottish Text Society
edition). The overdue reassessment will have to take all his work
into account, and not just the Palgrave's Golden Treasury part
of it. However, my concern here is with his translations.

Between the times of Douglas and Drummond the Renaissance ideas on Imitation are the great divide. To Douglas, Virgil
was Virgil, whether in Latin or in Scots – 'Go, wulgar [i.e. ver-
nacular] Virgill...' as he says at the end. But Drummond had
no hesitation in publishing as his own a large number of poems
which ran the gamut from close translation to loose imitation or
paraphrase, taken from Italian, French, Spanish, Latin, and even
English. Some of his best-known poems are in fact direct translations, though the average reader who comes across them in
anthologies will be unaware of the fact. A measure of moral
blame has attached to Drummond for this, especially as he quite
naughtily does label some poems 'translations', but never the
best ones. But this is an area we today have to walk in rather
warily. A property-conscious, copyright-conscious world is not
the best vantage-point for understanding the subtleties of the
Renaissance doctrine of Imitation, which by its nature implied
an invisible communion of European writers, a vast web of ideals
and traditions shading off in each country to finer and finer distinctions and measures of vernacular or personal variation.
Drummond relished these European blueprints not simply
because, as Ben Jonson claimed, he was conservative or old-
fashioned, but also because the doctrine suited the subtle and
delicate movement of his own mind: the making of small distinctions, the slight renewal or slewing round of established metaphors or comparisons, the infusion of a personality drop by drop
into a tradition – these are what Drummond wanted and got
from his habit of translation.

We are apt to forget that to a Renaissance theorist, Imitation
in its best or ideal state was far removed from plagiarism, which
implies an easy theft. Du Bellay, in his *Deffence et illustration de
la langue françoyse* (1549), insisted that the imitator who wanted
his work to last must 'sweat and tremble many times, as if dead
to himself, and... endure hunger, thirst, and long vigils' (Chap.
3). It had to be the right poem at the right time, the poem that

suited the translator's gifts, aims, and language. That Drummond had done some thinking about the varieties of imitation is shown by his triple versions of two Italian sonnets, where he writes out the original, then a fairly close translation 'in the same sort of rime', then another version 'in frier sort of rime', and a final version 'paraphrastically translated'. Even the fact that he got the idea of doing this from still another poet does not remove the interest of the exercise.

There are times when Drummond nods, when perhaps he chooses a poem that is less 'on his wavelength' than he had imagined. His version of Marino's sonnet on the prodigal son, 'Cangia contrada...', 'I Countries chang'd, new pleasures out to finde', substitutes a bland pietistic complacence for the bitterness of the original. Marino's prodigal begs God to excuse his faults, Drummond's prodigal is confident that 'thy love... / My faults will pardon'. Marino's oak-tree is big and has branches, Drummond's is feebly personified as 'aged' and has 'arms'. Marino's prodigal listens to the 'sozzo armento', the filthy herd of pigs chewing acorns, Drummond's herd is not filthy and his prodigal doesn't 'listen' – the youth and the pigs are lay-figures in a static conventional landscape.

But in other poems the changes may transform a conventional original into something much more interesting. Tasso's madrigal, 'Al vostro dolce azzurro', makes great play with blue eyes and blue skies, but Drummond's version of it boldly starts off with *green* eyes ('To the delighfull Greene / Of you faire radiant Eine') and then has to find green in the sky, in the sea, and in heaven itself. Or turning to Marino again, Drummond's otherwise close translation of his madrigal 'Fabro dela mia morte' gains a newly striking opening line:

> A Dedale of my Death,
> Now I resemble that subtile Worme on Earth
> Which prone to its owne evill can take no rest.
> For with strange Thoughts possest,
> I feede on fading Leaves
> Of Hope, which me deceaves,
> And thousand Webs doth warpe within my Brest.
> And thus in end unto my selfe I weave
> A fast-shut Prison, no, but even a Grave.

The alliteration in the first line, the rare noun 'Dedale' for 'fabro', add to the basic idea of being the maker or shaper of one's own death the more specific evocation of Dedalus the builder of labyrinths, and this leads right into the web imagery of the poem and enriches it.

And in one final example, where Drummond borrows from English poetry instead of Italian, the 'imitation' shows, in being not simply verbal but in drawing on the whole original context, how much Drummond was prepared to extract from what at first sight seems a mere filching of a choice phrase from a greater author. It's a well-known borrowing, in the song 'Phoebus arise': the lines towards the end, 'Night like a Drunkard reeles / Beyond the Hills to shunne his flaming Wheeles', which are based on *Romeo and Juliet* (II. iii), 'And fleckel'd darkness like a drunkard reels / From forth day's path and Titan's fiery wheels'. These lines come from a speech by Friar Lawrence as he goes out in the early morning, just before Romeo rushes in to tell him he's in love with Juliet and wants to be married. Drummond is using the tragic implications of Shakespeare's play to underline the sudden change of tone at the end of his own poem, which from being an ecstatic welcome to love finally admits the lady is not there, will not arrive: 'Here is the pleasant Place / And ev'ry thing, save Her, who all should grace.'

One point that stands out in Drummond's poetry is that in most instances it would be very difficult, if not impossible, to detect from a poem in itself whether it was original or translated. Ronsard, Tasso, Marino become Drummond. How far this is a strong argument in favour of Drummond's methods is no doubt open to debate. But what cannot be upheld is the view that he was no more than a sport, an exotic, an anomaly in the history of Scottish poetry – the view, unfortunately, of Kastner in his STS edition, and a view still found, despite the useful reappraisals by Dr Ronald Jack and others in recent years. Drummond's English verse was as important in its way as Douglas's Scots. It acknowledged the reality of the linguistic situation in Scotland, where Gaelic, Scots, and English had somehow to live together. Drummond showed that English could be used, and that others would use it after him.

Bards and Makars, ed. A.J. Aitken et al. (University of Glasgow Press, 1977).

Robert Fergusson

The bicentenary of Robert Fergusson's death in 1774 is being well marked in a number of ways, in lectures, in exhibitions, in books and readings, and this is particularly gratifying. The one thing we can say at once about Fergusson is that he was unlucky – unlucky in his short life, unlucky in being followed so soon by the more flamboyant Burns, unlucky in the fact that the distinctive kind of urban poetry he so much enjoyed writing did not establish a tradition which in the nineteenth century might have kept his name up as a forerunner. We are, gradually, making amends. He is now a highly respected poet, much more often thought about and written about than he used to be; and the more we look closely at his work the more we find to admire, often with a sense of surprise, in that it was different from what we had expected, and had greater range. He is his own man, and is not to be taken only as a John the Baptist for Burns. Burns was, in a sense, baptized by Fergusson's poetry, as he himself frankly admitted, and many of his poems as is well known were sparked off by or modelled on poems by Fergusson, not always improved in the process. But Fergusson was doing some things Burns didn't do, and it's our duty in a later century to see him as clearly as we can, doing our best to creep out from under the large shadow of Burns as a world-poet.

To see Fergusson clearly is not as easy as we would like. It is not that his poetry is difficult or obscure, though it may at times present a barrier through its local and contemporary references to names and places and historical events, and also it has an occasional awkwardness of syntax which holds up the sense. But just because it is so much the poetry of an exact place and time about which we know a good deal, and because we also know from external sources quite a fair amount about Fergusson's own life, we are constantly (and I would say naturally) searching for a unifying principle, something that would bring the man and his work together. And this, despite some of the obvious things one can say about it, is in the end difficult. There is something that resists the idea of an integrated view. It is perfectly possible, and profitable, to discuss the main themes of his poetry, but to see the man in his poetry, to understand the tones of his voice as he speaks with more or less directness or disguise – this is much harder. Most of Fergusson's work lies between two extremes which might be illustrated by two quotations from poems that are in English and are far from being his best writing. At one extreme, he writes in a drinking song (untitled):

> Hollo! keep it up, boys – and push round the glass,
> Let each seize his bumper, and drink to his lass:
> Away with dull thinking – 'tis madness to think –
> And let those be sober who've nothing to drink....
>
> Huzza, boys! let each take a bumper in hand,
> And stand – if there's anyone able to stand.
> How all things dance round me! – 'tis life, tho' my boys:
> Of drinking and spewing how great are the joys!
>
> My head! oh, my head! – but no matter, 'tis life:
> Far better than moping at home with one's wife.
> The pleasure of drinking you're sure must be grand,
> When I'm neither able to think, speak, nor stand.

Place that against this extract from a paraphrase he made from the Book of Job (Chap. 3), in rhyming couplets:

> Why then is grateful light bestow'd on man,
> Whose life is darkness, all his days a span?
> For ere the morn return'd my sighing came,
> My mourning pour'd out as the mountain stream;
> Wild-visag'd fear, with sorrow-mingled eye,
> And wan destruction piteous star'd me nigh;
> For though nor rest nor safety blest my soul,
> New trouble came, new darkness, new control.

We know that that 'wild visag'd fear' and 'wan destruction' did in fact come to Fergusson in the last months of his life when he went mad; we also know how much joy he took in conviviality, even the vulgarly expressed conviviality of the drinking song just quoted. What we don't know is how much of the whole man the conviviality was, how much it might have been an escape from solitude, a cover for loneliness or for feelings of rejection. And whether therefore there might come a breaking-point when feelings of guilt would appear, the guilt of a divided spirit more and more uncertain about the value of the life he was leading, getting no work satisfaction from the boring copying of legal documents by which he earned his living (and indeed making more and more mistakes in doing it), and yet also not getting all the expected satisfaction from the joys of drinking and talking in the Edinburgh clubs and taverns after office hours. Part of his nature was, we know, eager and sprightly and humorous, fond of pranks, wanting to entertain and be entertained, relishing the theatre, making friends with actors and singers, being a singer and a bit of an actor himself. His friend Thomas Sommers, who wrote his biography, tells us that

> in the course of his convivial frolics he laid a wager with some of his associates that if they could furnish him with a certain number of printed ballads (no matter what kind), he would undertake to dispose of them as a *street* singer in the course of two hours. The bet was laid: and the next evening, being in the month of November, a large bundle of ballads were pro- cured for him. He wrapped himself in a shabby greatcoat, put on an old scratch wig, and in this disguised form, commenced his adventure... In his going down the Lawnmarket and High Street, he had the address to collect great multitudes around him, while he amused them with a variety of favourite Scots songs, by no means such as he had ballads for, and gained the wager by disposing of the whole collection. He waited on his companions by eight o'clock that evening, and spent with them, in mirthful glee, the proceeds of his street adventure.

What is interesting about the incident is not just that he had a repertory of Scottish songs and ballads to sing, but that he par- ticularly enjoyed the acting of the part of the street singer and did it successfully, even to deceiving the lieges by selling them ballads he hadn't sung. Acting and singing are two of the things Fergusson might have done, instead of scraping a pen in a law office, if any possibility of such a career had offered itself. His fondness for acting and actors goes with his relative non-revela- tion of personality in his poems, his frequent dramatizations (Plainstanes and Causey, Herriot and Watson in 'The Ghaists',

Brandy and Whisky in 'A Drink Eclogue', the Sow of Feeling).
A psychologist might see him as involved in a search for identity,
particularly after the traumatic experience of being rejected by
(and at the same time rejecting) his rich uncle John Forbes in
Aberdeenshire and walking all the way back to Edinburgh in
1769 – a quarrel coming to a head on a point of social manners,
Fergusson being sent from the dinner-table because he was
improperly dressed. What price rank? what price society? what
price family relations? – these are questions he must have asked,
and since he lacked deep emotional involvements so far as we
know, the tendency would be for him to lose himself in social
company, to have a circle of friends as the focus of his life, and
by these means to stave off what he later came to call 'the horrors'
or 'the blue devils'. In an anonymous poem published in 1786,
an Epistle addressed to Burns but also referring to Fergusson,
the writer whoever he was puts very well this split which began
to appear in Fergusson's personality:

> Poor Fergusson! I ken'd him weel,
> He was a blythsome canty chiel;
> 'I've seen him roun' the bickers reel',
>   An' lilt his sang,
> An' crack his joke, sae pat an' leal,
>   Ye'd ne'er thought lang.
>
> O had ye seen, as I hae seen him,
> Whan nae Blue Devils did pervene him
> An' heard the pipe the Lord had gi'en him
>   In Scottish air
> Ye'd aiblins for an angel ta'n him,
>   He sang sae rare.
>
> But whan by these damn'd fiends attacket,
> His fine-spun saul they hew'd and hacket,
> Your very heart-strings wad hae cracket
>   To've seen him than;
> He was just like a headless tacket,
>   In shape o' man.

What those 'damn'd fiends' were we don't know exactly, whether
it was a manic-depressive psychosis, or syphilis, or possibly both.
What we do know is that he had acute feelings of guilt and

religious damnation. David Irving tells us in his biography of Fergusson (1799) how

> He was one day met below the North Bridge by a gentleman [William Woods the actor] with whom he had formerly been very intimately connected; and as he seemed to pass on quite regardless of every surrounding object, his friend accosted him, and demanded of him whither he was going. He replied that he had just discovered one of the reprobates who crucified our Saviour, and that in order to have him disposed of according to law, he was making all possible haste to lodge the information with Lord Kames.

This of course is a classic type of delusion: Fergusson really means that *he* is the reprobate who crucified our Saviour, and he is seeking to give himself up – something which to a modern psychiatrist would be a cry for help. His last days in the Edinburgh Bedlam are particularly moving because he alternated between bouts of violence and sanity. His friend Sommers visited him in his cell a few days before he died. 'We got immediate access to the cell,' he wrote, 'and found Robert lying with his clothes on, stretched upon a bed of loose uncovered straw. The moment he heard my voice, he instantly arose – got me in his arms and wept!' But although he was lucid then, and begging his friends to set him free, he died very soon after that.

This is the man who wrote the poems, the man we try to relate to the poems. It's an affecting story, and a story that makes us angry with some of the participants – with his uncle Forbes, with his friends who could have done more to help him at the end. But it's the poems that survive, and we have to define his achievement if we can. He has the vivid description that comes from his objectivity, his dry eye, his slight non-involvement: seen at its sharpest when he's dealing with city life, but by no means only there, as 'The Farmer's Ingle' shows. He has a considerable power for satire, applied to a great variety of subjects from Dr Johnson to the Town Guard. The satire is reasonably good-natured for the most part, but certainly can show its teeth when it wants to give a real nip. He has a command of parody and of imitation of dialects as well as styles, which goes with an interest in language that seems to be quite well developed. And, the thing that most of all was unfortunately cut off with his early death, he had and expressed in different ways a growing search for his identity as a poet, especially as a national poet who would be vigilant over Scotland, trying to define its culture, its values, its relation to England and the Continent. This search was far from easy or straightforward, because it was so much mixed in with his own real practical troubles and problems, as he reminds us in one of his last poems, 'To my Auld Breeks': his old patched pair of trousers has really had it, but he addresses them as intimate friends who must know that his life has been on a knife-edge of temperament:

> You've seen me round the bickers reel
> Wi' heart as hale as temper'd steel,
> And face sae apen, free and blyth,
> Nor thought that sorrow there cou'd kyth;
> But the niest mament this was lost,
> Like gowan in December's frost.

And he goes on to talk about poverty as well as temperament, and sees the auld breeks as a symbolic check to pride and materialism:

> Or if some bard, in lucky times,
> Shou'd profit meikle by his rhymes,
> And pace awa', wi' smirky face,
> In siller or in gowden lace,
> Glowr in his face, like spectre gaunt,
> Remind him o' his former want,
> To cow his daffin and his pleasure,
> And gar him live within the measure.

The strange, imaginative idea of the old trousers like a gaunt spectre glowering into the face of the successful poet 'in siller or in gowden lace' is Fergusson's way of both complaining about his poverty and yet claiming a kind of dignity or reality in it which can help to 'cow the daffin'.

Going back, however, to the simpler aspects of Fergusson's achievement, his gift for description and evocation could be lavishly illustrated throughout his writing. But there are some irresistible examples, such as his picture of the Highlander town-guards being shaved and dressed for the Leith Races: the rhymes are particularly clever in this stanza:

To whisky plooks that brunt for wooks
    On town-guard soldiers' faces,
Their barber bauld his whittle crooks,
    An' scrapes them for the races:
Their stumps erst used to *filipegs*,
    Are dight in spaterdashes,
Whase barkent hides scarce fend their legs
    Frae weet, and weary plashes
        O' dirt that day.

Where the description is straight and devoid of grotesqueness, Fergusson gets his effects both by placing the right and significant detail with economy in the right place and also by keeping in mind the whole picture he is building up stroke by stroke – working very like a good genre painter in fact: as in the picture of the farmer's wife preparing the evening meal for the returning ploughmen in 'The Farmer's Ingle':

Weel kens the gudewife that the pleughs require
    A heartsome meltith, and refreshing synd
O' nappy liquor, o'er a bleezing fire:
    Sair wark and poortith douna weel be join'd.
Wi' butter'd bannocks now the girdle reeks,
    I' the far nook the bowie briskly reams;
The readied kail stand by the chimley cheeks,
    And had the riggin het wi' welcome steams.

It brings out very well, through its appeal to the senses, the theme Fergusson wants, of the actual richness and value of this simple way of life – the meal has no complex or unusual components, but its total effect seems mouth-watering as well as nourishing – the big fire, the good strong beer, the bannocks covered with butter, the barrel of cream in the corner, the pots of broth steaming up to the rafters.

    Some of the best pieces of description include a satirical intent, which certainly does give an edge to passages like the picture of the drunken fop or macaroni lying in the gutter in 'Auld Reikie':

Whan feet in dirty gutters plash,
And fock to wale their fitstaps fash;
In pools or gutters aftimes sunk:
Hegh! what a fricht he now appears,

Whan he his corpse dejected rears!
Look at that head, and think if there
The pomet slaister'd up his hair!
The cheeks observe, where now cou'd shine
The scancing glories o' carmine?
Ah, legs! in vain the silk-worm there
Display'd to view her eidant care;
For stink, instead of perfumes, grow,
And clarty odours fragrant flow.

Fergusson takes what might not unfairly be called an unholy delight in the picture he draws. The contrast between the careful artificial finery of the dandy and the grim unlovely reality of his Edinburgh street is not only something that makes a dramatic picture – a touch of Brueghel verging on Bosch – but it does suggest a moral dimension: the macaroni is getting his come-uppance (a) for following alien unScottish fashions, and (b) for appearing to be effeminate in a very masculine environment. The rouge on the cheeks, the pomade on the hair, the silk stockings remind us of John Gay's poem *Trivia*, one of the sources of 'Auld Reikie', where in a passage on fops Gay advises his readers to give each of them a wide berth: 'Pass with caution by, / Lest from his shoulder clouds of powder fly'. It might be added that Fergusson had something of an obsession with fops and macaronis, and a lengthy article might be written about the clothes imagery throughout his poems – not only in obvious instances like 'To my Auld Breeks', 'Braid Claith', and 'On Seeing a Butterfly in the Street', but scattered through many poems from 'Ode to the Gowdspink' to 'Auld Reikie'. We know from several witnesses that Fergusson himself was extremely careless about his clothes; when he visited the douce people of Dumfries he astonished them by appearing more like a tramp than a distinguished poet. I have already mentioned the rankling effect of his being ejected by his uncle from the dining-room for being shoddily dressed. So probably there is something personal in his attacks on dandies and even on those who were decently and respectably dressed in good braid claith. But on the impersonal level he is of course using clothes imagery to make statements about hypocrisy and affectation, to underline once again the virtues of simplicity.

In Fergusson, description shades off into satire very quickly. He had a keen eye, he relished being the observer, and much of the immediate impact his poetry made on the public in Scotland when it began to be printed came from a delighted recognition that here was a poet who really had his gaze on Edinburgh (and other parts of Scotland). The very honesty of the eye inevitably threw up objects for mockery as well as scenes to be pleased with and praised. He has his own comment on satire near the beginning of 'Auld Reikie', when he's describing the early morning, and the housemaids pausing on the stairs with their chamber-pots before they empty them down into the street:

> On stair wi' tub, or pat in hand,
> The barefoot housemaids looe to stand,
> That antrin fock may ken how snell
> Auld Reikie will at morning smell:
> Then, with an inundation big as
> The burn that 'neath the Nor Loch Brig is,
> They kindly shower Edina's roses,
> To quicken and regale our noses.

After this he humorously denies that he's being satirical, though *some* (he says) would make it an occasion for satire – some 'hae gien auld Edinburgh a creesh' 'wi' satyre's leesh' – but he's not like that, because 'without souring nocht is sweet'. Most people, however, would regard the exaggeration of 'inundation', and the adverb 'kindly', as clearly satirical, though it's an easygoing, light, bantering satire. When he has a subject that engages rather more of his feelings, even when it's not the most serious of subjects, the satire becomes more unmistakable and vigorous and inventive. Dr Johnson was the target of his attack on more than one occasion, and he's attacked both for his anti-Scottish remarks (like the famous dictionary definition he gave for 'oats': 'A grain which, in England, is generally given to horses, but in Scotland supports the people') and for his heavily Latinate style of writing. The first of these offends Fergusson's awareness of the actual poverty of Scotland and at the same time seems to undermine his feeling that plainness and simplicity of life were valuable. The second (Johnson's style) was also an offence against simplicity and directness, but the way in which Fergusson dealt with it showed that he was paying a certain tribute to Johnson against his will. To take up that latter point first, in his poem 'To Dr Samuel Johnson: Food for a new Edition of his Dictionary', which is written in English in a parody of Johnson's style, Fergusson discovers, or rediscovers, a different kind of comedy from what he usually produces, a heavy, polysyllabic, elephantine comedy which nevertheless links back to Sir Thomas Urquhart and to Drummond's 'Polemo-Middinia'. The parody uncovers or releases something that Fergusson might not otherwise have found, and it shows (because of one of the books in the background which he almost certainly read before he wrote this poem) a more general interest in language than one confined to reviving and developing Scots. We, he says, addressing Johnson in mock praise, we

> who never can peroculate
> The miracles by thee miraculiz'd,
> The Muse silential long, with mouth apert
> Would give vibration to stagnatic tongue,
> And loud encomiate thy puissant name,
> Eulogiated from the green decline
> Of Thames's banks to Scoticanian shores,
> Where Loch-Lomondian liquids undulize.

Now, Fergusson's reference at one point to Johnson's 'Lexiphanian style' shows that he had been reading Archibald Campbell's book *Lexiphanes*, published when Fergusson was a student at St Andrews, and this work was a long parodic attack on Johnson, cleverly done, but also with preface and dedication where Campbell put forward his ideas about language and changes in language, and these Fergusson must have read with interest, because Campbell fears the swamping or loss of true English under a Latin and Greek invasion, in rather the same way as Ramsay and Fergusson felt about Scots threatened by English. In his other poem on Johnson, 'To the Principal and Professors of the University of St Andrews, on their Superb Treat to Dr Samuel Johnson', which is in Scots and is a very happy performance, Fergusson takes up the other theme, of the alienness of this visitor who is regaled at St Andrews in such a sophisticated and unScottish way – probably 'snails and puddocks mony hunder / Wad beeking lie the hearth-stane under' – but Fergusson if he had his way would have forced him to eat a very different sort of dinner, a dinner that would remind him he wasn't in London any more; it might even do him good, though he would hate it:

> *Imprimis*, then, a haggis fat,
> Weel tottl'd in a seything pat,

Wi' spice and ingans weel ca'd thro',
Had help'd to gust the stirrah's mow,
And plac'd itsel in truncher clean
Before the gilpy's glowrin een.
Secundo, then a gude sheep's head
Whase hide was singit, never flead,
And fowr black trotters cled wi' girsle,
Bedown his throat had learn'd to hirsle.
What think ye neist, o' gude fat brose
To clag his ribs? a dainty dose!
And white and bloody puddins routh,
To gar the Doctor skirl, O Drouth!
Whan he coul'd never houp to merit
A cordial o' reaming claret,
But thraw his nose, and brize and pegh
O'er the contents o' sma' ale quegh:
Then let his wisdom girn an' snarl
O'er a weel-tostit girdle farl,
An' learn, that maugre o' his wame,
Ill bairns are ay best heard at hame.

There is, in a passage like that, a very familiar kind of Scottish reductive humour at work – calling the distinguished Doctor a gilpy (a rascal), a stirrah (a fellow), and making all his actions basically offputting and dehumanized (he skirls, he pechs, he girns and snarls) – but the enormous gusto of the writing seems to come from Fergusson's bold knowledge that he is eating his cake and having it; it's like the soldiers' old joke about going back to a land fit for heroes to live in – only a hero could live in it. Those four black trotters clad in gristle *learning* how to slide (hirsle) down your throat produce a somewhat horrific effect; yet they are no doubt very nutritious. From scenes like these old Scotia's grandeur springs.

Poems like that one, and 'Hallow-Fair', and 'Leith Races', with their relentlessly extravert and bouncy tone, can be excellent fun but they tend to yield diminishing returns. The reader begins to long for a few darker tints among the broad strokes of the satire. Fergusson himself knows this, and has the range to encompass some harder and grimmer effects when he wants to. His dialogue poem 'The Ghaists', where the ghosts of George Heriot and George Watson, the famous endowers of Edinburgh schools, discuss the implications of the Mortmain Bill of 1773 which threatened to discourage charitable endowments by empowering or tempting trustees to put their funds into government securities at a poor three per cent, takes a difficult subject, recalcitrant perhaps to poetic treatment, but makes something powerful out of it because Fergusson is intelligent enough to understand the implications of the bill and because these implications rouse up very strongly the national and patriotic side of his character, as well as his feelings of disgust at the frustrating of charitable intent by government. The poem inevitably loses some communicativeness because of the historical facts it's based on, yet the poet does a remarkable job in explaining or expounding the situation clearly within the poem, and giving you most of the facts you need to know, and he also, very deliberately and cunningly, woos you into the poem by the dramatic presentation of the two ghosts meeting and talking in a sinister cold churchyard not long before dawn. The sense of a frightening, unnatural atmosphere is used to lead in to the subject of an unnatural change in Scottish history; and even when dawn comes, there's no cockcrow to announce the return of the ghosts to the underworld. Everything is outlandish, murky, shivery:

> Cauld blaws the nippin north wi' angry sough,
> And showers his hailstones frae the Castle Cleugh
> O'er the Greyfriars, whare, at mirkest hour,
> Bogles and spectres wont to tak their tour,
> Harlin' the pows and shanks to hidden cairns,
> Amang the hemlocks wild, and sunburnt fearns.

The ghosts talk, and Heriot tells Watson about the proposed bill. Watson has some hope, but Heriot is angry and pessimistic: he sees it all as specifically a blow at Scotland from an alien government in London:

> Black be the day that e'er to England's ground
> Scotland was eikit by the Union's bond;
> For mony a menyie of destructive ills
> The country now maun brook frae mortmain bills,
> That void our test'ments, and can freely gie
> Sic will and scope to the ordain'd trustee,
> That he may tir our stateliest riggins bare,
> Nor acres, houses, woods, nor fishins spare,
> Till he can lend the stoitering state a lift

Wi' gowd in gowpins as a grassum gift...
Hale interest for my fund can scantly now
Cleed a' my callants' backs, and stap their mou'.
How maun their weyms wi' sairest hunger slack,
Their duds in targets flaff upo' their back,
Whan they are doom'd to keep a lasting Lent,
Starving for England's weel at three per cent.

In that poem, although it is not entirely successful, Fergusson shows how well he can move in the area where entertainer merges into serious commentator, where the poet takes up a stance on a public issue affecting his society rather than himself. What I have suggested earlier about his search for an identity was also a search for a role. The role of social observer which he played so brilliantly was deepening into that of social commentator, through satire certainly, but also through a search for the positive values that would have to be found to offset satire. It was not like Pope writing in Augustan England, sure of certain settled values, conservative and conservationist, the spider at the centre of a well-built web. Fergusson's Scotland and Edinburgh were much less sure of values beyond the immediate and local righting of wrongs that leapt to the eye, but that they were thinking about them, and wondering how they might be defined or embodied, the poems of Fergusson clearly show. The rural values of plain living and high thinking expressed in poems like 'The Farmer's Ingle' were not enough, and it is of the greatest interest that Fergusson, as a man who had sampled country, town, and city life, saw this, and did attempt to bring the city as a node of values into his overall picture. Some of his best poems – 'On seeing a Butterfly in the Street', 'Mutual Complaint of Plainstanes and Causey', 'Braid Claith', 'Auld Reikie' – address themselves to this task. The results are often deeply ambiguous. There is no doubt at all that although Fergusson liked to be refreshed by the countryside, his place and home were in the city. Yet there is hardly an aspect of city life that he fails to satirize or attack in some poem, at some point. A poem that seems to have a particularly uneasy balance is the 'Butterfly'. The butterfly is identified as a 'daft gowk in macaroni dress' who is out of place, out of his element in the city street. He's 'Like country laird in city cleeding, / Ye're come to town to lear good breeding' – and further, he's like the Scottish laird who goes down to London, laughed at, mocked, gullible, vulnerable, poking his head into business in politics and at court which doesn't concern him, and making nothing of it in the end – the old story of Sawney who can't even speak English, what's he doing in London, why doesn't he stay in his own kailyard? And in fact Fergusson says that surely the poor butterfly can't really believe he has made a good exchange, trading in 'the mavis' note' for street-cries of 'penny pies all piping hot'? But Fergusson loved the street-cries, and he's not being true to himself in preferring the mavis. He was caught here in the dilemma of not wanting to praise the city environment if it merely encouraged affectation and trendiness (and also the hypocrisy of 'Braid Claith'), and he tries to get out of it by saying that although all the butterfly people, the beautiful people, the macaronis, will be scattered by the first heavy shower, others who are poor or used to adversity will survive all the bad weather a northern city has to offer. You can see Fergusson wriggling and struggling in this poem (which is still an attractive one), and this convinces you all the more of the reality of the search he was engaged on.

In 'Plainstanes and Causey', the mild flyting between the pavement and the road of a developing city is nicely used to sketch out the problems of busy sidewalks and growing traffic, the pavement complaining in a somewhat aristocratic and snobbish spirit that it should really be used for strolling beaux and ladies and is getting too much hard treatment from the new hordes of hurrying tradesmen ('mealy bakers, / Hair-kamers, creishy gezy-makers') and heavy Gaelic chairmen tramping it to pieces 'Wi' waefu' tackets i' the soals / O' broags', and the road in turn complaining that its new importance in the city, for traffic, is being frustrated by old-fashioned merchants and lawyers standing and blethering in the middle of the road. The solution they propose is a humorous one: fine both sorts of jaywalkers, and 'This might assist the poor's collection, / And gie baith parties satisfaction.' Even though it is humorous, the human touch of remembering the poor fits in also with a human touch in the elegant plainstanes, when he admits that his business is not only 'To fend frae skaith the bonny ladies' but also

> To keep the bairnies free frae harms
> Whan airing in their nurses arms,
> To be a safe and canny bield
> For growing youth or drooping eild.

In these different poems you can watch Fergusson gradually building up his own perilous, satirical humanism, with many touches of grimness and fear and frequent memento-moris (in the 'Butterfly', for example, he has the fine scornful couplet when he dismisses the butterfly's short-lived pretensions, trying to 'ding awa' the vexing thought / Of hourly dwining into nought' – *vexing* is just right). In 'Auld Reikie', which we must remember is an unfinished poem, he gives us an extraordinary mixture of straight observation, satirical comment, some moralizing, some pathos, some little nips at religion but at the same time an almost morbid dwelling on death and the trappings of death, and, towards the end, some serious and moving thoughts on Scottish history which are themselves immediately cut to comedy, the note on which the fragment ends (as it had begun). The poem uses, but doesn't consistently use, the organizing principle of the passing of time through day and night, and we tend to remember it more strongly for incidents in it than for the pleasure of following a forward drive of action or argument. The housemaids holding up their chamber-pots, the decayed prostitute at the lamp-post, the macaroni in the gutter, the hired mourners in the funeral procession, the 'joes and lasses' out walking on Sunday afternoon, the threadbare bohemians haunting the second-hand-clothes street, and above all the wonderful Caravaggiesque picture of the old bruiser reeling drunk out of the tavern accompanied by his cloud of attendant elegant young men, the best thing in the poem, full of the strongest reverberations and unexpected pathos:

> Frae joyous tavern, reeling drunk,
> Wi' fiery phiz, and ein half sunk,
> Behad the bruiser, fae to a'
> That in the reek o' gardies fa':
> Close by his side, a feckless race
> O' macaronis show their face,
> And think they're free frae skaith or harm,
> While pith befriends their leader's arm:
> Yet fearfu' aften o' their maught,
> They quatt the glory o' the faught
> To this same warrior wha led
> Thae heroes to bright honour's bed;
> And aft the hack o' honour shines
> In bruiser's face wi' broken lines:
> Of them sad tales he tells anon,

> Whan ramble and whan fighting's done;
> And, like Hectorian, ne'er impairs
> The brag and glory o' his sairs.

Both the bruiser and the feckless macaronis are creatures of the city, and it's in that environment that the poet can bring them together and through contrast say something about them both. But Fergusson is also, in this poem, at certain points, deliberately abstracting himself from the throng, looking back at or down on the city from a distance or from a height, and this is where he seems to be reaching for another dimension of meaning which perhaps the rest of the poem if it had been written would have developed. It has been pointed out by critics that one of the sources of the poem (as already mentioned) is John Gay's long poem *Trivia*, which presents the life of the streets of London, though in a different way, giving a sort of reader's guide to London, what to wear, where to go, where not to go, how to avoid pickpockets and so on. But there's a greater poet than Gay somewhere behind Fergusson's poem. That poet is Milton. Echoes of Milton are clear and strong in the important passage where Fergusson begins to talk about Scottish history, and it's the early Milton, the Milton of 'L'Allegro' and 'Il Penseroso', poems written when Milton was Fergusson's age, in the same metre as 'Auld Reikie', having many parallels in the presentation of the sights and sounds of a day and night, and obviously appealing to Fergusson in having (as two sides of the same coin) L'Allegro the joyous happy man and Il Penseroso the thoughtful melancholy man, both of whom he was. And just as the young Milton is anxiously searching for his destiny, his aim, his identity, so too is Fergusson. Milton climbs into the tower from which he can watch the stars: he is the poet as seer, thinking over man's fate. Fergusson climbs Arthur's Seat and looks over the landscape, the rain drives him down to Holyrood House, and *his* meditation is on more immediate things than Milton's, on Scotland, on – perhaps – his destiny as a national poet.

> Or shou'd some canker'd biting show'r
> The day and a' her sweets deflou'r,
> To Holyrood House let me stray,
> And gie to musing a' the day;
> Lamenting what auld Scotland knew
> Bien days for ever frae her view:

O Hamilton, for shame! the Muse
Would pay to thee her couthy vows,
Gin ye wad tent the humble strain
And gie's our dignity again:
For O, wae's me! the thistle springs
In domicile of ancient kings,
Without a patriot to regrate
Our palace, and our ancient state.

Fergusson did not live to become the poet he was feeling his way towards being, but the work he did leave is a concentration in a few years of very genuine, entertaining, strongly-rooted verse; it's achievement as well as promise; and we are right to mark his memory.

Bicentenary Lecture, University of Edinburgh, October 1974.

Scottish Poetry in the Nineteenth Century

It has never been the easiest of tasks to get nineteenth-century Scottish poetry into focus, and much of it resists order and categorization, to an uncomfortable degree. The absence of commanding creative figures in Scotland to whom other poets could relate themselves, even by way of opposition; the lack of good critics who might have stopped, at various points, a slide into sentimentality or derivativeness or mediocrity; the decline of the famously sharp literary journals like the *Edinburgh Review* and *Blackwood's Magazine* which tended to be replaced by family magazines such as *Chambers's Journal* and *The People's Friend*; a rapid turndown in the intellectual and cultural sprightliness of Edinburgh, leaving a vacuum not yet convincingly filled by the struggling giant of Glasgow, and presenting therefore a country without a true national centre; add to that a diaspora – Byron, William Bell Scott, George MacDonald, David Gray, Robert Buchanan, James (B.V.) Thomson, Robert Louis Stevenson, John Davidson – which leaves endless and largely unanswerable questions about a poet's 'Scottishness': and it is not hard to understand why Hugh MacDiarmid was so determined that the twentieth century should deliver, if he had anything to do with it, a more solidly based and recognizable Scottish poetry than the nineteenth had done. However, the present task is to see what was actually there.

At the beginning of the century, the poetry of Walter Scott and James Hogg enjoyed a popularity it has never been able to regain, and although it met (and largely created) the contemporary taste for historical romance it did not prove greatly seminal for later poets, and much of it seems to look beguilingly back rather than proddingly forward. When Lord Cockburn said in his *Memorials* that the 'eighteenth century was the final Scotch century' we do not necessarily agree with him but we can see what he means. Scott, in writing *The Lay of the Last Minstrel* (1805), prepares the way for statements like Cockburn's. In this creaky yet sombrely effective narrative, the old minstrel who tells the story, who chants it as Scott in fact had chanted it to the Wordsworths when they visited him in Jedburgh, is supposed to be living towards the end of the seventeenth century, having survived what to him were the hard and dangerous times of the Commonwealth and Civil War, and the events he relates are supposed to have taken place a long time before, in the Borders, at the middle of the sixteenth century, and even involving (with intentional anachronism) the wizard or early scientist Michael Scott who lived in the thirteenth century; and all this, of course, projected by the author to a nineteenth-century audience. It is a many-layered poem about Scotland, about the Scottish experience or spirit, with a great deal of nostalgia coming through the figure of the old 'last minstrel' himself and also through the suggested identification of Scott with him; he too is the last minstrel of the old history of Scotland which moves him so much. Similar qualities are found in *The Lady of the Lake* (1810), which deals with the clash between the centralising and unifying values of King James V and the admired but wild and uncontrolled values of the Highland chieftain Roderick Dhu, and which again presents a past that can be recreated, whatever its angers and follies at the time, in terms of drama, charm, and high romance. The fact that the long narrative poems of Scott do not on the whole stand up well to line-by-line analysis, the verse being filled out with expletives, sown with clichés, and propped up by fairly coarse-textured rhetorical devices, has told against him in modern times, but there is a case to be made, as one makes it with Edmund Spenser, for the large-scale cumulative effects a long poem can sustain, and Scott keeps some powerful and unexpected passages for those who can yield to his storytelling. Anyone who finds this difficult can still enjoy the more intimate style of the attractive autobiographical introductions to the six cantos of *Marmion* (1808), written as verse letters to different friends and talking in an easy familiar style about friendship and art and life and memory:

> Heap on more wood! – the wind is chill;
> But let it whistle as it will,
> We'll keep our Christmas merry still.

James Hogg, friend and colleague of Scott's, and a co-collector of ballads and folk-songs, described the difference between them as being that Scott was king of the 'school o' chivalry' whereas Hogg was 'king o' the mountain an' fairy school which is a far higher ane nor yours'. In spite of this claim, he actually does himself an injustice, since his remarkably varied work holds many surprises, as recent editions have made clear.[1] Legend and folklore and the supernatural do certainly feed into such successful and well-known poems as 'Kilmeny', with its mysterious brooding atmosphere and many critical interpretations, and 'The Witch of Fife' with its grotesque humour and alternative endings, but it is limiting to think of Hogg only in these terms. He was willing to try anything, and although he wrote too much, and often badly, his resolute belief in spontaneity and freshness of attack was coupled with a tantalizing sophistication that led him into areas where Scott had no entry. There is an astonishing contrast between the rollicking, traditional, satirical Scots of 'The Great Muckle Village of Balmaquhapple' and the quiet straight lyrical English and almost timeless magic of 'A Boy's Song'. English is also used to wickedly lively effect in *The Poetic Mirror* (1816-31), with its parodies of Wordsworth, Coleridge, Scott, Byron, and others, including the author himself; their complex mixture of mockery and tribute shows a kind of literary insight that is different from his more regularly credited insight into folk-song and folklore and oral poetry. In other poems like 'A True Story of a Glasgow Tailor', 'The Dominie', and 'Disagreeables', he developed a rough, bold, colloquial blank verse, in English but with snatches of Scots dialogue, which is racy and readable and entertaining – and not a mountain or fairy in sight. One of his 'disagreeables' is a creditor:

> I do remember once. – 'Tis long agone,
> Of stripping to the waist to wade the Tyne –
> The English Tyne, dark, sluggish, broad, and deep;
> And just when middle-way, there caught mine eye,
> A lamprey of enormous size pursuing me!
> Lord what a fright! I bobb'd, I splashed, I flew!
> He had a creditor's keen ominous look,
> I never saw an uglier – but a real one.

Byron's claim to be considered as a Scottish poet depends partly on his maternal parentage and his early upbringing in Aberdeen, partly on Scottish qualities of temperament which he claimed to have, and partly on the sheer problematics of regarding such a

European, mercurial, and in many ways anti-English figure as an English poet. (The pros and cons of this are usefully rehearsed in recent essays by Tom Scott and Philip Hobsbaum.[2]) T.S. Eliot, comparing the busts of Byron and Scott, thought he saw 'a certain resemblance in the shape of the head'. The huge popularity of Byron's verse narratives, from *Childe Harold's Pilgrimage* onwards, rolled on a wave that Scott had started, but quickly extended itself into exotic settings, contemporary history, and heroic identification of new *zeitgeist* and new individual, in ways that soon began to give Scott's narratives a distinctly dusty look. 'So much for chivalry,' says Byron in his *Childe Harold* preface, and 'these monstrous mummeries of the middle ages'. And as Scott's narrative poems became worse and worse, being naturally displaced by his prose fiction, so Byron's became better and better, culminating in the sustained brilliance of *Don Juan*. Rapidity and insouciance of composition link Byron to Scott and Hogg, but Byron had access to technical virtuosity that far surpassed theirs. Hogg, in a dedicatory poem to Byron which was far from sycophantic, put his finger on the spot in praising him for

> thy bold and native energy;
> Thy soul that dares each bound to overfly,
> Ranging thro' Nature on erratic wing –
> These do I honour.

'Bold', 'energy', 'dares', 'overfly', 'erratic' – these are the right words, and sometimes Hogg is uncannily perceptive. What is interesting is that Hogg adds 'native'; he still claims the mould-breaking energies as Scottish. The splendid digressionism of *Don Juan*, its many voices and tangents and recoveries, its daring shifts of tone, do seem to have something of that Scottish quality which so disconcerted and irritated Dr Johnson when Boswell left him to converse with those master printers the Foulis brothers at the Saracen's Head Inn in Glasgow: they were 'good and ingenious men', Boswell reports, but they had an 'unsettled speculative mode of conversation' and they 'teazed him with questions and doubtful disputations'. Also, what one might call the encyclo-pedism of *Don Juan* – and Byron shares this with Scott – its lists, its informativeness, its use of many languages, is a recurring Scottish preoccupation. When Byron looked back (in *Don Juan*, X.19) at *English Bards and Scotch Reviewers* (1809), his early squib against Francis Jeffrey and the *Edinburgh Review* and most other things Caledonian ('it being well known', as he says in a note, 'there is no Genius to be found from Clackmannan to Caithness'), he frankly admitted a necessary callowness, 'to show my wrath and wit', but 'I "*scotched* not killed" the Scotchman in my blood.' It is interesting that the admission quotes from an English writer's most Scottish play.

Although Byron, by leaving Scotland and never returning to it, ruled out any potential he might have had for providing a personal focus for other poets in the country, he did prove to be one of the influences (others were Shelley, Poe, and Whitman) taken up by writers who resisted the sentimental sub-Burnsian blandishments of the popular *Whistle-Binkie* anthologies (1832 and many later editions). Not that Scottish traditions were useless or exhausted: there is much charm in the songs and local epistles of Robert Tannahill the Paisley weaver-poet, and individual poems like William Tennant's lively fantasy of rustic merry-making, *Anster Fair*, and William Bell Scott's smilingly, dancingly sinister 'The Witch's Ballad', still deserve anthology space. *Anster Fair*, written in English in near-Spenserian stanzas, offers an unexpected link between Byron, who favoured similar metres, and the seventeenth-century Scots song, 'Maggie Lauder', on which the poem is based. If 'Scottish traditions' include the eighteenth-century James Thomson, we can add the author of 'The Luggie' to the list, since the rather formal, latinate, and by Victorian times distinctly old-fashioned descriptive diction of that poem, praising the countryside north of Glasgow, shows his strong influence; but the unfortunate David Gray, dead of tuberculosis at the age of twenty-one, did not live long enough to write underivatively, and his best poems are a group of personal sonnets owing much to Keats and Shakespeare, but delicate and moving within their limitations.

But for sixty years *Whistle-Binkie* must have thought it ruled the roost. Victorian morality took strong root in Scotland, and these tightly packed, assiduously produced, biographically anno- tated, and constantly revised anthologies, in which you would be hard put to find a dozen really good poems, but which seemed so innocuously comic and sentimental, were carefully devised as instruments of social control, as was made clear in the 'new and enlarged edition' of 1890. After lauding 'this broad, fresh, living stream of healthy Scottish song', the preface continues: 'When the first portion of *Whistle-Binkie* was issued from the press, our Scottish firesides were still greatly under the influence of the old chap-books, which, while they embodied much genuine poetic feeling, expressed in terse and graphic language, were yet permeated and marred by much that was coarse and indecent, – these last two characteristics being, indeed, the chief features of many of them. It was the purpose and glory of *Whistle-Binkie* to exhibit, to cherish, and to preserve all the tenderness, the refinement, and the genius of the national muse, without the coarseness and licentiousness by which it had been debased.'

During this period the real poets, minor though they may have been, had to look elsewhere. Those of them, like Alexander Rodger and William Thom, who contributed to *Whistle-Binkie*, kept their strongest verses for other pages. Life as it really was, and as it appeared to thinking and feeling spirits, comes to us fitfully but sometimes powerfully, sometimes with great pathos, sometimes with irony and wit, in the often imperfect work of half a dozen poets whose names ought not to be forgotten. Alexander Rodger, the 'Glasgow radical' mentioned above, gained notoriety from the anti-monarchist ballad he wrote at the time of George IV's visit to Edinburgh in 1822. Walter Scott, who helped to stage-manage the royal progress, produced a celebratory version of an old song, 'Carle, now the King's come', and Rodger promptly produced his anti-celebratory 'Sawney, now the King's come', advising ambitious Scots to 'kneel, and kiss his gracious bum'. He made a spirited attack on time-serving clergy in 'Black Coats, and Gravats sae White'. He wrote an incisively epigrammatic elegy for Thomas Paine, one of his heroes. And in the particularly interesting longer poem, 'Shaving Banks', he uses the Burns stanza with much skill to warn the ordinary working public that the grand new invention of Savings Banks, ostensibly a rainy-day protective device, is really just one more devious method of enslaving working people, of 'shaving' them of their hard-earned cash. Rather like Holy Willie, the speaker of Rodger's poem (a minister) is brashly and brutally self-condemnatory:

> Come, come, my lads, this is nae hoax,
> Here are our books – and here's our box,
> We'll put your siller in the stocks;
>   And when it's there,
> Confound you for a set o' blocks,
>   Gin ye see't mair;

What then? – Ye tim'rous, backward set,
The interest ye'll be sure to get,
The stock will help to pay some debt
   John Bull is awn,   [owed]
Or creesh the sair-worn wheels o' State,   [grease]
   To keep them gaun.   [going]

For look ye, it is our intent
To cleek you firm to Government...

Also associated with Glasgow were Alexander Smith and James Macfarlan. Smith tends to be remembered as the author of one very fine and resonant poem, 'Glasgow', which was among the earliest attempts to bring positive and powerful images of the industrial city environment so resolutely avoided by the Whistle-Binkians. A poet in the Romantic tradition, he extended romanticism into the machine age and found 'Another beauty, sad and stern' in the furnaces and foundries and shrieking trains which seem to thrill, terrify, and exalt the watcher in a strong and new transfusion of emotions. The city is the growing point, and the conservative somnolent countryside must learn to deal with 'The roar and flap of foundry fires, / That shake with light the sleeping shires'. And the whole country must learn that close-knit rural communities are not necessarily the ideal: 'A sacredness of love and death / Dwells in thy noise and smoky breath.' Smith's ambitious and overblown longer poems, 'A Life-Drama' and 'Edwin of Deira', scarcely survive, but 'A Boy's Poem', though somewhat laboured and over-descriptive in a Tennysonian manner, has some excellent passages reflecting love and loneliness in Glasgow and the Firth of Clyde.[4]

Smith, in his preface to *Golden Leaves from American Poets* (ed. J.W.S. Hows, 1866), was able to praise Edgar Allan Poe's poetry while deploring the man ('the most disreputable of poets'). Smith's Glasgow contemporaries might have felt the same way about the pedlar-poet, James Macfarlan. If alcohol, ingrained vagrancy, and general unreliability tended to make Macfarlan's death at the age of thirty another Victorian morality-story, the poet himself, autodidact as he was, used all his miseries to project something general and almost mythical about the individual, and especially the creative individual, in industrial society. Byron, he said, set him off into poetry; Poe, it is clear from the echoes, sustained him; and his work looks forward in some respects to

James (B.V.) Thomson's *The City of Dreadful Night*. He enjoyed a measure of fame, particularly for his rousing march-song, 'The Lords of Labour', where the workers are Titans drawing their 'steam steeds' through the 'triumphal arch' of tunnel-builders' skill; 'heroes who wield no sabre', their sweat-drops turned to jewels 'in the crown of toil'. His city poems, especially 'The Street' and 'The Midnight Train', resemble and rival Smith's 'Glasgow' (plagiarism, if any, could go either way). 'The Ruined City' is a powerful, Poe-like vision, in almost science-fiction terms, of a 'city's blasted heap' under a 'fierce, relentless sky', abandoned to reptiles and wild beasts. It ends:

> The sunset's wild and wandering hair
>   Streams backward like a comet's mane,
> And from the deep and sullen glare
>   The shuddering columns crouch in vain,
> While through the wreck of wrathful years
> The grim hyena stalks and sneers.

His most ambitious poem, 'The Wanderer of the West' (1856), constructed in ten sections with different metres, combines a Byronic wanderer-hero with the autobiographical story of a young poet trying to break out of poverty into art and fame. Here, 'The Lords of Labour' is turned over to reveal the dark side of the struggle, where 'the poor Boy-Poet grimes within a dismal den, / Piles the fire and wields the hammer, jostled on by savage men', where the forges are 'like great burning cities' (an astonishing image-reversal) and where 'the soul is dwarfed within him that was cast in Titan mould'. For all its imperfections, there is something very moving about Macfarlan's poetry.[5]

Janet Hamilton, a shoemaker's daughter from North Lanarkshire, was a remarkable woman who overcame many disadvantages – no education, marriage at fourteen and a large family to raise, blindness in middle age – in order to write poetry which would have a social function within communities in Scotland, especially outside the main cities, and which she dedicated to 'her Brothers, the Men of the Working Classes'. She wrote in both English and Scots (the earliest poems she came across were volumes of Allan Ramsay and John Milton, lying on a weaver's loom), but most of her best work is in Scots, and in a poem called 'A Plea for the Doric' she laid her finger on at least one of the Scottish poet's problems:

> I'm wae for Auld-Reekie; her big men o' print
> To Lunnon ha'e gane, to be nearer the mint;
> But the coinage o' brain looks no a'e haet better,   [not a bit]
> Though Doric is banish'd frae sang, tale, and letter.

Her subjects range from Garibaldi and Poland to *Uncle Tom's Cabin* and the Crimean War, but cluster strongly about the immediate and familiar issues of the family, work, education, and the place of women in society. Her Victorian earnestness is lightened by a humorous direct appeal that shows she really would like people to listen; working men, she says, don't respect themselves enough, and live in a dangerous ignorance:

> Ye've means, but want the wull to use them,
> Ye whiles neglec', an' whiles abuse them;
> Ye hae nae time for e'enin' classes;
> Ye've time to drink, an' see the lasses –
> Staun at hoose-en', or change-hoose door,
> An' smoke an' swear, an' raise a splore,   [uproar]
> An' play at cards, or fecht wi' dougs,
> An' whiles to clout ilk ither's lugs;   [ears]
> O wad ye no be muckle better   [much]
> To read a book, or write a letter?
> Had ye the wull, wi' book an' pen
> Ye'd fin' the way to mak' ye men.
>
> ('Rhymes for the Times – I')

She complemented her poems with essays on social subjects, which are also worth reading.[6]

Like Hamilton and Macfarlan, the Aberdeenshire weaver-poet William Thom enjoyed some contemporary fame, but in a life of general poverty and hardship. Among much mediocre sentimental work, which he placed in *Whistle-Binkie*, he also wrote some powerful satirical and grotesque poetry, a mode which unfortunately no critic encouraged him to develop. At least two poems, both in Scots (one modulating towards English), leave the impression of a fiery indignation, and an original cast of expression, that never spread themselves into what might have been an *oeuvre*. In 'Whisperings for the Unwashed', the early morning town drummer drums loud enough to physically waken the weavers in their hovels but never loud enough to waken them spiritually and shake them from their apathy; they are such craven nonentities to society that when they die 'They grudge the grave wherein to drap ye, / An' grudge the very *muck* to hap ye.' 'Chaunts for Churls' is a wild reel of rhythm and rhyme where Sawtan (Satan) and Sin have a dialogue about the gains they expect from the Disruption in the Church of Scotland in 1843. Thom ended his touching prose *Recollections*[7] with a strange image which sums up much of the desperate yet buoyant commitment to art which kept the self-taught poets going: 'Now, amid the giant waves of monopoly, the *solitary* loom is fast sinking. Thus must the Lyre, like a hencoop, be thrown on the wrecking waters, to float its owner ashore.'

Contemporary subjects are treated with a more ironic and detached intelligence by the elusive James Young Geddes of Dundee and Alyth, of whom little seems to be known beyond his books.[8] A favourite theme is art versus the machine. In 'A Work of Art' he praises a grocer's almanack on his wall, showing a Hartz mountain scene, a 'brilliant, glowing chromograph' which Ruskin and Whistler would despise but which he prefers to his 8-day kitchen clock protesting 'with prosaic knock'; yet both have their place, and 'Clock and picture argue on'. The machine makes a comeback in 'The Man and the Engine', where a mechanic feels he has become 'a part / Of the mill machinery' but

> I think I could find a poem here,
> Were I only blessed by a little wit,
> And my engine should be the theme of it.

Another nicely contrasting pair of poems is 'The People's Theatre' and 'Glendale & Co.' In the former, a mobile theatre arrives in Alyth, apparently ramshackle and dubious:

> It came within the bitter winter time,
> Thick was the ground with snow, the air with rime –
> It came in ruins on an ambulance,
> And we, the townsmen, looked at it askance.

(Anyone who could write that third line is no negligble poet!) But the poem comes round to see values in the temporary changeable art of the theatre which can be set against everyday material money-making. The long lines of Whitmanian free verse which characterize the remarkable 'Glendale & Co.' are devoted to demolishing, with sharp perceptiveness, step by step, the credentials of this *Metropolis*-like weaving conglomeration.

Glendale is methodical –
The works an enlargement of the man;
There nothing imperfect; no repairing, no patching –
The imperfect machine cast into the furnace;
Every machine with its duplicate prepared, ready to be
  put in its place.
Imperfect men and women cannot be recast – cannot be
  rejuvenated –
They could not endure the fiery furnace;
They must be discharged –
To do otherwise would be to break down the system:
The works are for workers;
The workhouses and benevolent institutions are for the
  old and infirm.
Why regret the harshness of the system?

If Poe made Macfarlan, Whitman certainly made Geddes. It becomes clear that three strands of influence are at work on nineteenth-century Scottish poetry: a minor one from America, in addition to the more important ones from the English Romantics and from the native Scottish tradition, whether in English (Thomson) or in Scots (Ramsay, Fergusson, Burns, Hogg).

During the last quarter of the century, more familiar names come on the scene, all exiles from Scotland: Robert Louis Stevenson, James (B.V.) Thomson, John Davidson. Even more familiar is the name of an 'internal exile' who outlived Thomson and Stevenson: William McGonagall. McGonagall has never been long out of print; the other three poets are not easy to obtain, and are probably, despite critical opinion in their favour, not very widely read. What can be said about this apparently unedifying situation? It is usually assumed that McGonagall is enjoyed because he is unintentionally amusing, and everyone likes a good laugh. True, if dubiously defensible. But we know, from tested public performance, that an actor with a good voice can read the best of McGonagall (e.g. 'The Little Match Girl') quite straight and with some pathos, as doubtless Dickens would have done. If voice seems to be the key, we perhaps direct ourselves to Hamish Henderson's argument[9] that the clumsy ametricality of the lines (on the page) can be related to McGonagall's Irish family background of 'Come-all-ye' folk-song, the value of his poems being no more than that of their originality in uniquely and consistently forming their style out of the detritus of folk poetry.

Perhaps anything carried to an extreme is attractive, as William Blake claimed. The obvious 'badness' of McGonagall also does not cancel the genuine popular appeal of someone who, unlike many of his poetic contemporaries, gave himself the function of commenting on the noted public events of the time.

McGonagall may seem a natural product of a Scotland which had so little sense of aesthetic, to say nothing of political, direction. The number of uprooted or exiled poets who went to England or elsewhere, with mixed fortunes of popular success and mixed posthumous reputations, can also appear a natural development in the latter part of the century – not helping the poetic situation in Scotland itself, yet showing, almost as in a scientific experiment, how much could or could not be made of the uprooting in terms of new poetic strength stimulated by new living environment. Robert Buchanan allowed his prickly combativeness to embroil him in endless literary controversies, to the detriment of his own literary art, which remained unexamined, derivative, turgid and repetitive. Fatally lured towards religious and philosophical heights which he could not command, he succeeded in only a handful of the poems of his voluminous output: some London genre sketches, one or two tragic ('The Scaith o' Bartle') and comic ('The Widow Mysie') idylls set in Scotland, and a few passages of light satire which one would have liked to see more of:

> Far is the cry from Byron's brandy
> To Pater's gods of sugar-candy!
> Lost the Homeric swing and trot,
>   Jingle of spur and beam of blade,
> Of that moss-trooper, Walter Scott,
>   Riding upon his border raid...
> And troubadours devoid of gristle
> Play the French flute and Cockney whistle.
>   ('The Outcast', Canto II, 1891).

Buchanan's Scottish experience was sandwiched between being born in England and returning to England as a young man, so the Scottish connection, although he felt it and acknowledged it, could hardly be paramount in his work. With Robert Louis Stevenson that connection goes much deeper into the fibre of the man, and he relished and experimented with Scots as well as English, and had thoughts about Scottish poetry as something that might still be distinct from English or 'British' poetry. The limitation of what he actually achieved goes with his having been more essentially a novelist than poet, but the variety and range of his verse are impressive nevertheless. When he uses Scots, he is aware that he is doing what he can with a thinned-out literary medium, and in the well-known note in *Underwoods* (1887) he makes it clear how sceptical he is that the mushrooming scientific study of dialects in his own time will help Scots to survive: he puts his faith neither in a close use of local speech ('Let the precisians call my speech that of the Lothians. And if it be not pure, alas! what matters it?') nor in a proleptic MacDiarmidism which would deliberately revive obsolete words as well as show no geographical favouritism (the latter he would go along with up to a point, in an easygoing sort of way). Perhaps the result of this is that many of his Scots poems are fairly conventional, some of them leaning to the kailyard ('Ille Terrarum') or once more rehearsing well-known religious objects of attack ('The Scotsman's Return from Abroad') or doing both together '(A Lowden Sabbath Morn'); but then we have also the delightfully nostalgic portrait of youth in 'A Mile an' a Bittock', the folkishly sinister ballad of 'The Spaewife', and the perfectly poised gentlemanly complaint of 'The Counterblast Ironical'. And in the famous valediction 'To S.R. Crockett' he achieves excellence by using only three Scottish words, but each one (whaups, howes, peewees) carefully placed in each of the three stanzas, to maximum effect. Stevenson was bolder in English than in Scots, and followed his mentors, Matthew Arnold and Walt Whitman, into convincing experiments in free verse.

> The narrow lanes are vacant and wet;
> The rough wind bullies and blusters about the township.
> And spins the vane on the tower
> And chases the scurrying leaves,
> And the straw in the damp innyard.
> See – a girl passes
> Tripping gingerly over the pools,
> And under her lifted dress
> I catch the gleam of a comely, stockinged leg.
> Pah! the room stifles me,
> Reeking of stale tobacco –
> With the four black mealy horrible prints
> After Landseer's pictures.
> I will go out.
>
> ('Storm')

Stevenson had his depths and darknesses, and although these received more extensive embodiment in his prose fiction, his verse too has some sombre moments, often coming out of the theme of exile which his own life exhibited in extreme form. To write firmly and strongly on that subject, avoiding the various kinds of sentimentality that lie in wait, is a good achievement for a Scottish poet, and Stevenson in his verse letter 'To S.C.' (his friend Sidney Colvin) sent a South Seas message guaranteed to make the recipient think. He asked Colvin, the next time he visited the British Museum, to have a long look at the huge Easter Island statues at the entrance – they too are exiles. Stevenson identifies himself with the displaced Pacific monoliths; they too must have known blood and violence, like the graves of the martyrs on the Scottish moors, and the Standing Stones behind that, in his poem 'To S.R. Crockett': 'So far, so foreign your divided friends / Wander, estranged in body, not in mind.'

James (B.V.) Thomson and John Davidson were exiles nearer home, and produced between them the last and strongest phase of the furth-of-Scotland poetry before Hugh MacDiarmid with his heroic heave turned the lever north again. Both have singular powers, but exercised them in very different ways: Thomson the author of one great poem, *The City of Dreadful Night* (1874), Davidson a prolific writer of lyrics, dramatic monologues, eclogues, 'testaments', verse dramas, and poems of contemporary social and political comment, in styles ranging from the colloquial to the latinate sublime. Both were examples of the Scottish type of religious atheist or religious materialist; they were both interested in science and evolution; they both took up themes from the struggles of ordinary people in industrialized society; and both had psychological problems that in Thomson's case led him virtually to drink himself to death, and in Davidson's fostered a frustrated megalomania that led to suicide. They attracted much admiration from modern poets like T.S. Eliot and Hugh MacDiarmid, who saw them as forerunners or prophets of a modern awareness, a modern sensibility. Eliot, another exile, brought something of them into English poetry; MacDiarmid in his poems brought Davidson at least back to Scotland.

The City of Dreadful Night is partly the reaction of an uprooted Scottish poet to Victorian London at the height of its expansion, but partly also it is a poem with a mental landscape, an attempt to exteriorise, through powerful nightmarish images, the inner struggles of a man's life. Passages of general comment alternate with passages describing action as the insomniac speaker wanders through the city and has various meetings and encounters. The city, doubtless based on London, and probably also using Thomson's early memories of Glasgow, is not to be identified: it becomes simply 'the city', any city that is very large and very old, it has huge buildings, great bridges, squares, cathedrals, mansions, slums, endless streetlamps. The night inhabitants, and the actors of the poem, are the outcasts of daytime society, the tramps, the drunks, the drug-addicts, the half-crazed, the homeless, the sleepless, the lonely. The speaker, the 'I' of the poem, is both a familiar and an intimate of this night world, who can align himself with its sufferings, and yet also an observer, an artist, a reporter, an imaginative reconstructor, who is able to stand apart and build up a poem, an art object, in organized sections, for an audience. Abstract and particular passages move in alternation towards an extremely powerful conclusion. The last section (XXI) takes us to the north of the city, where there is a bleak ridge or plateau looking over this metropolis, and on the ridge is a colossal bronze statue of a winged woman based on Albrecht Dürer's *Melencolia*. She is the embodiment of whatever it is that makes the night city dreadful, an image of alienation, lethargy, and apathy, frozen in brooding inward thought, but also suggesting great endurance and latent power – power under a spell which no one can yet break.

> The moving moon and stars from east to west
>   Circle before her in the sea of air;
> Shadows and gleams glide round her solemn rest.
>   Her subjects often gaze up to her there:
> The strong to drink new strength of iron endurance,
> The weak new terrors; all, renewed assurance
>   And confirmation of the old despair.

In so far as Thomson's city is London, the companion-piece by John Davidson which T.S. Eliot yoked with it in his mind is 'Thirty Bob a Week', the dramatic monologue of a London clerk with wife and family to support on that amount – not absolute poverty, but near it – who comes across as a heroic figure on the edge of despair:

> It's walking on a string across a gulf
>   With millstones fore and aft about your neck;

> But the thing is daily done by many and many a one;
> And we fall, face forward, fighting, on the deck.

But Davidson was no Cockney himself, arriving in London only in his early thirties, and he remained a more markedly Scottish writer than Thomson. Although a contributor to the *Yellow Book* in the 1890s, and a co-member of the Rhymers Club with W.B. Yeats, he brought something from outside, from the north, a hardness and roughness, a hammering quality, an obsessiveness with certain themes, especially some dealing with science and religion, which literary Londoners commented on and sometimes criticized. Yeats thought Davidson had too much 'violent energy, which is like a fire of straw... and is useless in the arts'. Perhaps so, but Davidson produced, among a mass of over-ambitiously grandiose writing, some very fine poetry: 'The Crystal Palace' with its brilliantly crisp and detailed mockery of the building and its visitors, 'The Wasp' with its nice imaginative projection into the feelings of a wasp trapped in a railway carriage, 'Snow' with a fusion of science and art worthy of MacDiarmid's later ideals; the wonderfully evocative urban landscapes of 'The Thames Embankment' and 'In the Isle of Dogs', the touchingly autobiographical 'The Last Journey' (Epilogue to 'The Testament of John Davidson'):

> Farewell the hope that mocked, farewell despair
> That went before me still and made the pace.
> The earth is full of graves, and mine was there
> Before my life began, my resting-place.

Much of his later work, the long blank-verse 'Testaments', which involve a search for a modern system of thought and a search for a hero, can be regarded as a surrogate world piled up by a desperate man; some of this poetry, dedicated to a Nietzschean 'will to live', is turgid and labyrinthine, some of it has great power both of image and of incident. It is a strange paradox in Davidson that one can turn from this darkly and brutally exalted arrogance to a moving awareness of the reverberations of the ordinary and everyday:

> An unseen roadman breaking flint,
> If echo and the winds conspire
> To dedicate his morning's stint,

> May beat a tune out, dew and fire
> So wrought that heaven might lend an ear,
> And Ariel hush his harp to hear.
>
> ('Matinée')

Davidson was not the only Scottish poet writing at the end of the century, and other writers and other styles would also feed into the new developments of the twentieth century, but with Davidson we can at least understand Hugh MacDiarmid's intense reaction to that

> small black shape by the edge of the sea,
> – A bullet-hole through a great scene's beauty,
> God through the wrong end of a telescope.
>
> ('Of John Davidson')

Notes

1 James Hogg, *Selected Poems*, ed. Douglas S. Mack (Oxford, 1970); *Selected Poems and Songs*, ed. David Groves (Edinburgh, 1986).
2 Alan Bold, (ed.) *Byron: Wrath and Rhyme* (London, 1983) pp.17-56.
3 Alexander Rodger, *Poems and Songs, Humorous, Serious, and Satirical*, ed. Robert Ford (Paisley, 1897).
4 Alexander Smith, *Poetical Works*, ed. William Sinclair (Edinburgh, 1909).
5 James Macfarlan, *Poetical Works*, with a Memoir by Colin Rae-Brown (Glasgow, 1882).
6 Janet Hamilton, *Poems Sketches and Essays*, ed. James Hamilton (Glasgow, 1885).
7 William Thom, *Rhymes and Recollections of a Hand-loom Weaver*, ed. W. Skinner (Paisley, 1880). See also Robert Bruce, *William Thom, the Inverurie Poet – A New Look* (Aberdeen, 1970).
8 James Young Geddes, *The Spectre Clock of Alyth and Other Selections* (Alyth, n.d., c.1885); *In the Valhalla* (Dundee, 1891).
9 Hamish Henderson, 'William McGonagall and the Folk Scene', in *Chapbook* vol. 2 no.5 (Aberdeen, 1965), pp.3-10, 23-34.

The History of Scottish Literature, Vol.3: Nineteenth Century, ed. D. Gifford (Aberdeen University Press, 1988).

Voice, Tone, and Transition in Don Juan

'Byron is a perfect chameleon', concluded his friend Lady Blessington, who recorded the gist of his frank conversations with
her. She thought he had 'no fixed principles' of conduct or of
belief, even if he had ruling sentiments (love of liberty, hatred
of cant). If the chameleon is an animal that changes colour for
self-protective purposes, is this how we are to see Byron? Certainly he gave no single constant impression. In company, he
could be constrained and withdrawn, or warm and loquacious,
depending on the size and congeniality of the group. Both reactions seem too spontaneous to be consciously self-protective, and
their main consequence was to increase the interest and curiosity
felt by observers of his unpredictable, tantalizing personality. If
his silence concealed nothing more than diffidence and being ill
at ease, it may be that his loquacity concealed more. He loved
wit and repartee, and in the right mood he could throw out a
chain of ideas of extraordinary richness, linked by lightning connections scarcely sensed by the hearer; but he disliked sustained
argument, and when Leigh Hunt once tried to persuade him that
good argument needed logic and reason, his answer was: 'For
my part, it is the last speaker that convinces me.' This eternal
impressionability, the lack of patience with reason, the search
for unknown links-forward rather than known links-back, is certainly zestful and creative, and one of the keys to his poetic
method, but it may at the same time be self-protective in a man
who is loath to expose a central jostle of unresolved beliefs and
counter-beliefs to the hard clear light that step-by-step argument
would place them in. He is quite capable of making a virtue of
contingency:

> The great object of life is Sensation – to feel that we exist –
> even though in pain – it is this 'craving void' which drives us

to Gaming – to Battle – to Travel – to intemperate but keenly felt pursuits of every description whose principal attraction is the agitation inseparable from their accomplishment.

(Letter to Annabella Milbanke, 6 September 1813)

This is the philosophy of a man of moods, who if often bored or abstracted enjoys the contrast that a sudden excitement brings. Those who expect to find the languid humours of a world-weary Romantic may be disconcerted by bursts of brisk no-nonsense wit; others, led to expect the wit, may find a dark immovable object they cannot even probe. John Galt, travelling on the same boat as Byron from Gibraltar to Malta in 1809, noted his general waywardness, which he thought partly a pose, but was struck more persuasively by a deeper contrast between the sociable 'day' Byron and the abstracted solitary 'night' Byron, the latter being like 'a man forbid', sitting on a rail in silence and staring into the darkness. When we say that Byron was temperamental and moody, then, we have many witnesses, not least himself. But the contrasts are not only between sensation and sensation, as the letter to Annabella might suggest, or between sensation and the lack of it, as Hunt observed. Sensation, feeling, craving, pursuit, agitation – to use the words of the letter – are not all in all. A different contrast emerges if one compares passages from two other letters. Writing to Thomas Moore on 2 March 1815, Byron is the very image of a man in a down mood:

I am in such a state of sameness and stagnation, and so totally occupied in consuming the fruits – and sauntering – and playing dull games at cards – and yawning – and trying to read old Annual Registers and the daily papers – and gathering shells on the shore – and watching the growth of stunted gooseberry bushes in the garden – that I have neither time nor sense to say more than

Yours ever,
B.

Yet the sharpest contrast to that passage comes in another letter to the same correspondent, five years later, from Ravenna (9 December 1820), and is not a report of the delights of some elated sensation or excitement but is concerned with right action, with duty. The local garrison commander is shot near Byron's house, and lies dying in the street. A crowd gathers, makes a great noise, but does nothing to help; there is even a doctor, who conceals the fact that he is one. Byron reacts instantly: disgusted, pragmatic, British, taking charge.

> As nobody could, or would, do any thing but howl and pray, and as no one would stir a finger to move him, for fear of consequences, I lost my patience – made my servant and a couple of the mob take up the body – sent off two soldiers to the guard – despatched Diego to the Cardinal with the news, and had the commandant carried upstairs into my own quarter. But it was too late, he was gone – not at all disfigured – bled inwardly – not above an ounce or two came out.... You are to know that, if I had not had the body moved, they would have left him there till morning in the street for fear of consequences. I would not choose to let even a dog die in such a manner, without succour: – and, as for consequences, I care for none in a duty.

This admirable practicality – and the splendid last phrase is set down with absolutely no self-consciousness – has the effect of almost, though possibly not quite, negating his remarks about 'sensation'. The incident *was* exciting, and in another part of the letter he describes, almost like a novelist, how the man 'only said, "O Dio!" and "Gesu!" two or three times' before he died. But mainly what he illustrates is the inculcation of certain moral ideas and habits of action which occupy an area of constancy, of reliability, in a character otherwise fluid and variable. The imprint of this, too, is seen in his poetry.

Byron in company; in the streets; in correspondence. But what of Byron in his room, writing his private journals – has he any helpful secrets? Not secrets, perhaps, but some instructive examples of association and transition, caught on the wing in a more purely unpremeditated way than in the famous digressions of *Don Juan*. Two are worth noting, and both are called 'strange'. The shorter one (*Ravenna Journal*, 2 February 1821) is a tribute to the sudden effect of music. After ruminating on his bad habit of waking too early in the morning, in a state of either despondency, or thirst, or anger, and wondering whether all this is hypochondria or a case of premature senility, he writes, without a break:

> Oh! there is an organ playing in the street – a waltz, too! I must

leave off to listen. They are playing a waltz which I have heard
ten thousand times at the balls in London, between 1812 and
1815. Music is a strange thing.

The music, utterly accidental as it is, makes him stop what he is
doing, and yet seems to carry forward, as if in another dimension,
his thoughts of time passing and place changing. In a longer
passage (*Ravenna Journal*, 12 January 1821), he is kept indoors by
bad weather, reading letters from England and a collection of
English poetry. Suddenly there is a change of direction, as his
reading of the song 'Sabrina fair' in Milton's *Comus* sets off an
unforeseen train of reminiscences about a dead friend of his
youth, Edward Noel Long.

> How strange are my thoughts! – The reading of the song in
> Milton, 'Sabrina fair' has brought back upon me – I know not
> how or why – the happiest, perhaps, days of my life (always
> excepting, here and there, a Harrow holiday in the two latter
> summers of my stay there) when living at Cambridge with
> Edward Noel Long, afterwards of the Guards, – who, after
> having served honourably in the expedition to Copenhagen
> (of which two or three thousand scoundrels yet survive in
> plight and pay), was drowned early in 1809, on his passage to
> Lisbon with his regiment in the St. George transport, which
> was run foul of, in the night, by another transport.

He goes on to evoke the summer days of an intense romantic
friendship when he and Long, as students at Cambridge, rode,
dived, swam, read, played music together, and crowns the story
with a reference to his even deeper attachment to the choir-boy
John Edleston. The associative triggering comes from water (the
element in which Sabrina, guardian nymph of the River Severn,
lived, in which Long and Byron dived and swam in the River
Cam, and in which Long drowned in the Atlantic Ocean) and from
music (the song invoking Sabrina, the intimate music-making
of the masque in which it is set, and the flute-and-'cello evenings
in Cambridge when Byron was his friend's audience); and
Byron's bisexual nature makes him see, at a flash, the features of
Edward Long under the wet 'loose train' of Sabrina's hair. He
calls the thought-sequence 'strange' because it has arisen so
quickly, 'I know not how or why'. But what is strange in the
prose of a personal diary may flourish naturally in the verse of a

long poem which delights in real or apparent spontaneity. Shelley, interestingly enough, used the same word to characterize the poetry as Lady Blessington had used of the poet. 'The language in which the whole [of *Don Juan* Cantos III-V] is clothed – a sort of chameleon under the changing sky of the spirit that kindles it – is such as those lisping days could not have expected' (letter to Byron, 21 October 1821). What does *this* chameleon change from, and to?

Byron said many, and sometimes contradictory, things about *Don Juan* in his letters. It was 'meant to be a little quietly facetious upon every thing' (September 1818); it was 'the most moral of poems' (February 1819); it was a '*human*' poem after so many '*divine*' ones (April 1819); he had 'no plan' but he did have 'materials' (August 1819); it was 'the sublime of *that there* sort of writing' and could not have been written by anyone 'who has not lived in the world' (October 1819); 'to how many cantos this may extend, I know not' (February 1821); but some day it would be recognized as 'a *Satire* on *abuses* of the present states of Society' (December 1822). The range of comments fits the fluidity of the man. The poem is both lightly facetious and highly moral; it has no plan and is a planned social satire; it is erotic but sublime. Clearly a poem of such great length, composed over several years, must have grown and developed in the conceptions that motivated it, but it is harder than usual to see any ruling structure, not only because the work is unfinished but because Byron never decided how many cantos it was to have (24? 100? 150? – these were all forecasts he made at different times) or what goal the narrative and chronology were making for (the French Revolution and its aftermath? the fight for Greek independence? – these he considered). Add to that the fact that the emotional and intellectual climax of the poem as we have it comes half-way (Canto VIII, the siege of Ismail), with a distinct slackening of interest in the last cantos dealing with Juan's visit to England, and any sense of a satisfying architectonic is postponed to the vista of a much longer poem where extremely powerful revolutionary or military scenes in France or Greece might have redeemed the slack and restored the balance. To a reader in the late twentieth century, however, architectonics is not everything, either in art or for that matter in life. *Don Juan* may indeed seem all the more appealing, with a kind of proleptic modernity, in its foretaste of so many later unfinished long poems, like Pound's *Cantos*, MacDiarmid's *Mature Art*, William Carlos Williams's *Paterson*, Olson's

Maximus Poems, Berryman's *Dream Songs*, and Lowell's *Notebook* and *History*. In all these examples, the poem eventually becomes, whatever its organizing principles may once have been (narrative, philosophical, epic), an accompaniment or doppelgänger of the poet himself, rising and falling with the fluctuations of the poet's life, a work not so much unfinished as unfinishable. There is an uneasy moment in *Don Juan*, near the end of Canto XII, when Byron realizes that this is exactly where a conventional twelve-book epic would end, and brazens out his awareness both of epic traditions (which indeed he has acknowledged and illustrated throughout the poem) and of his original way of breaking them:

> But now I will begin my poem. 'Tis
>   Perhaps a little strange, if not quite new,
> That from the first of Cantos up to this
>   I've not begun what we have to go through.
> These first twelve books are merely flourishes,
>   *Preludios*, trying just a string or two
> Upon my lyre, or making the pegs sure;
> And when so, you shall have the overture.
>
> My Muses do not care a pinch of rosin
>   About what's called success, or not succeeding:
> Such thoughts are quite below the strain they have chosen;
>   'Tis a 'great moral lesson' they are reading.
> I thought, at setting off, about two dozen
>   Cantos would do; but at Apollo's pleading,
> If that my Pegasus should not be founder'd,
> I think to canter gently through a hundred.
>
>   (XII. liv-lv)

'Success' would be *Paradise Lost*, *The Divine Comedy*; the great task conceived, mapped out, and completed. He is doing something else, which he cannot even define for himself, far less for his readers. But he offers them a jaunty ticket for the forward voyage.

This is an art of improvisation, though we have to use the term carefully. We know that Byron had watched, met, and talked to Tommaso Sgricci, the Italian theatrical *improvvisatore*, who strung together impromptu verses on subjects suggested by the audience, but this would interest him as a sort of parallel activity rather than influence his own style, which was already formed. He does, nevertheless, tip his hat in Sgricci's direction in *Don Juan*, when he defends what he mock-modestly calls his 'desultory rhyme' as chiming out the matters uppermost in his mind from moment to moment of writing, 'Just as I feel the *Improvvisatore* (XV, xx). And the fact that Sgricci's was an oral, public art, an art of the voice and not the pen, does help to remind Byron of the importance of 'voice' in his own art, of the effect of good lively free conversation he never had to destroy other qualities to obtain. He characteristically gives the impression of devaluing his own facility in this respect, when he says: 'I rattle on exactly as I'd talk / With anybody in a ride or walk' (XV, xix). Not exactly; nor is it really rattling on. But in so far as he conveys the sense and presence of a racy speaker, within the strict confines of his chosen metrical system, an achievement that is much more remarkable than his usually non-versewriting critics give him credit for, we cannot but feel the nearness of the man to his persona, so many accounts of his conversation, and of the tone and calibre of his voice, have been recorded, quite apart from the additional evidence of his extraordinarily frank, immediate, spirited, communicative, 'speaking' letters. Colonel Leicester Stanhope, one witness among many, described his conversation as 'a mixture of philosophy and slang, of everything, – like his *Don Juan*'.

The sense of an identifiable and 'modern' speaking voice, the voice of a worldly but well-read, playful but sharp and ardent British writer of the early nineteenth century, seems to have been desired by Byron for two contrasting purposes. The social reality of the 'I' in the poem, his knowledge of and comments on undisguised contemporary and recent events, helps to persuade the reader of *Don Juan*, if he is pondering the speaker's categorizing of it as an epic, that one way to accept the category is to see it as a 'true' epic, its material firmly based in the British and Mediterranean world, of the period from 1789 to 1823. On the other hand, 'documentary' is scarcely a word one would apply to it, and the vigorous, versatile, descanting, reader-conscious voice, with its sudden flights and digressions, helps to keep the poem opened up, as every poem must be, towards the imagination; an unmodulating, low-keyed, deadpan voice, or a voice restrained by decorums of rhetoric, would not meet the case, but Byron's own voice, transmuted only by being raised, as it were, to a higher power by the demands of the poetry, is ideal for the variety of pursuits and targets that appear, disappear, and reappear.

The historical reality is opposed to what he calls the 'labyrinth of fables' that swallows and numbs readers of earlier epics, and he sees himself as being in the epic succession only if readers will accept, as he buoyantly believes they will, one notable jolt to their expectations:

> There's only one slight difference between
> Me and my epic brethren gone before,
> And here the advantage is my own, I ween
> (Not that I have not several merits more,
> But this will more peculiarly be seen);
> They so embellish, that 'tis quite a bore
> Their labyrinth of fables to thread through,
> Whereas this story's actually true.
>
> (I, ccii)

One cannot push this too far. Even the most diligent historical novel needs fictional characters, including very often the hero or heroine. At the beginning of the first canto, the speaker admits that only Don Juan will suit his purposes, not (as he might have chosen) Nelson or Wolfe, Danton or Buonaparte. The mention of such names, however, and the accompanying references to 'gazettes' and 'Trafalgar', are sufficiently indicative of the 'truthful' aspect of the poem, and before long Juan is seen acting within the historical framework. It is not only the historical truth of great events that Byron is interested in: he has a conception of a true portrayal of 'human things and acts', a bird's eye view of 'that wild, Society', a glance 'thrown on men of every station':

> Besides, my Muse by no means deals in fiction:
> She gathers a repertory of facts,
> Of course with some reserve and slight restriction,
> But mostly sings of human things and acts –
> And that's one cause she meets with contradiction;
> For too much truth, at first sight, ne'er attracts;
> And were her object only what's called glory,
> With more ease too she'd tell a different story.
>
> Love, war, a tempest – surely there's variety;
> Also a seasoning slight of lucubration;
> A bird's-eye-view, too, of that wild, Society;
> A slight glance thrown on men of every station.

If you have nought else, here's at least satiety,
    Both in performance and in preparation;
And though these lines should only line portmanteaus,
Trade will be all the better for these Cantos.

(XIV, xiii–xiv)

Even the wry joke at the end somehow contributes to his sense that although he has now and again to explain himself to his uneasy readers ('For too much truth, at first sight, ne'er attracts'), he has the confidence of his own wide sweep and purview of real things. The truths may be well-observed facets of human conduct, human relationships; truths such as a novelist would use. They may be moral, within traditions of satirical stripping-down and exposure, as he warns the reader in a striking stanza:

But now I'm going to be immoral; now
    I mean to show things really as they are,
Not as they ought to be: for I avow,
    That till we see what's what in fact, we're far
From much improvement with that virtuous plough
    Which skims the surface, leaving scarce a scar
Upon the black loam long manured by Vice,
Only to keep its corn at the old price.

(XII, xl)

The double meaning of 'improvement', moral and agricultural, serves to remind the reader of recent changes in society and to sharpen the 'modern' edge of the attack, while not losing the older reverberations of 'plough' and 'loam' and 'manure'. Else-where, on a deeper level, the speaker envisages a universal mid-night unmasking, when the world as it really is would be seen as almost the exact opposite of what we customarily suppose it to be. In two forceful stanzas, he uses imagery from *Othello*, supreme play of deception, to illustrate the point:

'Tis strange, – but true; for truth is always strange;
    Stranger than fiction: if it could be told,
How much would novels gain by the exchange!
    How differently the world would men behold!
How oft would vice and virtue places change!
    The new world would be nothing to the old,
If some Columbus of the moral seas
Would show mankind their souls' antipodes.

What 'antres vast and deserts idle' then
  Would be discover'd in the human soul!
What icebergs in the hearts of mighty men,
  With self-love in the centre as their pole!
What Anthropophagi are nine of ten
  Of those who hold the kingdoms in control!
Were things but only call'd by their right name,
Caesar himself would be ashamed of fame.

(XIV, ci–cii)

But the poem, to be true to Byron, had to be true to his moods, to his waywardness. Here, too, he has valuable comments to make through his poem's speaker. At the beginning of the seventh canto he is in transition from a theme of love (the vengeful jealousy of the sultan's wife, Gulbeyaz, in Constantinople) to a theme of war (the Russian siege of the Turkish fortress of Ismail on the Danube). Love and Glory are invoked, but questioned. The possessive, ruthless love of Gulbeyaz, commanding that Juan and Dudù be sewn into sacks and thrown into the Bosphorus, was real enough, but hardly glorious; and the forthcoming battle, 'glorious' in conventional terms, was not going to be glorious either. This is not to say that true love and glory do not exist – the speaker is defending himself against a charge of cynicism – but that they are flickering, evanescent, hard to grasp or pin down, appearing to us as shows when we are searching for substance. To meet these shifting and inconstant visions, which flash or twist above us like a shower of meteors or the Northern Lights, the speaker's poetry will itself shift and flicker, constant in its inconstancy:

O Love! O Glory! what are you who fly
  Around us ever, rarely to alight?
There's not a meteor in the Polar sky
  Of such transcendent and more fleeting flight.
Chill, and chain'd to cold earth, we lift on high
  Our eyes in search of either lovely light;
A thousand and a thousand colours they
Assume, then leave us on our freezing way.

And such as they are, such my present tale is,
  A nondescript and ever-varying rhyme,
A versified Aurora Borealis,
  Which flashes o'er a waste and icy clime.

(VII, i–ii)

'Ever-varying' is the key word, in keeping with Byron's own voice and temperament. But the changes, like the changing, dancing, shimmering folds of the aurora borealis, are a change of patterns, or half-patterns, rather than some anarchic amorphousness. In the same way, he pauses to describe in some detail, and with great relish, the ever-changing rainbow which appears as a good omen in the sky shortly before Juan is saved from shipwreck in the second canto. It is not the fact that it might be a good omen which interests the speaker, who shows himself to be duly sceptical about sailors' superstitions while accepting their occasional usefulness ('It is as well to think so, now and then'), but the nature of the changing shapes and colours themselves – the transience that strikes a chord in his mind and makes him dissolve the rainbow in a scatter of comparisons ranging from the beautiful to the grotesque:

> Now overhead a rainbow, bursting through
>   The scattering clouds, shone, spanning the dark sea,
> Resting its bright base on the quivering blue;
>   And all within its arch appear'd to be
> Clearer than that without, and its wide hue
>   Wax'd broad and waving, like a banner free,
> Then changed like to a bow that's bent, and then
> Forsook the dim eyes of these shipwreck'd men.
>
> It changed, of course; a heavenly chameleon,
>   The airy child of vapour and the sun,
> Brought forth in purple, cradled in vermilion,
>   Baptized in molten gold, and swathed in dun,
> Glittering like crescents o'er a Turk's pavilion,
>   And blending every colour into one,
> Just like a black eye in a recent scuffle
> (For sometimes we must box without the muffle).
>
> Our shipwreck'd seamen thought it a good omen –
>   It is as well to think so, now and then;
> 'Twas an old custom of the Greek and Roman,
>   And may become of great advantage when
> Folks are discouraged; and most surely no men
>   Had greater need to nerve themselves again
> Than these, and so this rainbow look'd like hope –
> Quite a celestial kaleidoscope.
>
> (II, xci-xciii)

The metaphors and similes leap over one another in their eager-
ness, not to define a static object but to accompany a richly changing
one. The rainbow is a bridge; a banner; a bent bow; a chameleon;
a baby; a Turkish crescent; a black eye; a kaleidoscope. 'It
changed, *of course*'; otherwise, what use would it have been to
the speaker! Byron, no great lover of the static art of painting,
would have seen little virtue in the fixed, tubelike rainbow of
Millais' *The Blind Girl*, double though it is. But literature, like
life itself, flickers, infinitely tantalizing and suggestive, forming
and breaking up similitudes and patterns. The final 'kaleidoscope'
is a good illustration of Byron's sense of the language as a
developing and malleable medium. The kaleidoscope was
invented in 1817, and Byron saw one in 1818, just before he
wrote these stanzas. It is the quickness with which he sees the
potential of the new word that we notice, and his figurative use
of it, applied to the rainbow, is the earliest recorded in *N.E.D.*
The kaleidoscope's combination of pattern and change would
recommend it particularly to Byron.

Meteor – aurora borealis – rainbow – chameleon – kaleidoscope. Do we have our man there, our poem, or are they both

> like the borealis race,
> That flit ere you can point their place?

Byron's art has been found hard to define, and critics have often
expressed some dissatisfaction with it, not helped in their
enquiries by the poet's jokiness ('Hail, Muse! *et cetera.*' – III, i)
or by his reiterated praise of spontaneity ('Why, Man, the Soul
of such writing is its licence' – letter to John Murray, 12 August
1819). Yet some 2,000 stanzas of *ottava rima* had to be engineered,
rhymes had to be found, cantos had to be ended and begun, a
considerable range of characters had to be made psychologically
convincing, and the relation and balance between story and
digression had to be thought about. Too much organization
would have been death to the very spirit of *Don Juan*, but is the
art sufficient for Byron's unique purposes?

His best effects, like Spenser's (how he would have disliked
that 'like'!), may be appealed to, or experienced, but scarcely
quoted, since they emerge over many pages, out of the flux and
eddying of the poem, and are cumulative rather than pointed.
This is not to say that local felicities and virtuosities are not frequent, from single lines and phrases ('A mighty mass of brick,

and smoke, and shipping', 'that costive Sophy', 'But they will not find liberty a Troy', 'without risk or / The singeing of a single inky whisker', 'A lonely pure affection unopposed', 'Half naked, loving, natural, and Greek', 'Carotid-artery-cutting Castlereagh', 'gentlemen in stays, as stiff as stones', 'The calentures of music') to whole stanzas where he accepts and dispatches with éclat some peculiar challenge (the Latin prescription Juan is given when he falls sick in Russia, at X, xli; the flash or canting language used elegiacally as a tribute to the footpad Juan shoots on his entry into London, at XI, xix). His command of rhyme is a great pleasure: bold, ingenious, outrageous; he takes positive delight in extending all the normal expectations, rhyming with words from Latin, Greek, French, German, Italian, Spanish, Russian, Arabic, Turkish, Persian, Aramaic, Gaelic, and Scots. Sometimes it is what is *not* said, as in the wonderful pause between two connected stanzas at VIII, cix-cx, where – whether through the exigencies of *ottava rima*, or by a stroke of genius, or more likely a mixture of the two – the last-ditch defence of the Khan and his five sons during the siege of Ismail is given sudden pathos:

> Nay, he had wounded, though but slightly, both
>   Juan and Johnson; whereupon they fell,
> The first with sighs, the second with an oath,
>   Upon his angry sultanship, pell-mell,
> And all around were grown exceeding wroth
>   At such a pertinacious infidel,
> And pour'd upon him and his sons like rain,
> Which they resisted like a sandy plain
>
> That drinks and still is dry. At last they perish'd. . . .

And sometimes a brilliant passage is created out of the revitalizing of an ancient convention, as in the much-quoted *'ubi sunt'* of XI, lxxxi-lxxxvi, where the speaker, looking back on the decade before 1822, can hardly believe the changes that have occurred, in a time of political and social ferment. As befits the chameleon, he warms to the theme of change, but the remarkable characteristic of these eleven stanzas is the way in which they manage to be highly comic, witty, cutting, and 'modern' (in 1822, but the feeling is still there), and yet at the same time shadowed with intimations of mortality in the old *ubi sunt* manner. On the one hand all seems robust satire:

> Where's Brummell? Dish'd. Where's Long Pole Wellesley?
>   Diddled.
>   Where's Whitbread? Romilly? Where's George the Third?
> Where is his will? (That's not so soon unriddled.)
>
> (XI, lxxviii)

But somehow, and even within the robust tone, there is place for Edward Young, author of *Night Thoughts* and other works of edifying gloom and *memento mori*:

> 'Where is the world?' cries Young, at *eighty* – 'Where
>   The world in which a man was born?' Alas!
> Where is the world of *eight* years past? *'Twas there* –
>   I look for it, – 'tis gone, a globe of glass!
> Crack'd, shiver'd, vanish'd, scarcely gazed on, ere
>   A silent change dissolves the glittering mass.
> Statesmen, chiefs, orators, queens, patriots, kings,
> And dandies, all are gone on the wind's wings.
>
> (XI, lxxvi)

'A silent change dissolves the glittering mass.' Like the Love and Glory shining and vanishing at the beginning of Canto VII, contemporary history also, sharp and specific as it is, a whole world of manners and personalities and actions, nothing seeming to be more real, steals away from decade to decade, undermined by forces we cannot see or hear. It is surely a very uncommon art that can produce a hilarious *ubi sunt* which is an *ubi sunt* all the same.

The larger-scale effects, which are the least amenable to analysis and evaluation because they involve such abrupt shifts not only of subject-matter but equally of tone and atmosphere, are nevertheless important in a long poem, whose length might well be thought to accommodate its variety.

Having decided that he would not plunge *in medias res* as earlier epic poets had done but instead would 'begin with the beginning' (I, vii) because (with tongue positively rolling in cheek) the regularity of his design 'Forbids all wandering as the worst of sinning', the speaker seems to promise a straightforward, almost novelistic narrative. This, very obviously, was not to be, and the amount of 'wandering' becomes so great as the story progresses that it can be seen eventually as a sort of *in medias res*, with interruptions of the action not for flashback or explanatory purposes as in

Virgil or Milton but for expatiatory flights into another dimension, the mental dimension of the speaker's (i.e. virtually
Byron's) thoughts and opinions on a large variety of subjects.
Naturally he comes to admit and comment on these 'wanderings',
as he comments on almost every aspect of the poem at some
point within it (not from uneasiness but out of an exuberant
conviction that the reader will be interested in his originality – a
mighty maze, and all without a plan!), begging our indulgence
for many and unconscionable digressions. 'If I have any fault,'
he says (cries of 'No!' expected), 'it is digression' (III, xcvi),
neglecting his characters while he soliloquizes and gives his 'addresses from the throne'. The didactic function is developed in
a later canto:

> Oh, pardon my digression – or at least
>   Peruse! 'Tis always with a moral end
> That I dissert, like grace before a feast:
>   For like an aged aunt, or tiresome friend,
> A rigid guardian, or a zealous priest,
>   My Muse by exhortation means to mend
> All people, at all times, and in most places,
> Which puts my Pegasus to these grave paces.
>
>   (XII, xxxix)

That the digressions are very often didactic would not be dis-
puted, but the variety of mood and tone with which they are
presented gives them a much greater interest than 'grave paces'
might suggest. Much of Byron's art can be revealed from two
of the more extended digressionary passages, in Cantos I and III.

The artistic method may be said to be being tried out in the first
canto (I, cxv–cxxxvi). The youthful Juan is sitting in a summer-
house on a pleasant June evening with Julia, Don Alfonso's young
wife; as the sun sets, and the moon comes up, they embrace, and
she consents to be his lover. 'Here,' says the speaker, 'my chaste
Muse a liberty must take –', but the chaste reader, whether
relieved or disappointed, is quickly reassured that the 'liberty' in
question is not erotic but literary: a digression is coming, to fill
in the five months that we are to imagine elapsing between that
embrace and the next one to be described. The digression, after
the Sterne-like teasing of the previous stanzas, leads with a
straight lyrical listing of things that are sweet and desirable – the
distant song of a gondolier, the sound of a waterfall, a rich grape-

harvest – which modulates to a more mocking tone as the sweets and desirables widen to include a woman's revenge, a belated legacy, a quarrel with a tiresome friend, and then returns briefly to the lyrical mode with praises of the sweetest thing of all, 'first and passionate love'. Immediately a tangent offers itself: Adam's first love led to the Fall, the fruit plucked from the Tree of Knowledge has led to an 'age of oddities let loose', a welter of discoveries and inventions good and bad – the guillotine, galvanism, vaccination, rockets, polar voyages, miners' safety-lamps. Man is indeed a strange phenomenon, and – with a partial return to his setting-off point, though the digression is not finished yet – 'Pleasure's a sin, and sometimes Sin's a pleasure.' Man goes to his grave without knowing much about his meaning or his fate:

> What then? – I do not know, no more do you –
>   And so good night. – Return we to our story:
> 'Twas in November, when fine days are few. . . .

But this is a false start: wait for it! A little meditation on November follows, with evocative description of the season, indoors and outside: a dusting of snow on the far-off peaks, rough seas breaking on the promontory, 'sober suns' setting at five o'clock, the wind gusting while a family piles wood on the fire, the speaker's personal (and rather delightful) summing-up:

> There's something cheerful in that sort of light,
>   Even as a summer sky's without a cloud:
> I'm fond of fire, and crickets, and all that,
> A lobster salad, and champagne, and chat.

And then at last: ''Twas midnight – Donna Julia was in bed. . . .' And the story proceeds with Juan and Julia surprised and unmasked by the jealous Don Alfonso. There is a connecting thread, if one wants it, through the whole digression, but that thread is perhaps little more than the tight-rope on which Byron dances his various and unforeseen steps.

The third canto offers more developed, more rich transitions, in the long digression in its latter part (III, lxxviii-cxi). The action stops while Juan and his ideal love Haidée are enjoying a celebration on their island, just as her father, the pirate Lambro, unexpectedly returns and is about to put an end to their idyllic relationship, Juan banished and Haidée dead of despair and grief. The digression is therefore an interlude between love and death, and might be expected to show high seriousness; which indeed it does, yet a seriousness mingled with broad comedy, keen satire, and literary criticism, in a fairly audacious amalgam that tests the reader's sympathy and receptivity to the limit. There are, however, links and connections of a most interesting kind, some clear enough, others more oblique or subterranean.

Juan and Haidée, exotically dressed and surrounded by every Levantine luxury from iced sherbet to tame gazelles, have finished their feast and now sit back to enjoy a suite of entertainers – 'Dwarfs, dancing girls, black eunuchs, and a poet'. The presence of the poet, though natural enough in the circumstances, gives an initial signal to the reader that the story is going to be interrupted, and so it proves. The poet is described as well-known, and 'a very pleasant fellow' in company, but a time-server, a 'sad trimmer'. He will sing encomiums on the sultan and the pasha, or 'God save the King', or 'Ça ira', as the occasion demands. He is not devoid of grace, however, and the situation of the remote island, the friendly non-authoritarian audience, encourages him to be bold for once, so that

> without any danger of a riot, he
> Might for long lying make himself amends;
> And singing as he sung in his warm youth,
> Agree to a short armistice with truth.
>
> (III, lxxxii)

From this unworthy vessel there is then delivered the famous lyric, 'The isles of Greece, the isles of Greece!'. It well deserves its fame, and in writing it Byron had the brilliant second thought of changing the *ottava rima* to a scaled-down version of it – six lines instead of eight, four feet instead of five, but a rhyming couplet still closing the stanza – and by this means keeping both separateness and continuity. (It is one of the many features which show the hand of the artist, whatever Byron may say about his carelessness.) The poem is both a plangent elegy for Greece, once culturally and politically great and now sunk in apathy under foreign domination, and a muted call to arms. Like a Wagnerian motif, Byron's belief in the duty of a poet to act as precursor or harbinger of change sounds out here as it so often does when the authorial temperature is right. The singer of the poem is at once bitterly self-critical (the lyre of Sappho and Anacreon has grown 'degenerate' in his hands) and what we would call an 'extremist' in his nationalism (praising the ancient Greek tyrants because at least they were Greek, not Persian or Turkish). He wants the Greeks to remember their military history, and act on the recollection.

> The mountains look on Marathon –
> And Marathon looks on the sea;
> And musing there an hour alone,
> I dream'd that Greece might still be free;
> For standing on the Persians' grave,
> I could not deem myself a slave.

The fervent but guilt-ridden bard, having his moment of truth as he recites before Juan and Haidée, fades out and is replaced by a more general meditation on whether the pen after all is mightier than the sword. It begins straight and serious:

> But words are things, and a small drop of ink,
> Falling like dew, upon a thought, produces
> That which makes thousands, perhaps millions, think;
> 'Tis strange, the shortest letter which man uses
> Instead of speech, may form a lasting link
> Of ages; to what straits old Time reduces
> Frail man, when paper – even a rag like this,
> Survives himself, his tomb, and all that's his!
>
> (III, lxxxviii)

But then, with a characteristic modulation, as the speaker warms to his theme he begins to toss and turn it, look at it from unexpected angles, find modern examples which naturally resist a too solemn tone, and move it step by step towards specific literary criticism, though never quite losing the thread of a poet's obligations to society. 'Troy owes to Homer what whist owes to Hoyle.' But what state, what realm, what power owes anything to the Lake Poets and their friends? What are Wordsworth, Coleridge, and Southey but renegades whose names 'cut a convict figure, / The very Botany Bay in moral geography'? Wordsworth (who as we know heartily returned Byron's dislike) is the main target, mocked at for puerility, for tediousness, for provinciality, as against what the speaker would no doubt claim as his own adultness, readability, and internationalism. The attack, enter-

taining enough in the main, in a boisterous sort of way, ends on
a sour and savage note:

> 'Pedlars,' and 'Boats,' and 'Waggons!' Oh! ye shades
>   Of Pope and Dryden, are we come to this?
> That trash of such sort not alone evades
>   Contempt, but from the bathos' vast abyss
> Floats scumlike uppermost, and these Jack Cades
>   Of sense and song above your graves may hiss –
> The 'little boatman' and his *Peter Bell*
> Can sneer at him who drew 'Achitophel'!
>
> (III, c)

After this explosion, there could only be an abrupt change of
tack. At first, it is an apparent return to the story, though the
narrative does not in fact take up again till eighteen stanzas later
(IV, viii), and all that is happening is that the reader is temporarily
(helpfully!) reminded of the two lovers, now left alone at the end
of the revelry. 'T' our tale', says the speaker, but really this is
no more than a chord struck between two greatly different
sections of his huge digression. As the lovers watch the twilight,
an evocative lyrical mode suddenly emerges, the battle of the
books is forgotten, and an evening hymn in praise of nature,
with 'Ave Maria!' repeatedly punctuating it like a vesper-bell,
shows yet another side of the speaker, and of Byron. Woven
into it, with some cunning, are passages translated from Sappho
and Dante (whose names preserve continuities from the earlier
part of the digression), emphasizing the mysteriously softening
and healing influences of the twilight hour. These influences are
allowed to bring the passage to an end with an unexpected reference to Nero, a tyrant justly destroyed, but whose tomb, as
Suetonius records, was strewn with flowers by 'some hands
unseen'. The reference to Nero links back to the mention of the
Greek tyrants in the poet's song at the banquet, but makes of
course an entirely different point. Bravura carries off the 'Ave
Maria!' passage, but only just; examined closely, it has some
elements of the factitious, almost of kitsch. Its defence is made
more readily when one takes it in its place as one strand in a very
long poem, and in fact, reading the poem at a natural speed, and
coming to it in its context, one finds it strangely moving.

'But I'm digressing...' the speaker has the grace to add, and
closes the canto with a sardonic joke. Read Aristotle's *Poetics*,

he says, for a perfect defence of the length and variousness of epics.

The shorter digressions tend to be more manageable, involving fewer shifts of tone, but still make capital out of contrast, as for example the sprightly and perceptive discourse on money at the beginning of Canto XII, or the passage on literary fame and bluestockings at the end of Canto IV. At parts where the story is itself at its most intense and serious, as during the siege of Ismail in Cantos VII-VIII, digression is instinctively held in check, but never quite disappears. Canto VIII closes with a couple of highly effective transitions, from exalted prophecy addressing future generations to a light familiar address to the reader, and from that to straight narrative pathos in a very plain style in the concluding stanza. At the end of the carnage, when the Russians have at last taken Ismail, and Suwarrow has sent back his boastful and blasphemous rhyming message to the Empress, the speaker bursts out with his promise that he 'will teach, if possible, the stones / To rise against Earth's tyrants', adding:

> And when you hear historians talk of thrones,
>   And those that sate upon them, let it be
> As we now gaze upon the mammoth's bones,
>   And wonder what old world such things could see,
> Or hieroglyphics on Egyptian stones,
>   The pleasant riddles of futurity –
> Guessing at what shall happily be hid,
> As the real purpose of a pyramid.
>
> (VIII, cxxxvii)

But immediately he turns to the reader and reminds him how he has kept his word to write an epic with its promised 'sketches of Love – Tempest – Travel – War' – and all of it 'very accurate, you must allow'. However, this is a tone which will not do to end *that* canto with, so he swiftly closes the digression and returns momentarily to the story, on its most personal level, describing an ounce of good squeezed from the horror of war, as Juan goes off with the little Turkish girl he has saved:

> The Moslem orphan went with her protector,
>   For she was homeless, houseless, helpless; all
> Her friends, like the sad family of Hector,
>   Had perish'd in the field or by the wall:

Her very place of birth was but a spectre
　Of what it had been; there the Muezzin's call
To prayer was heard no more! and Juan wept,
And made a vow to shield her, which he kept.

(VIII, cxli)

The quiet proleptic assurance of the last three words is a fine touch, and one of those necessary positives which appear like beacons in the flux throughout the poem, reminiscent perhaps, in their emphasis on immediate, self-committing action, of Byron's encounter with the dying soldier in Ravenna.

Byron: Wrath and Rhyme, ed. A. Bold (Vision Press, 1983).

Carlyle's Style

My subject, Carlyle's style, is not the easiest subject to talk about, because it is rather abstract and needs to be fleshed out. So I shall be reading you a fair number of extracts from Carlyle's various works, extracts which I've chosen because they may help to bring out some of the points I want to make – though I hope that something more general about Carlyle's writing will emerge too.

There are many aspects of Carlyle's style which are of great interest, both to a writer and to a reader. But we do have to reckon with the fact that Carlyle is still not very widely read or enjoyed, despite the amount of scholarly and critical attention his work has been receiving in recent years. All the Victorian sages and prophets have suffered a great reversal of reputation, none more so than the two who at the time were most highly, even fulsomely, praised – Ruskin and Carlyle. It may be that their contemporary fame had something unreal about it and will never return. It is certainly very hard for anyone today to go through the voluminous works of Ruskin and Carlyle and not feel that our ancestors were to some extent taken in by a kind of rhetoric which could not survive because there is something hollow at the heart of it; it may be very splendid at first glance, but when you probe into it you find it doesn't stand up so well, begins to scatter and dissipate in a series of cloudy and confused and even contradictory grandeurs, and these confused grandeurs come from men who have not fully mastered their subjects – men who are still struggling to believe, right through the nineteenth century, that it was not impossible to be a universal sage, to express whole views of society's ills and hopes, past, present, and future, cultural, political, economic, religious, and who are encouraged in this belief by the Victorian public, which is hungry for wisdom, hungry for sages and prophets, unwilling to accept the specialization that was waiting in the wings. The efforts that Ruskin and Carlyle made were heroic, gigantic; the influence they had on their contemporaries was big and real – there's no argument about that. Historically, they are of huge importance. But we, a century later – and we have to remind ourselves that it's more than a century already, that Carlyle's *Sartor Resartus* is as far back from us as Bunyan's *Pilgrim's Progress* was from Carlyle – so we, after a century and a half, are required to ask our own questions about Carlyle, we have to try to estimate how much of him has truly remained, how much can still be salvaged, how much (to put it at its most blunt) can still be read.

This last point is quite a crucial one if we want to think about Carlyle's style. When Carlyle's reputation collapsed, this was due almost equally to his style and to his content. To his contemporaries, although his style was much criticized and sometimes mocked, it nevertheless had all the fascination of something new and strange, and younger readers especially found themselves haunted by its repeated phrases and used them as watchwords and stimuli and as counters in conversation. But later, once the freshness wore off, and the books had been widely discussed and analysed and criticized, the eccentricity of the style began to seem more and more wilful, and the question had to be asked, Did it really help the meaning? Or was its defence simply that it reflected the twists and turns of its author's mind and temperament – *le style c'est l'homme* – and therefore one must take it or leave it? These are questions that have not been by any means fully investigated, and they are interesting and important questions.

One of the difficulties in trying to define Carlyle's style (or styles) is that not only was he a highly individualistic character in himself but also he had wildly mixed (and one could say unhappily mixed) Scottish and English background and experience; in addition, he was a voracious reader in continental literature, especially German. When his books began to appear, and particularly after *Sartor Resartus*, his reviewers and critics did their best to find literary bedfellows for him – they mentioned the Germans of course, and Rabelais, and Laurence Sterne, and Swift, and the Bible and Shakespeare, and that was fine as far as it went. But there are many parallels to be found also in Scottish literature – Sir Thomas Urquhart, and the long satirical and flyting traditions, to say nothing of Scottish preachers or Scottish speech habits. Of course Carlyle lived most of his life out of Scotland, in London, and the Scottish/English dichotomy in him never meant much to his English reviewers and critics, but it is bound to interest us in Scotland. Edwin Muir thought he had both gained and lost by it, but he saw him mainly as a prime, powerful example of the awful *strain* behind the Scottish/English split.

> The style of Carlyle... was taken bodily from the Scots pulpit;
> he was a parish minister of genius, and his English was not
> great English, but great Scots English; the most hybrid of all
> styles, with some of the virtues of the English Bible and many
> of the vices of the Scottish version of the Psalms of David...
> He took the most difficult qualities of the English language
> and the worst of the Scots and through them attained a sort
> of absurd, patchwork greatness. But – this can be said for him
> – his style expressed, in spite of its overstrain, and even
> through it, something real, the struggle of a Scots peasant,
> born to other habits of speech and of thought, with the English
> language.   (*Latitudes*, 1924)

There are a number of things in that view of Edwin Muir's which
one wouldn't necessarily agree with; but words like 'hybrid' and
'patchwork' and 'overstrain' are not without point. The question
is whether they are the whole picture.

The Victorians thought that Carlyle had the ability to produce
an overall, prevailing effect which was very grand and which
was in some sense poetic or epic. He might be vulnerable when
looked at closely, but if you stood back, the genius of the man
suffused the whole work. Emerson said of *Past and Present*: 'Here
is Carlyle's new poem, his *Iliad* of English woes'. John Stuart
Mill said of *The French Revolution*: 'This is not so much a history,
as an epic poem.' One can see what they meant, and Carlyle did
strive after large-scale effects in prose which have a certain parallel
to the large-scale effects of epic poetry. But he was too much of
a lover of language not to relish detail, and he would want you,
if you were going to defend him, to defend him in small as well
as in large contexts. We know how good he was at turning a
phrase even just to fix one of his contemporaries, not always
maliciously but certainly with bite and sharpness. Coleridge was
'round, fat, oily, yet impatient'; Hazlitt was a 'thick-headed and
discourteous boor'; Charles Lamb and his sister were 'a very
sorry pair of phenomena'; Newman had the 'brain of a rabbit';
George Eliot was 'neither amusing nor instructive, but just dull';
Whitman wrote as if the 'town bull had learned to hold a pen';
Disraeli was an 'abominable stump-orator and "impenitent
thief"'; Queen Victoria 'sailed out as if moving on skates'.

One of the most interesting early comments on his style is in fact much concerned with detail. This is the letter his friend John Sterling wrote to him in 1835, about *Sartor Resartus*. He did have some general criticisms: he spoke of the 'headlong self-asserting capriciousness', the 'lawless oddity, and strange heterogeneous combination and allusion', the 'jerking and almost spasmodic violence' – but he also praised the 'depth and fervour of feeling, and a power of serious eloquence'. These are all things one would find it hard to disagree with. Sterling also talked, however, about details, about the 'positively barbarous language', misuse of words, use of new words, use of German-style compound words, etc. Examples of words he disliked as new and barbarous: 'environment', 'talented', 'stertorous', 'visualised', 'complected', all of them acceptable today. This is not to say he could not have found more relevant examples: owleries, riancy, hierogram, Baphometic, galoon, lavation, deliquium, super-hirundine. But are we to blame Carlyle for these rare words? If they occurred in pedantic and highly artificial contexts, we might. But in fact they are almost lost in the stream of the speaking voice – eccentric though it may be – which is Carlyle's greatest contribution to the prose style of the period. Carlyle when he wrote back to Sterling accepted some of the criticisms but made a spirited defence of his neologisms and thought Sterling (like Swift before him and a lot of people after him) was barking up the wrong tree by trying to insist on purity of style.

> But finally, do you reckon this really a time for Purism of Style; or that Style (mere dictionary Style) has much to do with the worth or unworth of a Book? I do not: with whole ragged battalions of Scott's-Novel Scotch, with Irish, German, French, and even Newspaper Cockney... storming in on us, and the whole structure of our Johnsonian English breaking up from its foundations, – revolution there as visible as anywhere else!   (letter of 4 June 1835)

This remarkable outburst shows much perception and takes the argument out into a far wider area than that of self-defensiveness. Carlyle rushes out to pitch his tent among the rumble and hubbub of what a fastidious critic like (say) Matthew Arnold would regard as a place of total disaffection. It is hard not to admire his boldness.

But let's look at some actual examples of Carlyle's style. One of the obvious points to make is that he does not have a monolithic style which he carefully nurtures and preserves; his style in fact varies a great deal according to the occasion. If he's writing a private letter, or anything else which is not meant for immediate publication, he will use a very free, familiar, racy, conversational style, with little formal syntax, but with many of the characteristics of his more developed and deliberate public style, i.e. lots of parentheses, dashes, exclamation-marks, asides, touches of quirky humour, word-play. One of the most quickly-written pieces of prose he ever produced, an account, almost like a diary, of a brief visit to Paris in company with the Brownings in the autumn of 1851, was not meant for publication but was printed posthumously in *Last Words of Thomas Carlyle* in 1892; he gave it the title 'Excursion (Futile Enough) to Paris; Autumn 1851: Thrown on Paper, Pen Galloping, from Saturday to Tuesday, October 4–7, 1851.' Sunday in Paris proved a trial:

> All rather *rusty*; crowds not very great; cleanness, neatness, neither in locality nor population, a conspicuous feature. Champ de Mars all hung round with ugly *blankets* on Pont d'Iéna side; a balloon getting filled; no sight except for payment. Against my will, we dismounted at another entrance and went in. Horse-holder with brass badge vehement against another without: 'Sergent de ville!' – at length *he* got possession of the horses, and proved a very bad 'holder'. Dirty chaos of cabriolets, &c., about this gate: four or five thousand people in at half-a-franc or, to the still *more* inner mysteries, a franc each. Clean shopkeeper people – or better, unexpectedly intelligent – come to see this! A sorry spectacle: dusty, disordered Champ de Mars, and what it now held!

In private letters, he keeps his correspondent very much in mind. The following extract, from a letter written to his wife Jane on 24 July 1836, is characteristic, with its mixture of comic and serious, its parentheses and exclamations and quick-spoken phrases, its spotlighting of whatever is interesting in the mundane, and above all its engaging quality of showing its sense of the addressee throughout – the style is for her, it's meant to please her, it has words like 'Womannie' (the letter begins 'My Dear Womannie'), 'Goody', it has German ('hellen Blick'), it has Scots ('greet'):

> One night also, being determined to *order* myself a pair of shoes

(*trash* beyond utterance; ugly and *dear*, are my late pairs), I called on Allan Cunningham to ask: Not in. Then forward to Willis to ask: Not in. Wherefore, home; – and the shoes are still unordered. Jack has offered me an old pair; which I think I shall accept. By the bye, James Aitken has a pair of lasts lying ready, and a *cast* of my foot ('roots of trieys' [trees] and all), and considering it deeply, and consulting with James who is a judicious man, see if you cannot order me a pair of shoes to be made off them? See if you cannot, Goody with that *hellen Blick* of yours! Poor James has sent me two pounds of Mundell's Tobacco by Jack; a sort of thing which, I know not why, almost made me *greet*: it was in huge coarse paper; the poor Brother had earned it by the toil of his right-hand: I remembered him a tow-headed judicious herd-boy; and so many chancings and changings had gone on since then. Thank him *heartily* from me (but not in the sad mood). – I believe you had also better choose me a pair of winter trousers; you: and set Shankland on them, if he have the measure: wide enough, long enough: not too heavy, and of a dim colour! I shall then have nothing to do with Cockney snips for another blessed Winter, – perhaps never more in Time?

A third example is a little similar to those two passages, in that it was again not intended for publication but was written more deliberately – from his *Reminiscences*, published just after he dies in 1881. In these autobiographical sketches the style is very vivid and sharp, often the style of a good observer, a good journalist (which in a sense is what Carlyle was). It has much of the immediacy of talk, the talk of a man remembering his early years, but it's not so free or so loose as the last two examples, because I think Carlyle knew it *was* likely to be published even though he said it was too personal and would have to be edited. It contains some portraits of well-known people whom Carlyle had been acquainted with (friendly with is too strong!). One of the best of these is his account of Francis Jeffrey, lawyer and editor of *The Edinburgh Review*, a generation older than Carlyle, whom he got to know in the 1820s. It shows particularly the pithy journalistic command of observation, it's verbally interesting, has well-chosen adjectives, is often satirical, has good illustrations in detail of general points being made; the style never runs away with the subject:

I heard gradually that he was not reckoned 'successful' in Public Life; that as Lord Advocate, the Scotch with their multifarious businesses found him irritable, impatient (which I don't wonder at); that his 'great Speech' with 'the cheers of that House', etc. etc., had been a Parliamentary failure rather, unadapted to the place, – and, what was itself very mortifying, that the Reporters had complained of his 'Scotch accent' to excuse themselves for various omissions they had made! His accent was indeed singular, but it was by no means Scotch: at his first going to Oxford (where he did not stay long), he had peremptorily crushed down his Scotch (which he privately had in store, in excellent condition, to the very end of his life, producible with highly ludicrous effect on occasion), and adopted instead of a strange swift, sharp-sounding, fitful modulation, part of it pungent, quasi-latrant, other parts of it cooing, bantery, lovingly quizzical; which no charm of his fine ringing voice (*metallic* tenor, of sweet tone), and of his vivacious rapid looks and pretty little attitudes and gestures, could altogether reconcile you to; but in which he persisted through good report and bad.

For a less straightforward, less journalistic, more rich and developed style, here is an example from his long essay 'Count Cagliostro' (1833). The eighteenth-century Italian quack and so-called alchemist made a fortune out of gullible high society, but was eventually unmasked and given life imprisonment. Carlyle takes him as a fascinating super-scoundrel, his life a kind of poem, delivering something other than the expected lessons. Here is how the essay on this remarkable character ('as large as life, and as esurient') ends:

But in fine, look at this matter of Cagliostro, as at all matters, with thy heart, with thy whole mind; no longer merely squint at it with the poor side-glance of thy calculative faculty. Look at it not *logically* only, but *mystically*. Thou shalt in sober truth see it (as Sauerteig asserted) to be a Pasquillant verse, of most inspired writing in its kind, in that same 'Grand Bible of Universal History'; wondrously and even indispensably connected with the Heroic portions that stand there; even as the all-showing Light is with the Darkness wherein nothing can be seen; as the hideous taloned *roots* are with the fair *boughs*, and their leaves and flowers and fruit; both of which, and not one of which, make the Tree. Think also whether thou hast known no Public Quacks, on far higher scale than this, whom a Castle of St Angelo never could get hold of; and how, as Emperors, Chancellors (having found much fitter machinery), they could run their Quack-career; and make whole kingdoms, whole continents, into one huge Egyptian Lodge, and squeeze supplies of money or of blood from it at discretion? Also, whether thou even now knowest not Private Quacks, innumerable as the sea-sands, toiling as mere *Half*-Cagliostros; imperfect, hybrid-quacks, of whom Cagliostro is as the unattainable ideal and type-specimen? Such is the world. Understand it, despise it, love it; cheerfully hold on thy way through it, with thy eye on higher load-stars!

The grand periods build up to a carefully designed cumulative effect, but do not lose the reader in abstraction or remoteness; indeed there is no let-up on the reader's involvement, with the direct imperatives of 'look' and 'think' and 'understand' and 'hold on thy way'.

The two most interesting books from the point of view of style are *Past and Present* (1843) and *Sartor Resartus* (1836, Boston). The first of these has more clarity because it addresses itself to a more specific social and political problem; the other book, being more philosophical, shows Carlyle's style at its most fully developed, most idiosyncratic, often at its most obscure. *Past and Present*, dealing with 'the condition of England', opens its theme of the paradox of a wealthy country's strange malaise by presenting the reader with one easily-grasped central metaphor – some evil enchantment has frozen the goods and products the nation has to hand, made them untouchable, unusable, and the problem, as in an old fairy-tale, will be to find some means of undoing the spell:

England is full of wealth, of multifarious produce, supply for human want in every kind; yet England is dying of inanition. With unabated bounty the land of England blooms and grows; waving with yellow harvests; thick-studded with workshops, industrial implements, with fifteen millions of workers, understood to be the strongest, the cunningest and the willingest our Earth ever had; these men are here; the work they have done, the fruit they have realised is here, abundant, exuberant on every hand of us: and behold, some baleful fiat as of

Enchantment has gone forth, saying, 'Touch it not, ye work-ers, ye master-workers, ye master-idlers; none of you can touch it, no man of you shall be the better for it; this is enchanted fruit!' On the poor workers such fiat falls first, in its rudest shape; but on the rich master-workers too it falls; neither can the rich master-idlers, nor any richest or highest man escape, but all are like to be brought low with it, and made 'poor' enough, in the money sense or a far fataler one.

In the medieval interlude of Book 2, a twelfth-century way of life is contrasted with the present, to the disadvantage of the nineteenth century, because of the absence of the later dreaded cash-nexus. A passage from this part shows a style which is still clear, with hard clear-cut concrete detail, well-chosen little pic-tures giving a vivid immediate effect, yet not only pictures, since there's a verbal interest too, little touches of etymology, a sense of history, yet nothing pedantic, a strong thrust of urgent feeling through the passage:

> The Ribble and the Aire roll down, as yet unpolluted by dyers' chemistry; tenanted by merry trouts and piscatory otters; the sunbeam and the vacant wind's-blast alone traversing those moors. Side by side sleep the coal-strata and the iron-strata for so many ages; no Steam-Demon has yet risen smoking into being. Saint Mungo rules in Glasgow; James Watt still slumbering in the deep of Time. *Mancunium*, Menceaster, what we now call Manchester, spins no cotton, – if it be not *wool* 'cottons', clipped from the backs of mountain sheep. The Creek of the Mersey gurgles, twice in the four-and-twenty hours, with eddying brine, clangorous with sea-fowl; and is a *Lither*-Pool, a *lazy* or sullen Pool, no monstrous pitchy City, and Seahaven of the world! The Centuries are big; and the birth-hour is coming, not yet come. *Tempus ferax, tempus edax rerum.*

But when we come to Book 3, 'The Modern Worker', where Carlyle makes his attack on the 'Mammonism' of the nineteenth century, there is a deployment of almost grotesque fantastic images, even though they are based on things actually seen in London, the method of the grotesque being used to startle people into awareness, a comic approach for initially funny but then very much not funny purposes:

The Hatter in the Strand of London, instead of making better felt-hats than another, mounts a huge lath-and-plaster Hat, seven feet high, upon wheels; sends a man to drive it through the streets; hoping to be saved *thereby*! He has not attempted to *make* better hats, as he was appointed by the Universe to do, and as with this ingenuity of his he could very probably have done; but his whole industry is turned to *persuade* us that he has made such! He too knows that the Quack has become God. Laugh not at him, O reader; or do not laugh only. He has ceased to be comic; he is fast becoming tragic. To me this all-deafening blast of Puffery, of poor Falsehood grown necessitous, of poor Heart-Atheism fallen now into Enchanted Workhouses, sounds too surely like a Doom's-blast! I have to say to myself in old dialect: 'God's blessing is not written on all this: His curse is written on all this!' Unless perhaps the Universe *be* a chimera; – some old totally deranged eightday clock, dead as brass; which the Maker, if there ever was any Maker, has long ceased to meddle with?

Sartor Resartus is Carlyle's most extraordinary book, partly a disguised autobiography of early years, crisis, and coming through; partly it's a so-called 'Philosophy of Clothes' in which the whole universe is surveyed from the one central metaphor of clothes and what lies beneath them; partly it's a book about writing, its subject might be said to be language itself, and the nature of fictions and fictionality. The author hides, first behind a supposed editor, and then behind an imaginary German professor, and the book offers a running dialogue between the editor and the professor; the professor is quoted but his quotations are undermined by ironic comment; and the stylistic interest of this, the interest of *doing* this, the element of intellectual play and virtuosity it involves, all this is part of the driving motive force of the book, i.e. it's a book for writers as much as for readers. But not entirely; like *Past and Present*, it is concerned with a crisis in modern society, especially in the nightmarish vision at the end, of the future of the grotesque figures of the Dandies versus the Drudges (like the Eloi and the Morlocks in H.G. Wells's *The Time Machine*). An apocalyptic clash of social revolution is foreseen through metaphor and simile, and in one of the images the haves and the have-nots, the 'money' and the 'hunger', interlock in a cataclysmic flood which has been caused by two adjacent whirlpools finally overwhelming the land between them, the picture being vividly brought home for Scottish readers (whom Carlyle never quite forgets) by reference to the Bullers of Buchan (where the North Sea shoots up through natural blowholes in the cliff):

> I could liken Dandyism and Drudgism to two bottomless boiling Whirlpools that had broken-out on opposite corners of the firm land: as yet they appear only disquieted, foolishly bubbling wells, which man's art might cover-in; yet mark them, their diameter is daily widening: they are hollow Cones that boil-up from the infinite Deep, over which your firm land is but a thin crust or rind! Thus daily is the intermediate land crumbling-in, daily the empire of the two Buchan-Bullers extending; till now there is but a foot-plank, a mere film of Land between them; this too is washed away: – and then – we have the true Hell of Waters, and Noah's Deluge is out-deluged!

This is only a sample of the vision which Carlyle, through his professor character, gives us towards the end of the book. In writing which is stylistically so fascinating, does it almost become style for style's sake, is the meaning, the real social warning, overlaid by the richness of the language? (And we have to remember that he was writing only a decade before the year of revolutions all over Europe, 1848.) Is he making an impossible double demand of his readers? It may be that his readers sort themselves out into two groups. Engels admired Carlyle; so did James Joyce. To Engels, it was necessary to penetrate through the surface of Carlyle to find the serious and important social analysis. To Joyce, Carlyle was one of the great liberators of language and style, which is why he uses Carlyle so much in *Ulysses*, both in the Yes, the Everlasting Yea, of the conclusion, and in the remarkable parody of Carlyle which he brings in at the crucial moment of the birth of Mrs Purefoy's baby in the maternity hospital, again taking Carlyle as a celebrator, an anti-Malthusian, a yea-sayer to life. What may not be so easy is to bring the Engels and the Joyce together, a task for which we may judiciously blame Carlyle at least in part, and not merely human frailty.

Centenary Lecture to the Carlyle Society, Edinburgh, March 1981.

The Poetry of Robert Louis Stevenson

Stevenson is generally regarded as a very minor poet who nevertheless produced a handful of poems which have been well known and well liked for quite a long time. Even this nucleus of famous poems would scarcely meet the most rigorous demands of the modern critic for a poetry that is really earning its keep from word to word, and Janet Adam Smith in her edition of the collected poems had to admit that: 'If we are looking for poetry that has mature passion and mystery, that explores sensibility, that drills down into the subconscious, we shall not come to Stevenson.' But she also said, in that edition, that she hoped her book would 'stimulate some real criticism, and encourage readers to take Stevenson's poetry seriously', and she seems to have felt that a due appreciation of Stevenson had in fact been blocked by the popularity of a few poems. That was twenty years ago, in 1950, and the situation has changed a little since then, but it could change a good deal more, in bringing a new range of Stevenson's poems to people's notice. When Douglas Young brought out his collection *Scottish Verse 1851-1951* in 1952, he was evidently hoping to follow up Janet Adam Smith's remarks, and included a fair number of poems which were less familiar; but they were not particularly well chosen to make the right kind of impact, and later anthologists have tended to revert to the tried favourites – 'In the Highlands', 'To S.R. Crockett', 'Requiem', 'The Spaewife', 'A Mile an' a Bittock', 'Ille Terrarum' – and of course there is no reason why they should not return to these poems if they are the best. But one anthologist who has been more adventurous, and who has given a genuinely fresh look at Stevenson which has to be taken into account, is George MacBeth in his *Penguin Book of Victorian Verse* (1969). In this collection he prints five poems, all of them worth reading, none of which are in any of the Scottish anthologies, and he also makes fairly large claims for Stevenson in his introductory note, saying that in some ways his verse is deeper, more personal, more piercing than his prose, and that he has quite a central importance in Scottish literature for his 'love of clandestine violence'. Mr Mac-Beth himself is not unknown for a love of clandestine violence, and you may want to discount something for that reason, but he is also Scottish and is pointing to a demonstrably Scottish preoccupation. These are subjects I shall return to; at the moment I want merely to indicate that there are aspects of Stevenson's poetry which have still to be illuminated and which are worth illuminating. It is extremely unlikely that any revaluation would make him more than a minor poet, but he can and should be shown to be a much more varied and interesting minor poet than his reputation suggests. Like his near-contemporaries James Thomson and John Davidson, he badly needs some proper critical attention, especially in Scotland.

Stevenson does not seem to have thought very highly of his own abilities as a poet – though one always has to be careful in evaluating comments of this kind. In one of his poems – 'To Dr Hake' – he talks about himself as trying to write poetry in the image of a sparrow feebly chirping in the wood before the better singers have roused themselves:

> Thus on my pipe I breathed a strain or two;
> It scarce was music, but 'twas all I knew.
> It was not music, for I lacked the art,
> Yet what but frozen music filled my heart?

This suggests that he thought he had the matter of poetry in him, but simply lacked the skill he knew was required to bring it out. In some other comments he shows a sort of exasperated puzzlement over the reaction of people to his poems, but seems largely to accept their verdict, as if he had little confidence in his own way of writing. The volume called *Ballads*, published in 1890, was badly received, and Stevenson gave a joky, uneasy half-defence of these poems in a letter to H.B. Baildon in 1891: 'They failed to entertain a coy public, at which I wondered; not that I set much account by my verses, which are the verses of Prosator; but I do know how to tell a yarn, and two of the yarns are great.' And in another letter to his friend Edmund Gosse about the same time he says: 'By the by, my Ballads seem to have been damn bad; all the crickets sing so in their crickety papers; and I have no ghost of an idea on the point myself: verse is always to me the unknowable.' Here he seems just to throw up his hands; both the public and the critics – or crickets – have rejected him, and yet he had thought that because he knew how to tell a great yarn he could hold them all enthralled in their seats. But the tone is humorous; there is no analysis of the shortcomings; he has other fish to fry. (These Ballads are not in fact good poems, with the exception of one short one called 'Christmas at Sea', and usually it's fairly clear why: he writes in a long rough lolloping rhyming couplet which quickly becomes tedious in a lengthy narrative poem.) In this instance, it is obvious that his wonderful command of narrative movement in prose fiction misled him into thinking that poetry presented no special problem if you wanted to tell a story in verse; but of course it does, as even a minor cricket could have told him. All this might suggest that Stevenson had never done much thinking about his art, but this is not true. He had quite a lot to say about the technical aspects of poetry, especially its sound-effects, which he discusses in his essay 'On Some Technical Elements of Style in Literature'; he experimented in a considerable range of verse forms from imitations of classical metres to the most up-to-date exercises in the free verse of Walt Whitman and Matthew Arnold; he gave some thought to his own native problem of language, whether, when, and how to use Scots instead of English; he wrote essays on a fair number of poets, both English-language and foreign, and was far from ignorant of the main movements of poetry in his time, even if these movements were not to him a matter of passionate concern. I would like to comment, in illustrative fashion, on two of these interests: the use of free verse, and the use of Scots.

To take Scots first of all. Stevenson, like Thomson and Davidson, may have been exiled from his native place, but he never regarded himself as anything but a Scotsman and a Scottish poet. Writing to J.M. Barrie from the South Seas, he gave this pen-portrait of himself:

Exceedingly lean, rather ruddy, black eyes, crows-footed, beginning to be grizzled, general appearance of a blasted boy – or blighted youth... Past eccentric – obscure and oh we never mention it – present industrious, respectable and fatuously contented... Cigarettes without intermission, except when coughing or kissing. Hopelessly entangled in apron-strings. Drinks plenty. Curses some. Temper unstable... Has been an invalid for ten years, but can boldly claim you can't tell it on him. Given to explaining the Universe – Scotch, sir, Scotch.

One feels about that devastating portrait that it isn't only the last sentence which is Scotch, there is something Scotch in the whole approach, mocking and reductive, relentlessly truthful, down to the apron-strings which most authors would be ashamed to admit. In the subjects of his poems, then, it is hardly surprising that Scotland and Edinburgh should recur again and again, or that both should draw from him very strong reserves of feeling. The two great opposing, unresolved, often interlocking themes of his poetry are the desire for travel and the desire for home, and although in the end home in the physical sense became Vailima, mentally it was Scotland more deeply than ever because of time and distance, and the most popular poems of all are the ones that voice this feeling, such as 'To S.R. Crockett':

> Blows the wind today, and the sun and the rain are flying,
>   Blows the wind on the moors today and now,
> Where about the graves of the martyrs the whaups are crying,
>   My heart remembers how!
>
> Grey recumbent tombs of the dead in desert places,
>   Standing-stones on the vacant wine-red moor,
> Hills of sheep, and the howes of the silent vanished races,
>   And winds, austere and pure:
>
> Be it granted me to behold you again in dying,
>   Hills of home! and to hear again the call;
> Hear about the graves of the martyrs the peewees crying,
>   And hear no more at all.

The longing that is expressed there is of course not only a longing for a place but for a place with its history, even for a place as history. It wouldn't be a poem without the wind and the moors and the sheep and the whaups crying, but a steady look at it convinces you that its centre is not these things, its centre is blood, as its subject is death, the poet's own tiny nineteenth-century death merging into the blood of the martyrs of Scotland's hideous religious history and even that merging in turn into the far more distant prehistoric blood of the sacrifices at the standing-stones. It's Lewis Grassic Gibbon in twelve lines. And having said that, one is surely reminded of George MacBeth's point about the love of clandestine violence?

But 'To S.R. Crockett', although it is about Scotland, is not written in Scots, except for one Scots word in each of its three stanzas: whaups, howes, peewees. In a fair number of poems, though it is not a large percentage of his total output, Stevenson did use Scots, most of the Scots pieces being collected in one section of the volume *Underwoods* in 1887 with an important and interesting explanatory note. The main argument of this note is a defence of an eclectic use of Scots. He knows this eclecticism has to be argued because he is writing in one of the heydays of dialectology, when the examination and description of local dialects was having an influence which can be seen in several poets from Barnes and Hopkins to Doughty and Hardy. Dialect is not what Stevenson wants; he wants language; and if that language does not truly exist he must do what he can to give it a workable body. Here is what he says:

> I note again, that among our new dialecticians, the local habitat of every dialect is given to the square mile. I could not emulate this nicety if I desired; for I simply wrote my Scots as well as I was able, not caring if it hailed from Lauderdale or Angus, from the Mearns or Galloway; if I had ever heard a good word, I used it without shame; and when Scots was lacking, or the rhyme jibbed, I was glad (like my betters) to fall back on English. For all that, I own to a friendly feeling for the tongue of Fergusson and of Sir Walter, both Edinburgh men; and I confess that Burns has always sounded in my ear like something partly foreign... Let the precisians call my speech that of the Lothians. And if it be not pure, alas! what matters it? The day draws near when this illustrious and malleable tongue shall be quite forgotten: and Burns's Ayrshire, and Dr Macdonald's Aberdeen-awa', and Scott's brave, metropolitan utterance will be all equally the ghosts of speech. Till then I would love to have my hour as a native Maker, and be read by my own countryfolk in our own dying language: an ambition surely rather of the heart than of the head, so restricted as it is in prospect of endurance, so parochial in bounds of space.

What is rather striking about that passage is the way it seems to foreshadow the whole twentieth-century argument in Scotland about language and poetry. It looks forward to Hugh MacDiarmid in its determination to be eclectic, and yet it looks forward to Edwin Muir in the underlying pessimism with which it links the continued decline of Scots to that fatal separation of heart and head which was there in Allan Ramsay's day, to say nothing of Stevenson's. Stevenson could not foresee the revolution in poetry which was to take place after 1900 and which would be able, because of a new attitude to language, to induce or educe new attitudes to Scots; nor could he foresee how a new kind of political nationalism would help to conspire towards the same result. In his time, he could only see his place at the end of a long line, and although it is true that by going back behind the nineteenth-century versifiers to Fergusson and Burns he was able to refresh the tradition and at his best to write better Scots poetry than most of his contemporaries, there was no real renewal of the existing traditions in such a way as to broaden the intellectual basis of Scots and to make it meet the demands of full expression. He wanted a language, but all he had was a relatively thin medium which he used with some skill and humour to produce late nineteenth-century variations on earlier Scotch themes. It is interesting to see him starting both with confidence and with a sense of inevitable limitations. In his poem 'The Maker to Posterity' he imagines some auld professor in the future coming across his Scots poems and scratching his head over them:

> 'What tongue does your auld bookie speak?'
> He'll speir; an' I, his mou to steik:
> 'No bein' fit to write in Greek,
> > I wrote in Lallan,
> Dear to my heart as the peat reek,
> > Auld as Tantallon.

> Few spak it then, an' noo there's nane.
> My puir auld sangs lie a' their lane,
> Their sense, that aince was braw an' plain,
> > Tint a'thegether,
> Like runes upon a standin' stane
> > Amang the heather.

'Dear to my heart as the peat reek.' This suggests that the kailyaird is not going to be very far away, and in fact superior kailyaird is what we find in a poem like 'Ille Terrarum' – literally kailyaird in being written in praise of the house and garden of Swanston cottage, but literarily kailyaird in its telltale vocabulary: the *auld housie weel happit* in its garden trees, its chimneys smoking *couthy and bien*, and when the poet thinks about its homely delights from the distractions of the city he says *I mind me on yon bonny bield*. All these images of the snug cosy homely place-to-return-to or place-to-dream-of are really felt by Stevenson, and so the poem remains not a bad one, but its vulnerable points are very near the surface, like the threadbare arms of a chair that has been a bonny bield just too often. A much better poem is 'The Spaewife', where, despite the use of an ancient ballad dialogue form, something original and memorable has been produced, with its mysterious Yeatsian beggar figure giving her classically comfortless refrain-line at the end of each stanza:

> O, I wad like to ken – to the beggar-wife says I –
> Why chops are guid to brander and nane sae guid to fry.
> An' siller, that's sae braw to keep, is brawer still to gi'e.
> – *It's gey an' easy speirin'*, says the beggar-wife to me.

Equally successful, and again because it has managed to control its romantic material in a classical way, is 'A Mile an' a Bittock', a completely convincing hymn to youth and friendship, soaked in the kind of nostalgia for the lost country of the young that goes so deep in Stevenson and then miraculously dried out again through realism and humour.

Many of the Scots poems, unfortunately, deal in a fairly conventional way with religious satire, owing a lot to 'Holy Willie's Prayer' and ringing the changes on being anti-Calvinist, anti-clerical, and anti-hypocritical. As might be expected by Stevenson's date, the effects he obtains are often quite entertaining but hardly very subtle or new. Stevenson has a favourite character, one of his 'masks', an ex-elder of the kirk called Mr Thomson, and in the poem called 'The Scotsman's Return from Abroad', Mr Thomson comes back from 'uncovenantit' foreign parts to see if his old church is still the same: he has his doubts about some of the innovations, but these are all dispelled once the minister launches into his sermon:

> O what a gale was on my speerit
> To hear the p'ints o' doctrine clearit,
> And a' the horrors o' damnation
> Set furth wi' faithfu' ministration!
> Nae shauchlin' testimony here –
> We were a' damned, an' that was clear.

> I owned, wi' gratitude an' wonder,
> He was a pleisure to sit under.

Stevenson's Scots poetry is always competent, and obviously written with a good deal of enjoyment. Its limitations are not hard to define and within these limitations it can give a lot of pleasure.

To turn now to Stevenson's use of free verse, where he was moving out into much less charted territory, though it was also being explored at the same time by his friend W. E. Henley. Even today this side of his work is not represented in the anthologies (including George MacBeth's), and I dare say some people are surprised when they discover that he did write free verse, and good free verse at that, long before the days of imagism and the modern movement. By free verse I mean poetry which has neither metre nor rhyme but which uses irregular effects of musical cadence and rhythm. It is essentially a twentieth-century phenomenon, but its forerunners are in the nineteenth century, and Stevenson was influenced by two of them, Matthew Arnold and (more importantly) Walt Whitman. Despite his uneasy and at times rather patronizing essay on Whitman in *Familiar Studies of Men and Books* (1882), Stevenson clearly fell under Whitman's spell, at least for a time, and in another essay, 'Books Which Have Influenced Me', he gives us some indication of what Whitman meant to him by including *Leaves of Grass*, between the New Testament and Herbert Spencer, as one of the seminal works in his reading experience. 'A book', he says, 'of singular service, a book which tumbled the world upside down for me, blew into space a thousand cobwebs of genteel and ethical illusion, and, having thus shaken my tabernacle of lies, set me back again upon a strong foundation of all the original and manly virtues.' So *Leaves of Grass* blew his mind, and at the same time blew his metric. In Stevenson's poetry, Whitman tends to show in his long lines, Arnold in the short. The two influences can be seen together in an attractive poem called 'Song at Dawn':

> I see the dawn creep round the world,
> Here damm'd a moment backward by great hills,
> There racing o'er the sea.
> Down at the round equator,
> It leaps forth straight and rapid,
> Driving with firm sharp edge the night before it.

Here gradually it floods
The wooded valleys and the weeds
And the still smokeless cities.
The cocks crow up at the farms;
The sick man's spirit is glad;
The watch treads brisker about the dew-wet deck;
The light-keeper locks his desk,
As the lenses turn,
Faded and yellow.

The girl with the embroidered shift
Rises and leans on the sill,
And her full bosom heaves
Drinking deep of the silentness.
I too rise and watch
The healing fingers of dawn –
I too drink from its eyes
The unaccountable peace –
I too drink and am satisfied as with food.
Fain would I go
Down by the winding crossroad by the trees,
Where at the corner of wet wood
The blackbird in the early grey and stillness
Wakes his first song.
Peace, who can make verses clink,
Find ictus following surely after ictus,
At such an hour as this, the heart
Lies steeped and silent.
O dreaming, leaning girl,
Already are the sovereign hill-tops ruddy,
Already the grey passes, the white streak
Brightens above dark woodlands, Day begins.

There is real quality in that poem, and the freedom of the verse
seems to have helped Stevenson to bring romance and reality
together, to have as a framework traditional images of sunrise
but to insert into the landscape a few details which can be very
moving: the figure of the lighthouse-keeper locking his desk
when his huge lenses grow faded and yellow as the natural light
grows (this lighthouse-keeper comes into other free-verse
poems, and Stevenson is obviously thinking of his father and of
his difficult relationship with him), and then the figure of the

dreaming, leaning girl, unexplained, half-symbolic yet very real, held like the poet by this moment of beauty and calm before time starts up again and moves them away from the scene, and also from youth.

I wanted, in quoting that poem, with its quiet, winding, subtle movement, to emphasize the enormous difference of effect between it and the banging satire of the passage previously quoted from 'The Scotsman's Return from Abroad', with its cheery thoughts on universal damnation. Both poems work, but the distance between them is one measure of what even a minor poet can do.

If we want to ask whether there is anything central, anything between or among the various extremes in his work, anything at least that can be defined, this is not easy to answer, since so much of his effectiveness as a poet comes precisely from the thrill or pathos of oppositions – adventure versus the bonny bield, casting off versus landfall, present experience versus memory, sailor and hunter versus housebuilder and paterfamilias, the delicate and productive tensions of a prolonged immaturity of which he was well aware. Only in a few images, like that of the lighthouse-keeper, do the opposites seem to be temporarily resoved: the man in the lighthouse is both at sea and on land, he is both in great danger and unusually snug, he leads a solitary life but would not be employed if he was by nature unbalanced or morbid, and so he moves between loneliness and family, between the wild elements and the humdrum streets. Stevenson's father's occupation as a lighthouse-designer fascinated Stevenson, quite apart from the already close and tense relation that existed between them. George MacBeth is right in seeing this father-son relationship as being very important in Stevenson, and some good poems are concerned with it in one way or another. The boy's feelings towards his father were a mixture of guilt, envy, admiration, and love, but whatever the feelings were they were strong. When his father eventually became senile, a sick man, unable to recognize the members of his family, Stevenson wrote this short poem about him. It is called 'The Last Sight':

> Once more I saw him. In the lofty room,
> Where oft with lights and company his tongue
> Was trump to honest laughter, sate attired
> A something in his likeness. 'Look!' said one,
> Unkindly kind, 'look up, it is your boy!'
> And the dread changeling gazed on me in vain.

The remarkable power of that last line comes from the fact that the natural order of things *both* seems to be taking its course *and* seems to be turned upside down; the father has become helpless, like a child, in his senility, but unlike a child he has become an object of terror rather than pity to his son looking at him; he is a 'dread changeling' in whom something horrible has been planted from outside. And there is the further irony that Stevenson himself might well have been called the changeling, in so far as he seemed doomed in his early years to disconcert his parents. The poem is curiously reminiscent of Hugh MacDiarmid's short poem about *his* dying father, 'The Watergaw', with its 'last wild look ye gied / Afore ye dee'd!', and suggests a similar bond of family experience from which both poets drew some power.

Parents and children áre therefore not an unexpected theme to find in Stevenson, and the poems in *A Child's Garden of Verses* (1885) fit very well into his preoccupations. They have been described as about rather than for children, though some children do like them. Reading them today, one can see them as looking straight forward to Ian Hamilton Finlay, who has many affinities with Stevenson's period and whose pre-concrete poems particularly have many of the same qualities as *A Child's Garden of Verses*. I am thinking especially of Stevenson's 'My Bed is a Boat', 'The Lamplighter', 'The Cow', 'Singing', and 'Rain', all of which have not only the sort of subjects Mr Finlay likes but also the same not-quite-innocent eye asking us humorously and gently to look at simple things.

> The rain is raining all around,
>   It falls on field and tree,
> It rains on the umbrellas here,
>   And on the ships at sea.

Opinions have varied about this part of Stevenson's work, especially as he also wrote a mass of self-confessedly light verse for which no poetic claims were to be made. The *Child's Garden* poems seem to me to have great charm, and not to be light verse in a pejorative sense. The note of his light verse, perky and devil-may-care, is quite different, as in this example from his 'Rhymes to Henley' (VIII):

> We dwell in these melodious days
> When every author trolls his lays;

And all, except myself and you,
Must up and print the nonsense, too.
Why then, if this be so indeed,
If adamantine walls recede
And old Apollo's gardens gape
For Arry and the grinder's ape;
I too may enter in perchance
Where paralytic graces dance,
And cheering on each tottering set
Blow my falsetto flageolet.

Well, Stevenson did blow his falsetto flageolet quite a lot, and it is no great thing, though even here 'paralytic graces' is good. But the poems in *A Child's Garden* are different, and of better calibre. Are they all, however, boats and rain and cows and lamplighters? Is everything in this garden lovely? There are a surprising number of soldiers and guns and battles around. 'Now, with my little gun, I crawl / All in the dark along the wall'... What is Stevenson doing with his little gun? In another poem, called 'The Dumb Soldier', he tells a very fey tale of how he buried one of his lead soldiers underground in the lawn, and means some day to dig him up again to ask him what it was like lying alone in the dark of the earth. And when, in another poem, he looks for pictures in the fire, what does Stevenson's child see? Armies and burning cities.

Armies march by tower and spire
Of cities blazing, in the fire;
Till as I gaze with staring eyes,
The armies fade, the lustre dies.

Then once again the glow returns;
Again the phantom city burns;
And down the red–hot valley, lo!
The phantom armies marching go!

Blinking embers, tell me true
Where are those armies marching to,
And what the burning city is
That crumbles in your furnaces!

Every boy, perhaps, plays with soldiers and sees armies in the

fire. But there does seem something particular, something underlined, in these poems of Stevenson's – notably the one where he
buries the unresisting soldier in the lawn. It was not for nothing
that A.E. Housman found himself so strongly attracted to
Stevenson, and looking at it from a wider angle one can think
back to George MacBeth's remark about the 'love of clandestine
violence'. The fact is that there is an aspect of Stevenson to which
violence appeals, and in this he is linked to a number of his
contemporaries, including Housman, Henley, Kipling, and
Davidson. A full picture of Stevenson must therefore take this
into account. Under the velvet jacket, the arm is covered with
thick black hair. In his essay on Edgar Allan Poe, Stevenson says
of his story 'Berenice': 'Horrible as it is, [it] touches a chord in
one's own breast, though perhaps it is a chord that had better be
left alone.' In his prose, as we know, he could not leave it alone,
and so we have *Dr. Jekyll and Mr. Hyde, Markheim, Thrawn Janet*,
and many other intimations of a dark sub-world which was
extremely real to him and of which he gives a powerful account.
But in the poetry too, the violent world now and again looks
out at us and makes us wonder about the sources of Stevenson's
art. In one of the poems included by George MacBeth in his
Penguin Book of Victorian Verse, a poem called 'To S.C.' (that is,
Sidney Colvin) Stevenson writes his friend a verse letter, a verse
meditation, from the South Seas, looking back from a night scene
of throbbing sea and flailing palm-trees to the calm London streets
near the British Museum. But the familiar exile's poem is given
a strange twist: what he asks Colvin to do, the next time he goes
to the British Museum, is to stop and gaze at the huge Easter
Island statues at the entrance – they too are exiles, though exiles
of a different kind:

> One moment glance, where by the pillared wall
> Far-voyaging island gods, begrimed with smoke,
> Sit now unworshipped, the rude monument
> Of faiths forgot and races undivined:
> Sit now disconsolate, remembering well
> The priest, the victim, and the songful crowd,
> The blaze of the blue noon, and that huge voice,
> Incessant, of the breakers on the shore.
> As far as these from their ancestral shrine,
> So far, so foreign, your divided friends
> Wander, estranged in body, not in mind.

It is a firmly controlled and striking passage where Stevenson, in the South Seas, identifies himself with the displaced Easter Island gods, and what he associates these blank mysterious gods with is human sacrifice, 'the priest, the victim, and the songful crowd'. Like the graves of the martyrs on the Scottish moors, and the Standing Stones behind that, the Easter Island monoliths move and disturb him in a way that he does not want to analyse.

But although he does not analyse it, he lets the evidence appear again and again. In one of the longer poems in his posthumous volume *Songs of Travel* (1896) he lets us into a larger area of this experience. This poem, 'The Woodman', takes as its subject the clearing of jungle overgrowth in Vailima when he was building his house there. It was very hard and difficult work, and he felt increasingly, as he hacked away at the lianas, that nature was not indifferent but hostile to man, and had a frightening life of its own which could never be understood but could only be combated, to the death if necessary. He ends up in a position that might be described as exactly the opposite of Wordsworth's, bearing out rather neatly the argument that 'Wordsworth in the tropics' would be a very different man. Of course Stevenson is writing after Darwin, and Darwin is in the poem too. But mainly it is the reflection of personal experience, and the reader gets the impression that Stevenson, by the time he reaches the last section of the poem, has almost frightened himself with the discovery of his own ruthlessness and ruthless enjoyment of the struggle. The battle here is only against vegetable nature, yet he senses, unmistakably, that his feelings reverberate outward into the whole human struggle, into human society both at peace and in war. Here is how the poem ends:

> The common lot we scarce perceive.
> Crowds perish, we nor mark nor grieve:
> The bugle calls – we mourn a few!
> What corporal's guard at Waterloo?
> What scanty hundreds more or less
> In the man-devouring Wilderness?
> What handful bled on Delhi ridge?
> – See, rather, London, on thy bridge
> The pale battalions trample by,
> Resolved to slay, resigned to die.
> Count, rather, all the maimed and dead
> In the unbrotherly war of bread...

Why prate of peace? when, warriors all,
We clank in harness into hall,
And ever bare upon the board
Lies the necessary sword.
In the green field or quiet street,
Besieged we sleep, beleaguered eat;
Labour by day and wake o' nights,
In war with rival appetites.
The rose on roses feeds; the lark
On larks. The sedentary clerk
All morning with a diligent pen
Murders the babes of other men;
And like the beasts of wood and park,
Protects his whelps, defends his den.

Unshamed the narrow aim I hold;
I feed my sheep, patrol my fold;
Breathe war on wolves and rival flocks,
A pious outlaw on the rocks
Of God and morning; and when time
Shall bow, or rivals break me, climb
Where no undubbed civilian dares,
In my war harness, the loud stairs
Of honour; and my conqueror
Hail me a warrior fallen in war.

'A pious outlaw on the rocks / Of God and morning'. This is a very different Stevenson from the rather precious and namby-pamby figure we sometimes, though wrongly, persuade ourselves we are beginning to see in him; it is different even from the self-portrait quoted earlier; the constant imagery of war and warriors is partly the invalid's quite natural desire for action and adventure, it is partly the husband's equally natural protective gesture over his property and environment, and yet again it is something more, and 'the love of clandestine violence' is a phrase that although loaded is not entirely off the mark. As Housman loves the soldiers he kills in his verse, so Stevenson seems to be attracted by what he calls 'the man-devouring Wilderness', and by that 'handful' that 'bled on Delhi ridge'.

I have tried to show that Stevenson's poetry is not all of the surface, though even the surface has more variety than is commonly supposed. He has his depths, his surprises, his shocks for the unwary reader. He was writing at a time when it was difficult for poetry to be good, and one must not fall too hard on short-comings which he often shares with his contemporaries. When one compares him with Gerard Manley Hopkins, who lived at the same time and also died in his mid-forties, then of course it is impossible not to see the difference between a man who was a poet to his finger-tips and one who like Stevenson was an occasional poet whose main work lay elsewhere, in prose. But Hopkins is dazzling and it is important to give Stevenson his due. His verse is a genuine part of the tradition of Scottish poetry, which it extends in more than one direction, and in addition to that it holds out a range of poetic effects and pleasures which is, I believe, a good deal wider than we have been accustomed to assume. The hunter may be home from the hill, but at least he brought something back.

Edinburgh Stevenson Lecture, 1970.

James Bridie's The Anatomist *and* John Byrne's The Slab Boys

The Anatomist (1930) and *The Slab Boys* (1978) are obviously two very different plays, but they do have certain things in common, and they make an interesting comparison. They both have clear links with their authors, who know what they're talking about. Bridie was a doctor, and his play is about doctors and medicine and medical research. John Byrne was himself a slab boy, mixing paint for the designers at a carpet factory, and his play is about slab boys in a carpet factory. So in this sense both plays carry and convey a kind of authority and confidence which is notable and convincing. Also, you could claim that both plays are comedies. Certainly *The Anatomist* has a large element of tragedy and melodrama, but the beginning and end seem to indicate that the play is some sort of comedy – a serious, exciting, thoughtful comedy, full of ideas and arguments, containing horror but somehow managing not to leave that as the final impression. *The Slab Boys* is more obviously and continuously comic, but it too has tragic undercurrents and serious ideas, and is, if you like, a 'portrait of the artist as a young man', with a great deal to say, or suggest, about the struggles of a working-class artist in post-war society. And finally, both plays are good theatre. Both were successful with audiences from their first production, and both have shown that they can be revived successfully. This is not unconnected with the fact that both Dr Knox and Phil McCann, the two heroes, are strongly theatrical characters. The main difference between the two plays is that they belong to different eras of Scottish theatre. Bridie was writing mainly before the Second World War, in the 1930s, and his appeal was in general that of a middle-class writer to middle-class theatregoers. Byrne is writing after the war and in the wake of the post-war change of emphasis towards realistic and often socially committed working-class plays – the tradition of plays like Ena Lamont Stewart's *Men Should Weep*, George Munro's *Gold in his Boots*, Roddy McMillan's *All in Good Faith* and *The Bevellers*, Bill Bryden's *Willie Rough*, Hector MacMillan's *The Sash*. (*The Bevellers* seems particularly close to Byrne's play.) And going outside Scotland, one interesting difference is that John Byrne is asking his actors and director to show, as far as is practical on stage, the actual process of mixing paint for carpet designers – it's a very physical play, you can't mime it! Now this is what you also get in other plays of the period, like Arnold Wesker's *The Kitchen*, where the play is set in the kitchen of a large restaurant, as realistically as possible, or David Storey's *The Contractor*, where a huge marquee for a wedding reception is gradually set up, bit by bit, realistically and correctly, in the first part of the play and dismantled in the latter part. Both Wesker's kitchen and Storey's marquee are no doubt images or metaphors for something else, but from the audience's point of view there is a great fascination in watching people at work. *The Slab Boys* comes into this category of play, and that is a part of its hold on the audience. Plays have tended in the past to be about what their characters did or said when they were *not* at work, but since 1950 work has itself often become both a setting and a theme. Of course there is work in Bridie's play too, in the background, but the work there is anatomical dissection, and this might have strained theatre resources or audience reaction!

Bridie, to look at him first, died in 1951, but in the thirty-odd years since his death we don't seem to be much nearer any really agreed assessment of his place and value as a dramatist. His plays are not very frequently performed, and are, you may say, out of fashion. Yet when the best of them, like *The Anatomist*, are revived, they prove to be very good theatre. So what is the problem? Bridie was himself a somewhat impish and enigmatic character. He wrote plenty about himself, for example in his autobiography *One Way of Living* (1939), but he likes to provoke and play with and tantalize the reader, using a good deal of mockery and irony and sometimes claiming to be less serious than he really was. The way he begins his autobiography is very typical (and I should add that he calls it among other things the History of a Happy Bourgeois – is *that* ironic?):

> '*The Lowland Scot is the fine flower...*'
> '*To consider curiously the Scottish Character...*'

> *'Whatever we may think of the general characteristics of the Lowland Scot...'*
> *I found I had put in the carbon paper wrong side up. I tore out the sheet and began again.*

> The Lowland Scot differs from the rest of mankind in that he has no Unconscious Mind. He is aware and critical of all the levels of his consciousness, even when he is asleep or tipsy. He is expert upon himself, if upon no other matter...One result of this is that the Scotsman is a good biographer but a bad autobiographist. His remarkably objective view of himself brings the recording of his own acts and experiences out of the field of art and into the field of mathematics. The story of an instrument of precision has poor appeal to the emotions. I am a Lowland Scot...So far as I know there is not a drop of English or of Highland blood in my veins. I am thus ill-qualified to write the story of my life or of any part of it.
>
> (pp.4–5)

You will notice how even that simple beginning contains an elusive note: if the story of an instrument of precision has poor appeal to the emotions, then the autobiography will be incomplete.

In trying to (or trying not to!) define himself, he takes up a number of themes: education, religion, politics, nationalism. Of these, it might be worth quoting what he says about religion, since *The Anatomist* is in its way a play that keeps raising religious issues, especially the opposition between conventional Christian disapproval of 'interfering with nature' and the new 'religion of science' which doctors and other researchers were drawn into. Religious issues and references and images do indeed recur throughout Bridie's plays, but he disclaimed belief, and tells us how much he hated, as a boy, having to attend services in the Pollokshields Free Church in Glasgow:

> I hated the dreadful smell of varnish and damp cushions and moth balls and hot pipes and the lavender and eau de cologne on the ladies' handkerchiefs...I hated the creak of the minister's boots on the pulpit stairs...I hated the nippit faces and reverent bronchitis of the worshippers. I hated the abominable, snivelling voice with which the parson addressed his maker. I disliked most of the hymns and practically all the psalms...

I hated the cruel, stone-eroding monotony of the sermon...
I liked only the elders when they came round with the plate.
Some of them, I knew, were pleasant men; and I had a sense
that I was paying my threepenny-bit to get out of Purgatory.
When the time came when my mother asked me to join the
Church these early terrors must have fought for me and I
remained an outlier and a heathen in spite of all appeals to my
honour, my religious sentiment and my affection.

(pp. 15-16)

On the matter of nationalism, and language, and the English
and the Scots, Bridie was in part forthcoming, and in part unde-
cided. He was very much concerned with the establishment of
a Scottish National Theatre, but when it comes to nationalism
in the larger sense he is not so ready to be pinned down; what
he is quite sure of, however, is that the English and the Scots are
different – that is the basis you have to start from – and the
difference is what he and Moray McLaren investigate in their
letters in the book called *A Small Stir* (1949). It is instructive to
remember how mercilessly the poor Englishman Mr Raby is
mocked in *The Anatomist* for his inability to understand Scots
accents; even the genteel Edinburgh delivery of the Misses Dishart seems to flummox him ('Are you fond of Naples, Mr Raby?'
'Yes, ma'am. I like them very much.'). The play uses English
(Raby), Scottish-English (Knox, the Disharts), Irish-English
(Burke and Hare), and various kinds of Scots (Mary Paterson,
Davie Paterson). Bridie relishes the variety, as a dramatist, but
he also enjoys pointing to the fact that a Scotsman and not an
Englishman wrote the play. In one of his letters in *A Small Stir*
(pp. 137-43) he comments:

A week or two ago, a Sunday newspaper offered me some
money and I wrote them a playful article about Scotland...
I hinted that God, from time to time, had been very lavish in
providing Scotland with perfervid and original minds. I
suggested that Scotland was waking up, now... [1949] I
expressed the fantastic wish that some of Scotland's remarkable men should come out of the land of Egypt [i.e. exile in
England] and sport their kilts of many colours in the land of
Scotland, where they were born and where, presumably, they
could still flourish.

He went on to describe the reaction to his article: letters of praise from Scottish Nationalists, and a spate of vicious letters from England about Scottish ingratitude for all the good things England had done for the Scots since 1707. This English view of history he won't accept – even though a lot of his own income as a dramatist came from London theatres. As he puts it, 'any serious resistance to their kindly despotism brings out the worst side of the English.' And he warns us, finally, not to underestimate them, if we do resist or oppose them. 'Moscow has nothing on the English in making adverse witnesses talk nonsense. They do it without drugs, or hypnotism or torture, or even the use of mirrors. They do it by magic.'

So overall you have the picture of a moderate-minded, non-religious, ironical, middle-class Lowland Scot from Glasgow who discovers his talent for writing plays during a period of renascent nationalism, and also a period of violently clashing ideologies such as Communism and Fascism, and who – perhaps this is the most we can say – is enormously interested in the ideas and movements of the time but finds it hard to commit himself to any of them. His characters toss ideas about, playfully or sceptically or seriously; and often the drama is set in motion through a contrast or opposition between a mocking or reductive spirit and some character who is possessed and obsessed by some new idea pointing to the future, like Dr Knox in *The Anatomist* who sees the necessity for regular dissection in medical training and research, or the young medical student Charles Cameron in *A Sleeping Clergyman* who studies the germs of his own disease under the microscope although he's dying of tuberculosis. And the temperament of Bridie does not permit even these two characters to come through as unsullied heroes: the attitude to Knox, in his involvement with the Burke and Hare murders, is highly ambiguous, and any virtues in the desperate Charlie Cameron have to work themselves out three generations later as the play moves in time from the 1860s to the 1930s.

In *The Anatomist*, the medical subject of body-snatching and dissection suited Bridie as a doctor, but it also leads him right into highly dramatic human situations involving murder, prostitution, crisis of conscience, dedication to an ideal, the place of love in life, the place of the scientist in society – many themes emerging from realistically presented human dilemmas. Yet there is something more, in that Dr Knox (as I mentioned earlier) is highly theatrical, he is if you like an actor in his own drama –

it's not for nothing that he feels he's like Hamlet, engaging in banter with Mary Dishart as Ophelia, near the beginning: 'You are facetious, Mr Knox.' 'Your only jig-maker.' A jig-maker is a deviser of little theatrical interludes or epilogues, as Hamlet is, and perhaps Knox is too. Bridie was attracted by the theatrical possibilities of someone who was himself theatrical: the interest to the audience of an outwardly rather bizarre figure, unhand-some, bald, with an eye-patch, yet dressed like a dandy, fasci-nated by and fascinating to women, commanding a loyal follow-ing of students, full of playful or cynical or brutal conversation yet totally and knowledgeably committed to medical teaching and research, a man who plays the flute so badly yet so engagingly in Amelia Dishart's drawing-room that she doesn't know whether to laugh or cry, and yet the very man who is unwilling to question the true provenance of the bodies brought to him for dissection – a man of so many sides, so many contradictions, that he becomes a perfect focus for Bridie's ambiguous purposes. The actual difficulty of knowing what Knox was like in real life in early nineteenth-century Edinburgh (and this difficulty remains, despite the book on him by Isobel Rae, *Knox the Anatomist*, 1964) is precisely what draws Bridie to him as a drama-tic subject. In Bridie he is a great anatomist; he is a tragi-comic, half-ludicrous lover; and there are suggestions that like Faust he has a touch of the Devil, as in the conversation between Paterson and Raby at the end of Act 2: 'It's a nice morning, Mr Raby.' 'Yes... I say, he's a cool fish, the Governor.' 'Robert the Devil they· call him.' 'Deep, ain't he?' 'As deep as the pit.' 'What do you think? Does he think they knocked that girl on the head?' 'His Maker only kens what yon man's thinking.'

These contrasts in the main character are then built up by Bridie into a *play* of contrasts, and especially the movement from the genteel Edinburgh drawing-room of the first act to the low-life scenes in the Canongate tavern in Act 2 and back to the Disharts' drawing-room in Act 3; and the use of the Disharts' house as an impromptu lecture-theatre for Knox and his students at the end is a brilliant final contrast, bringing the medical and non-medical themes together. The middle act, with Walter getting drunk, and Burke and Hare luring the beautiful Mary Paterson to her doom ('Don't you worry, you'll sleep sound this night,' as Hare says), and then the tea-chest brought in with a lock of red hair caught in the lid – all this has so much inherent melodrama that it presents a real challenge to the producer: but it can be done, it can give us a genuine pathos, and the pathos is helped by the fact that Mary is no shrinking waif but a very robust character, strong-armed and strong-mouthed, so that her becoming a victim of the murderers is all the more striking and effective. This pathos makes Knox's possible guilt, in turn, all the more strong as a dramatic theme. Indeed some critics have blamed Bridie for not making Knox, at the end, a complete villain, perhaps being condemned in court for complicity in murder, or alternatively, for not giving him a clear vindication as an innocent sufferer in the cause of science. But I think Bridie was right in not making it a morality play. The ambiguity is essential. The end, in its own way, is in fact very positive, even frighteningly so, in the emphasis it places on the sheer power of Knox's personality, his Nietzschean imperturbability, and the comic undercurrents in his last speech never undermine its near-grotesque yet heroic stance.

> With you I shall take the liberty of discussing a weightier matter... 'The Heart of the Rhinoceros.' This mighty organ, gentlemen, weighs full twenty-five pounds, a fitting fountainhead for the tumultuous stream that surges through the arteries of that prodigious monster. Clad in proof, gentlemen, and terribly armed as to his snout, the rhinoceros buffets his way through the tangled verdure engirdling his tropical habitat. Such dreadful vigour, gentlemen, such ineluctable energy requires to be sustained by no ordinary forces of nutrition...

Turning to *The Slab Boys*, we can see that John Byrne does not want or need the strong contrasts of scene or environment you find in Bridie. The two acts of the play are both set in the slab room of a carpet manufacturer in Paisley in 1957, and the action takes only one day. There is a sort of classic concentration or unity about this that seems to suit Byrne's double purpose: to use a fairly claustrophobic setting ('a small paint-spattered room') where his characters will constantly be forced to interact, and to suggest the idea of escape, whether into the dubious promotion of the design studio or out into the 'real' world where an apprentice designer might become a real artist. And whereas Bridie wants to have moments of calm or quietness interspersed among the loud or argumentative or violent passages – variety of pitch as well as variety of tempo – Byrne's play goes fast and hardly ever lets up. There's a curious sort of paradox in the fact that although *The Slab Boys* is a very funny play, almost continuously so, and might therefore be thought somehow to be indulgent or easy-going compared with the high drama of a play about body-snatching, it has a hard edge, a rawness that hits a few nerves, even through all the fantastic and often black humour, whereas it could be argued that Bridie sometimes falls back on stereotyped emotional triggers that seasoned theatregoers may resist. But perhaps that is only because Byrne is our contemporary, and we really feel the thrust of *how* he says what he has to say about work or art or hospitals or growing up or growing old in our time – there's no historical escape back into 1828. (When I say 'in our time' I realize of course that the events of the play are already thirty years back, and Byrne has an acute sense of period; but it is still a good deal nearer to us than Bridie's Burke and Hare world.)

The quickfire inventiveness of the verbal humour is what immediately hits the audience. It spreads all through the play, but its power centre is the hilarious double act of Phil McCann, the would-be artist, and his friend Spanky Farrell, both nineteen and both from beautiful downtown Ferguslie Park. There is a great joy in these exchanges, either with each other or more usually against a third character. Sometimes when they gang up on poor Hector or puzzled Alan or the unfortunate Jack 'Plooky Chops' Hogg, they remind us a little of Pinter's Goldberg and McCann (another McCann!) in *The Birthday Party*. At other times their backchat and standup routines are more like the clowning in Beckett's *Waiting for Godot*. They relish – and this is not at all unrealistic, though exaggerated; teenagers do it all the time – putting on other voices, becoming other characters, acting out satirical scenarios through their imitations, e.g. their fondness for contrasting Ferguslie Park and Stobo's carpet factory with the Frank Richards world of Greyfriars School and the Owl of the Remove and all its pukka hierarchies.

HECTOR: My bloody wireless! That was for my Maw's Christmas present.
PHIL: Bless my boater, did you catch that, Cherry? A yuletide cadeau for the squirt's Mater and blow me if old Quelch ain't went and confiscated the blighter!
SPANKY: Christ, Nugent, that's torn it.
PHIL: Buck up, Pygmy Minimus... Cherry and I'll think of

something. Any ideas, Cherry, old chap?
SPANKY: How about a set of cufflinks?
PHIL: I'll wager that beast, Bunter, had a fat finger in this...

(p.5)

Or at the very end, Phil and Spanky left on stage, Phil dismissed from the factory and still hoping to get to Art School sometime, Phil has the last word, distancing himself from his misfortune by putting on the public school persona once again.

PHIL: I wonder what the Guv'nor's got for one's tea t'night? Plate of jolly fine mince, perhaps? Or a shoulder of lamb to cry on? Best fling the leg over the trike and zip back to Fairyland... find out, eh? Confront the old duffer... break the news about the scribblin' school, the sack, and... oh, yes, the Old Dear's impromptu dip, what? Might stop off en route and chuck a bottle of bubbly in the boot... cheer the little tike up.
(*Picks up dustcoat*) Would you mind stuffing that down Quelch's throat as you leave, old bean? Thanks. Oh, and do pop a few of Bunter's boils for me, there's a good chap. Think I've got everything...? Yes. Gosh, and All Serene, what a bally day. Started off pleasantly enough... one's Mater off for a few days in the country... but, fuck me, if it ain't gone downhill since then. Fuck me, if it ain't! (*Pause*) Christ, I've just remembered something... (*Takes a couple of steps and executes a cartwheel*) Giotto used to be a Slab Boy, Spanks!

(pp.43-44)

Phil gives the play a positive, hopeful conclusion (only just, but he does), in his own voice, and by his own action, his physical cartwheel being the equivalent of the perfect circle which according to legend Giotto was able to draw.

There's also the running humour of their attack on the middle-class Alan with his Parker pen – they refuse to give him any real identity by calling him everything but Alan (except once): Archie, Eamonn, Albert, Adam, Arthur, Alfie, Aldo, Agnes...

And apart from verbal humour, there's the use of classic physical farce situations, like the number of times Hector is bundled back into the cupboard in Act 2 – funny, if a bit overdone, though it fits in with the general physicality of the play.

As regards what I called the 'hard edge' of the play, there are two points I would note. The first concerns the fact that Phil McCann, the hero of the play, is a talented nonconformist who is trying to tell us something about the system in which he feels he's caught, or in danger of being caught. Whether he will ever make it as an artist we don't know (he's still an unsuccessful artist at the end of *Still Life*, the third play in the trilogy), but we do know that he has real talent and that he cares about matters of art. With all the joking and fooling around we might not be sure, but it's made clear at one or two particular points. Near the beginning of Act 2, Jack the designer criticizes him for apparently taking no interest in the business, in the details of carpet designing, and Phil is angry because Jack has assumed he would not be interested in some design magazines he's going to lend Alan. It's a social thing as well as an artistic thing. Jack's unspoken assumption is that slab boys from Ferguslie Park don't read design magazines. Phil bursts out:

> PHIL: Ach, pish, Jack! 'Some of us take a pride in what we do' ... You? You lot! You're a bunch of no-talent no-hopers, arse-licking your way up the turkey-runner to Barton's office, a fistful of brushes in this hand and the other one tugging at the forelock... 'Good morning, Sir Wallace, by Christ but that's a snazzy Canaletto print up there on the wall next to that big clock that says a quarter to eight... Suffering Jesus, is that the time already? My, but how time flies when you're enjoying yourself. Pardon me, while I flick this shite off my boot... Just after stepping on one of Jimmy Robertson's sketches... it'll wash off, I'm sure. What? No, no, not at all, Sir Wallace... of course I don't mind putting in a bit of unpaid overtime... it's results that count, isn't it?' Jack, you wouldn't know a good design from a plate of canteen mince. Interest? As soon as Barton starts revving up his Jag you're the first one out the door and the leg over the bike before Miss Walkinshaw's even got her teeth out of her waterjug!
>
> (p.24)

The other area where the play has a bite and isn't merely entertaining concerns Phil's mother. This comes out especially in relation to Alan and his happy family background. In Act 2 Phil learns that his mother has vanished from hospital and might be anywhere. Alan enters, and Phil takes it out on him (unfairly – but that's the play!):

SPANKY: Leave him alone, Phil...he doesn't know what you're talking about.

PHIL: I bet you he doesn't. (*To* ALAN) What do you know about getting up in the middle of the night in your shirt tail to say five decades of the rosary over your Maw's open wrists? What do you know about screaming fits and your old man's nut getting bopped off the Pope's calendar? What do you know about razor blades and public wards and row upon row of gumsy cadavers all sitting up watching you stumble in with your Lucozade and excuses? Christ, what one's mine? Is that you, Maw? What do you know about living in a rabbit hutch with concrete floors and your old man's never in and you're left trying to have a conversation with a TV set and a Maw that thinks you're St Thomas Aquinas? What do you know about standing there day in, day out in the Factor's office asking for a move and the guy with the shiny arse on his trousers shakes his head and treats your Old Dear like dirt??

(p.36)

This again, like the outburst on art and design, is a social outburst as well as a personal one, and it's strong. It brings across the vividness of Phil as the central character and it also makes him a spokesman, without being soapboxy or strained – what he says comes out of his actual teenage experience. It is still, in the way he talks, comic; but it bites.

Like *The Anatomist*, *The Slab Boys* has been criticized for not having a real climax. At the end, the characters are getting ready for the Staff Dance. Hector has been promoted to designer, Phil has been sacked, Phil's mother has been found, fished out of the river safely ('the grappling hooks did not break the skin' as the ambulance man says in a last flick of black humour), and that's it. Perhaps the answer is that it's the first play in a trilogy? But even the trilogy as a whole lacks a really convincing climax. Things are still open-ended. Perhaps there is more to follow? Middle-aged one-time slab boys? It's interesting that Byrne's more recent play, *Tutti Frutti*, which for most of the time seems very slow and unstructured, does have an undoubted climax, a literal *coup de théâtre*, with an aging rock star setting fire to himself in his leathers in the Pavilion Theatre in Glasgow. But that was television. Maybe Byrne likes to do things differently in the theatre. At any rate, there seems no doubt that in *The Slab Boys* he wrote something which combines a lot of entertainment with some pungent comments on the world we live in, and perhaps the unfinished action is a part of the comment.

Note

Quotations from the plays are taken from James Bridie, *The Anatomist*, Constable, London, 1931 (second edition, revised, 1932), and John Byrne, *The Slab Boys*, Salamander Press, Edinburgh, 1982. The other plays in Byrne's trilogy, *Cuttin' a Rug* and *Still Life*, were also published by Salamander in 1982.

Text of a talk given to a conference on Scottish literature organized by the Association for Scottish Literary Studies, University of Strathclyde, 3 October 1987.

James Joyce and Hugh MacDiarmid

I ought perhaps to begin with the apology, or at least the warning, that my essay may seem to be more about MacDiarmid than about Joyce, but I have written it under the umbrella of the collection title of 'James Joyce and Modern Literature', and I hope that my use of Hugh MacDiarmid will give a new perspective to some of the wider issues of Joyce's work. I shall not be writing about any personal relationship between the two writers, since that did not exist; but the absence of such a relation may even help in seeing more clearly such relations as obtain between their *oeuvres*. Now that the writing of both men is complete – MacDiarmid died in 1978 and his *Complete Poems* was published in the same year[1] – we can survey them from the vantage-point of history, and begin to map out some remarkable points of contact and overlap as well as some instructive differences.

Although they were near-contemporaries, and had many literary acquaintances in common, Joyce and MacDiarmid never met. Meetings were set up several times, but for various accidental reasons failed to materialize. We have MacDiarmid's word for it that Joyce knew his poetry and in particular *A Drunk Man Looks at the Thistle* (1926)[2], but the influence that can be documented goes in the other direction, and is shown most obviously in the title of MacDiarmid's long poem *In Memoriam James Joyce* (1955)[3]. Lack of documentation, however, does not rule out the interesting possibility that *A Drunk Man Looks at the Thistle*, which appeared while Joyce was working on *Finnegans Wake*, may well have contributed something to the shaping of that novel. There are a number of suggestive similarities: *A Drunk Man* is a long, multi-layered, stylistically diverse poem, set at night, using much interior monologue, bringing in historical as well as contemporary figures, frequently fusing the local and the universal, climaxing in a vision of the Great Wheel of History which makes its complete turn every 26,000 years, having a hero who if not a publican is a drunk man, and closing with the words

169

of the hero's wife. Drink, in *A Drunk Man*, takes the place of dream or nightmare in *Finnegans Wake*, and has the same effect both of liberating the deeper levels of thought and experience and of encouraging the emergence of startling verbal juxtapositions and incongruities. As we try to read the mysterious letter scratched from the dump in *Finnegans Wake*, so we struggle to see clearly the shaking moonlit thistle which the Drunk Man confronts, and which is metamorphosed dozens of times, from an actual thistle emblematic of Scotland to Yggdrasil the World Tree to a pickled foetus to Christ on the Cross to the speaker himself as a Jekyll-and-Hyde. And MacDiarmid's wheel image seems to have much the same function as Joyce's Viconian cycles, in that it serves to telescope history, although MacDiarmid stops short of the complete identificatory device of the pun which allows Joyce to condense more material more continuously.

> The skippin' sparks, the ripples, rit   [scrape]
> Like skritches o' a grain o' grit
> 'Neth Juggernaut in which I sit.
>
> Twenty-six thoosand years it tak's
> Afore a'e single roond it mak's,
> And syne it melts as it were wax.   [then]
>
> The Phoenix guise 't'll rise in syne
> Is mair than Euclid or Einstein
> Can dream o' or's in dreams o' mine.
>
> Upon the huge circumference are
> As neebor points the Heavenly War
> That dung doun Lucifer sae far,   [dashed]
>
> And that upheaval in which I
> Sodgered 'neth the Grecian sky
> And in Italy and Marseilles,
>
> And there isna room for men
> Wha the haill o' history ken
> To pit a pin twixt then and then.
>   (*Complete Poems*, p.159)

I am sure that Joyce, when he read a passage like that, must have appreciated the way in which MacDiarmid planted his little seeds of information and 'point', though he himself would have brought them even closer together: 'Juggernaut' and 'Euclid' reminding us of the Great or Platonic Year of Hindu and Greek astronomers, after which the heavenly bodies would return to their original places, the 'sparks' of the heavily rolling wheel leading to its final phoenix-like melting and resurgence, the datable autobiographical reference to MacDiarmid's service in the Mediterranean during the First World War juxtaposed against a War in Heaven which is out of time altogether, so that the wheel is suddenly seen to be both historical and metahistorical. It would not be surprising if *Finnegans Wake* showed a measure of influence from *A Drunk Man*, but in any case there has clearly been some parallel development going on in the two authors which encourages us to look at them together, and also to think of them as belonging to a period when such contemporaries as Ezra Pound and David Jones were exploring history and ideas about history in large-scale works of a similar ambitiousness and inclusiveness.

Joyce and MacDiarmid both emerged from social and literary environments where they felt impelled to adopt a critical, single-minded, often lonely role. They laid on themselves a weight of responsibility which Joyce dealt with almost entirely in terms of art and which in MacDiarmid issues in ceaseless journalistic and publicistic activity as well as in art but which in both men had deep roots in their national feelings about Ireland and Scotland as places presenting challenges and problems quite distinct from those of England or (if there is such a thing) 'Britain'. Not only Stephen Dedalus wanted to 'forge in the smithy of my soul the uncreated conscience of my race' (*A Portrait of the Artist as a Young Man*, p.257); Joyce himself wrote in a letter to Nora in 1912 that he was 'one of the writers of this generation who are perhaps creating at last a conscience in the soul of this wretched race' (*Letters*, II, p.63). This is very much in keeping with MacDiarmid's lines in *A Drunk Man*: 'A Scottish poet maun [must] assume / The burden o' his people's doom, / And dee to brak' their livin' tomb' (*Complete Poems*, p.165). The 'living tomb' that MacDiarmid saw the Scottish people imprisoned in at the beginning of the twentieth century is a close cousin of the 'paralysis' Joyce saw gripping Ireland: a mixture of complacence, sentimentality, provinciality, and philistinism, differing only with the Catholic background in Ireland and the Protestant background in Scotland. Both authors sought to dent the provinciality by looking first not to writers in England or America but to notable figures of Northern Europe: Joyce going to Ibsen, MacDiarmid to Dostoevsky and Blok and Shestov. This aim at the Europeanizing or internationalizing of two small peripheral nations (re-Europeanizing and re-internationalizing would be more accurate, since both countries had had rich international contacts in their history) has to be seen in a political context of nationalism as well as in a cultural context of revitalization. With MacDiarmid the nationalism was overt, committed, and life-long (he was one of the founder members of the National Party of Scotland), though his international interests made him an uneasy bedfellow in a largely inward-looking nationalist movement. That Joyce's feelings about Ireland were divided and often problematic is well known, but there is no mistaking their intensity or their continuing active presence. Revisiting Dublin from Trieste in 1909, he wrote to Nora:

> I felt proud to think that my son – mine and yours, that handsome dear little boy you gave me, Nora – will always be a foreigner in Ireland, a man speaking another language and bred in a different tradition.
>
> I loathe Ireland and the Irish. They themselves stare at me in the street though I was born among them. Perhaps they read my hatred of them in my eyes. I see nothing on every side of me but the image of the adulterous priest and his servants and of sly deceitful women. It is not good for me to come here or to be here.   (*Letters*, II. p.255)

To Joyce, a straightforward nationalism like MacDiarmid's was impossible, and his exiling of himself from his own country – something which MacDiarmid could never have done – gave the clearest indication that so long as Irish nationalism implied continued support for the Catholic Church and continued faith in the revival of Irish Gaelic as the native tongue, it could never command his loyalty:

> I confess that I do not see what good it does to fulminate against the English tyranny while the Roman tyranny occupies the palace of the soul. . . . Ancient Ireland is dead just as ancient Egypt is dead. . . . The old national soul that spoke during the centuries through the mouths of fabulous seers, wandering minstrels, and Jacobite poets disappeared from the world with

the death of James Clarence Mangan....It is well past time for Ireland to have done once and for all with failure. If she is truly capable of reviving, let her awake.   ('Ireland, Island of Saints and Sages', 1907[4])

Despite his moods of impatience and revulsion, however, Joyce could not help retaining a painful interest in Irish politics, especially during the gestation of the Irish Free State, and Dominic Manganiello has usefully traced the details of his complex position in *Joyce's Politics* (London, 1980). Clearly Joyce was pro-Irish in being anti-English, but he saw his Irishness as working on a more modern and international level than the Irishness of those who made a virtue of their patriotism and sense of tradition. His scathing comment in a letter to his brother Stanislaus in 1906 underlines this distinction:

If it is not too far-fetched to say that my action, and that of men like Ibsen &c, is a virtual intellectual strike I would call such people as Gogarty and Yeats and Col[u]m the blacklegs of literature. Because they have tried to substitute us, to serve the old idols at a lower rate when we refused to do so for a higher.   (*Letters*, II, p.187)

MacDiarmid, without going into exile and without Joyce's fear of the implications of the word 'nationalist', had nevertheless a similar sense of isolation from, and frequent opposition to, what his co-nationalists in Scotland appeared to stand for. His anti-wet intellectualism, his extreme pro-Gaelic language platform, and most of all his espousing of communism in the early 1930s, left him with a constant fight on his hands. It is the Gaelic cause which particularly interests us here, because this is one of the links with Ireland, though not with the Ireland that Joyce wanted to see. In his autobiography, *Lucky Poet* (London, 1943), MacDiarmid has a recurrent awareness of Ireland as the great Celtic motherland, and claims that 'a Scottish Scotland must be a Gaelic Scotland' (p.201). Scottish Gaelic, like the Irish Gaelic from which it had originally diverged, was on the retreat, but MacDiarmid was nothing if not quixotic, and called for a resurgence of all the Celtic languages, going hand-in-hand with a cultural and political self-determination until there was a united and steely 'Celtic crescent' of workers' republics from Scotland down through Ireland, the Isle of Man, Wales, Cornwall, and

Brittany, which would eventually become a pincer movement and squeeze the English into final submission. Finnegan wakes! That is not, I think, a James Joyce scenario. Yet the imaginative as distinct from the practical appeal of such an awakening is by no means alien to Joyce's concerns. Both Finn and Finnegan, after all, to say nothing of that rex futurus Arthur, were chosen by Joyce as chief exemplars of reawakening, and all are Celts. And as a codicil to any evocation of the broken barrows of Arthur and Finn, let me mention another small and curious Joyce/Mac-Diarmid link, which if accidental is surely ben trovato. Not only the giant Finn of Irish legend, but the Finns of Finland, could be expected to emerge from burial-mounds. It was a part of European folklore that Finns – and the name was applied to people of the remote north even if they were not properly speaking Finnish – had magic powers, including the unnerving ability to spring up from the burial-barrow. So famous were they for this Lazarus-like behaviour that in the dialect of Shetland (the part of these islands nearest to Finland) the phrase 'hjokfinni body' means an odd, uncanny person who might well be a witch or wizard, like a Finn from a hjok or hog (= burial-mound). In *Lucky Poet*, MacDiarmid writes near the end (p.379):

> If I were asked by someone, who was finding it difficult, to describe in a single sentence – or express in a brief parable – just what the sort of life I have had, as described in or implied by the foregoing chapters, amounts to, I would probably reply: 'It's all just a matter of a Hjok-finnie body having a ride on a neugle'.

Later, he explains (in a very Joycean phrase) that a Hjok-finnie body is 'a buried Finn up again', and that a neugle is a water-horse, a creature which only a Finn could safely ride. This is MacDiarmid's view of himself as shaman, ethnic trickster, prankster, male prankquean. That the image has, however, a heroic as well as a comic aspect is shown elsewhere in *Lucky Poet* (p.186), when he writes: 'Like David Jones, I have always "had in mind the persistent Celtic theme of armed sleepers under the mounds".'

Joyce and MacDiarmid seem frequently to meet, therefore, in the dream-ridden, deep-imaged, mythological areas of creative experience, especially but by no means only against a background of Celtic culture and history. But this does not explain the initial impact, and to a large extent the continued impact, of Joyce upon MacDiarmid, which was linguistic. MacDiarmid does not appear to have taken any great interest in *Dubliners* or *A Portrait*, but the publication of *Ulysses* in 1922 took him by storm. There are reasons for this which are quite separate from the general *réclame* of that book. MacDiarmid was at a moment of crisis and decision in the development of his own poetry, which had not yet been published in a personal collection in book form. In that year he turned from writing in English to writing in Scots, and discovered in the process that he had released a totally unexpected but amazingly fresh and original vein of poetry – the short lyrics of *Sangschaw* (1925) and *Penny Wheep* (1926) and the long philosophical poem *A Drunk Man Looks at the Thistle*. Even though he did not attempt to imitate it, it was the bold and innovative use of language in *Ulysses* that encouraged him to take equal risks in giving new life to what had become the effete tradition of writing in Lowland Scots (or Lallans, or simply Scots, which is now the preferred term). The followers of Robert Burns in the nineteenth century were a maudlin, pawky crew who reduced poetry to light verse and left it there. Despite attempts at a more serious Scots poetry from Robert Louis Stevenson, Lewis Spence, Violet Jacob and some others, the situation was still far from healthy when MacDiarmid began to write and publish just after the First World War. At first he associated the use of Scots with a provincial nostalgia for old simplicities which had gone for ever, and attacked it much as Joyce mocked the use of Irish Gaelic. But then he had a good look at the language in dictionaries and grammars, became more and more excited by what he found, and put this excitement to the test by deploying the rich and largely forgotten vocabulary of Scots in a series of new poems written from 1922 onwards. In doing this he felt that somehow Joyce was at his elbow, and he tried to say why, in an article in his own magazine, *The Scottish Chapbook*.[5] After remarking that he had been greatly struck by a 'moral resemblance' between Joyce's *Ulysses* and Jamieson's *Etymological Dictionary of the Scottish Language*, he went on:

A *vis comica* that has not yet been liberated lies bound by desuetude and misappreciation in the recesses of the Doric: and its potential uprising would be no less prodigious, uncontrollable, and utterly at variance with conventional morality than was Joyce's tremendous outpouring.

(You will notice that the image of the sleeping and resurrected giant is not too far from that passage either.) A liberation through language and, interestingly, a liberation that will please the spirit of comedy: MacDiarmid, like Joyce, is to a considerable extent a comic writer, and also like Joyce, he sees an effect of moral catharsis in comedy. And the language had to be fresh, surprising, unconventional, far from the homely cliché-dropping humour of post-Burnsian verse; that was why Jamieson's dictionary was important to him. In these early poems he showed an extraordinary ability to mix convincingly together English words (to be spoken of course with a Scottish accent), Scottish forms of words which are still commonly heard and understood, and then suddenly the startling dictionary word given a new life in a new context, rising from the grave like a hjokfinni, rising like the word hjokfinni when MacDiarmid uses it. He would have liked to add Gaelic, as Scotland's third language, but knew too little to employ it creatively as he employed Scots and English.

What MacDiarmid was doing was unlike what Joyce was doing, yet it was parallel to it, as it had links also with the work of Eliot and Pound and with modernist writing in other countries wherever the revolution and restoration and 'making new' of the word were to be found. MacDiarmid's Scottishness and Joyce's Irishness were perfectly compatible with this instinctive feeling for the age, both as a period of climactic general change and as a period when language had become and would continue to be a matter of central importance. In a 1932 article on 'Problems of Poetry Today',[6] MacDiarmid wrote to defend Joyce against attacks which had been made on him after magazine publication of sections of *Work in Progress*:

> In *Work in Progress* Joyce, using about a score of languages, becomes not less, but more, Irish. 'Anna Livia Plurabelle' may look incomprehensible on the printed page; but on the gramophone record, in Joyce's own voice, it gets right over to every hearer above the level of a mental defective.

This view of MacDiarmid's, that it is the native or national aspect of an international modernist writer which keeps the wolf of incomprehension from the door, has an element of paradox about it, but it is a theme to which MacDiarmid often reverts, and I am not sure that Joyce would have disagreed with it. I believe most people will confirm that hearing Joyce reading from

Finnegans Wake is a revelatory experience, and this not only because it suddenly does become more comprehensible, but also because the very marked Irishness of the voice and indeed of the whole performance makes one think again about the purpose and meaning of the whole work. (A more recent example of this sort of reaction is the record of William Burroughs reading from *The Naked Lunch*; hearing that very American voice, with its sardonic deadpan humour, you suddenly realize that he is in the tradition of great American storytellers, nearer Mark Twain than Schwitters or Dada.)

MacDiarmid's enthusiastic response to the fragments of *Work in Progress*, as they appeared during the late 1920s, elicited at least one direct tribute in his own poetry. 'Water Music', included in *Scots Unbound and Other Poetry* (Stirling, 1932), is a lyrico–musical, alliterative, onomatopoeic recognition of the 'Anna Livia Plurabelle' section of *Finnegans Wake*. Here is how it begins:

> *Wheesht, wheesht, Joyce, and let me hear*
> > *Nae Anna Livvy's lilt,*
> *But Wauchope, Esk, and Ewes again,*
> > *Each wi' its ain rhythms till't.*

> Archin' here and arrachin there,
> > Allevolie or allemand,
> Whiles appliable, whiles areird,
> > The polysemous poem's planned.

> Lively, louch, atweesh, atween,
> > Auchimuty or aspate,
> Threidin' through the averins
> > Or bightsom in the aftergait.

> Or barmybrained or barritchfu',
> > Or rinnin' like an attercap,
> Or shining' like an Atchison,
> > Wi' a blare or wi' a blawp.

> They ken a' that opens and steeks,
> > Frae Fiddleton Bar to Callister Ha',
> And roon aboot for twenty miles,
> > They bend and bell and swaw.

Brent on or boutgate or beshacht
    Bellwaverin' or borne-heid,
They mimp and primp, or bick and birr,
    Dilly-dally or show speed.

Brade-up or sclafferin', rouchled, sleek,
    Abstraklous or austerne,
In belths below the brae-hags
    And bebbles in the fern.

Bracken, blaeberries, and heather
    Ken their amplefeysts and toves,
Here gangs ane wi' aiglets jinglin',
    Through a gowl anither goves.

Lint in the bell whiles hardly vies
    Wi' ane the wind amows,
While blithely doon abradit linns
    Wi' gowd begane anither jows.

Cougher, blocher, boich and croichle,
    Fraise in ane anither's witters,
Wi' backthraws, births, by-rinnin's,
    Beggar's-broon or blae – the critters!
                   (*Complete Poems*, pp.333–4)

    MacDiarmid was brought up in the Scottish Borders, and in his autobiography he recalls (*Lucky Poet*, p.219) the delight he took in the countryside as a boy, the forests and heather hills and moorlands, the 'strange and subtle relationships of water and light', and above all the 'multitude of rivers, each with its distinct music'; these, he says, were 'the champagne days – these long, enchanted days on the Esk, the Wauchope, and the Ewes'. Memory of a happy childhood chimes in with his delighted reading and hearing of Joyce's Anna Livia Plurabelle as he makes use of the *topos* of praising one's little-known native place and saying that it deserves artistic immortality at the side of places already made famous. His method is to scour the dictionary for Scottish words, many of them rare or forgotten – which will describe the appearance, movements, moods, colours, and sounds of rivers. These words – and you may have caught the fact that they are taken from the A, B, and C pages of the dictionary, which would have appealed to Joyce as an example of virtuosity – are mostly unfamiliar. What happens therefore is that a certain degree of onomatopoeia, and the alliteration which combines with well-marked rhythmic effects to convey impressions of movement and speed, help to give the poem an interesting mixture of imitative form (which facilitates at least some entry into the landscape content) and the linguistic and extraneous ABC element (which acts as a distancer and reminds us that this is a poem about poetry and not merely about rivers). As he says, the 'polysemous poem' is planned to move on its different levels, at different rates, with different characteristics, and in this it is working like Joyce's fiction. Yet to most readers (even Scottish ones!), and this too would be in line with statements made by Joyce about Anna Livia Plurabelle, it must come across as 'polysemous' mainly in the way that music could be called polysemous, as a complex exhilarating flux of sound, and one comes back to the title, 'Water Music'. Richard Ellmann reports[7] how when Nino Frank was discussing an Italian translation of Anna Livia Plurabelle with Joyce in 1937, Joyce's 'whole emphasis was again on sonority, rhythm, and verbal play; to the sense he seemed indifferent and unfaithful, and Frank had often to recall him to it.'

But with one central Joycean device MacDiarmid has little to do; the pun he leaves aside, under Joyce's trademark. In the fourth line of the poem quote above, Joyce would not have missed the latent pun in 'till't', which means 'belonging to it, attached to it' but could also suggest the River Tilt in Perthshire, one of the rivers Joyce does in fact refer to in Anna Livia Plurabelle. In the poem, however, that added meaning would be an irrelevant import. MacDiarmid admitted frankly, in another 1932 essay, 'The Case for Synthetic Scots',[8] that his 'synthetic Scots has not touched the fringe of Joycean experimentation' and that 'the small innovations I have already attempted do not go nearly far enough'. 'A Joycean amalgam,' he adds, 'of Scots, Gaelic, and English, plus Gothic, Sanskrit, Old Norse, seems to me a medium through which a great deal could be done to advance this world-wide experimentation and bring language abreast of modern psychological requirements.' Such an amalgam, although it brings its variety of languages together as a collage or mosaic rather than in the Joycean melting-pot of punning, was MacDiarmid's final tribute, *In Memoriam James Joyce* (1955).

This '*hapax legomenon* of a poem', as its author calls it, is described on the title-page as being only a part of a larger unpublished work, 'A Vision of World Language', but is itself over 6,000 lines long, and is decorated, like the Book of Kells or *Finnegans Wake*, with indignant Celtic whiplooplashes, prudently blocked rounds, whirligig glorioles, and tiberious ambiembellishments by the Scottish artist J.D. Fergusson, including James Joyce's name set forth in best stubby ogam. Joyce would doubtless have accepted such a majestic and pan-Celtic memorial as no more than his due. But is this enormous poem, like so many elegies, a work that tells us more about its author than about its subject?

The poem has six sections. The first and longest has the actual title In Memoriam James Joyce and aims to describe, by every direct and indirect means, the kind of poetry MacDiarmid likes and would like to write; and it is a poetry which he relates specifically to the major work of Joyce. Particularity of language, and range of knowledge and of reference, are important to it. Plenitude and richness of the linguistic texture, however, should not be so continuous as to rule out moments of silence, absence, abstracted vision, black holes in the text through which we can suddenly peer into alternative worlds:

> So beyond all that is heteroepic, holophrastic,
> Macaronic, philomathic, psychopetal,
> Jerqueing every idioticon,
> Comes this supreme paraleipsis,
> Full of potential song as a humming-bird
> Is full of potential motion.
>
> (*Complete Poems*, p.771)

('So beyond all that is of non-standard pronunciation, that compresses many ideas into a single word, that combines different languages, that loves learning, that homes in on the mind like a target, that ransacks every dialect and jargon dictionary, comes the supreme emphasis of non-emphasis, of omission, of absence, which is full of potential song as a humming-bird is full of potential motion.')

The second section, 'The World of Words', moves in roughly the same territory as the first, but is directed more towards the psychology of readers' reception and perception of words, the reactions we have to names, images, sounds, colours, letters, metres, syntax, symbols, spelling, calligraphy, shibboleths, secret languages – everything involved in the complex relations between writing, speech, and thought. The third and fourth parts, called

'The Snares of Varuna' and 'The Meeting of the East and the West', bring in a theme that is important to MacDiarmid and to a lesser extent to Joyce also – the significance of oriental and especially Indian thought and the necessity to move beyond a Europe-centred idea of culture to a world-literature overview. The fifth section is a satirical scherzo called 'England Is Our Enemy' where MacDiarmid parades what in *Who's Who* he liked to define as his Anglophobia (a characteristic not unknown to Joyce either), attacking English literature and criticism for that very bland, anti-extremist insularity – 'a stone-heap, a dead load of moral qualities' – which he and Joyce had been doing their best to discredit by bypassing Anglosaxondom, jumping from Vico Road to Vico or from Ecclefechan to eternity. In the sixth and last section, 'Plaited like the Generations of Men', the poem tries to draw all its strands together, admits it can have only a partial success in doing so ('Have I failed in my braid-binding?'), but establishes its main positive theme of belief in human evolution, with the evolution of language persistently contributing to it and with the work of Joyce masterfully contributing to the evolution of language.

The poem, like *Finnegans Wake*, is full of 'quashed quotatoes, messes of mottage' (p.183). It is to a great extent a mosaic of extracts from MacDiarmid's reading of books, articles, and reviews, the prose being rewritten as verse, with quotations from many languages although the main body of the writing is in English. Like Joyce and Rabelais and Swift, MacDiarmid makes much use of the catalogue: he has lists of languages, of poets, of scholars, of books, of dissertations, of philological terms, of styles of Chinese writing, of Shetland words for the sea, of mathematical theories, of archaisms, of tropical woods, of translators of Sanskrit. In Joyce, such catalogues have that mixture of the comic and the tiring which seems inseparable from the device, but in MacDiarmid, because he *can* be very humourless where his hobby-horses are concerned, one is not so sure of the comic component. Joyce, an arch-hypertrophist, loved to mock the hypertrophies of scholarship, as in the Book of Kells pages of *Finnegans Wake*: see, he says, '*Some Forestallings over that Studium of Sexophonologistic Schizophrenesis*, vol.xxiv, pp.2-555', and compare *Later Frustrations amengst the Neomugglian Teachings abaft the Semi-unconscience, passim*' (*Finnegans Wake*, p.123). MacDiarmid seems to me now to be more aware of the comic potential of such lists than I thought at the time when the poem first appeared, but he has still more of the didactic than Joyce. Both comic and didactic aspects slide into this passage:

> Kroh's 'Eidetiker unter Deutschen Dichtern,' too
> And Martin's exhaustive study of imaginal traits,
> 'Die Projektionsmethode und die Lokalisation visueller
>   und anderer Vorstellungsbilder,'
> And, of course, the 'Vergnügliches Handbuch der
>   Deutschen Sprache'
> Parts of which might well have been written
> By Edward Lear and Wilhelm Busch
> With occasional advice from Lewis Carroll
> – Yet a mine of information about German life and
>   habits.
>
> (*Complete Poems*, p.806)

Joyce in the poem is to some extent a Virgil to MacDiarmid's Dante. His presence is strongly felt, to anyone who knows his work, even when he is not being mentioned, but periodically MacDiarmid will interrupt his narrative, exclaim 'Ah, Joyce...', and engage the novelist in direct address, sometimes expressing solidarity, sometimes admitting differences, sometimes praising him as innovator and forerunner. This was a favourite method of MacDiarmid's; you can see other examples of it in his various 'Hymns to Lenin' and in his 'Letter to Dostoevsky' in *A Drunk Man*. Three of the passages addressing Joyce are of special interest.

In the second section, 'The World of Words', there is a long passage beginning 'Ah, Joyce, this is our task' which goes on to define the linguistically central labour – 'So this is what our lives have been given to find, / A language that can serve our purposes' – and finally brings everything together in a striking illustration, not unlike an epic simile in the remoteness and elaborateness of the ground of comparison. The labours of writers like Joyce and himself in the world of words remind him of stories of the difficult physical exploration of the Greenland icecap:[9]

> When climbing on to the ice-cap a little south of Cape
>   Bismarck
> And keeping the nunataks of Dronning Louises Land on
>   our left
> We travel five days

On tolerable ice in good weather
With few bergs to surmount
And no crevasses to delay us.
Then sudd~nly our luck turns.
A wind of 120 miles an hour blows from the East,
And the plateau becomes a playground of gales
And the novel light gives us snow-blindness.
We fumble along with partially bandaged eyes
Our reindeer-skin kamiks worn into holes
And no fresh sedge-grass to stump them with.
We come on ice-fields like mammoth ploughlands
And mountainous séracs which would puzzle an Alpine
    climber.
That is what adventuring in dictionaries means.
                    (*Complete Poems*, p.823)

Superficially this might seem to be not far from Eliot's 'intoler-
able wrestle / With words and meanings' in 'East Coker', or
indeed with the wrestling with his material which every serious
writer has to undergo, but in fact MacDiarmid, and by implica-
tion Joyce, are taking it a step farther back, back into the dictionary,
the store of all human words, which is waiting to unlock its
treasures but is guarded, as treasure-mounds are, by dragons: of
strangeness, of difficulty, of unfamiliarity, of over-familiarity,
of jargon, of technicality, of unpronounceability, of semantic
elusiveness, of phonic unhelpfulness. With this Joyce would
surely agree. From the 'paralysis', 'gnomon', and 'simony' of 'The
Sisters' in *Dubliners* (p.7) to the 'alfrids, beatties, cormacks and
daltons' of *Finnegans Wake* (p.19), he invests the individual word
with an almost magic power, and it is a power which is not won
easily.

    In a second passage, from the last section of the poem, and
with a pretty instance of that paraleipsis he had mentioned earlier,
MacDiarmid exclaims, 'Ah Joyce, enough said, enough said!'
and then proceeds to bombard that vacuum with illustrations of
his favourite theme of continuous evolution. Science synthesizes
new colours; human consciousness is growing in secret 'like a
mango tree under a cloth'; Schönberg was right in saying it was
not for the evolution of music to wait on the human ear but for
the human ear to catch up with the evolution of music; and Schönberg, Joyce, and MacDiarmid himself are evolutionary forces –
articulators of the new – in music, prose, and poetry. In another

of his remarkably applied, lengthy similes, drawn from Sir Charles Sherrington's *Man on his Nature* (Cambridge, 1940), MacDiarmid suggests that Joyce's work is prospective, it is not for these present generations but for the future:

> Even as nerves before ever they function
> Grow where they *will* be wanted; levers laid down in
>   gristle
> Become bone when wanted for the heavier pull
> Of muscles which *will* clothe them; lungs, solid glands,
> Yet arranged to hollow out at a few minutes' notice
> When the necessary air shall enter; limb-buds
> Futile at their appearing, yet deliberately appearing
> In order to become limbs in readiness
> For an existence where they *will* be all-important;
> A pseudo-aquatic parasite, voiceless as a fish,
> Yet containing within itself an instrument of voice
> Against the time when it *will* talk;
> Organs of skin, ear, eye, nose, tongue,
> Superfluous all of them in the watery dark
> Where formed – yet each unhaltingly preparing
> To enter a daylit, airy, object-full manifold world
> They *will* be wanted to report on. Everywhere we find
> Prospective knowledge of needs of life
> Which are not yet but are foreknown.
> All is provided. As Aristotle says,
> 'To know the end of a thing is to know the why of it.'
> So with your work, vastly outrunning present needs
> With its immense complication, its erudition,
> (The intricacy of the connections defies description.
> Before it the mind halts, abased. *In tenuis labor*.)
> But providing for the developments to come.
>
> (*Complete Poems*, pp.886-7)

This claim opens very large questions, to which I shall return in a moment. Let me first quote the last of these 'Ah, Joyce!' passages, where near the end of the poem he thinks of Joyce's death and prepares to take his leave, in a mood of gratitude and optimism. With its use of English, French, German, and Greek it brings us back to the multilingual theme, but what is most notable about it is its dramatic, excited style, which itself enacts the splendid exit of Joyce's soul from this world to the next,

seen first from our side and then by a sudden twist, rather like
that of *Alice Through the Looking-Glass*, from the other.

> Ah, Joyce! We may stand in the hush of your
>   death-chamber
> With its down-drawn blind
> But those who were on the other side
> When you passed over would find
> It (despite the general view: 'Another queer bird gone!')
> As when – no! Not the Metaphysical Buzzard!
> (*C'est un numéro! C'est marrant* – in both senses!)
> But the peacock flew in through the open window
> With its five-foot tail streaming out behind,
> A magnificent *ek-stasis*
> Counterpart of your great *Aufhebung* here,
> *Der Sinn des Schaffens* completely seen at last.
> – The supreme reality is visible to the mind *alone*.
>   (*Complete Poems*, p.888)

So as a peacock, ancient symbol of immortality, Joyce makes
his ecstatic exit from the poem, the meaning of the creative act
(*der Sinn des Schaffens*) seen finally as a flash, an epiphany, a sudden
revelation, without which all the painstaking accumulation of
detail would be in vain.

But what of evolution, what of MacDiarmid's view of the
artist as someone creating for, and in a sense truly creating, the
future? I am not sure that anyone knows, even yet, what Joyce
was doing with language, in the steps he took from *Dubliners* to
Finnegans Wake. That there is a steady evolution in his own work
is clear. But how did he see himself and his function? Did he
have a sense of function at all, or does MacDiarmid foist this
upon him because of his perhaps Scottish didacticism? In a letter
to Nora in 1909, Joyce spoke of 'those boundless ambitions which
are really the leading forces in my life' (*Letters*, II, p.256), but he
did not say what the ambitions were. In later years he usually
deflected enquiry by saying he wrote to make people laugh, or
to give them pure music, not literature, or to keep critics busy
for centuries to come. 'The green wothe botheth,' as the child
Stephen Dedalus sang, and it was 'his song', no one else's, but
how did that green rose, that Hibernian blue guitar, come into
being from the 'wild rose blossoming on the little green place'
of the 'real' song? (*A Portrait*, p.7) Is this a pointer towards artistic

creativity, or to the fact that Joyce was to become a pillar of the Berlitz, able to answer his correspondents in fluent French, German, Italian, or Triestine dialect? MacDiarmid's argument, throughout *In Memoriam James Joyce*, is that he and Joyce were both working towards world-consciousness, and that this was in fact the next general evolutionary step. Values in national cultures isolated by their individual languages were often neglected or lost or unknown, and it was the function of the artist either to engineer fruitful confrontation of cultures or deliberately to mingle them. In an epigraph to *In Memoriam James Joyce*, MacDiarmid quotes the Russian philosopher Vladimir Solovyov: 'The true unity of languages is not an Esperanto or Volapük or everyone speaking French, not a single language, but an all-embracing language, an interpenetration of all languages.' That last phrase would apply to Joyce better than to MacDiarmid, who uses collage rather than interpenetration. But it is very doubtful if Joyce reached the 'unity of languages' for the evolutionary or social or humanistic reasons Solovyov and MacDiarmid put forward. This is not to say that Joyce has no interest in the future, or that *A Portrait*, *Ulysses*, and *Finnegans Wake* are not in some sense forward-looking and even optimistic works. The welcome to life and the forging of the uncreated conscience at the end of *A Portrait*, the affirmative and lyrical 'yes' of Molly Bloom, and the strong feeling of moving out into the unknown, into something more than the expected cycle of nature, at the end of *Finnegans Wake*, are not as passive or as self-enclosing as they are sometimes made out to be. But for all that, it is hard to resist the conclusion that MacDiarmid did to some extent create the Joyce he praised. The way he did it is what draws us to take a new look at both writers.

Notes

1 Hugh MacDiarmid, *Complete Poems 1920-1976*, ed. Michael Grieve and W.R. Aitken, London, 1978.

2 I owe this information to Dr Donald Low of the University of Stirling, who showed me a letter written by MacDiarmid to Dr Low's wife, answering a query about his contacts with Joyce.

3 Hugh MacDiarmid, 'In Memoriam James Joyce: from "A Vision of World Language"', Glasgow, 1955.

4 *The Critical Writings of James Joyce*, ed. Ellsworth Mason and Richard Ellmann London, 1959), pp.173-4.

5   'A Theory of Scots Letters', *The Scottish Chapbook*, 1 (1922), pp.180–4 (p.183).
6   Hugh MacDiarmid, *At the Sign of the Thistle: A Collection of Essays*, London, 1934, p.118.
7   Richard Ellmann, *James Joyce*, New York, 1959, p.713.
8   Hugh MacDiarmid, *At the Sign of the Thistle*, pp.184–7.
9   The passage is drawn from John Buchan's novel, *A Prince of the Captivity* (1933).

James Joyce and Modern Literature, ed. W.J. McCormack and A. Stead (Routledge, 1982).

MacDiarmid's later poetry against an International Background

In an anthology of American poetry, *The American Long Poem*, which appeared in 1977, the editor, Stephen Fender, addresses himself particularly to the point that many American poets – and he's thinking especially of Ezra Pound and William Carlos Williams – have incorporated large amounts of non-poetic material into their verse, that's to say, prose taken from books, magazines, newspapers, letters, indeed any documentary source that the poet wants to use. It was Fender's discussion of puzzled reactions to such incorporated material, and the solution he offers to the problem, that started me thinking again about Hugh MacDiarmid in the same connection. In his selection from Pound's *Cantos*, Fender deliberately includes unpopular, non-lyrical cantos dealing with American history, with Jefferson and Van Buren and the politics and economics of the eighteenth and nineteenth centuries (Cantos 31 and 37); he does this partly as a challenge to the reader, partly because they are important and little-read, and they're little-read because they incorporate many passages of prose taken from histories, biographies, autobiographies, letters and documents of the period, extracted, slightly altered, and printed as verse by Pound. What Fender does is to reprint, on the facing page, all the relevant original documents, because he believes that without that we are not getting what Pound wanted. What he argues is that the original documents are in a real sense a part of the poem. As he says:

> Pound exploits his sources so profoundly that they cease to be 'sources' and become part of the poem. I do not mean this in any figurative sense. I mean that the poems as we have known them up to now are fragments only, conveying merely the vaguest impression of, say, men of many interests busy making a country, and that the complete poems emerge only

when the historical documents are also seen. Thus, to find the relevant passages in these documents is actually to experience a metaphor, where the 'thing' is the poem on the page and the 'thing compared' is the document.

(p.92)

The idea of a text outside the text, a sort of dark doppelgänger which haunts the text and should be seen to haunt it, might seem to be something special to Ezra Pound, but the more we look at the whole business of collage in twentieth-century writing the more pervasive it appears to be, and it is something which criticism has not yet properly got to grips with. It may be argued that the thing itself is not new. Shakespeare could be said to have pillaged the prose works of his contemporaries, and if there had been stringencies of copyright in the modern sense he might have had some trouble with North's Plutarch and might not have been able to retire to Stratford so early. But there is some difference between Shakespeare's straightforward use of narrative material or sketches of historical character, and on the other hand the modern writer's multiplex, far-ranging, and often ironical juxtaposition of original and non-original matter. In the modern writer, it is often difficult to know whether the context that he uses or quotes from is itself important: in Eliot's *The Waste Land*, for instance, some of the quoted contexts are highly significant, some are of no significance whatsoever, and many are in an uncertain area in between. Another problem peculiar to our time is that whereas in past centuries a poet might have a wide spread of allusions, sometimes involving quotation, as in Milton and Spenser, the allusions being mostly a part of the general cultural baggage an educated reader might be expected to carry, so that if he did not have it it was not something he would boast about or be indifferent to, in modern writers the allusions and quotations will usually and deliberately *not* be an expected part of general culture; often they will be deliberately informational rather than cultural, with the aim of winkling the reader out of an accepted tradition, mainly the classical/biblical/romantic, and forcing him to take stock of another tradition (either existing or potential), or of the idea of the healthy absence of any tradition. If you are ignorant about banks and credit and economic history, Pound wants you to consider these things and to believe that poetry is right to deal with them; if you have not read the Bhagavadgita and the Upanishads, Eliot wants you to read them and to believe that all wisdom does not come from Jerusalem, Athens, and Rome; if you have not thought about the relation between mythology and real life, William Carlos Williams tries to get you to do so by embedding in his long poem *Paterson* actual letters he has received from Allen Ginsberg and from a woman referred to by the initial C., and by giving these letters contexts which are not merely autobiographical, or even autobiographical at all.

In all this, the reader is being asked to adjust to what may seem to be a strange approach to poetry, or to something which may not look like poetry. There are problems. There may be irritation, rejection. What is perhaps surprising therefore is the number of writers, well-known writers, in both verse and prose, who have taken the risk of using non-original material, either overtly or without acknowledgement. Apart from Pound, Eliot, and Williams whom I have mentioned, and the extreme case of William Burroughs who makes collage the central technique of his style, writers who make particularly interesting use of non-original material would include David Jones, Robert Lowell, and the German poet Hans Magnus Enzensberger. David Jones, like Ezra Pound, is a writer whom MacDiarmid has expressed admiration for, and he is possibly the one who comes closest to MacDiarmid in technique, though not in his view of life. In his two long poems (or prose-poems), *In Parenthesis* (1937) and *The Anathemata* (1952; subtitled 'fragments of an attempted writing'), he deals with what might seem the very traditional subject of British history, but it is slewed round, with a strong emphasis, towards its Roman and Welsh Celtic elements, so that in the end it has the disturbing effect, not unlike the effects of Eliot and Pound, of presenting us with a new tradition; and this new tradition ('new', he would say, only because forgotten and unfamiliar) is explained (if that is the word) or perhaps expounded through a highly elaborate network of quotation and allusion and by the provision of notes by the author. But that is not all. Jones (like MacDiarmid) loves detail, loves to get it all in, and he draws on many specialisms for the precise informational details of things and actions. In his preface to *The Anathemata*, after acknowledging many books he has drawn from, he has this passage (and it might almost come from *Lucky Poet*):

> There are, however, many others to whom I may be as, or more, indebted. Who should say how much may be owing to

a small textbook on botany; a manual of seamanship; various items in the magazine *Wales* edited by Mr Keidrych Rhys; a guide to the Isle of Wight; a child's picture-book of prehistoric fauna; a guide-book to the parish church of Cilcain, Flintshire, by a local antiquary, 1912; a glossy 1949 bookstall purchase on the pontifex Isambard Kingdom Brunel; a brochure on the composition and permanence of colours; a pamphlet on the prevention of collisions at sea; a paper read before a London conference of psychologists; the text of a guide to a collection of Welsh samplers and embroideries; a catalogue of English china or plate; a neglected directive from Rome on the use of the Chant; a reference in *The Times* to the cry of a bittern in Norfolk, or to the bloom on a thorn-bush in Herefordshire, or to an Homeric find on Karatepe ridge?   (p.38)

– So you have here a catalogue which mentions catalogues: an endless recession of detail, an accumulation of things apparently unrelated, but perhaps to be, somehow, related. The link with MacDiarmid is that the things accumulated are not primarily cultural, they are part of the general informational background of the time, with a leaning towards the technical and the scientific. And to Jones it matters that they should become a part of the reader's knowledge as well as (hopefully) his pleasure. As he says in his preface to the earlier book *In Parenthesis*: 'I would ask the reader to consult the notes with the text, as I regard some of them as integral to it.' (p.xiv) To Jones, as to MacDiarmid, there was a strong sense of the informational bombardment of the twentieth century, and the feeling that somehow someone should be attempting to bring some of this material into poetry, whether on the back of existing myth or not. Jones saw the shift from culture to information as a great difficulty for poets, and he confessed that he didn't really know how to deal with it, but he felt that it was a problem not to be swept under the carpet. As he wrote in the preface to *In Parenthesis*:

> We stroke cats, pluck flowers, tie ribands, assist at the manual acts of religion, make some kind of love, write poems, paint pictures, are generally at one with that creaturely world inherited from our remote beginnings... Yet we must do gas-drill, be attuned to many newfangled devices; some fascinating and compelling, others sinister in the extreme; all requiring a new and strange direction of the mind, a new sensitivity certainly, but at a considerable cost.' (p.xiv)

This 'new direction of the mind' that David Jones speaks of seems to demand a less ordered, less assured, less prescriptive view of history, including the history of one's own time. It seems positively to want juxtaposition, collage, montage, spatial rather than linear effects. It views, or tends to view the work of art as almost infinitely expansile, because there is so much, from life as well as from art, that the writer wants to include in it. *The Anathemata* is an unfinished poem, as are *The Cantos*, and *Paterson*, and the long poems of MacDiarmid. – And, one might add, many of the poems of Robert Lowell, especially the long sequences *Notebook* and *History*, ceaselessly altered, added to, rearranged, and cannibalized by the author under the pressure of the history of his times and of himself. Lowell had the reputation when he died of being a very distinctive American poet, a very distinctive and original voice, and yet it is a curious fact that that voice was many voices, that Lowell was a determined and highly experimental user of other people's works, to a degree that is beginning to be known now to critics but is probably not suspected by the wider public, except where Lowell has himself called attention to some borrowing. He confesses much, but conceals more. In *Notebook* (1969) he has an 'Afterthought' at the end, where he comments on his many borrowings:

> I have taken from many books, used the throwaway conversational inspirations of my friends, and much more that I idly spoke to myself. I have no wish to sleuth down my plagiarisms, but want to say that 'Hell' is taken from two paragraphs of Glenn Gray's 'The Warrior'; ideas and expressions in 'Half a Century Gone' come from Simone Weill; ideas and expressions in 'Obit' and another poem, from Herbert Marcuse. Two poems steal distortedly from the Urdu poet Ghalib... The intelligent and not the stupid quote belongs to R.P. Blackmur in the poem dedicated to him. The borrowings from Plutarch [still going strong! – E.M.], Sir Thomas More's son-in-law, Emerson, Coleridge, Goethe, Sir Kenneth Clark and Stonewall Jackson are easier to spot... I had good guides when I began. They have gone on with me; by now the echoes are so innumerable that I almost lack the fineness of ear to distinguish them.

This is an extraordinary confession of what he himself calls his 'plagiarisms'. And yet there is much, in all his volumes, that he does not mention. Perhaps the most striking example is in the splendid 'The Quaker Graveyard in Nantucket' from his early book *Lord Weary's Castle* (1946): in the prefatory note to that volume he refers to some borrowings, but not to the most remarkable one: as critics have pointed out, the very strong opening section of 'The Quaker Graveyard', describing the drowned sailor, is modelled closely on the opening chapter of Henry Thoreau's book *Cape Cod*, which describes a shipwreck; many of the famous phrases – 'the sea was still breaking violently', 'matted head and marble feet', 'lustreless deadlights' – are taken directly from Thoreau. Here, a good piece of prose is transformed into an even better piece of poetry. Why then does Lowell not acknowledge it? Can it have been accidental? Hardly likely. If he does not acknowledge it, this must mean that the collage 'metaphor' between the two texts is not important to him, yet to anyone who thinks about it it could easily seem to add a dimension to the poem to place Lowell's Nantucket against Thoreau's Nantucket of a century before. This is a puzzle, and there doesn't seem any answer to it.

No such puzzle attaches to the poetic sequence by Hans Magnus Enzensberger called *Mausoleum*, published in an English translation by Joachim Neugroschel in 1976. This is a sequence of poems about famous persons who in one way or another have helped to mould the modern European and worldwide consciousness – it includes for example Machiavelli, Newton, Gutenberg, Leibniz, Campanella, Darwin, Lenin, Goya, Chopin, Babbage, Semmelweis, and Bakunin. Each poem is printed as a very clear collage of original poetry and documented writings or utterances of the great man in question, the latter being in italic and the former in roman type. Sometimes the effects are reinforcing, sometimes highly ironic or critical. Enzensberger is using the collage device as a concentrated, clever, hard–hitting method of bringing together a range of social and scientific comment.

Collage, then, seems to have established itself; it continues, and it continues to be revealed. One of the strangest recent revelations, in Deirdre Blair's biography of Samuel Beckett, is that Beckett included in his plays and novels paragraphs copied from his own private letters to his friend Thomas McGreevy. Thrift, thrift, Horatio!

What I have sketched in is a background, one of the many backgrounds against which Hugh MacDiarmid may be set if we want to build up a whole picture of his work. It applies especially to the period from the late 1920s to the early 1940s, although in MacDiarmid's own case we must remember that his collage was well established in *Annals of the Five Senses* in 1923, and his later work is in that sense a return to his own beginnings. What we know about the long poems of his late work is that they subsist very pervasively on quotations, mostly from prose, and largely informational rather than cultural prose. Books, journals, reviews, letters, newspapers, speeches, advertisements are all used; some sources are indicated, many are not; and as with T.S. Eliot, some of the source contexts are highly relevant, some are mere faceless ragbags of ransacked information, and some are hard to decide. If there is any key to this activity – the poet sitting surrounded by a rising sea of thousands and thousands of cuttings and notes and journals – it is perhaps best seen in something he wrote in *Annals of the Five Senses*, in the last prose section, 'Limelight from a Solitary Wing':

> So his tendency was always to the whole, to the totality, to the general balance of things. Indeed it was his chiefest diffi-culty (and an ever-increasing one that made him fear at times cancellation to nonentity) to exclude, to condemn, to say No ...He was always fighting for the absent, eager for forlorn hopes, a champion of the defeated cause, for those portions of truth which seemed to him neglected...' (p.194)

The portions of truth which seemed neglected were of course what he had found, in the writings of others, and much of his later work would come into the technical category of 'found poetry' as we now employ that term. Very little of it, however, is found poetry in the strictest sense – the sense in which William Carlos Williams would embed a transcribed letter into *Paterson* – and perhaps the term 'treated text' which is now used would be nearer the mark, i.e. almost always when material is taken over, and this of course applies in the main to prose, it is altered, 'treated', both through line-division and through little omissions and additions, and sometimes through rearrangement of compo-nent parts, and even though these alterations may be slight, they are thought-out and often quite subtle, as Kenneth Buthlay rightly pointed out in his comments on the Karl Kraus passage in *In Memoriam James Joyce*. (And following up another suggestion by Kenneth Buthlay, one would argue that when MacDiarmid makes up his poem 'Reflections in a Slum' out of entries in André

Gide's *Journal* for 3–4 August 1935, the fact that he displaces the order in which Gide's material is presented would repay study.) An indignant correspondent wrote to the *Times Literary Supplement* in 1965 complaining that the Kraus passage had been lifted from an anonymous review in that journal, and he took it for granted that there was no possible defence of this – unaware, obviously, that Buthlay had given a careful defence of it a year before, in his book on MacDiarmid, pointing out that anyone going from MacDiarmid to the original article would see that the article was written by someone with a fine feeling for rhythm, but that 'the point is that MacDiarmid saw it first, and brought out the rhythmical pattern of some parts of the prose by cutting them into verse-lines'. And also: 'Anyone who looks closely at the little changes, including word-substitutions, that have been made in the original, will recognize that the hand of the poet has not lost its old cunning.' (*Hugh MacDiarmid*, 1964, p.106)

So what we have is not so much found poetry as a series of treated texts. And I believe that where we can make the comparison between the original and MacDiarmid's transformation of it, the changes are nearly always meaningful and I would say 'careful' except that the lucky poet can be careless and still produce through a quick insight the right new effect. (The best example of that is the series of little changes by which prose from a short story by Glyn Jones became the short poem 'Perfect'.) But what we still also want to know, when we can, is what lies behind the collage, what metaphor, to use Stephen Fender's term, is being created between the two texts. I would like to look at a couple of examples, one from *In Memoriam James Joyce* and one from *The Kind of Poetry I Want*, to see what light we can throw on this.

In the last section of *In Memoriam James Joyce*, 'Plaited like the Generations of Men, there is a fine passage describing the human embryo and how it already has, in the womb, in minute form, the organs it will someday need to use, though at the moment they are useless to it. The passage is an analogy, beginning with 'even as', and it is meant to put MacDiarmid's case for an avant-garde in art. 'Even as' the human embryo, far too complex for its present dim life in the womb, is preparing for a future existence it cannot yet imagine, so Joyce in prose, Schönberg in music, MacDiarmid in poetry are preparing through the complex nature of their art for a future time, a future audience which will naturally accept their work as if it was made for them. This is quite an important idea in MacDiarmid, and it is of some interest that for

where they *will* be wanted, they make the 'right' connections. We all drop into this mode of thought; we adopt it as we dissect. In the particular prodigy before us now, that of a microscopic cell becoming a man, we incline to read the whole story in that way. We say 'it grows into' a child. Grows? Levers laid down in gristle, becoming bone when wanted for the heavier pull of muscle which *will* clothe them. Lungs, solid glands, yet arranged to hollow out at a few minutes' notice when the necessary air shall enter. Limb-buds, futile at their appearing and yet deliberately appearing, in order to become limbs in readiness for an existence where they will be all-important. A pseudo-aquatic parasite, voiceless as a fish, yet constructing within itself an instrument of voice against the time when it *will* talk. Organs of skin, ear, eye, nose, tongue, superfluous all of them in the watery dark where formed, yet each unhaltingly preparing to enter a daylit, airy, object-full world which they *will* be wanted to report on. A great excrescence at one end of a nerve-tube, an outrageously outsized brain, of no avail at the moment but where the learning of a world which is *to be* experienced will go forward. Living structure is a mass of Aristotle's final causes. All is remembered; no detail is forgotten, even to the criss-cross hairs at entrance to a cat's ear which keep out water and flies. Had antiquity or the Middle Ages been acquainted with the facts, they would have been set down to Natural Magic. Fernel's Preface (1542) wrote 'as Aristotle says to know the end of a thing is to know the why of it'.

(Pelican ed., pp.106-7)

In the second, very brief passage used by MacDiarmid, Sherrington is quoting from the Spanish neurologist, Cajal, who made a special study of the nerve-structures between an insect's eye and its brain, and wrote:

> The intricacy of the connexions defies description. Before it the mind halts, abased. *In tenuis labor.*   (p.117)

When we reach the last (Latin) words, we have a multiple recession: MacDiarmid quoting Sherrington who is quoting Cajal who is (mis)quoting Virgil's *In tenui labor* in the Fourth Georgic – 'the subject (of bees) may be small (but has great effect)' *In tenui labor* indeed! So the quotation from Sherrington is well used;

but we can trace a wider meaningfulness in MacDiarmid's going to Sherrington in the first place. This book, *Man on His Nature*, was originally the text of the Gifford Lectures on Natural Theology at the University of Edinburgh in 1937-38. 'Natural theology' is perhaps as good a description as any for MacDiarmid's own area of belief, but I would want rather to make the point that Sherrington had a mind which was highly speculative and imaginative as well as being the mind of a man trained in scientific method; his writing is attractive, and he had the ability to make technical matters clear; he was generally cultured, and his chapters have epigraphs from poets and philosophers as well as from scientists – and the quotations are not trite but often unexpected and showing an unusually wide and impressive range of reading. His book, in fact, sets its scientific description of man within a context of man's history and man's potential which is fully aware of, but does not accept, the so-called science/art dichotomy. And in this connection, if I may return to the triple perspective of quotation in the phrase *In tenui labor*: this is a triple reinforcement, in an extremely unexpected way, of MacDiarmid's desire to bring art and science together. Sherrington's part in this I have mentioned; the Spanish neurologist, Cajal, whom Sherrington quotes, was a Nobel Prize-winning scientist who nevertheless wrote in his *Recollections of My Life* (1937): 'The garden of neurology holds out to the investigator captivating spectacles and incomparable artistic emotions. In it my aesthetic instincts found full satisfaction at last' (p.363). And finally, when Cajal quotes from Virgil's Fourth Georgic, which describes the life of bees, he is quoting from a poet who is writing as a scientist, and finding wonder in the truth of things. So the collage method, if we follow it up by looking at quoted contexts, can certainly reveal more of the inner life of the poem than we might suspect from a surface reading.

The other passage I want to refer to is on pages 36-37 of *The Kind of Poetry I Want*, a shorter passage but interesting because of its provenance. It is one of the many analogies, here putting the case for a poetry of exact and powerful description, with full attention to detail, instead of a poetry of broad general diffused impressions:

> In photographic language, 'wide-angled' poems
> Taking in the whole which explains the part,
> Scientifically accurate, fully realized in all their details,

As Prudentius's picture of the gradually deputrefying
   Lazarus,
Or Baudelaire's of the naked mulatto woman,
Or Pope's most accurate particularities
In the Epistle to Lord Bathurst...

This passage, apart from the first two lines, is taken from Aldous
Huxley's book *Texts and Pretexts* (1932, pp.212-15), and indeed
the context here is really needed to see precisely what MacDiarmid has in mind. Huxley's book is itself put together on a collage
principle, being a very personal anthology of poetic extracts
linked by a commentary. The present passage comes from a chapter called 'Descriptions', and what MacDiarmid has done is to
omit the quoted poetry and take over a part of the commentary,
hoping no doubt that the mere reference to Prudentius, Baudelaire, and Pope will economically make his point. But the original
Huxley context not only fills out the theme but also adds something which we might not suspect from the MacDiarmid passage
itself. The lines from Prudentius, the fourth-century Latin Christian poet, give a detailed physical description of the raising of
Lazarus from the dead, the 'deputrefying' process involving the
return of colour to the cheeks, the eyes becoming clear again
instead of dripping with pus, the stink of the body being transformed into a sweet exhalation, the dried limbs being suffused
again with the vital liquids – the description oddly enough being
about as horrific as a description of the original putrefying would
have been. The Baudelaire poem ('La très-chère était nue...')
describes the naked body of his mulatto mistress, Jeanne Duval,
laid out before him in the firelight in a stupefyingly inviting
position which arouses the speaker's desire and admiration,
aesthetic as they are, to the very edge of disgust. And the Pope
quotation begins:

In the worst inn's worst room, with mat half hung,
The floor of plaster and the walls of dung,
On once a flock-bed, but repaired with straw,
With tape-tied curtains, never meant to draw,
The George and Garter dangling from that bed,
Where tawdry yellow strove with dirty red,
Great Villiers lies – alas, how changed from him,
That life of pleasure, and that soul of whim!...

Huxley goes on to comment on these lines: 'I remember, the first time I read Pope's lines, being profoundly impressed by those walls of dung. Indeed, they still disturb my imagination. They express, for me, the Essential Horror. A floor of dung would have seemed almost normal, acceptable. But *walls* – Ah, no, no!' Well, we know from *A Drunk Man Looks at the Thistle* as well as from the early lyrics that MacDiarmid likes things with a scunner in them. The fact that he has chosen these three references, and one of the later ones in Huxley's chapter which are taken from pleasant and charming love-poems, seems almost to add the significance that you prove a case at its hardest point: if you can stomach Prudentius, Baudelaire, and Pope, you really do believe that immediate detailed description is good. And again, as with Sherrington, if you consider the whole of what Huxley is doing in this book, you learn something else and you can see why MacDiarmid was attracted in the first instance. In his introduction, Huxley gives his collagist's apologia:

> So I must content myself with picking up these broken and half-forgotten fragments from the past and fitting them, one here, another there, into their appropriate places in the jumbled mosaic of contemporary experience... There is too much raw material, of too many kinds; and some of the kinds (as, for example, the experience of the urban industrial or clerical worker) seem almost too hopelessly mechanical ever to be given style. And yet it is only by poets that the life of any period can be synthesized. Encyclopaedias and guides to knowledge cannot do it, for the good reason that they affect only the intellectual surface of a man's life. The lower layers, the core of his being, they leave untouched.   (p.4)

The relevance to MacDiarmid of what Huxley says is I think very clear. And when we remember that Huxley, like MacDiarmid and Sherrington, was a man who frequently moved across the two worlds of art and science, and believed that it was important to do so, we can perhaps begin to sense that MacDiarmid's later work is less isolated and less quixotic in its aims than is sometimes supposed. It is not only that the collage technique, as we have seen, was widely employed by other writers, but that the basic underlying art/science collage, a collage in idea rather than in technique, finds many echoes in the period from the late 1920s to the early 1940s. Alexis Carrel's book *Man, the Unknown*

(1935) was a much-discussed study by a biologist, like Sherrington, which attempted to give a full picture of man as seen by the science of the 1930s but including a recurring, emphasized sense of man's extension in time and evolution and covering aesthetic and philosophic aspects. In a passage dealing with beauty, Carrel has no doubts – and this is characteristic of the period – that whatever beauty is it is not a prerogative of the world of art. As he writes:

> It animates the bloody art of the surgeons, as well as that of the painters, the musicians, and the poets. It is present also in the calculations of Galileo, in the visions of Dante, in the experiments of Pasteur, in the rising of the sun on the ocean, in the winter storms on the high mountains. It becomes still more poignant in the immensity of the sidereal and atomic worlds, in the prodigious harmony of the brain cells...
>
> (pp.130-1)

Another writer, now largely forgotten but widely read in his time, was Martin Johnson who published with Faber a series of books on themes interlinking science and the arts: *Art and Scientific Thought* (1944), *Time, Knowledge and the Nebulae* (1945), and *Science and the Meanings of Truth* (1946). In his preface to the first of these books Johnson described his main theme as 'the relatedness between scientific and imaginative mentality'. He writes as a mathematician and physicist, but his book has an interesting and surprising foreword by Walter de la Mare. And to these names we might add that of J.W. Dunne, whose explorations of the idea of time exerted a strong imaginative fascination, and that of Olaf Stapledon in science-fiction, and especially his book *Last and First Men* (1930), where questions of science and art are brooded over into the distant future. But the writer who for all his obvious differences seems closest to MacDiarmid's interests and methods is the American Charles Fort (1872-1932), whom he refers to in *Lucky Poet* as a kindred spirit. As he writes there:

> I have acquired and have at command an enormous amount of out-of-the-way knowledge – though I cannot claim yet in this respect to be like Charles Fort of New York, of whom Orage used to tell me, who had accumulated a tremendous library of cuttings, &c., recording happenings all over the world traversing accepted scientific laws of all kinds or com-

pletely setting at naught the most generally accepted ideas on the subjects in question.   (pp.267–7)

Whether MacDiarmid had read Fort or not I am not sure, but he has certainly described him accurately in that quotation. Fort's four books, *The Book of the Damned, New Lands, Lo!* and *Wild Talents*, which were published together in a mammoth volume in 1941, are like a vast MacDiarmidesque notebook in prose, prose with flashes of poetry, science with flashes of art, fact with flashes of speculation and wonder. Here is the opening of Chapter 16 of *Wild Talents* (1932), where he takes up the theme of data and the collecting of them, and of how data do and do not allow themselves to be organized:

But why this everlasting attempt to solve something? – whereas it is our acceptance that, in a final sense, there is, in phenomenal affairs, nothing – or that there is only the state of something-nothing – so that all problems are only soluble–insoluble – or that most of the social problems we have, today, were at one time conceived of as solutions of preceding problems – or that every Moses leads his people out of Egypt into perhaps a damn sight worse – Promised Lands of watered milk and much-adulterated honey – so why these everlasting attempts to solve something?

But to take surgical operations upon warders of Sing Sing prison, and the loss of rectitude by lace curtains, and the vanishing man of Berlin; 'Typhoid Mary', and a Chinese hair-clipper, and explosions of coal, and bodies on benches in a Harlem Park –

Robert Browning's conception was to take three sounds, and make, not a fourth, but a star.

Out of seven colors, not to lay on daubs, but to paint a picture.

Out of seven million Americans, Russians, Germans, Irishmen, Italians, and on, so long as geography holds out, not to pile a population, but to organize – more or less – into New York City.

Sulphur and lava in a barren plain, and a salty block of stone, shaped roughly like a woman – signs of erosion on rocks far above water-level – a meteor that had set a bush afire – the differences of languages of peoples – and all the other elements that organized into *Genesis*.

Data of variations and heredity and adaptations; of multiplications and of checks and of the doctrine of Malthus; of acquired characters and of transmissions – and they organized into *The Origin of Species* –

Just as, once upon a time, minerals that had affinity for one another came together and took on geometrical appearances.

But a crystal is not supposed to be either a prohibition or an anti-prohibition argument. I know of a crystal of quartz that weighs several hundred pounds. But it has not been mistaken for propaganda.

There is a convenient myth which we all fall into and use, but it is a myth, that the 1930s were above all a political and socioeconomic decade. It is true that superficially politics and economics pressed hard on people's concerns. But in terms of the life of the mind, in terms of intense intellectual ferment and speculation, it was a decade when other things were more central: in particular, biology and time, the link between these being probably the idea of evolution, though there was also much interest in dreams and precognition. There was a new attempt to see man in the round, in a cosmic rather than a social setting. There was a sharp sense of the multifariousness of data, and a feeling that if any key was to be found to the ordering of the data it would have to be aesthetic and philosophical as well as scientific. Advances in microscope and telescope techniques were pushing the microcosm and the macrocosm further and further apart, so that Sir James Jeans was able to call his famous astronomy book of 1930 *The Mysterious Universe* and mean it, despite its being in no sense obscurantist. The books of Jeans and Eddington, of Sherrington and Huxley; the encyclopedic compilations of Charles Fort; the many popular encyclopedias which began to appear at that time in weekly parts, with their extraordinary juxtapositions of subjects and illustrations; the remarkable anthologies of Walter de la Mare, unjustly forgotten like so much from that period, subtle creative scrapbooks of prose and verse on a huge range of material, aesthetic and scientific – these are the background of MacDiarmid's later verse and his collage technique, quite as much as his reading of poetry by Pound or Eliot or David Jones. What he actually read, and what he actually used, from all this background, will take some sorting out for many years to come. In this paper I wanted merely to indicate some of the threads that link him to that time, and to suggest that both his technical and his philosophical concerns were shared by others, in ways that may help us to consider them more seriously if we are somewhat predisposed against them, as it is easy to be. There is little danger, in doing this, that we shall knock the bottom out of his mystery. As he himself remarked long ago, in *Annals of the Five Senses*: 'The sources of certain of my quotations I unfortunately cannot now trace.'

Scottish Literary Journal, vol.5, no.2, December 1978.

MacDiarmid at Seventy-five

The great temptation, in talking about Hugh MacDiarmid's poetry, is to try to sum up its quality by picking out the best pieces and rejecting the rest fairly firmly. At its most extreme, this method produces the view of some, that MacDiarmid has only six good poems, all very short and all written before 1926. No one wants to say that the best of the early lyrics are not among the best things he's ever done; but it isn't necessary to depress the early poems in order to stake out claims for the later work. What is troublesome and difficult is to show the relation of both earlier and later work to any enduring or overriding conception of what poetry is. The poems in *Sangschaw* and *Penny Wheep* are concentrated and laconic, they use regular metrical forms, they are clearcut completed objects, and they have a great originality – partly of viewpoint and perspective but also simply of verbal juxtaposition. The late poems like *In Memoriam James Joyce* and *The Kind of Poetry I Want* are long and discursive, they're in free verse, they're not complete but only the top parts of a still larger, submerged, unpublished poem, and although they're original in their total appearance they're made up to a great extent as a patch-work of facts and quotations. It's maybe not surprising that he himself has spoken of this change as a 'violent break', a 'crisis', a 'new departure'. Yet something continues and remains, from the first work to the last, and the present occasion seems a good one to throw a few pointers towards defining what it is.

It's worth remembering that his first book is not *Sangschaw* but *Annals of the Five Senses* which came out in 1923. This strange collection of prose and verse is both hard to read and hard to describe, but what one can say about it is that a good deal of the later MacDiarmid is already there in essence – so much so, in fact, that one might think it was *Sangschaw* which provided the interruption, rather than the later work which drove him off the rails. This is a book of – what? Autobiographical sketches in the third person? Studies in morbid psychology? Experiments in a convoluted prose style? Reflections on the recent war, on sex, on God, on clothes, on eternity and destiny? It's all these and more, it has the omnivorous and encyclopedic quality of the later MacDiarmid, the same lack of concern for the reader's comfort, the same interweaving of quotations and references – Swinburne and Chesterton, Donne and Hopkins, Conrad and Galsworthy, Bacon and Edward Carpenter, Browning and Wordsworth, Henry James and William James, the Bible and the *Saturday Westminster Gazette*: all is swept in, all is ransacked, indiscriminately, as a habit of mind already. He calls it a book of 'mosaics' – a word that would apply later to *A Drunk Man Looks at the Thistle* and *The Kind of Poetry I Want* – and he uses in his introduction two similes to indicate his line of defence in such a literary method or anti-method:

> As fish are seen through an aquarium so these perhaps strange fish of mine are discernible almost entirely through a 'strong solution of books' – and not only of books but of magazines and newspaper articles and even of speeches. What I have done is similar to what is done when a green light on a railway replaces a red light, or *vice versa*, in a given lamp.

Annals of the Five Senses is a pretty indigestible book taken as a whole, but it has some remarkable passages, and it establishes at once some of his leading characteristics: his simultaneous fondness for grand themes and catalogues of minute particulars, his uncritical amassing of material from every source, his belief that the evolution of life does not and cannot stop at social betterment. There is something engaging about this super-Autolycus, this lover of loose ends, but he's not so magpie-minded, even in this early book, as to be unaware of the difficulties such a person faced if he wanted to commit himself to a cause. He describes how he 'used to plunge into the full current of the most inconsistent movements, seeking – always in vain, until he was utterly exhausted, not having failed, however, to enrich every one of them – to find ground upon which he might stand foursquare'. When he came later to write his 'Second Hymn to Lenin', part of his friendly argument with Lenin centres on just this point, that the politician can be ruthlessly singleminded, but the poet can't:

> For a poet maun see in a' thing,
> Ev'n what looks trumpery or horrid,

A subject equal to ony
– A star for the forehead!

. . . . . .

He daurna turn awa' frae ocht
For a single act o' neglect
And straucht he may fa' frae grace
And be void o' effect.

Why, one may ask, should the poet 'fall from grace' if he neglects what looks like a 'trumpery or horrid' subject? The answer to this would seem a superstition to a Marxist critic but it is deeply true to MacDiarmid's nature. In *Annals of the Five Senses* he defends his all-inclusiveness by saying that he recognizes 'in that prodigiousness of the universe a safeguarding excellence, since it must hold infinite resources and he might allow it some credit without accusing himself of improvidence.'

To regard the prodigiousness of the universe as being excellent is merely a Shakespearian view, but to add that this is a *safeguarding* excellence is much more striking and provocative. What, after all, is being safeguarded? Multiplicity is being safeguarded from classification, mystery is being safeguarded from reason, vision is being safeguarded from theory. Can we add that nature is being safeguarded from art? It's certainly being protected from any art that goes too quickly for design and order without having accepted the aleatory discipline. MacDiarmid's view could lead to a completely aleatory conception of art, and this is in fact borne out by the interchangeability of large parts of his later poetry, by mosaic or anti-organicist methods of composition as in *A Drunk Man Looks at the Thistle*, by the widespread use of long, direct, and often unacknowledged quotation which although it is an act of choice on the poet's part increases the element of chance in the total product. All this is no doubt largely untheorized and undeliberate on the part of MacDiarmid, who hardly sees himself as a forerunner of Burroughs and McLuhan. But what he has done, all through his life, is to insist on the importance of the multiplex, as against simplistic solutions, and this involves paying tribute to chance. His fondness for dictionaries and word-lists, for instance, shows this. There are quite a number of passages in his poetry which are bristling with uncommon words beginning with the same letter or with letters from the same part of the alphabet, and it's clear that these passages make use of lists of words which have been collected by the poet for their richness and curiosity value. Many of the words will have no apparent semantic connection with the theme that's being dealt with, but they're given relevance by the ingenious way they're worked in – often by a brilliantly unexpected use of metaphor. So a purely chance connection of rare words is transformed into an apparently and of course temporarily ordered and meaningful connection. There's a passage in 'Cornish Heroic Song for Valda Trevlyn' where in the space of fourteen lines we get the words *resipiscence, reptant, raphe,* (un)-*rabbetable, réseau, retitelarian, rempli,* and *rhabdite*; and the last few lines of 'On a Raised Beach' give us *ébrillade, enchorial, encrinite, entrochal,* and *epanadiplosis.* All these words are, by virtuosity, built into their respective contexts.

It's this longing for fullness, this fear that values may escape by being buried in dictionaries, which to a large extent lay behind his attempt to develop Scots. The national, patriotic aim was secondary to his discovery of the sheer expressive richness of the Scottish language, with its surprisingly large vocabulary of words that unfortunately were often obsolete or obsolescent. As he wrote in *The Scottish Chapbook* in 1923:

> The Scots Vernacular is a vast storehouse of just the very peculiar and subtle effects which modern European literature in general is assiduously seeking...It is an inchoate Marcel Proust – a Dostoevskian débris of ideas – an inexhaustible quarry of subtle and significant sound.

These are high terms for something that in practice wasn't so easy to carry out. The storehouse of effects and the quarry of sound are admirably rifled in his onomatopoeic tribute to James Joyce, 'Water Music', or in the strong, swinging, shaggy stanzas of 'Tarras'; but antiquarian enthusiasm tends to overrun a poem like 'Scots Unbound', with its subtitle 'Divertissement Philologique'. The possibilities and the limitations could only be found by trial and error, and it will always surely be in MacDiarmid's favour that he took these enormous risks with vocabulary, whether in English or in Scots.

These are the risks of plenitude, the heady pleasures of excess. Much of MacDiarmid's work, where this extraordinary plenitude is to be found, will never please those who want a pared-down muscular poetry, or a watertight poetry, or a non-referential poetry. But it has its own particular surprises for anyone who's eager to write it off as boring, and these surprises couldn't be sprung by any other means. The means are wasteful, but one must simply add What is wrong with that? – Consider, in the following passage from *The Kind of Poetry I Want*, how the fish seem to keep slipping off the hooks and yet there they are laid out before us at the end:

> As it was in the beginning
> So it is again at the end of life.
> Think of the decrepit old human being,
> Bent over, head bowed,
> Seated in a weary, curled-up position
> Exactly similar to the unborn babe's.
> The cycle of life begins and ends
> In the same design. Only the proportion,
> Size, and shape of the human being
> Change as he passes through the stages
> Of babyhood, youth, maturity, and old age,
> The eternal oval, the egg itself.
> A poetry therefore to approach with two instruments
> – Which, being mutually destructive,
> Like fire and water, one can use
> Only one at a time
> – Even as one may attempt to describe
> The relative positions of the Imperial Palace,
> Hagia Sophia, and the Circus, in Constantinople.
> On the one side the Palace was connected,
> By open arcades and paradoxical gardens,
> With the Golden Egg of Hagia Sophia;
> On the other side an intestinal system
> Of passages and winding stairs
> Led to the Circus. But as regards
> Byzantium in especial, these things are merely
> The elements which combine to form
> A stupendous life pregnant with symbolism.
> Because the theme of that life
> Was the world-embracing mystery
> Of God and man
> It stands supreme
> Above its ingredients.
> The ingredients resemble the things
> For which a woman with child longs.

> Like the juice of the oyster,
> The aroma of the wild strawberry,
> The most subtle and diversified elements
> Are here intermingled to form
> A higher organism.

Opposites are always meeting in MacDiarmid. Although he has this passion for inclusiveness and multiplicity of ingredients, he's been equally attracted by emptiness, silence, space, the alien and the inhuman, and some of his finest poetry is a confrontation of these things. This also runs all through his work, from the bare worlds like mammoths' bones in *Sangschaw*, through the powerful geological meditation of 'On a Raised Beach', and the elegies on Rilke and Charles Doughty, to the elemental rock and water of 'Direadh III' and 'The North Face of Liathach'. But what is the nature of the attraction? What draws the poet, in these poems and others, to the mountain-top, the Arabian desert, the Shetland island, the glaciers of Greenland, the craters of the moon? A man may want to go to Mars or Venus because there is the possibility of finding new forms of life there. On the other hand a man may want to go to the moon because the possibility of life can almost be ruled out. Most people I suppose would grudgingly admit that they can understand the former, but when they think about the latter they tend to encounter a blank. Yet the rock, the desert is a challenge not only to man's physical exploration and endurance but also in a curious way to his intelligence. Looking round the subhuman forms of life, we can make something of a monkey, a dog, a frog, even an oak-tree or a sunflower; but what about a stone? We think of Martin Buber staring into his cat's eyes, of Edwin Muir and his Orkney horses; but where does MacDiarmid on the raised beach get us? Like Robbe-Grillet, he is determined to emphasize the alienness, the non-humanness of so-called inanimate nature, and he's searching for its value in its very expressionlessness, its silence and incommunicability: these, he says, are to remind man of the importance of a permanent and awe-inspiring openness to experience, to time and weather and chance and change. As one line puts it: 'There are plenty of ruined buildings in the world but no ruined stones'. So our only bond with the geological earth is that it reminds us, shatteringly, how far we have gone from it, and therefore how far our remote descendants, to whom we shall be no better than stones, will one day be from us.

The figure of Doughty in the Arabian desert exerted a strong appeal for MacDiarmid. Doughty was explorer, geologist, word-collector, epic poet, man of independent mind – everything that MacDiarmid admired – but he was also a man who exposed himself to the elemental things, to the most ancient and unassimilable part of the human environment. The end of Mac-Diarmid's elegy on Doughty, *Stony Limits*, puts this with great persuasiveness:

> I know how on turning to noble hills
> And stark deserts happily still preserved
> For men whom no gregariousness fills
> With the loneliness for which they are nerved
> – The lonely at-one-ment with all worthwhile –
> I can feel as if the landscape and I
> Became each other and see my smile
> In the corners of the vastest contours lie
> And share the gladness and peace you knew,
> – The supreme human serenity that was you!
>
> I have seen Silence lift his head
> And Song, like his double, lift yours,
> And know, while nearly all that seems living is dead,
> You were always consubstantial with all that endures.
> Would it were on Earth! Not since Ezekiel has that far
>   sun ringed
> A worthier head; raw as Adam you stood
> In the desert, the horizon with vultures black-winged,
> And sang and died in this still greater solitude
> Where I sit by your skull whose emptiness is worth
> The sum of almost all the heads now on Earth
> – By your roomy skull where most men might well spend
> Longer than you did in Arabia, friend!

Between the poems of emptiness on the one hand, and the poems of plenitude on the other, there's an enormous gap of ordinary human experience which MacDiarmid's poetry scarcely represents at all. Hardly ever, in any poem, do you get a sense of a man who is committed emotionally to something other than ideas, words, or landscapes. The beautiful and terrible bonds that are not geological but between individual persons, bonds of love or friendship, of desire, misery, doubt, or forgiveness – these are strikingly absent. This is the greatest lack in MacDiarmid's poetry – though he would hardly agree. He must be the most unexistential poet ever to have written. The deficiency would cripple any writer who had less to fall back on, in himself and in books, than MacDiarmid has always had. I said he wouldn't agree with me, because this deficiency goes hand in hand with a polemic. He would regard it as an essential part of his historical mission as a Scottish poet to undo the over-reliance on human feelings and human situations in Burns and his Victorian successors. As he remarks disgustedly in the Foreword to *The Kind of Poetry I Want*: 'Almost all modern Scottish poetry gives off a great sense of warmth and offering, like a dog when it loves you.' Well, this is fair enough in the sense that we don't want a wet poetry. But a poetry of human feeling is not necessarily wet, and one would suspect that an inadequacy as well as a polemic lay behind this rejection of warmth.

The compensations however are extraordinary enough: a poetry which gives itself the liberty to turn without notice from Sacco and Vanzetti to God's Recording Angel, or to use the reproductive self-eviscerations of the Guinea worm as an unforgettable analogy for poetic creation, or to attack A. E. Housman for praising an army of mercenaries (and how seldom is an angry poem successful): in other words, a poetry that has managed to bring together science, religion, politics, aesthetics, and certainly polemics, and to devise its own Pisa-like tower of simile and allusion, cemented with the loosest syntax known to Christendom, and yet to stand, as impressively in the end as any twentieth-century verse. Eccentric and often maddening genius he may be, but MacDiarmid has produced many works which, in the only test possible, go on haunting the mind and the memory and casting Coleridgean seeds of insight and surprise. He has shown once more, and against much twentieth-century doctrine, that the *anima poetae* is what matters.

Broadcast on the BBC Third Programme 10 and 11 August 1967. Reprinted in a shortened version in the *Listener*, 10 August 1967.

Edwin Muir

It is a world, perhaps; but there's another.

It is always interesting, and often valuable, to examine the work of a poet who is out of the main stream of his contemporaries' verse. Edwin Muir was little interested in the technical innovation and linguistic experiment that characterized the literature of his period, and his poetry failed to make much impact until, towards the end of his life, the fading of the 'modern movement' allowed his plainer virtues (like those also of Robert Graves) to come into some prominence. Muir himself came late to poetry, and owing to his scrappy education had many initial difficulties to surmount, some of them difficulties a younger man might have taken in his stride in the natural excitement of discovering, following, and discarding poetic models. As he says in his *Autobiography*: 'I had no training; I was too old to submit myself to contemporary influences...Though my imagination had begun to work I had no technique by which I could give expression to it.' It may be fairly said, I think, that he never did develop an entirely sure-footed technique; even his last poems are liable to be flawed by some awkward rhythm, some clumsy inversion, some flatness of vocabulary: yet by going his own way he establishes the point that what is awkward or flat is not necessarily more fatal to poetry than what is tediously admirable in accomplishment. Without wanting to praise slackness over slickness, a reader can find himself admitting that a thought-provoking piece remains a thought-provoking piece, even when its critical viability is well under proof. Muir of course has many drab, dull poems which don't come to life at all, and that is another matter. But the best of them have a quiet, persistent, winning quality which overcomes the occasional stammering of the voice.

Although in his reliance on traditional verse-forms and avoidance of startling or broken imagery Muir was out of step with his time, his search for a usable mythology links him to his con-

213

temporaries. In this very recalcitrant problem his solution is no more successful than that of Yeats, Pound, or Eliot. Instead of casting a wide net like these poets, he practised economy and restraint, relying on a narrow range of recurrent images – road and journey, labyrinth and stronghold, living and heraldic animals – and a handful of unrecondite myths in which the chief figures are Hector and Achilles, Odysseus and Penelope, Oedipus and Prometheus, Adam and Abraham. It is through such legendary and often heroic figures (supplemented now and again by such later historical characters as Knox and Calvin) and such Kafkaesque imagery (drawn frequently from his own dreams, which were at various periods of his life obsessionally powerful) that Muir projects his experience and vision of the world of time against the imagined world of eternity. But with what success?

> My childhood all a myth
> Enacted in a distant isle...

As P. H. Butter points out in his very useful introduction to Muir's work,* Muir was the last born of a fairly large family on an Orkney farm and so grew up in a seemingly solid, secure, timelessly established environment: a glowing self-sufficient world that too readily lent itself to the myth of an Eden, once its charm had been shattered by the luckless family migration to Glasgow. The idea of Eden, a Fall, and a search for reconstituted unity and harmony, is central to Muir's poetry. As an idea it is overworked, and often brought in unconvincingly, but clearly the poet was haunted all his days by the contrast between his protected Orkney boyhood and the harsh realities of industrial Glasgow he was plunged into as a youth, and a philosophy so rooted in early personal experience needs careful watching if a poet is to persuade others of its value. Muir took to myth too eagerly. His poetry would have been strengthened by a greater realism and materiality. Powerful material which he is able to make use of in his prose (e.g. his memorable description of the Fairport bone-factory in his *Autobiography*) he cannot allow into the world of his poetry. Perhaps by a natural modesty or diffidence, he seldom presents his experience directly – despite his admiration for Wordsworth – and this sometimes results in

---

* *Edwin Muir*, Writers & Critics Series, Oliver & Boyd, Edinburgh and London 1962.

muted or shadowy effects where we feel an unexpressed resonance beating vainly back from the poem towards the past instead
of outwards towards us. Professor Butter assumes, for example,
that in the early 'Ballad of Hector in Hades', which is based on
a childhood recollection of being rather frighteningly chased
home from school by another boy, the mythologizing of the
experience into the hunting of Hector by Achilles 'has enabled
him to objectify his personal experience, to universalize it and
make it into a work of art'. But I feel on the contrary that this
very Wordsworthian incident would have taught Muir more as
a poet if he had tried to say more directly and sharply what it
meant or seemed to mean to him. To translate it into the terms
of classical mythology is, in a poetic sense, too easy, even if the
resulting poem is not a bad one.

It is only fair to add that to Muir himself the 'fable' accompanied
and brooded over the 'story' at almost every moment of life: not
only, as most obviously, in Orkney, where as he tells us 'there
was no great distinction between the ordinary and the fabulous;
the lives of living men turned into legend', but later as he motored
through the desolate *paysage moralisé* of the slag-hills around Glasgow –

> dwarf-like and sinister, suggesting an immeasurably shrivelled
> and debased second-childhood... I saw young men wandering
> in groups among these toy ranges, and the sight suddenly
> recalled to me the wood-cuts in *The Pilgrim's Progress* which
> I had read as a boy; perhaps because this scene really seemed
> to be more like an allegorical landscape with abstract figures
> than a real landscape with human beings.
>
> (*Scottish Journey*)

We must grant him the reality of this feeling, and yet we can be
disappointed that he moves so quickly into the abstract, allegor-
ical landscapes. He confesses in the *Autobiography* that 'dreams
go without a hitch into the fable, and waking life does not.' This
means in practice that his poetry does not always fully 'earn' the
mythology it presents. And conversely, when Muir does want
to comment on contemporary life he may be rather at a loss,
wanting to mythologize but being too timid to euhemerize.
Muir's chief weakness, indeed, is that he came to use Good and
Evil as flags of convenience. The poem 'The Good Town', for
instance, leaves a melodramatic impression because one knows

very well what the poet is talking about but one simply doesn't accept the 'universalizing' black-and-white opposition between the Danny Kaye 'streets of friendly neighbours' where lock and key were 'quaint antiquities fit for museums' while ivy trailed 'across the prison door' and their later metamorphosis into a place where

> If you see a man
> Who smiles good-day or waves a lordly greeting
> Be sure he's a policeman or a spy.

In his *Essays on Literature and Society* Muir attacked Alexander Blok for being too responsive to historical change, but Blok could with some justice have blamed Muir for deliberately muffling his own very real responsiveness to change and for persuading himself – against all the evidence, not least the evidence of his own Christian faith – that 'Nothing can come of history but history.'

What Muir felt most deeply and expressed most movingly was the sense of aftermath – the slow passage of time after some great or terrible event, the endurance or patience or suffering of survivors, the crumbling of wasted cities: Eden after the Fall, Troy after it was sacked, Penelope remembering Odysseus and Telemachos remembering Penelope, Oedipus old and blind, Prometheus on the rock and later in his grave, Abraham the wanderer, Scotland with its long annals of 'wasted bravery idle as a song', the world after an atomic war. Muir's acute sense of time in its relation to action is seen in the fine 'Telemachos Remembers' –

> The weary loom, the weary loom,
> The task grown sick from morn to night,
> From year to year. The treadle's boom
> Made a low thunder in the room.
> The woven phantoms mazed her sight.
>
> If she had pushed it to the end,
> Followed the shuttle's cunning song
> So far she had no thought to rend
> In time the web from end to end,
> She would have worked a matchless wrong.

Instead, that jumble of heads and spears,
Forlorn scraps of her treasure trove.
I wet them with my childish tears
Not knowing she wove into her fears
Pride and fidelity and love.

– and in a larger, geological context in his remarkable poem 'The Grave of Prometheus':

Yet there you still may see a tongue of stone,
Shaped like a calloused hand where no hand should be,
Extended from the sward as if for alms,
Its palm all licked and blackened as with fire.
A mineral change made cool his fiery bed,
And made his burning body a quiet mound,
And his great face a vacant ring of daisies.

In the poem 'Troy', the aftermath of calamity is chosen, not the moment of destruction itself, and this gives a peculiar horror to the situation: an old Trojan warrior, gone mad, is living in the sewers under the city, fighting hordes of rats; he is discovered by a band of robbers and dragged to the surface; he sees the city like a graveyard

With tumbled walls for tombs, the smooth sward
    wrinkled
As Time's last wave had long since passed that way,
The sky, the sea, Mount Ida and the islands,
No sail from edge to edge, the Greeks clean gone.
They stretched him on a rock and wrenched his limbs,
Asking: 'Where is the treasure?' till he died.

Muir's emphasis on the pointlessness of history was not always as cruel as this, but it is a theme that was never very far from his mind. Connected in part with his consciousness of a lost Eden, it also owes something to his dreams and nightmares with their fears of 'eternal recurrence', and to his own lack of sympathy with contemporary history, which he saw as a series of defeats, disappointments and growing threats. There is a strand of pessimism in his reflections on human destiny which his religious hope was never quite robust enough to dismiss, and he outgrew such early belief as he had in economic and political solutions.

This does not mean that the pessimism is not shot through with hope and longing, often a stoic hope and a metaphysical longing. The nightmarish poem 'The Combat', based on dream material, describes an endlessly recurring fight between a powerful and an apparently defenceless animal in which the 'soft brown beast' is mauled and savaged but always manages to escape and live to fight again; neither animal 'loses', but

> The killing beast that cannot kill
> Swells and swells in his fury till
> You'd almost think it was despair.

One might say that if this is an image of life, of man's fate, life would hardly be worth living on such terms. Yet on second thoughts one can see history through the eyes of the poem, and man not unlike the 'undefeatable' animal in the fable, whether the huge opponent has been monstrous beasts, natural calamities, oppressive rulers, or even some less visible enemy. The least visible, of course, may be the worst of all, and Muir's poetry shows, for all his 'gentleness' which critics have perhaps stressed too much, great awareness of the latent cruelties and inexplicable attacks that life – and man, and Muir himself – seem to guard as sources of pride and assurance. One short poem gives forcible expression to this.

The Face

> See me with all the terrors on my roads,
> The crusted shipwrecks rotting in my seas,
> And the untroubled oval of my face
> That alters idly with the moonlike modes
> And is unfathomably framed to please
> And deck the angular bone with passing grace.
>
> I should have worn a terror-mask, should be
> A sight to frighten hope and faith away,
> Half charnel field, half battle and rutting ground.
> Instead I am a smiling summer sea
> That sleeps while underneath from bound to bound
> The sun- and star-shaped killers gorge and play.

'A sight to frighten hope and faith away.' Muir had undoubtedly felt such presences, and his later poetry, some of it on themes of atomic war, is much concerned with it, but he persisted obstinately on his journey ('The heart in its stations/ Has need of patience') and was rewarded with those lyrical gleams of quiet meditative joy or hopefulness which are among his most personal utterances – poems like 'The Bird' (a beautiful Bridges-like counter-poem to 'The Face'), 'The Question', 'A Birthday', 'In Love for Long', 'The Debtor', 'The Poet' and 'I have been taught by dreams and fantasies'. The particular sweetness of Muir's lyrical style when it is successful is like the sudden scent of some wild flower which a freer inspiration has allowed to break through the rather abstract and heraldic character of his verse.

> I never felt so much
> Since I have felt at all
> The tingling smell and touch
> Of dogrose and sweet briar,
> Nettles against the wall,
> All sours and sweets that grow
> Together or apart
> In hedge or marsh or ditch.
> I gather to my heart
> Beast, insect, flower, earth, water, fire,
> In absolute desire,
> As fifty years ago.
>
> ('A Birthday')

The group of brooding prophetic reflections on future war and destruction which he wrote in the 1950s – 'The Horses', 'After a Hypothetical War', 'The Last War', 'Petrol Shortage', 'The Day before the Last Day' – is a powerful though imperfect last attempt by Muir to speak more directly than through myth and symbol on issues that haunted and distressed him. Perhaps because he is looking forward – however doubtfully – instead of back, perhaps because in these poems the air of science-fiction lends paradoxically a greater reality and urgency than is usual with Muir, this group of poems leaves a strong impression (a much stronger impression, for example, than the poems on specifically Christian themes which he was also developing in the 1950s).

'The sun rises above the sea, and they look and think:
"We shall not watch its setting." And all get up
And stare at the sun. But they hear no great voice crying:
"There shall be no more time, nor death, nor change,
Nor fear, nor hope, nor longing, nor offence,
Nor need, nor shame." But all are silent, thinking:
"Choose! Choose again, you who have chosen this!
Too late! Too late!"
And then: "Where and by whom shall we be
        remembered?" '

('The Day before the Last Day')

These poems form, as he says, an 'imaginary picture of a stationary fear', the fear that a possible atomic devastation would destroy not only what is physical but human values as well ('No place at all for bravery in that war'). Yet by a curious closing of the circle he brings this fear round to his own intimations of hope, by suggesting in 'The Horses' and 'Petrol Shortage' that a post-devastational return to primitive pastoral life might restore man to the protection of the earth he had become increasingly estranged from. Men who have no tractors begin to tame wild horses: 'Our life is changed; their coming our beginning.' Butter describes this as 'a vision of a more hopeful kind' and also quotes John Holloway's statement that though in Muir's vision 'the powers of evil were great, ultimately the powers of good and goodness were greater; and they were greater because they were also humbler, more primaeval, nearer to life in its archaic simplicity'. Well, one man's hope is perhaps another man's despair. Muir's primitivism, returning all post-atomic mankind to an Orkney farm, not without a certain austere satisfaction, seems to me to be more insulting than comforting to man's restless spirit and aspiring brain. Let your survivors tame the horses of the Moon, the dragons of Mars: I would call that hope. But Muir was in search of a simplicity which the future was unlikely to reveal unless by a return to the past, and even the simplicity of the past is more myth than reality. So weakness mingles with strength in his search: the weakness of an underlying evasion and escape, the strength of a sincere and moving desire for good. Muir retreats from the wonderful challenge which the apparent menace of the scientific and political future has thrown down to us in mid-century, but he expresses the menace in unforgettable images.

I see the image of a naked man,
He stoops and picks a smooth stone from the ground,
Turns round and in a wide arc flings it backward
Towards the beginning. What will catch it,
Hand, or paw, or gullet of sea-monster?
He stoops again, turns round and flings a stone
Straight on before him. I listen for its fall,
And hear a ringing on some hidden place
As if against the wall of an iron tower.

The Review, 5 February 1963.

Garioch Revisited

Robin Fulton's edition of Robert Garioch's *Complete Poetical Works* (Macdonald, 1984) offers a useful opportunity to take a further look at Garioch's work. This edition replaces the *Collected Poems* of 1977, adding to that volume some forty pages of poems taken from Garioch's Notebooks and more than doubling the number of his translations of Belli's sonnets. The writer includes explanatory and textual notes, and some photographs of Edinburgh and of the poet's MSS. Garioch's own non-chronological rearrangement of his poems in the *Collected* has been further rearranged by Robin Fulton, still non-chronologically and in seven untitled sections; this hardly seems a good idea (despite the admitted problems attending a chronological printing), since in the absence of an index of titles or first lines it becomes irritatingly difficult to locate individual poems, and even more difficult to study the poet's development if one should want to do so. Another criticism must be that half a dozen poems in the *Collected* have been silently omitted in the misnamed *Complete*. (On this, see Alexander Scott's review in *The Scottish Review*, no.31, August 1983, and subsequent correspondence in no.33.) Many, indeed most, of the poems from the Notebooks are rather slight, and it does not seem logical to include them while excluding (without comment) poems which Garioch had himself collected. For example, it is a pity to lose an early piece like 'For the Bloomsbourgeoisie' (from *17 poems for 6d*, 1940), since it shows an aspect of the poet otherwise unrepresented. But with these qualifications, it is excellent to have this volume which keeps Garioch's work before us, and it stands up well – craftsmanlike, entertaining, varied, often moving. Nevertheless, shifts of emphasis and interest, and of values too, are bound to affect our views as time passes. The hard-edged 1980s are not the ebullient 1960s. Sisyphus may still be among us, but who is 'shair of his cheque at the month's end'?

Although it would be quite wrong to take up the view that one cannot be serious through comedy, the more straightforwardly serious poems of Garioch stand strongly and indeed seem to gain in interest, suggesting that there might be more of a balance between the 'serious' and 'comic' aspects of his work than used to be assumed. It would not be impossible to take twenty of his best poems and find them dividing equally into these two categories – an artificial exercise, but perhaps instructive. In the former group we could have 'The Muir', 'The Wire', 'Brither Worm', 'My Faither Sees Me', 'Lesson', 'Letter from Italy', 'At the Tattoo', 'To Robert Fergusson', 'At Robert Fergusson's Grave', and 'Rullion Green Tercentenary'. The other ten could be: 'The Percipient Swan', 'Sisyphus', 'The Canny Hen', 'Perfect', 'Cooling-aff', 'Dr Faust in Rose Street', 'I'm Neutral', 'Heard in the Cougate', 'Did Ye See Me?', and 'And They Were Richt'. The immediately communicative humour and wit and sly social comment of the latter group are never in doubt, and are qualities that will still be linked in many people's minds with recollections of the poet's own readings, so distinctive in their mixture of audience-awareness on the one hand and on the other a 'classical' desire to articulate the internal structure of the poem. The clearly indicated spondees at the ends of the hexameters of 'Sisyphus' were both didactic and a part of the entertainment. But Donald Campbell recalls, in his memoir of Garioch in *Lines Review* (no.77, June 1981), how on at least one occasion the poet decided that audience expectation was due for a thwarting, and for a long sharp shock.

> I remember once chairing a poetry reading that had been organised at the New Town Hotel by the Heretics. We had a large, lively audience who were obviously out for a good time and ready to laugh. Before he read, I suggested to Garioch that he read from the Edinburgh Sonnets, knowing that such reading would bring the house down. He simply nodded and smiled. When his turn came to read, he chose just one poem – 'The Muir', a long, complex contemplation of Hell! Instead of acclaim, he got polite applause: that was the way he wanted it.

'The Muir' is a difficult enough poem on the page, all the more so at a public reading, but it is a poem one comes back to, and it has both depth and intensity. Garioch must have felt it was time, at whatever risk to his popularity as a performer, to remind people of the darker, more darkly questioning side of his work. What happens to Dante's Hell, the poem asks, in an unbelieving age? Has Hell become terrestrialized, as in Hiroshima, or do we still need metaphysics? Has modern physics not dematerialized the solid world in any case, so that we no longer know what is most 'real'? At the heart of the poem is Robert Fergusson, in his last days in the madhouse, howling in his mania, fearing a religious Hell that of all people he would be most unlikely to end up in.

> Melancholia it was they cried
> Fergusson's dool, an attribute at that
> of makars, and langsyne a sign of pride
> in men that wore the melancholy hat,
> but no in hummil Fergusson, wha sat
> gowlin in grief amang the Darien strae;
> yon skeelie makar, aince articulat,
> that used to sing "The Birks of Invermay",
> howled like a cuddy his falsetto bray
> wi nae wrocht artifice of poesy
> or music; here was truth, and it was wae.

That last line recalls a line in his poem about prison-camps, 'The Wire': 'here / the truth is clear, and it is wae.' Both poems were written in the early 1950s, when memories of the Second World War – of prison-camps and death-camps, of the atomic bomb – were still recent and sharp, and when Garioch's own experience as a prisoner-of-war, recounted with measure, reticence, and irony in his autobiographical book *Two Men and a Blanket*, must have been in his mind. His choice of Fergusson as a central character, 'gyte, gyte in Darien', is particularly meaningful not merely for the Edinburgh connection but because Fergusson, like Garioch himself, loved music and song and verse and good company, yet ended in that terrible 'wae' which may indeed be 'the truth'. He is moved especially by the fact that Fergusson's fine poet's and singer's voice has degenerated to an animal howl: the thing that gave most joy to him and to others has gone; and the same could happen to anyone. In the atomic era the change could be even quicker and show even less cause and effect. 'Sae whilk of us is gyte and whilk is wyce?' Against these troubled thoughts he does not find much to console or assuage – but something. In another prison-camp poem, 'Letter from Italy', it is the recognition of a familiar constellation (so that at least he is not 'gyte', and the constellation is at least free):

> Perimeters have bounded me,
> sad rims of desert and of sea,
> the famous one around Tobruk,
> and now barbed wire, which way I look,
> except above – the Pleiades.

Those who have heard him read that poem, which was one of his favourites, will I am sure confirm how strangely affecting he made that last line, which with the lightest of touches seems to bring together the classics and astronomy and the ordinary nostalgias of separation. In a parallel passage in *Two Men and a Blanket*, he describes another night in the Italian camp when something more positive begins to emerge from the suffering and the separation:

> As we thought of the people at home, each man's own misery projected itself into that of his wife or his mother or father; and out of this thought came a strange emotional anguish, a pity for those whom we loved so intensely, and a knowledge of that intensity which we did not possess in normal times. Even enforced asceticism has its effect upon the spirit: I will not try to say what effect it will have, but the power is perfectly real, as many good men have known from early times, and it may be turned to use in making us at least wish to be good men; which is a notable victory over pride.

All this may seem a far cry from the guttural verbal gymnastics and rollicking lèse-majesté of 'Heard in the Cougate'. But it is not really so surprising if the whole figure of Garioch as man and writer should take time to materialize, with various facets of a not unenigmatic character slipping into and out of focus. Three examples of the problematic, not from his poetry but from prose or conversation, may be given. He has an amusing story, in his autobiographical essay 'Early Days in Edinburgh' (in *As I Remember*, ed. Maurice Lindsay, 1979), about the time when, as a Scottish Episcopalian boy, he was due to be confirmed, and as part of the process had to confess which of the Seven Deadly Sins he was prone to commit. With humble but honest self-examination he goes through the list without finding anything, from Pride to Gluttony, that rings a bell. 'The Rector grew

impatient. "You don't mean to tell me you're perfect?" he said.
I said no, but whatever was wrong with me, it was not on the
list.' That 'whatever was wrong with me', giving and withdrawing complicity in a religious guilt-system with the same breath,
is very characteristic. Another small spanner is thrown into the
works in the conversation he recorded with Donald Campbell
in March 1977 (printed in *Cencrastus* no.6, Autumn 1981). Much
is often made of Garioch as an observer of Edinburgh life, and
it is the first point Donald Campbell makes, that his poems start
from the particular and the local and tend therefore, to anyone
who knows the city, to be recognizably true. But Garioch
demurs. 'Some of them are and some of them are pure invention.'
And later on in the interview he reiterates the point, with specific
reference to the Edinburgh Sonnets. 'A lot of them are pure
invention, while others were based on actual incidents.' Without
being quite as provoking as John Donne ('I did best when I had
least truth for my subjects'), he is quick to resist pigeonholing,
even at the expense of an offered kudos. If both of these instances
suggest an element of the escapologist, a third reference might
be taken to clinch the point. Garioch's autobiographical article
in Scots, 'I shuik hauns wi Houdini' (*The Scotsman*, 7 July 1979),
is typically subtle in the way it lures our expectations into believing we are about to learn some hard facts about the great escaper
from someone who had actually sat beside him and talked to him
as a boy – but then enjoys cauterizing these expectations and
allowing the escaper to escape once more. Did the blacksmith
friend of his father's who made locks and chains for Houdini
include 'quirks of joukerie-pawkerie' in them? He never found
out. Was it true that Houdini could narrow his hands and slip
out of handcuffs? Despite feeling his grip, he never found out.
And so the secrets of his craft, the mystery of his power, remain
elusive, and Garioch obviously identifies with the elusiveness.

The humours, the delight, the play, the ironies of the half-
revealed character, yes; but also a certain existential terror, half-
veiled. In 'My Faither Sees Me' he is led to 'steik my shutters
guid and ticht' when he imagines his father's face staring in at
him through a dark window. In 'Brither Worm' the soft innocent
persistent worm pushing through a crack in the flagstones is
succeeded unexpectedly by a rat; the rat looks at him and gives him
a 'sudden grue'. And in 'Day-Trip' the about-to-be-slaughtered
pig cries out, like Fergusson in Bedlam or the non-Christians of
Hiroshima under the Christian bomb, to the wrong god:

gey sonsy-lukan wemen here and there,
tow-heidit bairns doukan ablow the brig,
twa-thrie bodachs, bien, wi naethin adae
but blether awa, and bide till denner-time,
while a wud-feart pig, wi a voice like an auld wife
scrauchs til the wrang gode, Help! Help!

Garioch's Translations

Translation occupies a notable segment of Garioch's output. He translated mainly from Latin and Romanesco, with side-forays into French, German, Greek, Gaelic, and Anglo-Saxon. In these poetic versions he used a range of Scots from the aureate and formal to the colloquial, and a range of metrical effects from free verse and alliterative stress-metres to the strict grip of the Italian sonnet. It is obvious that he took this part of his writing seriously, enjoyed the variety of challenges it offered, and spent much time and effort searching for those solutions to the near-insoluble which the art of translation epitomizes.

As any translator knows, the author one happens to deal with may be there by choice (one's own enthusiasm) or by accident (a suggestion or a commission from outside), but if the resulting versions are felt to be successful and are published, there is usually some reason for the success which can be traced back from translation to translator. Little did the Scottish Latin poet Arthur Johnston (1587-1641) think, when he referred to the 'Gariochaeos tractus' of his native Aberdeenshire that he would be turned into Scots three centuries later by a poet calling himself Robert Garioch. The racy, light-hearted elegiac couplets of 'A Fisher's Apology' had been given an English prose rendering in Hugh MacDiarmid's *The Golden Treasury of Scottish Poetry* (1940), but in Garioch's version, using Scots and an imitative metre, this delightful defence of Sunday fishing against Presbyterian interdict came alive for the first time as far as Latinless readers were concerned. The fact that Garioch was brought up as an Episcopalian may have helped! But Johnston's sly arguments, the detailed account of salmon-catching, and the appeal against authority were all aspects of the poem that Garioch must have found congenial.

> If religion wad jist graunt me leave to gie in to this ae
> temptation,
> Oh, gie me indulgence on Sunday, that I may set my lines!

The sin duisnae last owre lang, nae mair nor ae short
  simmer,
   That's aa the length of my hairst, ye may tak my word
   fir that.

An imitative metre is also used to good effect in 'The Traivler',
Garioch's version of the untitled Anglo-Saxon poem usually
called 'The Wanderer'. He keeps the mid-line break as well as
the alliteration, hoping that the modern reader will find the
interest of the poem overriding the unfamiliar look of the lines:

   The wine-haas are rubble,   the rulers liggan
   by joy forhowit;   bonnie fechters hae faan
   by the waa in their pride;   weir killed some,
   reivit them on faur roads;   ane the ravens tuik
   owre the gret sea;   ane the grey wolf
   did til deid;   ane in the grund
   a dowie hero   hid in a hole.

Garioch was aware, in translating from Anglo-Saxon, that the
alliterative tradition acquired a Scottish dimension in medieval
times, becoming for some reason much more popular in the
north of England and in Scotland than in the Chaucerian south.
He used the longer medieval alliterative line (as in Dunbar's 'The
Tretis of the Tua Mariit Wemen and the Wedo') as a supple yet
forceful equivalent of the Greek hexameter in 'Anatomy of
Winter', his version of the famous description of a farmer's winter
in Hesiod's *Works and Days*. The wintry subject also allowed him
to latch onto a naturally recurring strong feature of Scottish
poetry, with vivid results:

   It garrs the bestial grue; their tails in the grooves
   of their hurdies are steikit weill hame. The hairy yins and aa,
   wi coats of guid cleidin, it cuts richt throu them;
   the weill-happit hide of an ox, that duisnae haud out the
     cauld.
   And it gangs throu a gait's lang hair. But gimmers and
     yowes
   wi fouth of fleece, the wund flegs them nocht,
   tho it bends an auld man's back, bow'd like a wheel.

Turning from these poets of earlier centuries to Guillaume

Apollinaire whose life overlapped with Garioch's own, and whose work was part of the modernist revaluation of poetic style, may seem a strange leap for him to have taken. And he translated Apollinaire closely, unpunctuated *vers libre* and all. Apollinaire in Scots is, to begin with, an unexpected thought, but when we look at the translations we can see reasons why Garioch was attracted to the French poet. In 'Victory', Apollinaire's plea for a revitalized language, in effect a new language, for poetry accommodates very well with Garioch's desire, and the desire of other Scottish Renascence writers, to re-energize Scottish poetry through an extension of the possibilities of Scots. To Apollinaire, the old languages are 'près de mourir', and it is only through habit and 'manque d'audace' that poets continue to use them; man is already 'à la recherche d'un nouveau langage'. So what does he want?

> We want new souns new souns new souns
> We want consonants wi nae vowels
> Consonants that gie smorit farts
>   Imitate the soun of a peerie
> Firk out a non-stop noise frae your neb
> Mak clicks wi your tongue
> Mak yuis of the stranglit noise of folk rudely slorpan
>   their meat
> The aspirat hechyuch of spittin wad mak anither bonnie
>   consonant

That *hechyuch* (Apollinaire's 'raclement') Garioch had himself brought into poetry, in his 'Heard in the Cougate', a few years earlier: 'Chwoich! Ptt! Hechyuch! Ab-boannie cairry-on.' A different link suggests itself in the poem 'Ferlie of the Weir'. Apollinaire and Garioch had each served in a major war, and both came to terms with the experience without the anguish of an Owen or a Rosenberg. 'J'ai creusé lé lit où je coule,' says the French poet:

> I hae howit-out the bed whaur I snoove ramifeean in a
>   thousan wee burns that gae aa airts
> I am in the front-line trench and yet I am aawhair or
>   raither I begin to be aawhair

And Garioch, in his own poem 'Letter from Italy', makes his

bed in the prisoner-of-war camp, in the open, and lies back: 'and now barbed wire, which way I look, / except above – the Pleiades.' In a third translation, 'A Phantom of Haar', in which Apollinaire touchingly describes a performance of street-acrobats, Garioch not only opened up something which was to make its appearance in his own poem 'Lesson', some years later, but also joined – how consciously it is hard to say – a chain of influences and empathies that began with Picasso's wonderful paintings of street-acrobats at the beginning of the century, and included Rilke's Fifth Duino Elegy, based on one of the Picasso paintings. In 'Lesson', Apollinaire's 'gey wee acrobat dressed-up in pulmonary pink' becomes a go-go girl 'in a see-throu pink gounie', dancing on the dusty floor of a Leith dockside pub:

> The folk lookit on calmly, wi interest, respect and pleisor,
> tho wi the faces of men, had luikit aa day at the side of a ship,
> as yon lassie's clean taes acceptit the ordinary stourie flair.
>
> Guillaume Apollinaire, wad ye hae gliskit here
> a phantom of Leith haar? Duis it still glimmer thair?

With his versions of George Buchanan, we move into one of the two main areas of Garioch's devoted labour as a translator. The huge contemporary reputation of the learned but devious sixteenth-century humanist has never been sustained, though it must seem an unnecessarily cruel fate that he should have become a buffoon-hero of the chapbooks. (I have before me, as I write, a Glasgow-printed *Witty and Entertaining Exploits of George Buchanan, Commonly Called the King's Fool*.) Rescue-operations have been mounted at different times for the best of his Latin poems, including the 'Epithalamium for Mary Stuart and the Dauphin of France' with its high encomium on Scotland and the Scots, but it cannot be said that he looms large in modern Scottish consciousness. Garioch, more than most, made a valiant attempt to resurrect the *inter sapientes sapientissimus* son of Killearn.

As a reluctant schoolmaster, Garioch felt well qualified to translate what is probably the most approachable of Buchanan's poems, 'Elegy I', his lament for the hard life of the poet-teacher in Paris. 'The Humanists' Trauchles in Paris' is a brilliantly sprightly rendering, in a sort of extended Burns stanza, of the more formal, though still quite pointed and humorous catalogue of exasperations in the original. The difference of tone can be seen from the opening line, where 'Ite leves nugae, sterilesque valete Camoenae' becomes 'Muses, fareweill! Fikefacks, awa!' In the same way, when Buchanan describes how a large part of the drowsy body of students is apt to snore in class, his simple 'stertit' is playfully amplified in Garioch's 'snore like grumphies'. And at the end, when Buchanan is bidding a wry farewell to his vocation, his 'nos alio sors animusque vocat' becomes a more jaunty, less elegiac 'As for me, I'll caa / anither jig'. But it would be unfair to Garioch to claim that our suspect old friend the Scottish reductive idiom was somehow vulgarizing the Latin. The Latin which Buchanan produces, however 'correctly' deployed it may be, according to sixteenth-century knowledge and/or development of classical Latin rules (and Buchanan has been called 'one of the summits of the Renaissance in matters of versification', by whose achieved standards other neo-Latin poets can be judged[1]) is nevertheless a virtually dead language, keeping only a semblance of life through its use in university teaching. Whether elegantly written or not, it therefore needs all the help it can get. What Garioch does for 'Elegy I' – and he remains close to the poem – is to draw out in a recognizable and communicative form the wit and pith that are really there.

Of the volume containing his Scots versions of Buchanan's plays *Jephthah* and *The Baptist* (1959), Garioch once wrote in a letter: 'I love that book better than the *Selected Poems*.)[2] He was convinced that not only were existing translations in English inadequate, but even 'the unco-dowie logic o the Hebrew Jephthah juist doesna maik wi English conventions, and the Baptist's thrawn Jewish threipin o ill-faur'd sooth seems mair naiteral whan he flytes in Scots.' And if the use of Scots helped to make the plays vigorous, the result was that he would 'dearly like to see and hear thae tragedies presentit on the stage.' He in fact deliberately kept the orthography moderate, so that actors could flesh it out with whatever further Scots they desired. These remarks, from the preface to his book, can surely be agreed with and sustained. Although both tragedies are short on action and suspense, and contain some very lengthy speeches, they have much powerful argument on meaty subjects taken from that area where politics and religion overlap (an area as relevant today as it was then, though what rationalist or utopianist of recent times would have foreseen it?), and the paucity of intellectual argument on the contemporary stage might make a stylish and confident production welcome. We know that the plays were written for performance by the students of the Collège de Guyenne in Bordeaux, where Buchanan was teaching in the early 1540s, and we have Montaigne's word for it that the dramas were well received (as a boy of twelve he had played some of the chief parts).[3]

Both plays have a subtitle (not translated by Garioch): *Jephthah* has *The Vow*, and *The Baptist* has *Calumny*. This moral interest is central in Buchanan's naturally didactic concern in writing plays which were to be part of the boys' education, but tragic effect is not thereby ruled out, nor is pathos. The human dilemma of Jephthah, who has promised to sacrifice the first living thing he sees on returning from a successful campaign, and is met by his own daughter, is a powerful one, and had entered folklore and balladry, as Garioch no doubt knew. (Hamlet, for example, quotes for Polonius's benefit the popular ballad of *Jephthah, Judge of Israel*, in Act II, Scene 2.) There is less pathos in *The Baptist*, but it has a more genuinely dramatic interplay of character, in the exchanges between Herod and his Queen, Herod and John, and John and Malchus. Each play stands up, in its own way.

In his translations, Garioch sticks fairly closely to the text, not rendering every phrase, but happily avoiding the feeble prolixity of the Revd Archibald Brown's English blank verse translations of 1906, which in his preface he politely acknowledges have been of 'muckle help' to him (muckle help in doing otherwise, one may jalouse). There are many excellent solutions, and even where the ethnically Scottish transfers might seem to intrude into stories taken from *Judges* and *Matthew*, they do not jar, for example, 'strang wi monie sons, or a feck o ghillies' ('gravem /Turba clientum, liberisve turgidum'), 'my hairt grues wi horror' ('pectus horrificat timor'), 'mang coronachs' ('inter funera'), 'cantie rumour' ('secundis rumoribus'), 'green straths' ('convalles virides'), 'wappenshaw', ('armis...paratu bellico'), 'serried schiltrouns' ('densae phalanges'), 'and ye wanchancy weirds' ('fataque infelicia'), 'by nae dirk nor claymore' ('haud ense, haud jaculis'). Garioch obviously relished, and perhaps exaggerated for purposes of grim humour, the formidably awful Herod's wife, whose opening words, addressed to the vacillating king, are 'Are ye that dozent' ('Tu lentus usque'). But he also rose to the eloquence of the last speech of Jephthah's daughter, when she has come to accept her sacrificial death:

> Syne nae man may deny, in days to come,
> that I was ding to be Jephthah's dochter;

hae me gruppit, dae it, gie the order
to drag me awa. I am dedicat til daith,
consecrat as a victim; I hae coost frae me
my luve o the warld's licht. Delay is laithsom:
and nou, my dearest mither, fare ye weill,
fareweill, my faither's hame, whaur I hae spent
sae monie cantie days, kindly brocht-up
in weill-faur'd hope, sune to be nobly weddit.
Fate, oh fate, and my forbears fordone by daith,
receive in peace a sawl gien as a pledge
for her country's safety; and ye licht o the sun,
new ilka dawning, taen frae my een, fareweill.

Although Garioch expressed great confidence in his work on
George Buchanan, and felt it was important to restore such a
largely forgotten Scottish literary figure, he also had to recognize
that by common consent it was his versions of 120 sonnets by
Giuseppe Belli which crowned his activities as a translator. In
Belli he found a congenial spirit, to whom abuses in society and
the pomposities of power were targets of witty and constant
attack, and in Belli's tightly constructed yet at the same time
bold and original verse he found a challenge to his own virtuosity
which he took up with increasing energy and enthusiasm. The
tendency has been to assume, because the results were so vigorous
and inventive, that this was a perfect match of poet and translator.
Belli might have thought differently. He was writing in a closely
defined, keenly observed urban dialect, Romanesco. Garioch,
however, was not writing so strictly in the urban dialect of Edinburgh; his Scots was more diffused and eclectic, and perhaps had
to be, if Edinburgh could not supply him with what Rome gave
to Belli. When we read, in Belli's introduction to his own poems,[4]
how he sees his city's language, we are irresistibly reminded of
Glaswegian, and when we further read his comments on the
relation of language to status and authority, we imagine his ideal
translator might be Tom Leonard. After defending the 'insubor-
dinate and licentious spirit' that shows through popular Roman
speech, he describes the people as inclined 'towards sarcasm,
towards the epigrammatic, towards the proverbial and the pithy,
towards the decisive forms of a gallus ('manesco') genius, not
speaking at length in regular and expository discourse... a fondness for ironies and ambiguities.' And his business, he says, is
'to extract a rule from chance, a grammar from usage'; he wants

to present in his pages 'not popular poetry, but popular speech unfolded into my own poetry'. The people, he says, have no art, no poetry, no oratory; the values he finds in them 'issue spontaneously from their own nature'. And his declaration is: 'I have resolved to leave, as a monument, what the people of Rome are today.'

Garioch's joyfully accepted task was to be as faithful as he could to the re-presenting of that picture of Belli's Rome, acknowledging that he could not Edinburghize Rome by a complete transference, linguistic or otherwise, keeping many of the Italian names (Doria, Nunziatina, Patta, Respiscitto, Monte-Mario, Campidojo, Terracina) and finding Scottish equivalents for others (Craigmillar, Wamphray, Maistress MacIlwhannie, Jock McPhee, Sairey, Sandy, Portobelly), and guarding a balance between the real preservation of Belli's nineteenth-century concerns and an ingenious use of twentieth-century parallels. Being a less acerbic satirist than Belli, Garioch worried at times whether he 'could find some more religious, but not anti-clerical sonnets, to balance things a bit' (letter to Antonia Stott, 18 March 1976). And as regards Belli's most outspoken and obscene poems, which he reluctantly accepted he ought to translate, but which he died before he could work on, he said: 'No, I daresay we can't exclude the obscene sonnets altogether, I agree. In an American university they would work out the right ratio by computer, but maybe we could have the obscene ones a little below the correct proportion' (letter to Antonia Stott, 12 March 1981). These were temperamental differences which every translator must come up against even when translating a poet he has eagerly chosen.

Working from literal translations made for him by Antonia Stott, but also examining each sonnet carefully by himself, Garioch saw his main problem was not how to avoid error but how to be as fair as he could, employing all his expertise, to the totality of each poem. He relished the variety of Belli's subjects, though his greatest successes are usually in dealing with themes and attitudes that made a strong appeal to him. In 'The Wee Thief's Mither' (No.740), a boy who has stolen a few watches and umbrellas is defended in court by his mother, who asks what all the 'cufuffle' (Romanesco 'ghetti', Italian 'strepiti') is about:

> Plenty fowk, Excellency, that git on fine,
> steal hunners mair nor him, and niver falter,
> and they win reverence, and dine and wine.

> I've aye gien this advice til him: Son Walter,
> lift hauf a million; fir the churches, syne,
> ye'll be a sanct, wi lilies on yer altar.

But the people do not always take the war into the enemy camp like the thief's mother, and their passivity and compliance in the face of confidently contemptuous power is nicely expressed in 'The Rulers of the Auld Warld' (No.361), where all that the translation misses is the double meaning of Romanesco 'vassalli' ('vassals' and 'rascals'):

> Yince on a time there was a King, wha sat
> screivan this edict in his palace-haa
> til aa his fowk: 'Vassals, I tell ye flat
> that I am I, and you are buggar-aa.'

After seeing the whole contents of the blistering edict, the people are too cowed at the end of the sonnet to do anything but ludicrously agree to their enslavement, saying *That's richt, that's richt.* More ambiguous in its attitude to the people is 'Ritual Questions' (No.1479), where the reader has to decide whether the almost meaningless conversation between two old friends is an example of a ritualized and therefore enfeebled mode of communication, or on the contrary an indication of the satisfyingly subtle laconicism of a code developed over generations by ordinary people. Giorgio Vigolo, one of the main commentators on Belli, calls it 'ecclesiastical ritual applied to social encounters: pure formalism' – but this still leaves the question open. The translation is beautifully close to the original, even down to the sweaty shirts and the snuff.

> Whan thae twa meet, mind whit I say, Maria.
> Staund roon a corner, listen to their spiel.
> 'Eh-ach, ma guid auld frien, Maister MacNeill.' –
> 'The same, yir hummil sairvant, Maister McKay.'
>
> Says he: 'Some sneeshin?' – 'Thanks,' he says, 'I'll try
> ae pinch. Hou're ye?' – 'Braw, and yirsel?' – 'Gey weill,
> thank ye.' – And syne he says: 'Hou dae ye feel,
> this weather? – 'Garrs me cheenge ma sarks, och aye.'

Says he: 'And hou's yir health?' – 'Soun as a bell,
and yours?' – 'Thank Gode, I'm's weill as maist of men.' –
'Yir fowk?' – 'Graund; yours?' – 'The same, faur's I can tell.' –

'I'm glaid of that.' – 'And I, as ye may ken.' –
'Aweill, Maister MacNeill, luik eftir yirsel.' –
'Maister McKay . . . till we meet again.'

There are many poems about the Pope and papal matters, and
Garioch takes these in his stride. Belli, though he died in the
bosom of the church, chafed under the reactionary Gregory XVI
and wrote during his papacy the splendidly outrageous sonnet
'A Suggested Ceremony' (No.1517). There are not enough papal
ceremonies, says Belli, and since the Pope keeps claiming he is
the Vicar of Christ, why should he not act out his office in earnest?
Cardinals, well-known thieves of the people, could help to complete the tableau:

Let's pit in the Paip's neive some kinna wand
or cane, slap on his heid a croun of thorn,
whup him agin a post, treat him wi scorn,
try him and syne condemn him out of haund . . .

And up there, ilka year, at Eastertide,
we'll nail Christ's Vicar on that halie day
forbye twa cardinals, ane on ilka side.

Belli, like Garioch, had an eye for the offbeat story, the bizarre
character or incident that sticks in the memory not because it
suggests a moral but merely as a reminder of the rich and strange
variety of human experience. The eccentric priest of 'The Reminder' (No.358), with his love of funerals and his long thin legs
'like twa parritch-spirtles' (scotticized from the 'bird-net poles'
of the original), is found one day, hanged from the crucifix-hook
above his bed – nothing much in that, you may say, until you
come to the last lines of the sonnet:

And this wee ploy of his meant sic a lot
to him, to keep the maitter in his heid,
he'd even tied his hankie in a knot.

A great virtue in Belli is that he can deal with the grandest of religious subjects in a spirit that seems fruitfully open, sometimes fantastic or playful, yet at the same time unmistakably committed to the seriousness of the theme. In 'Judgment Day' (No.273), one of the most striking of the sonnets, even though he is using phrases from the book of Revelation, and discussing our final consignment to heaven or hell, the tone is an extraordinary mixture of the familiar, the frightening, and the humorous, with images of children's games (the translation misses this), farmyard hens and chickens, swarms of insects, blowing out of candles, voices saying goodnight. A little reminiscent of seventeenth-century Metaphysical poetry, it is different in that it moves towards a mysteriously suggestive and unresolved conclusion that is more Romantic than Metaphysical. Why is it the angels who blow out the candles? Who says goodnight to whom? Is the whole house, from its infernal cellar ('cantina') to its celestial roof ('tetto'), to be left in darkness? If so, what does that mean?

> Fowre muckle angels wi their trumpets, stalkin
> til the fowre airts, sall aipen the inspection;
> they'll gie a blaw, and bawl, ilk to his section,
> in their huge voices: 'Come, aa yese, be wauken.'
>
> Syne sall crawl furth a ragment, a haill cleckin
> of skeletons yerkt out fir resurrection
> to tak again their ain human complexion,
> like choukies gaitheran roun a hen that's clockan.
>
> And thon hen sall be Gode the blissit Faither;
> he'll pairt the indwellers of mirk and licht,
> tane doun the cellar, to the ruiff the tither.
>
> Last sall come angels, swarms of them, in flicht,
> and, like us gaean to bed without a swither,
> they will blaw out the caunnles, and guid-nicht.

It is clear that in turning from the relentless moral dialectics of *Jephthah* to the sprightly Bakhtinian carnival, both linguistic and intellectual, of Belli, Garioch enjoyed a sense of liberation. The technical difficulties only increased his involvement. He made an interesting remark, after translating Sonnet No.1723 ('The Bronze Horse', where he rhymes 'atrabilious' with 'kill yese' and 'yo-yo' with 'Campidojo'): 'Here is a new Belli translation, No.1723, still with the translator's sweat glistening on it: art is to conceal art, aw'rite, but sometimes anguished effort may show through and give a kind of aesthetic pleasure' (letter to Michael Schmidt, 16 October 1972). Wrestling with the materials of their art is a joy that too few poets know, these slack days. Garioch shows it can be productive, given the right circumstances, and without downgrading the more plain and direct style he found fitting for Buchanan's tragedies.

Notes

1 Philip J. Ford, *George Buchanan, Prince of Poets* (Aberdeen University Press, 1982), p.36.
2 Letter to David Black, 26 November 1969, in *A Garioch Miscellany*, ed. Robin Fulton (1986), p.43.
3 Montaigne, *Essays*, Book I, Chapter 26.
4 Belli, *Sonetti*, a cura di Pietro Gibellini (Milan, 1984), pp.5-15.

Critical Essays on Robert Garioch, ed. R. Ross and J. Hendry (Edinburgh University Press, forthcoming).

The Poetry of Norman MacCaig

Norman MacCaig has not been prolific of statements about him-self or his art, but what he has said is perhaps all the more interest-ing on that account, and it might be a good place to start from. In an interview in *Scottish Field* in April 1972 he said:

> I'm a sprinter, not a long-distance runner…I'm a spontaneous, hit-or-miss writer, and mind you I'm only talking about my own methods. I never know what I am going to write about. I just feel like writing a poem – in the way that one feels hungry so one eats something. I sit down with a blank sheet of paper and a blank mind. And a phrase or a word is given, but don't ask me from where. I think it's the unconscious mind; I don't believe in White Goddesses and doves descending, because I think it's all in oneself.

One doesn't want to pin anyone down to what he says in inter-views, but this is the sort of statement MacCaig has made elsewhere, and he evidently feels it is one way of describing how he approaches the writing of poetry. It is an unpretentious stance, and the dislike of pretension is very characteristic. There is a dislike of the idea of inspiration from Muse figures outwith the poet's knowledge, and there is dislike of the idea of intellectual preparation for a poem, or coming heavy with forethought about its structure. Spontaneity is the virtue. And with spontaneity goes the habit of writing short poems, since a long poem needs preparation and forethought of a kind he is unwilling to give. It is a modest, clear-sighted approach.

In an earlier article which he himself wrote in *Scottish Field* in September 1957, 'Living in Scotland', he tells us a little more about this fondness for smaller rather than larger scale.

> I don't like big mouths, I don't like Big Business, I don't like Big Brother. Except in my more athletic moments, which

may be my best, I prefer small pictures, short poems, the Chaconne in D minor to the Mass in E minor. In a big-scale country you walk your legs off for a trifling re-arrangement of the scenery Around Lochinver a couple of hundred yards means a split new view. And I have often seen a little hill in Harris collapse to half its size when a cow appeared on the top of it. It needed the intrusion of the known, ordinary object to show the hill at its proper height. I think it is a part of patriotism to stare at the hill till there's a cow on it.

Here, the small poem is seen as in keeping with the small scale of Scotland as a country, the small scale of its landscapes (as compared with those of, say, America or Russia). As the story of the hill and the cow illustrates, the cow suddenly giving the right scale by deflating the pretensions of the apparently huge hill, he is especially attracted by the honesty and truthfulness of seeing things as they are – and he doesn't care whether they are small or not. He likes the Highlands, but he would hate to do a Macpherson's Ossian with the landscape, glamourising its mists and peopling it with shadows.

A third comment is useful in that it shows him taking up, in a mild way, a point of criticism he has at times received: that his poetry does not deal with the 'great' issues of the times, and in particular the more grim issues of politics and war. In 1973, when his book *The White Bird* was made a 'Recommendation' of the Poetry Book Society, he wrote in the society's Bulletin:

> I don't agree at all with those tho think that in these terrible times one must write only 'terrible' poems, that it is a sort of treason to the million suffering people in the world to write about the pleasures and graces that happen to one's own self. I should suppose, in fact, that while it is a very solipsistic creature indeed who can shut his mind to that suffering, it is all the more important in this sad world to notice, record and praise the good things that are still there.

This again is a theme he has returned to elsewhere, either because a charge of escapism catches one on the quick or because he wanted to put forward a view of the work of art (like Ian Hamilton Finlay in this, if in nothing else!) as a small oasis of order and happiness and beauty against the dark chaotic background of untransformed reality. However, these views don't quite carry forward (as we shall see) into his latest work, where death and suffering receive greater prominence.

One last quotation: MacCaig's autobiographical essay in Maurice Lindsay's *As I Remember* (1979) ends with what is perhaps the nearest he has come to a credo, an artist's credo.

> Poetry teaches a man to do more than observe merely factual errors and measurable truths. It trains him to have a shrewd nose for the fake, the inflated, the imprecise and the dishonest. So, it compels him to resist stock responses, because it compels him to examine the emotional significance, as well as the rational significance, of whatever comes under his notice. To have unexamined emotional responses is as immature, as dangerous, as to have unexamined beliefs. And what proportion, I wonder, of the misunderstandings and miseries in the world are due to no more than the stock use of big words – liberty, patriotism, democracy and all their dreary clan – and the stock response to them?

What strikes you most about this is the modesty of its claim for art, it sees art mainly as a corrective, a chastener, a reminder, a test for false ideas and unexamined ideals. If you can sometimes define a man by his opposites, MacCaig might appear as the opposite of Shelley, who in his *Defence of Poetry* called poets the 'unacknowledged legislators of the world' and the 'mirrors of the gigantic shadows which futurity casts upon the present'. Mac-Caig would have an instinctive suspicion of such large claims. Both attitudes obviously have their limitations: Shelley would not have the patience to measure out the small-scale cat-like precision of movement and imagery in a MacCaig poem; MacCaig, for his part, lacks the wonderful sense of letting go, of continuous long-distance spiritual drive and energy, which you get in Shelley.

But having mentioned Shelley, I am reminded of the fact that MacCaig did not reach these views of precision and fastidiousness and unpretentiousness and modesty of claim without a struggle. He now of course, as I'm sure you know, completely disowns his early poetry, but I'm afraid observers of his work have to be at least aware of it, even if they come to reject it too. (I remember once in conversation with MacCaig, quite a while back, happening to remark that I possessed all his books, including the two from the 1940s, *Far Cry* and *The Inward Eye*, and his immediate reaction was 'You should burn them, boy!') These two books were heavily influenced by the New Apocalypse movement of the early 1940s, and MacCaig also appeared in New Apocalypse anthologies at that time. This was a neo-Romantic movement, reacting against the socio-political poetry of Auden and his followers of the later 1930s; it stressed free emotion, and myth, and the unconscious; it admired D.H. Lawrence; its best-known adherent was Dylan Thomas. Nothing, you might think, could be further from the MacCaig we know, and of course you're right. But there are two points to be made. Although the New Apocalypse was based in London, it had a strong Scottish following, and its members included, in addition to MacCaig – at various times and with varying degrees of advocacy – Tom Scott, J.F. Hendry, G.S. Fraser, and Maurice Lindsay. In fact, if you add in Dylan Thomas, you could say the movement was more Scottish and Welsh than English; so that is a point of historical interest. The other point is that there is in fact *some* continuity from MacCaig's New Apocalypse poems of the 1940s forward into his later and very much better work. The early poems have a thick, rich, but almost meaningless deployment of metaphor and simile, irrational, undirected. The later poetry, from *Riding Lights* in 1955 onwards, is still noted for its imagery, but the scalpel has been at work, and although decorative effects can be found, there is a progressive paring away of all excess. The physically lean MacCaig is gradually matched by his poetry. (Is there a psychosomatic theory of art lurking about there?)

One of the noted features of MacCaig's poetry is a fascination with the self, how to define it, how to use it, how to disguise it, how to reveal it. The autobiographical article already quoted from Lindsay's *As I Remember* is called 'My Way of It'. The record he made for Claddagh Records in 1971 is called *The Way I Say It*. The film made about him by Films of Scotland in 1977 is called *A Man in My Position* – which is also the title of one of his books and one of his poems. And yet many people would say that the self they see in the poems is fairly elusive, perhaps because the poet's habit of being an observer – of nature, of animals and birds and fish, of places – has carried over into his observation of himself, giving an ironic distancing effect more often than anything skin-peeling or confessional. Yet the vulnerability of the self, of any self, does show – increasingly as his poetry develops. He expresses very well the idea of the complexity of the self, as something which both changes through time and yet remains constant too, in 'Summer Farm', where the speaker after describing himself lying in the grass on a hot summer day, watching ducks, a hen, a swallow, a grasshopper, abstracted from thought, suddenly imagines he's lifted above the landscape, looking down on it:

> Self under self, a pile of selves I stand
> Threaded on time, and with metaphysical hand
> Lift the farm like a lid and see
> Farm within farm, and in the centre, me.

The title he has used three times, 'A Man in My Position', presumably represents an idea that appeals to him. It really means 'not myself but someone like me or placed like me', it's like a third-person version of 'myself'. Yet at the same time it can also mean 'myself', e.g. 'how strange that this should happen to a man in my position'. It is a phrase that allows him to turn over various facets of the idea of self-consciousness:

> Hear my words carefully.
> Some are spoken
> not by me, but
> by a man in my position.

It is not hard to move into the idea of a divided self, or of a self with a mask. Is the mask protective? We are taunted. Is the self better without it? Don't believe it!

> How my friends would turn away
> from the ugly sounds coming from my mouth...
> How they would wish back
> the clean white bandages
> that hid these ugly wounds.
>
> ('Private')

The occasional suggestion that there is a darkness underneath, that the true self is perhaps better kept within its wraps, comes almost as a preparation for the contrast between poems like 'A Sort of Blues', where the speaker complains ironically that he is a 'failed St Sebastian', vainly trying to attract the arrows of suffering, condemned by all because he is too happy. 'My luck to live in a time / when to be happy / is to have no neighbours' – and (say) the much more recent poem 'Every Day', where

Sebastian's arrows have come home at last, and where there's a grim but finely expressed presentation of the aged self thinking of death:

> What's that cart that nobody sees
> grinding along the shore road?
>
> Whose is the horse that pulls it, the white horse
> that bares its yellow teeth to the wind?
>
> They turn, unnoticed by anyone,
> into the field of slanted stones.
>
> My friends meet me. They lift me from the cart and,
> the greetings over, we go smiling underground.

The self of the later poems is not by any means uniformly sombre, but it's interesting that even in a humorous and affectionate animal poem like 'Toad' – one of the best of his animal pieces – the poem is deepened by the bringing in of the darker self at the end:

> A jewel in your head? Toad,
> you've put one in mine,
> a tiny radiance in a dark place.

Animals, and the whole world of nature, are of course a central feature of MacCaig's poetry. Sometimes it's a matter of brilliant observation: the goat 'with amber dumb-bells in his eyes', the cows 'swinging / A silver slaver from each chin', the sheep half in and half out of the pen which 'makes a white hourglass in the sun', the pigeons that look like 'wobbling gyroscopes of lust', the collie that 'flowed through fences like a piece of black wind', the charging bull like a 'big black hunchback / with a small black boy running behind him'. Sometimes, in a mood of disgust, he praises the animal world at the expense of the human, praises it for its lack of morality and hypocrisy; only man suffers from these. This misanthropic note comes into quite a few of the later poems, e.g. 'Outsider' (not one of his best), where he envies the direct aggression and killing of the natural world, of the jungle and the sea, and describes this world of beasts as 'a free world, a world without hypocrisy, without masks. / Cramped with humanity, I envy them.' Some of the most successful of the animal poems simply use the world of nature to give man a jolt, to make him think, make him ask questions. Two good examples are 'Basking Shark', where the well-adapted hyper-ancient monster encountered on a rowing expedition makes the 'decadent townee' wonder whether jumped-up *homo sapiens* 'on a wrong branch of the family tree' is more truly the monster, and 'Lesson', in which a man studying an old fishbox learns nothing until it flies into his head when he is asleep and Disney-wise 'crams the sleeper inside it':

> And when the hammer hits
> the first nail on the head,
> he wakes with a scream, he knows
> what a fishbox is, he knows
> what a rope is, or a seagull standing
> at its horrible attention.

Poems more directly on human themes range widely in their effects, from the pathos and indignation of 'Assisi' to the comic but nicely perceptive elegy on MacDiarmid, 'After his Death', from the Wallace-Stevens-ish complexities of a poem on art ('No Consolation') to the straightforward pessimism of a poem on politics ('A New Age'). As with most poetry, the more concrete tends to win, over the more abstract. The deep dislike of cruelty and injustice which underlies much of his poetry is much less convincingly expressed in 'A New Age', with its imaginary and generalized horrors – 'How could we express our thankfulness / when the mass graves were filled / only with the dead?' – than in the immediately vivid perceptions of 'Assisi', where every detail helps to accumulate the meaning and nothing is forced or irrelevant, even though he risks sarcasm as well as anger and pity: everything is held in a web of echoes and parallels.

Perhaps I could end by quoting one of the later poems where MacCaig returns to all his earlier ideas about honesty and modesty and unpretentiousness of approach to both life and art, to his sense of the importance of the here and now and his dislike of ideologies and what he would regard as superstition (since he is not religious), to his belief that art must have impersonality if it is to avoid being sentimental – but now, in his latest poetry, adding to that a certain controlled but personal pathos, the feeling of someone who is in his seventies and whose friends die around him, leaving him as a survivor. It's called 'Recipe':

> You have to keep stubbornly saying
> This is bread, though it's in a sunset,
> this is a sunset with bread in it.
> This is a woman, she doesn't live
> in a book or an imagination.
> Hello water, you must say. Hello, good water.
>
> You have to touch wood, but not for luck.
> You have to listen to that matter of pitches and crescendos
> without thinking Beethoven is speaking
> only to you.
>
> And you must learn there are words
> with no meaning, words like *consolation*,
> words like *goodbye*.

Shortened version of a talk given to a conference on Scottish literature, organized by the Association for Literary Studies, at the University of Strathclyde, 6 October 1984.
Books in Scotland no.16, Autumn 1984.

On Sydney Goodsir Smith's 'Perpetual Opposition' and 'Deviation Tactics'

These two very characteristic poems by Sydney Goodsir Smith appeared together in *Figs and Thistles* (1959) and are evidently companion pieces. The first poem was originally longer by Parts II and III, but these were later dropped in the *Collected Poems* (1975), presumably as repetitive and unnecessary. Smith's footnote to the title 'Perpetual Opposition'* refers to a passage in Hugh MacDiarmid's poem 'Talking with Five Thousand People in Edinburgh', published in *Poetry Scotland* no.2 (1945):

> For I am like Zamyatin. I must be a Bolshevik
> Before the Revolution, but I'll cease to be one quick
> When Communism comes to rule the roost.

The idea of the poet as one who by his nature ought to be in perpetual opposition, and not merely in opposition to certain perceived phases of history or social development, appealed strongly to both Smith and MacDiarmid. Yevgeny Zamyatin, whom MacDiarmid refers to, was indeed a Bolshevik before the 1917 Revolution, and suffered for his political beliefs, but only three years after the Revolution he wrote his striking anti-utopian novel, *We*, which called into question the whole doctrine of human perfectibility through social engineering to which the Revolution was so deeply committed. Yet Zamyatin regarded himself as more, not less revolutionary than those who were

---

* Whether I read this pregnant thocht in ane of his works or heard the bard tell it in conversation I canna jist richtlie mynd: for all that, it's an *immortel* or evergreen in Hugh MacDiarmid's life and work. Mair's the pitie, neither he nor I can track it doun til a richt context – but it byles doun til this: MacDiarmid is a dour and unregenerate Scots Republican, but (says his theorie) gin siccan government wan throu til the seats of the michtie the morn's morn, his sel wad be the firstmaist gangan intil opposition.

transforming Soviet society and who expelled him from it in 1931. 'Revolution is everywhere, in everything. It is infinite. There is no final revolution, no final number. The social revolution is only one of an infinite number of numbers: the law of revolution is not a social law...Heretics are the only (bitter) remedy against the entropy of human thought' (essay 'On Literature, Revolution, Entropy and Other Matters', 1923).

These are high matters, strongly expressed. But is perpetual opposition not perhaps, from another point of view, an easy option? Smith's first poem begins with what looks like a worldly-wise scepticism, a pessimistic acceptance of the failure of revolutions to deliver what they promised; whatever 'the richt o the cause', you end up with winners and losers: '– Tyrants up and beggars doun / As you and I weill ken.' But this does not lead him to disgust, or alienated withdrawal, or a snobbish, 'sensitive' sniping at the imperfections of political arrangements. He still has his 'traist in betterment', the 'will to sort the ills', and even as he familiarly allies himself with 'Auld Chris' in opposing any programmatic perfectibility he alters his refrain lines and claims that through opposition the tyrants may 'feel the smairt' of what the beggars suffer in silence. In the last stanza, he falls back more positively on instinct, on the instinct of rebellie men whose reason may well tell them that revolutions cannot guarantee 'richt freedom', but 'reason's no the bard's concern'; his faith that a beam in the eye of one generation may recede to a mote in the eye of the next – a gradual progressivism or a progressive gradualism – needs and is fed by a 'divine discontent' like that of republican Milton living and writing in the dark days of a restored monarchy. The refrain becomes even more optimistic: '– Tho beggars walk and tyrants ride / In beggars' hairts find freemen's pride!' Smith's final throwaway '*Mebbe!*', maddening as it must be to political activists, and perhaps confirming them in a belief that poets are flibbertigibbets and not to be trusted, is nevertheless, for those willing to think about it, a salutary confirmation of the poet's questioning and opposing function. Smith, admittedly, was never tested by events, any more than MacDiarmid was. Is it not better to give perpetual support (Mayakovsky) than perpetual opposition (Zamyatin)? In general, I think it is (though not if one is a homosexual poet in Cuba). But this does not mean that large modern revolutions, solemn, imperial, hierarchical, heavily bureaucratized, would not be the better for reinstating that post of the ancient kingdoms, the court jester, or even (can you imagine it?) a Lord of Misrule.

'Deviation Tactics' shows the same rejection of utopian programmes. To those who are oppressed, all talk of Erewhon is meaningless, and the heart 'gies nocht for braw new worlds'. We should beware of 'the mongers' – a favourite Smith word, meaning the traffickers, the manipulators, the peddlers of stopgap ideas – who dangle idealistic short-cuts in front of us, 'black, pink, or reid', in order to make us deviate from our real singular vision, our 'aefauld sicht' of a better state. And with an interesting final twist, he warns us that even if the good revolution should come, and the beam in our eye be removed, the mongers will still be around, with deviation tactics so powerful as to endanger the martyrdoms of the revolutionary process. Whether Danton or Robespierre was right in the France of 1793, whether Michael Collins or Eamon de Valera was right in the Ireland of 1921 – these may be important questions, but watch the motives of those who keep asking them.

Radical Scotland, no.20, April/May 1986.

The Poetry of W.S. Graham

Although he has not reprinted all his early poems – there are a fair number omitted from *Cage Without Grievance* and *2nd Poems*, and *The Seven Journeys* is not represented at all – the uncompromising chronological arrangement of his *Collected Poems 1942-1977* presents Graham's readers with a dense initial verbal blast or barrage redolent of the whole heady iconolatry of the 1940s, and they must persist through these vatic voluntaries until they reach the clearer air of *The White Threshold* (1949), *The Nightfishing* (1955), and the later work of the 1970s. In the early poems, the word is king but meaning is not; and yet, as in the similar poetry of Dylan Thomas, there are frequent lines which stand out and refuse to be forgotten: 'Gone to no end but each man's own', or 'Through all the suburbs children trundle cries', or 'O gentle queen of the afternoon', or 'I walk as a lonely energy at large through my host' – the last of these in a poem unfortunately omitted from the *Collected Poems*. In an essay published in this early period (*Poetry Scotland*, no.3, July 1946), Graham wrote:

> The most difficult thing for me to remember is that a poem is made of words and not of the expanding heart, the overflowing soul, or the sensitive observer. A poem is made of words. It is words in a certain order, good or bad by the significance of its addition to life... Let us endure the sudden affection of the language.

He did not escape the obvious dangers lurking in that view, the overtaking of sense by sound, the over-estimation of subconscious and chance elements, the frustrating of argument and persuasion. Yet no one can say that sound, and the subconscious, and the progress of a poem through something other than logic, are not important features of poetry, and we have to be clear that Graham's continuing faithfulness to the Word is what gives his whole work its integrity, in that he is a great and cunning craftsman, with a very particular skill in rhythm, and in the movement of a poem from line to line, a skill that stood him in real stead from *The White Threshold* onwards, when control and clarity began to attract him more than they had done when he set out. A good Graham poem is an exceedingly well made poem (and hearing him read it impresses this fact even more strongly).

The White Threshold and *The Nightfishing* contained examples of the new clarity in fine lyrical pieces like 'Since all my steps taken' (where 'hobnail on Ben Narnain' and 'the creak of the rucksack' accompany the speaker's own quest to find himself and his poetic language) and 'Letter VI' (a love poem); in suggestive, memorable, powerful, almost-understood short poems like 'Night's fall unlocks the dirge of the sea':

> The surge by day by night turns lament
> And by this night falls round the surrounding
> Seaside and countryside and I can't
> Sleep one word away on my own for that
> Grief sea with a purse of pearls and debt
> Wading the land away with salt in his throat;

and in the two longer title-poems 'The White Threshold' and 'The Nightfishing', both of which combine Graham's obsessional interests in the sea and in trying to define the communicative act and art of poetry itself. The former poem, as its title suggests, envisages the sea as a vast source of beginnings, of voyages and discoveries physical and mental, of life and livelihood and yet equally of death and fear and awe, a place stained with the blood of hunted whales and rich with the bodies of drowned sailors yet also and perhaps inexplicably 'always the welcome-roaring threshold' – and this sea is also the perilous medium of language the poet sets out on, again and again, filled with the 'drowned' writers and works of the past and with the submerged, struggling, ascending hopes and cries of the poet himself which call up, in their turn, the memories and hopes of his readers:

> Always these all sea families felled
> In diving burial hammocks or toppled
> Felled elm back into the waving woods,
> Wear me my words. The nettling brine
> Stings through the word. The Morven maiden cries.

Your heartlit fathoms hurl their ascending drowned.

Very end then of land. What vast is here?
The drowning saving while, the threshold sea
Always is here. You may not move away.

'The Nightfishing', generally and rightly regarded as the better poem of the two, gives itself the benefit of a largely narrative structure – leaving the quay at night on a herring boat, casting the nets, waiting, hauling the catch in, returning in the morning through rough seas to a calm harbour – and by this method hopes to keep the reader less anxious, to make of him a companion, a co-voyager, a co-fisherman who will feel that he has seen and brought back his catch. The poem is carefully put together, with a night bell striking on the quay at the beginning to mark the time of setting out, and a bell at the end heard striking from a buoy far out at sea, as the speaker now back home remembers where he has been. Both bells are described as 'gentle' or 'faint', and this seems important. The poem, for all that it is concerned with a rough, cold, sometimes dangerous, often noisy human occupation has as its aim the extraction of an almost mystical stillness. It may be the stillness of a moment when a man bends to blow out an oil lamp, and with the exhaling of his breath is suddenly made aware of the whole chain of time and history, and of himself as no longer even the same person rising from the lamp as the one who bent down:

> I bent to the lamp. I cupped
> My hand to the glass chimney.
> Yet it was a stranger's breath
> From out of my mouth that
> Shed the light. I turned out
> Into the salt dark
> And turned my collar up.

Or it may be the stillness at the centre of the poem, at the point when the boat has stopped and the men have cast their nets and are sitting back waiting, not long before daybreak. Describing this pause, this moment (as it appears) out of time, a very Eliotian moment one might call it (and the passage has echoes of Eliot's 'Marina'), the poet is at his most vulnerable, since he has virtually to say why the nightfishing is important to him, and in what way it is something more than a nightfishing. The abstractness of the language, and the repeated use of rather question-begging words like 'grace', show his struggle, his self-consciousness. On the naturalistic level, the pause is a period of inactivity between the skilled work of casting and hauling in the nets; on the level on which the nightfishing is 'going out to catch a poem', the pause represents the moment at which much of the work has been done, and from which the end can perhaps be glimpsed but has still to be fought for, a moment of brooding survey, a kind of 'death' within the 'life' of the material, a necessary abstraction. But how to write about it without making the self-absorption seem extreme, even imperceptive?

> And I am illusioned out of this flood as
> Separate and stopped to trace all grace arriving.
> This grace, this movement bled into this place,
> Locks the boat still in the grey of the seized sea.
> The illuminations of innocence embrace.
> What measures gently
> Cross in the air to us to fix us so still
> In this still brightness by knowledge of
> The quick proportions of our intricacies?
> What sudden perfection is this the measurement of?
> And speaks us thoroughly to the bone and has
> The iron sea engraved to our faintest breath,
> The spray fretted and fixed at a high temper,
> A script of light.

As Norman MacCaig says in his 'Culag Pier', another poem about herring-fishing, 'And ropes seem tangled, but they are not so'. No doubt the 'intricacies' have 'proportions'. But what is the 'sudden perfection', what are the 'illuminations of innocence'? Is there an innocent pause between the hunt and the kill? At that very moment of stillness on the boat, the sea underneath is beginning to churn and twist with thousands of living creatures, some already caught on the meshes, some realizing in panic that their swimming-area is no longer free, all about to die in half an hour's time. This is not the fishermen's worry, since it is their livelihood, since people eat fish. Yet the poet is not a fisherman, and it might be argued that his use of words like 'innocence' and 'grace' and 'perfection' is likely to be counterproductive, making the reader restless, by their withdrawing of imaginative sympathy, at the very point where the reader's co-operation is most needed. But whether or not that objection is sustainable, I think it is certainly true that Graham has found the greatest difficulty in stitching together the outer and inner demands of the poem at some points, whereas at other points they may swim easily and beautifully into our acceptance. Whatever its faults, 'The Nightfishing' has seriousness and grandeur, and it remains for me at the centre of his achievement, even if excellences of other kinds were attained in his later volumes.

This seems not to be the general critical view, especially on the part of those of a younger generation who came to discover or rediscover Graham during the 1970s, after the appearance of *Malcolm Mooney's Land* and *Implements in Their Places*, both of which were Poetry Book Society Choices. Although there were many poems in both volumes which I liked and admired, I found some disappointment in these books – and I believe this disappointment was shared by others of my generation, the generation contemporary with Graham, which had grown up with his poetry – because they contained so much repetition of themes familiar from his earlier work: the problems of communication, the relation between poet and reader, the nature and status of language. I thought that someone who came from Greenock and Glasgow ought not to have lived so long in a telephoneless cottage in the wilds of Cornwall. In this, I feel on reflection that I was partly right and partly wrong. Having sea, wife, cat and kitchen table for sounding-board may be no bad thing; one can concentrate on essentials. Yet concentrating on essentials may become a bad thing. Integrity is a lone star state. The struggle to use isolation (Hopkins; Dickinson) is always admirable and instructive, but sometimes the hostages of involvement and mundanity turn out to be good hobgoblins who actually sweep the house and stoke the fire. But as Keats said, 'A man's life of any worth is a continual allegory – and very few eyes can see the mystery of his life'. Without the distancing of Cornwall, Graham would not have brought to fruition the Scottish and family material which is threaded through all his books but which finds its most moving expression in the volumes of the 1970s.

In an early volume like *The White Threshold* he establishes a sort of map of varied recollections of childhood and youth in Scotland. He climbs Ben Narnain in 'Since all my steps taken', recalls high tenement and peevered pavement and 'Clydeside, / Webbed in its foundries and loud blood' in 'The Children of

> In that high tenement
> I got a great grave.

Although the speaker, in becoming poet and not engineer, is a 'turncoat', the very metaphor he uses ('in a welding flash') pays its tribute to the early environment, and the ambiguous and striking phrase at the end implies that whether or not he died to Greenock and the Clyde, and whether or not it was a great loss, the grave he got from it and carried away from it was 'great' in the fecund sense of filling him with images and memories he would never cease to draw from, and in the precise sense of imbuing him with an engineer's love of good construction. 'What's he to me?' Answer: everything.

In the volumes of the 1970s, 'The Dark Dialogues', 'Greenock at night I find you', and 'To Alexander Graham' stand out. The second section of 'The Dark Dialogues' evokes in a masterly way the disturbing power of memory to interfuse with the present, and with a Wordsworthian simplicity (but not really simple – a very skilled hand is at work!) and with the sharp pathos Graham's poetry sometimes achieves, it links the accidental visitations of memory into the theme of human communication and understanding:

> I sit with the gas turned
> Down and time knocking
> Somewhere through the wall.
> Wheesht, children, and sleep
> As I break the raker up,
> It is only the stranger
> Hissing in the grate.
> Only to speak and say
> Something, little enough,
> Not out of want
> Nor out of love, to say
> Something and to hear
> That someone has heard me.

'Greenock at night I find you' opens with a perhaps unfortunate late obeisance to Dylan Thomas ('loud Greenock long rope-working / Hide and seeking rivetting town of my child / Hood') but immediately settles down to the speaker's imagining, at night, as in a dream, that he is revisiting the town of his early years, hearing the rattle of the yards, smelling the bone-works, watching the blue welding lights, walking along Cartsburn Street:

> See, I am back. My father turned and I saw
> He had the stick he cut in Sheelhill Glen.
> Brigit was there and Hugh and double-breasted
> Sam and Malcolm Mooney and Alastair Graham.
> They all were there in the Cartsburn Vaults shining
> To meet me but I was only remembered.

The sudden but particularly effective last two lines of the poem suggest many readings: 'I went away as a young man, so all they had was memories of me', 'Even if they are dead now, I like to think they remember me', 'They could not meet me – I was only remembering'. The father who makes his brief appearance in that poem takes the centre of the stage in 'To Alexander Graham', the best of the three. Graham's favourite firmly-written three-stress line without rhyme is used here with a wonderful confidence and delicacy. The speaker dreams he is back in Greenock, at the harbour, and meets his father who seems glad to see him and who tries to speak to him although the words have no sound. The dream is so vivid that the dreamer can smell the tar and the ropes on the quay. It reminds him of the time when he left Greenock as a young man, and his father wanted to say something to him but did not do so. He wonders what his father would think of him now – whether he would be proud of him. The bond between them is strong, perhaps all the stronger for being broken. It is almost like an endless recession of images, or repeated shots from a film, of two figures meeting and parting, trying to say what they want to but cannot say, the younger haunted by the older until when he himself is old he dreams of the father as a handsome and still young man.

> You stopped and almost turned back
> To say something. My father,
> I try to be the best
> In you you give me always.
>
> Lying asleep turning
> Round in the quay-lit dark
> It was my father standing
> As real as life. I smelt
> The quay's tar and the ropes.

I think he wanted to speak.
But the dream had no sound.
I think I must have loved him.

If there is a repetitiveness in Graham, which comes from the relative thinness of the material he uses, this is something he seems to have wished to qualify in the books of the 1970s, which spread out into a much greater variety of subject than was usual before: poems on friends like Peter Lanyon and Roger Hilton, a poem about first arriving in literary London, a poem in 'ten shots' about a refugee from the concentration camps, a poem about operating a fruit machine. Of such poems, the most impressive is the totally unexpected but delightful sequence 'Johann Joachim Quantz's Five Lessons', in which the eighteenth-century German flutist (and composer for the flute) is made to give a series of instructions to a young pupil, 'a lout from the canal / With big ears but an angel's tread on the flute', who is something more than promising. The background of the place and time is lightly but deftly sketched in, and the advice reverberates well beyond flute-playing.

But you will be all right. Stand in your place
Before them. Remember Johann. Begin with good
Nerve and decision. Do not intrude/too much
Into the message you carry and put out.

One last thing, Karl, remember when you enter
The joy of those quick high archipelagoes,
To make you keep your finger-stops as light
As feathers but definite. What can I say more?
Do not be sentimental or in your Art.
I will miss you. Do not expect applause.

Graham's *Collected Poems* is a fine volume, and ought to establish his reputation on a firm basis. His is one of the most distinctive and distinguished voices in modern Scottish poetry.

Cencrastus no.5, Summer 1981.

W.S. Graham: a Poet's Letters

Rather than attempt any sort of memoir, I would like to let Graham himself speak, through extracts from his remarkable and often moving letters. Although I first met him when I was seventeen, and therefore knew him for about fifty years, our meetings (in Glasgow, Blantyre, London and Edinburgh) were infrequent. Yet, as is sometimes the case, our relationship remained deep and committed even without personal contact. Each respected and believed in the other's work, and wrote about it freely and hard-hittingly without offence. He was my first poet, and only a year and a half older than myself, so the bond between us was close. I now regret the fact that after I was called up in 1940 I destroyed all my correspondence, including many letters from Graham. All that survived was a crumpled fragment of an undated letter from 1938, which I discovered many years later and which I now quote. It shows two things which were always important to Graham: the reading aloud of poetry, and the influence of music.

13 Brisbane St.,
Greenock.

Dear Morgan,

It is indeed myself, Graham. I was reading over some of your poems the other night, aloud. The room was singing and dreaming with the sound of them. Three of the dream poems fused into me and made me cry – They must be good – 'or what does this signify to you'. Mozart's 'Jupiter' plays upon............I feel I am disintegra............

The next extract I give is from the period of the Second World War. Graham's first book, *Cage Without Grievance*, came out in 1942, and I read it when I was in the Forces, in Egypt. I was disappointed by the collection, and wrote to say so. It may be that my feeling that the contents were escapist was unfairly sharpened by a consciousness of my own position in the middle of the desert campaign, whereas Graham had deliberately avoided conscription at the beginning of the war by going to live and work in Eire, and was never in the army. At any rate, he wrote back, some time later, and gave an eloquent defence of himself. I quote a part of his long letter. His reference to 'Cataracts are ephemeral to this fall' is to a poem of mine written in 1940, which he liked.

> 22 9 43 Wheelhouse, Pengersick Lane, Germoe,
> Marazion, Cornwall.

Dear Morgan, I am pleased to hear from you and sorry you are disappointed for I mind what you think of my poetry. Mostly I dont care what people say about my poetry. You are one of the few poets I have talked to whose poetry was poetry. Now, at this time (is it 3 or 4 years later) what have we changed to? For me, Edwin, your letter goes on so much a stream of vague and complicated ingredients that poetry must have that maybe it is different things we want to make out of words and find in the poetry of others. I must try to answer parts and point out some values. Now, at this time, I know what is my poetry in all I do, I have the feel of it more, I know what I want to make more nakedly and in its element than ever in my life. And yet at this time I feel it a great risk to write against your say. I promise it will not be so long again.

... My successes or failures are my own. Indoors they run riot and ruin or create and no one knows them even their names or for what they are and on them I sink and swim. 'unreal, without meaning, severed from true and naked emotion and shy of true thought'. People write and write so sweating that it should say something worthy and valueable to humanity that some comparative wisdom is tortured into the world, recognisable and able to be valued on its plane of the world's philosophy, so that the poet is assured and a bit certain that it is good (for it does not measure favourable with the things we know) and the public are a bit certain they are not being hoaxed (for here is something we understand) and another bad poem is made, a nice rivetted up wagon whose wheels all go silently round over the tested and known-to-be-good rails with its cargoes of 100 tons Thought which is known to be a good weight. The poet does not write what he knows but what he doesnt know. At this time I am more alive and creative in my thinking and intellect than I have ever been. I have read more, there are more things I am more sure of, I am more single and more constantly in my days a poet....

You say you dont see how I can but admit your criticism but I dont. What you say is yours, and what I say about my poetry does not agree with it. What you say about poetry I agree with. But the strange thing is that I would point out to people how in this line there is real poetry and quote 'Who longingly for violetcells prospect the meads'. or maybe 'Birches erect The ephemeral mechanism of welcoming'. And think of it with 'Cataracts are ephemeral to this fall' (because of 'EPHEMERAL') or quote all of O Gentle Queen, I, no more real than evil and Here next the chair I was when winter went, the three poems in my book which I would firstly let stand. So when I agree about poetry with you I then turn to my poems and say ... yes thats right. I am always so first to say love the words the single words that have a heart and a world in them which beats and changes to a new rhythm in every new position of context. And I think now words are saying more for me....

CAGE WITHOUT GRIEVANCE is a first book of poems. It's all right, better than most first books, because I am potentially a greater poet than most today which does not make me very great but I am.... The chief value is the realisation that my voice is heard and the involuntary responsibility which comes down on me and makes me more hard working at my poems....

Have you any new poems I can see? I dont know why you joined the forces. When do you come back? Have I an unavoidable bias? (I'm looking through your letter before I finish.) Christ its a great letter Morgan you can fairly write like a wee minister of a good gospel. I dont know what you want to be there for. I have my self said and then all you say I still say its when it comes to my poetry, theres the bother. 'There are innumerable things to speak of and questions to ask.' I hope you write soon. It was Norman [Thomson] told me you wrote to him. Right, here's the end and I cant write more. I seem to not be stimulated up to replying good to your letter. I dont know why. It seems not to matter. Yet it does matter to me very much that you are disappointed. Its raining now on the roof. I'm living in a caravan a friend's lent me in Cornwall, lonely and by the sea. I fish and gather mushrooms and write and cook.

Yours sincerely   W.S. Graham

After the war, our creative tracks seemed always to be out of phase. The decade from 1945 to 1955 was among Graham's most assured and productive times, and saw the publication of two of his most powerful books, *The White Threshold* (1949) and *The Nightfishing* (1955). For myself, it was a period of restless readjustment and unsatisfactory achievement. Conversely, when the 1960s proved happily productive for me, Graham's work was at its lowest ebb. So each of us had times of puzzlement, of silence, of admiration, for the other, but the thread of the letters was never snapped. I give an extract from a long ten-page letter he sent me in 1949, in reply to several letters of mine which had been piling up. He has striking things to say about 'The White Threshold' (it is not always clear whether he is referring to the book or its title-poem, or both), and about critics and editors; and I quote some of his candid criticism of my own poem 'Dies Irae'.

> 23 Cliff St.,
> Mevagissey,
> Cornwall
> England   14 4 49

My Dear Edwin,

Here are some notes, some kind of reply, to your good letters which I have here. And I'll go through them putting down answers to questions or questions implied.

Your letters are always so very live & civilised & sensitive. Though I have hardly replied I have often thought about you and what you've said about my poetry and what is in the letters, 'The Morgan Letters'.

Here I begin on the June 48 one. This must have reached me in America. You'll hardly have remembered what youve said. Still, I'll try to be clear.

I cant remember very well your 'Egypt Letter' which you say was 'carping' and which I defended. Probably I would now agree to most of it but say that it was a necessary and wholesome display of energy (to a degree which let it become valid, at times, as poetry) and point out its signs of a rich potential. I remember you using the word – 'stevedoring', about how I was manhandling & twisting words. It was so true. The 'distortion' is legitimate but in those early poems it was so often done rudely and not 'with grace'....

The sea in The White Threshold is a changing symbol. It is

variously – the continual Arrival from 'otherness' – the element
through which we all move and with the urge to really contact
and share with the other 'inner sea' of other people and break
the centre aloneness. Yet the centre aloneness is the greatest joy
and gift from Him. If showing it were easy it would be nothing.
– the mingling, always moving, spontaneous morality of the
'heart' as opposed to the outside constructions of order because
we are a world and live together. – and the sea with no exactness
but with nonetheless intensity and positivity – moving mingling
with a storm 1000s of miles away having affects and movements at our door –. Edwin, I really love being on the sea.
There I have a feeling of freedom & cleaness & being part of
a great energy which has nothing to do with any morality and
is completely unhuman....

First let me say, there are no editors I know of that I respect
at all as people of any real taste in poetry. Why they reject and
accept is not important. The only ones whose sympathy to my
poetry I respect are those who write poetry also and in whose
poems there is evidence of that relation to language as a dialogue
taken part in, going on in the very centre loneliness. I quickly
think who I care about liking or disliking my work. About half
a dozen. And I know that if I become wellknown and at all
'famous' in my lifetime it will not be, at all important but will
just mean that that larger public, who draw a certain selfcon-
scious and nostalgic excitement from running their eyes along
the words in my poem; believe I am a poet of some magnitude
because 'the few' believe so (from Eliot down to, say, Read),
and can read my work knowing they are not being 'taken in'
whatever that may mean. Art can not be fake. It either unites
with us to our advantage or doesnt unite with us at all. By 'to
our advantage' I mean to our enlargement of spirit. So, more
& more, I realise the aloneness is a joy to live in and talk there
to the most marvellous listener which is within my imagination and the limitations of that listener are the limitations of
my poetry. So certainly now I think – if I hadnt poetry – that
place to be in the act of making poetry – what would I do?
Where would there be the least peace in my life?...

The DIES IRAE is like nothing in contemporary poetry. As a
whole poem for me it is not successful. The listing & cataloguing
goes on too long. Phrases lines and some parts are very moving.
In fact, Edwin, I find it very moving anyhow as a whole poem
though I think it isnt successful. You would know I would like

the strong physical action language which seems to be kept out of contemporary poetry as much as possible, maybe thought as a sign of naivety. As you would notice in the TWT excerpt I, like you, am drawn very much to Anglo-Saxon words and language with that basic strong feel about it and recently in this poem I am working on ['The Nightfishing'] I've been going through all the Anglo-Saxon poems and earlier .... But I want a certain kind of strength in my work from the Anglo-Saxon poetry and even a certain faint echo but I must speak in the idiom of the language at its present point. To use archaisms (and you have) they must be used very self-consciously so that the knowledge that they are used by the poet to carry all their archaic associations in itself goes towards the success of the poem. It is usually as a montage value in a poem that archaism occures. Except in Pound. And Yeats is a curious instance and very special. Here, Edwin, it would have to be successful in the Pound way of The Seafarer or an earlier 'troubadour poem'. So, then, in some ways this would be like the best kind of translation of A.S., yet would be original? But there are phrases and words which have by now taken on too tarnished a poetic diction to be very often used freshly and I am apparent [sic] of them fairly soon. – God's <u>wrath</u> – sea of time – – groaning shores of wrath – faced the blast – poor coat threadbare. Now – no matter how thought out the reason – or how cunningly constructed into the organic of a poem, it's almost impossible to carry the weight of this worn out stuff. [There follow two pages of detailed critical analysis of the rhythm and vocabulary and rhetoric of 'Dies Irae.]...

Dear Edwin – I must stop now – thumb sore with writing and 4 a.m. but I'm posting this because I know myself and dont be hard on this letter. – Is there any chance of you getting down here to Mevagissey for a week maybe if I found some landlady would take you a week cheaply? Myself, I cant and am broke so cant move but would be happy to see you and we could talk & write & get the sun. (I know bits of your Horizon trans. [of the Anglo-Saxon poem 'The Ruin'] very well.) best wishes – let me hear from you soon, I'll go on with this letter soon, Sydney.

Later that year, Graham was living in London and having a series of lunchtime meetings with T.S. Eliot, who admired his poetry and apparently got on well with him. Graham was by that time on Faber's poetry list.

3 Warwick Gdns., London W14.
23 11 49

Dear Edwin

Here I write just a wee note not to answer ever yet your good letter but to say hello and give you a little news about myself. Though I write to you so little I think you would be surprised if you knew how often I think of you and your good seriousness in the middle of this frantic place. Also (if I can suppose that I write for some serious audience), in the temptation of a weak moment, when I am tempted to say the easier more attractive thing instead of trying harder to say the more difficult thing; you are one of a halfdozen people I might think of who would see it as a lesser statement. So hello there, and how are you and is there at all a chance of you being near London in the next three months or so? It would be nice to see you and talk....

A nice thing. I have been seeing Eliot quite a lot and what a real comfort (strengthening) it has been. We have talked mostly about verse and what he remarked about my own was cheering. Again, it is good to realise that, if one had been lazy or deceitful (though I am guilty enough and should try harder) in one's verse he would have known. We talked a lot about the structure of the long poem (I've just finished mine) and 'the purity of criticism' which I am almost a crank about. I mean that the criticism of poetry in Britain today is so bad and trite often through the 'critic' not bringing pure critical canons to bear on the subject, but bringing in outside values (which are incidental) of morality, ethics or even politics. Or they write so, what they call, 'impressionistically' that there is no need for them to think. Or they write about everything but the object because they have no elementary knowledge of what such an object is made of or how it works. I am not pleading for a dead, mechanistic criticism, but for a criticism which will enable the reader to understand the new special language of the new poet and which will more or less leave the reader to weigh and value and use the statement without the critic saying what he imagines the statement is (in paraphrase) and telling the reader it is good or bad accordingly. What cheered me was, he said that I had 'a good sense of form and a wonderful sense of rhythm'. He suggested that my poetry was 'intellectual' poetry and would go slow because people just were lazy about thinking. He thought no young poet had produced a long poem with any formal structure, which he thought was necessary. My poem's been finished a month and though I made about 11 drafts before then I've been changing words and lines a little till yesterday and now I really think it's finished. I'll try to get it on the BBC and published in some periodical, though it is 520 lines, and when it's ready to go in the next book for Faber I'll be able to see it better from the greater distance. If I can whip up any money to get it typed with 6 copies I'll send you one. I would like to know what you think about it. It's called – THE NIGHT-FISHING....

Some news – I've been pretty ill and out and in hospital here having xrays and treatment. I feel a little better and must scurry round for a job. I dont want to go back to Mevagissey. I've had enough of the country for a long time. I feel that me living always in the country has in some ways been an evasion for certain personal social problems in my relation to people generally. So now I'm going all out to get a job here and stick here a year or two or, if I get any money anywhere, I would like to go to Europe. Your letter was good and what you said about my verse was useful as always....

love,

Sydney

In the summer of 1950 I received another long letter, undated, from Cornwall, which is perhaps the most self-revealing of them all. In a frustrated between-poems mood; recently ill; and chronically short of money: somehow he transformed everything through the act of writing, through the appeal to a listener, and through a liberating undertow from Irish song, and Robert Burns, and *Finnegans Wake*. I wish I had space to quote the whole letter, which is really of a piece.

Higher Carn Cottage, Zennor. A grey evening not long till dark and low long wisps of cloud blowing past the windows. Dear Edwin hello. You'll just have to read this anyhow. And I have just got to write about how I feel at the moment or go quite mad. So I am writing you though I've all kinds of letters I owe but somehow I think I'll feel better after I say how 'No worse' this time seems to be. And I might not even send it when I finish.

A letter from Joke Grim, the desert of a laugh. Forgive this using you. I sit here with all my pieces of started poetry on the table by me and with the mist thick at the window and the light rapidly going. What do I write to say? I dont know. I havnt spoken to anyone for five days. I've been working hard, notes and beginnings etc. yet I havnt begun a poem yet in all this time.....

All things drag one down at once. Or – It never rains but. Stomach fucked. Not a soul, not even in St Ives, that is (apart from knowing anything about poetry) able to talk with a brain humbly and seriously about anything. Christ! Hardly a soul that can talk straightforwardly with a humble enthusiasm. So many cant talk for thinking about what kind of impression theyre making and if theyre 'winning' or not. And at the same time Eliot hasnt started any negotiations for a possible grant because my doctor hasnt sent the report yet and I've written the doctor three times and no reply and I just dont know what is going on maybe he's on holiday and so I try to borrow five-shillings's for paraffin and try and try hard not to feel bitter or persecuted when I see the people in St Ives who dont want to do anything much getting money for nothing. What a place this is we are all living in. (This is a list of complaints, Edwin, let it be and dont mind me having a revel in them) And I havnt found a cottage because I cant go ahead and say I'll take it because I might have not received the grant and I'm supposed to have this to the end of August. This is, I suppose, at the moment the NO to life. Down down down. I cant remember ever having been so deep. This surely must be the lowest before the ascension again. I dont know but writing it is like talking it and talking it must surely help. Poor target. I have procured a new battery for my radio 'on tick' and so I am able to sit here between sentences to you and listen to a woman talking in French, the cadences very sad and falling, and I dont know the slightest school French. Yet what a complication of emotions she arouses. Christknows what she's talking about. Maybe a cookery talk.

'When with his hunting dog I see a cloud' – the beginning of a Canto by E.P. So authentically poetic.

A joke or jock among the talking empties. Now on the radio –

The harp that once through Tara's halls
The soul of music shed
Now hangs as mute...

A great song. It has always affected me strongly. When I served my apprenticeship as an engineer I used to have to get up at 6.30 to catch the early train to Glasgow and I remember those dark cold mornings and me with no more wish to be in that screeching bedlam of tortured metal than die but strangely Radio Eire started gramophone records early and they always started with McCormick singing The Harp That Once and he was so good I never tired of it. What a story to tell. Dont mind much. Let it be. Let me go on for it's easing to talk at the moment. I've had my mind go steadily at verse day after day from 10 to around 7 at night that I just dont seem to know anything about it any more.....

A man called Whichcoat has an aphorism which goes –
We naturalize ourselves to the employment of eternity.

I'm crossed with light in this immortal space.
Maybe I shall encounter my own corruption,
Crossed with the scorch of The Iron and The Fire.

Position itself is a language, like selection
Whose pandemonium medium creates the tyrant.

That was two bits of verse from an old notebook I kept in Mevagissey. And naturally this quotation appeals to me –

The wan moon is setting behind the white wave
And time is setting for me oh.

Yes what a pass for me, the hawk-heart braced in the epic's hero, to come to. Better – The thick-heart based in the comic's peeriot. And I see that's not the spelling of a Canio but I've did my laughal best. Here's twelve midnight. It's some poor hurt but ever rejoyces. Morgan the Mighty or McMorgan the Michty. A lament on the moothiamonium. Or, to spoke police-lightly, a sonneteer of Soong will noby had from Muster Edinbro Moomorgan. Play jest yin metrefor o' muse-hicks for Jocky Gramfunny, Juke Grumf, Wullie Grum, Trouble-youas Greyhim, Sadknee Graham, Willheyum? Groom and

Ankle Bum Kidney and all. Rejoyce in the word. In the be grinning wiss the worried. An wan o'cluck o'moornin soughs roon awe. Gret but still grey gusts lowed an daunert abane the gabble. Way nay lea-rug or esstrung ster,

Moan kine drear hurrah.

Thus Tom Mick a Muse-meant for yews elf use Jams Joss – BUST IN HELL WARLID. Thus double in boy mucks goo. Ruskin wee day illso. O mush as end glims nigh so snorely noire arain the chummies' gabbles sleepin bemoth an a'ster lauft. Lay mint. Sick cloth to Waly Greymoo. Nare doed tae deid. Wi sear a stormache it he hid he laugh would turn his fuss tae the leal. A's hour an din o triprighter lits ruts drum nslumber saw slopy fell ma shudders than that Blackmanned Mirtheus approached see siftly lully tongued. An hour me blent so sablebodied big booth disindid drown tae tar me oot. Me Fah Lah Fah So Fah dinty floure. Doonfle aslap to luck's lap. An ss leapt and ss leapt sweat lay wrathin a dram dram oh fear wozzem no no entercoarse jest plandaft.

Thus entertuned to purefact pitch by instant Aeneas lie tupping erotter godybaby Awaya. Bony Churlie's noa byby. Illtaegather gatruddy. Lest and last lay if all tae haunchache still taegather. Men laudies liedies maysons frownds fumen chilldears rushouters dourshiters darecapers munswiwimens munswayoot glumfers and a' skittish barbs tae dull by Doric Ontwaddle. An yore silf Sadneigh listed a bit not least. Yawn vice rift up encore us. Tinderly armagirlo an besad or stunned say lavingly carrousing whore hair or heehaw seeks zone hairs a lust tae stir by. That wade myth an partied laps read cuin canny sham. The knack hair sulky a wee uncome nape weasely mad hypnoteased. Bit of coarse spute out the papple pips. There you'll rose badlimbs you'll pant the teen red. And on to ither ethers. Whit? Noosing noo. She-dolled a quintense beaf or get

Handover brute amend　　　　　　　Write soon, Edwin and

and say what youre doing and send

any new poems. Is there anything going on in literary Glasgow?

as ever,

Sydney

By way of contrast, here is what Graham himself calls a 'businesslike' letter, which I quote entire. He had begun writing and publishing again, after a long break, towards the end of the

1960s, and his wary gladness that this has happened is very characteristically expressed in the last paragraph.

> 4 Mountview Cottages,
> Madron, Penzance,
> Cornwall.   14 10 69

Dear Edwin,

Yes it is me, Sydney, after this long time. You will have probably noticed that I am putting out poems again after some years. This new book, MALCOLM MOONEY'S LAND is coming out in March. I have this extra proof which I enclose thinking you might like it enough to help its outcome either in Scotland or England by writing something somewhere on the development or lack in my work from earlier books. You certainly would be the boy to do it and I would rather be slain by you than praised by a fudge-brain. I am well aware I write to you for my own furtherance but I do not know now what is done or what is not done in these matters. I never see or talk to writers down here. The thing is, if you like MALCOLM MOONEY'S LAND, what can be done? In Scotland or England or America (POETRY CHICAGO seem very much *for* me.). Edwin, this is me deciding to be a bit businesslike for once.

I will be getting in touch with MacBeth soon who I think might put either a reading on again or maybe a discussion. Could anything be down [done?] there? Also, when you reply, I would be pleased if you could give me any suggestions about Scotland. I dont know what magazines are going about there. I dont even know whether my poetry is seen at all in Scotland. I am doing a reading of my poetry on March 3rd (a new idea sponsored by the publisher of the poet) at the POETRY SOCIETY in London. They have asked Nessie up too. And that is about all of selfish that. ENOUGH.

You will realise that coming from a lesser man than me or going to a lesser man than you, to say anything about your own work now after the selfish bit of the letter would be suspect. But let me say that I have followed your good real flight with great pleasure. You have my best respect, Edwin, and if that sounds pompous I say it at that risk but I dont think you will think that.

I hope this reaches you through the University. I seem to be able now at last to write more easily. New poems are coming out. I am now able to speak about things I always wanted to speak about but hadnt the equipment. That bitch muse seems to be at the moment a wee bit kind. Cheerio child of Lanarkshire.

love,
Sydney

The last letter I had from him was written in 1981, in a very shaky hand which gave me a pang, since his handwriting had always been so bold and splendid. The reading he refers to, in Edinburgh, also turned out to be our last meeting.

4 Mountview Cottages,
Madron,
Penzance
Cornwall.   15 9 81

Dear Edwin,

Great to hear your poetry.

Whatever happened at the end? I thought I was going to see you afterwards and have a talk for a while after all that long time? That woman with that dress seemed to whisk you away in a great rush.

If I can get up next year I hope we really meet.

best wishes,
Sydney

Note

I have retained Graham's idiosyncratic spelling and punctuation, but have corrected a few obvious typing slips. Omissions are indicated by five dots . . . . . Round brackets are Graham's; square brackets are used for occasional comments or information of my own. E.M.

The Sea, the Desert, the City: environment and language in W.S. Graham, Hamish Henderson, and Tom Leonard

I wish to consider three Scottish poets whose work has been strongly marked by a specific environment, each environment being topographically identifiable and describable, but at the same time being the occasion for great extensions of meaning. W.S. Graham (1918–86) was born and brought up in Greenock, on the Firth of Clyde, but then moved south and lived for the rest of his life on the coast of Cornwall. In both environments he was on the edge of the sea, and the sea dominates his poetry, as both a literal and a metaphorical presence. Hamish Henderson (b.1919) served as an officer with the Highland Division in North Africa during the Second World War, and his poetry starts out by dealing with the actual conditions of desert warfare but also opens more widely into thoughts and feelings about 'the desert' as such. Tom Leonard (b.1944), born and brought up in Glasgow, has committed himself to developing a Glasgow poetry which will not only recreate a range of social experience within that city but will frequently use the language(s) of Glasgow speech; all this within a broader recognition of the meaning and importance of 'the city'.

The three environments, although two are natural and one is man-made, hold tensions and oppositions which make them attractive to poets. The sea is the most alien, the most uninhabitable except briefly (in boats) or under special conditions (on oil-rigs); yet a source and image of both life (fishing; biological evolution) and death (drowning). The desert, dangerous and precarious to live in, a challenge to resourcefulness and survival, baffling in its dune-shifting and mirages, can yet be magnetic to certain temperaments for its colours, its silences, its starry skies, its strange extremes of heat and cold, its buried or half-buried relics of ancient cultures. And the city, which for some may be

273

as dangerous and precarious as the desert, is also a wonderfully varied and vigorous arena for every sort of human relationship and action and voice; alienating to some, and to others as natural as the sea is to fish.

W.S. Graham began publishing his poetry in the early 1940s, when the New Apocalypse movement was in the ascendant and when James Joyce had recently brought out *Finnegans Wake*. Linguistic intoxication made this early poetry almost impenetrable and, although an inchoate poetic force was always felt to be there, it was only with the appearance of *The White Threshold* (London, 1949) and more especially *The Nightfishing* (London, 1955) that his full talent could be recognized. It is significant that a powerful group of poems in *The White Threshold* took up seriously for the first time the subject and theme of the sea which were later to become so much his trademark, as if this particular concentration had effected a release of feelings previously blocked and confused behind thick verbal entanglements. He has done his exercises, he has packed his luggage, and now he is ready to set out into the unknown, to cross the white threshold, to go on a nightfishing. That the idea of such a release was important to him can be seen in his essay 'Notes on a Poetry of Release' (*Poetry Scotland*, 3 (July 1946), 56–58), where the sense of unbinding or uncaging is applied to the reader rather than to the poet, except that without the potential of release with which the poet has charged the poem from his own experience, using the flux of always–changing language as a sailor uses the flux of the always–changing ocean, no release would be carried across the gap to the reader:

> The most difficult thing for me to remember is that a poem is made of words and not of the expanding heart, the overflowing soul, or the sensitive observer. A poem is made of words. It is words in a certain order, good or bad by the significance of its addition to life.... The poem itself is dumb but has the power of release.... A poem is charged to that power of release that even to one man it goes on speaking again and again beyond behind its speaking words, a space of continual messages behind the words.

This 'space of continual messages behind the words' became very characteristic of Graham's poetry. Even when he is most directly evoking memories of his early days on the Clyde and his move from training as engineer to training as poet, as for example in 'Letter II' from *The Nightfishing* (*Collected Poems* (London, 1979), p.110), he gives the reader the bonus of grappling with the idea of a continuous shedding of selves, an involuntary sloughing of each dead 'I' as the next living 'I' is resurrected from it, all this summed up in the startling last two lines with his claim that his long-dead Clydeside tenement days are still fecund in a way that cannot be spelled out:

> Younger in the towered
> Tenement of night he heard
> The shipyards with nightshifts
> Of lathes turning their shafts.
> His voice was a humble ear
> Hardly turned to her.
> Then in a welding flash
> He found his poetry arm
> And turned the coat of his trade.
> From where I am I hear
> Clearly his heart beat over
> Clydeside's far hammers
> And the nightshipping firth.
> What's he to me? Only
> Myself I died from into
> These present words that move.
> In that high tenement
> I got a great grave.

Where more than reminiscence is at work, as in the sudden eruption of sea themes in *The White Threshold*, with poems like 'Night's Fall Unlocks the Dirge of the Sea', 'At Whose Sheltering Shall the Day Sea', 'Three Poems of Drowning', 'The Voyages of Alfred Wallis', and the title-poem, the sea itself, accompanied fairly quickly by its metaphorical possibilities, moves to the centre of the picture to interlock with problems of language, art, and communication. In the very fine 'Night's Fall...' the speaker lies at night listening to the sea breaking on the shore, and although he is 'Dressed warm in a coat of land in a house' he can neither write nor sleep, thinking about the ambiguous image the ocean presents, morally innocent and aesthetically beckoning yet filled with drowned people and sunken treasures, the 'Grief sea with a purse of pearls and debt / Wading the land away with salt in its throat'. In the elegy on the Cornish naive painter Alfred

Wallis (1855-1942), whose pictures celebrate seas and ships and coastal towns, the artist is presented through fantastic images, his death a keelhauling to Heaven, the land he leaves behind floating past him like a ship with gulls in the rigging of the roofs, he himself both sailor ('waved into boatfilled arms') and keel ('grounded on God's great bank'). This poem is one of several in which Graham pays tribute to painters who have lived and worked on the Cornish coast (Peter Lanyon, Roger Hilton, Bryan Wynter) and whom he sees as fellow-strugglers with the idea or the reality of the sea, whether they make of it something representational or something entirely abstract.

The title-poem, 'The White Threshold', is a longer piece, in five sections, strong and striking in parts but less than clear in overall structure; a first run, in a sense, for the more solidly achieved 'The Nightfishing'. The title does not mean, as George Barker once in friendly banter with Graham translated it, the well-scrubbed doorstep (though it might almost imply that too, Empsonianly) but, of course, the wave-crests and foam, the 'pacing white-haired kingdoms of the sea', that lure the watcher on the shore to enter, to cross the threshold, to cast off, to try that other kingdom, and then (deepening the metaphor) to descend and rise again, to announce the creative abyss to others, to welcome others at the threshold, to bring the messages and memories of the drowned, the dead (the real dead, or one's own dead selves), to show that Melville's harpooned whale is also the human heart, the 'caaing thresher' in its 'splendid blood'. And the speaker, the poet, is like the Ancient Mariner who has a tale to tell you: 'I walk towards you and you may not walk away.' The poem ends with a statement: the poet is at the threshold of his own ambitious and distinctive conception of poetry, the sense of his potential being stirred up as the sea stirs up the sand, the nature of the power being an interaction of present and past not unlike that of Wordsworth:

> This midnight makes, more than the sea its sand,
> My daily dead puff up an ambitious dust
> Through native pain endured and through my earliest
> Gesture towards the first fires of my past.
>
> (*Collected Poems*, p.83)

That ambition shows itself most fully and satisfactorily in 'The Nightfishing'. Here, structure and underpinning are provided by a narrative, the story of a boatload of fishermen (who are present but scarcely mentioned: there is only one observer/speaker) sailing out at night, casting their nets, waiting, hauling the herring catch aboard, and returning to the harbour in the morning through rough seas. The oddly solipsistic effect of the invisibility of the crew has been criticized, and the only defence must be that the realism of the poem is deliberately meant to go so far and no further. There are plenty of clear and straightforward references: 'The cross-tree light, yellowing now', 'the rudder live and gripped in the keel-wash', 'a sailing pillar of gulls', 'we cut the motor quiet', the nets 'sawing the gunwale / With herring scales', the rope 'feeding its brine / Into our hacked hands'. But we are never allowed to forget that, while all this perfectly recognizable fishing activity is going on, the boat is at the same time sailing through dark seas of language for a shimmering catch of poetry (that is, the poem), and even beyond that, for a catch of near-mystic experience that may feed the speaker's poetry in the future. The moment of pause after the nets have been cast is the centre of the poem, and as the men rest back, and the bilges slap in the first faint grey light, and gulls settle on the water, there is a strange abstracted stillness which is described as 'grace arriving'. Echoes of Eliot's 'Marina' accompany the sense of an unexpected, inexplicable moment of happiness and joy:

> This grace, this movement bled into this place,
> Locks the boat still in the grey of the seized sea.
> The illuminations of innocence embrace.
> What measures gently
>
> Cross in the air to us to fix so still
> In this still brightness by knowledge of
> The quick proportions of our intricacies?
> What sudden perfection is this the measurement of?
>
> (*Collected Poems*, p.97)

These unanswered questions, and the rather forced quality of the writing, make it hard to believe that the poem comes sufficiently sharp and clear at its most crucial point, and only the power of the surrounding narrative permits us to take on trust at least something of the 'still brightness', the 'instant written dead', the 'script of light'. Perhaps, when one thinks of the bilges slapping at the speaker's feet, the abstract language, continuing for several stanzas, has imposed a too conscious abreption from the story for the reader to be other than slightly suspicious of it; and perhaps, in that sense, the poet should have kept closer to the concrete imagery he uses so well. But, whatever one's momentary reservations, this remains an impressive poem, not easily forgotten.

'The Nightfishing' represents the furthest or deepest point of Graham's exploitation of sea imagery. After publishing the volume of *The Nightfishing* he had no book till fifteen years later, when *Malcolm Mooney's Land* (London, 1970) appeared, and his next volume after that, *Implements in Their Places* (London, 1977), was his last. In these late collections the sea is still present from time to time, but it is no longer the commanding obsession it was in his middle period. The Old Quay in Greenock where he 'smelt the tar and the ropes' is used as a setting in a moving poem about his father, 'To Alexander Graham', and in the title-poem, 'Malcolm Mooney's Land', there are allusions to the heroic Arctic voyages of Nansen in his ship *Fram*; the great virtue of Nansen, as Graham records elsewhere and would doubtless apply to the creative artist too, was that 'he knew when to allow himself to be drifted and when to act'[1]. The seventy-four quasi-epigrammatic sections of the title-poem in *Implements in Their Places* have a habit of adverting or reverting to the sea, at times wryly or humorously, at times with what seems like a consciously valedictory note, at times with literary references to other 'sea' associates (Shelley, Crane, Melville, 'Maybe even Eliot'). Two moods come across strongly, and with the same economy. One is grim, though not lacking in a final touch of black humour:

> From my bunk I prop myself
> To look out through the salted glass
> And see the school of black killers.
> Grampus homes on the Graham tongue.
>
> (*Collected Poems*, p.250)

The other is light, playful, self-perceptively resigned:

> When I was a buoy it seemed
> Craft of rare tonnage
> Moored to me. Now
> Occasionally a skiff
> Is tied to me and tugs
> At the end of its tether.
>
> (*Collected Poems*, p.237)

The death of Graham early in 1986 gives this piece an added pathos, but its well-cut outline remains typical of the engineer who did not go to sea but wrote about it instead.

It could be argued that Graham's devotion to the sea had both positive and negative aspects, in that it instigated most of his best poetry in the post-war years to 1955 but may also have encouraged him into an isolation which cut him off from too many human sources of feeling, his late attempt to recapture these (largely through reminiscence) and also to write more 'communicatively' through clearer meaning or lighter tone, being heroic but fragmented. When we turn to Hamish Henderson a similar question poses itself. Although he has published poems intermittently in magazines over the years, Henderson's only volume of his own poetry is *Elegies for the Dead in Cyrenaica* (1948; second edition, with some added material, Edinburgh, 1977), and that book sums up his experience of the desert, and of desert warfare, so intensely, in poems written between 1942 and 1947, that it must have been deeply problematic whether the desert, like Graham's sea, could somehow be carried forward to integrate with other and more ordinary facets of experience.

Hamish Henderson has become extremely well known as a collector, writer, and singer of songs, and his work with the School of Scottish Studies in Edinburgh, on ballads and folklore and indeed everything connected with oral tradition, has made him a revered figure in that area of culture where scholarly and popular can meet. There is some disagreement as to the continuities between his *Elegies* and his later songs. The *Elegies* use in general a 'high' literary style, with a recurring suggestion of the classical hexameter as well as hints of Pound and Eliot in line-breaks and in international vocabulary, yet there is also a fair amount of colloquial language, there are snatches of song, and the reader is certainly not being held at arm's length. For all that, the book stands out very distinctively in his work, and has been undervalued for what it is in itself.

The desert, in these poems, is shown as having such a powerful presence that it controls the reactions of soldier and poet to the war being waged. In his original 'Foreword', Henderson relates how the main theme of the sequence was suggested to him when he heard a captured German officer say: 'Africa changes everything. In reality we are allies, and the desert is our common enemy' (p.59). It is, on the one hand, a perfectly real North

African desert, and the book abounds with place-names: Sollum, Halfaya, El Adem, El Eleba, Himeimat, Munassib, Cyrene, Alexandria, Libya, Egypt. But it is also 'the dead land...insatiate and necrophilous', 'the brutish desert', 'the limitless / shabby lion-pelt', 'the heretic desert' with its bad trinity of 'sand rock and sky', 'this bleak moon-surface / of dents and ridges, craters and depressions', an 'imbecile wasteland', 'the unsearchable desert's / moron monotony', 'The tawny deadland' under silent 'African constellations', 'the envious desert', 'the ennui / of lime-stone desert', 'the benighted deadland', 'this barbarous arena', 'the lunar qattaras, the wadis like family trees'. It is a brutal, animal place, a pseudo-Trinity of material elements. Also, in the desert warfare within that barbarous arena (the Latin derivation is perfect), the shifting sands, the violent winds, and the mirages add a disorientating effect, so that the enemy appears as a *doppel-gänger*, a mirror reflection of oneself, as the battle swirls back and forward:

> And these, advancing from the direction of Sollum,
> swaddies in tropical kit, lifted in familiar vehicles
> are they mirage – ourselves out of a mirror?
> No, they too, leaving the plateau of Marmarica
> for the serpentine of the pass, they advancing towards us
> along the coast road, are the others, the brothers
> in death's proletariat, they are our victims and betrayers
> advancing by the sea-shore to the same assignation.
> We send them our greetings out of the mirror.
>
> (p.22)

If the 'other' is the 'brother', it is not only because the killed of both sides must join 'death's proletariat', it is equally a feature of the curious quasi-camaraderie of the desert campaign, where each side would take, use, and have retaken equipment or stores belonging to the other; where the haunting song 'Lili Marlene' was on Axis and Allied lips indiscriminately; and where Rommel was a German general whom his enemies could respect in a half-legendary way. So the desert is both alien and familiar, both savage and reconciling. The humanitarianism of the sequence, which would at first sight surely seem bizarre to anyone who had fought on the Russian front or been sent to a concentration camp, is strongly qualified at certain points. Although one of the best of the elegies, the seventh ('Seven Good Germans'), gives a sympathetic but unsentimental thumbnail sketch of the seven dead Nazis under their crosses at El Eleba, the interlude ('Opening of the Offensive') between the fifth and sixth elegies, which describes the fearsome barrage at Alamein in October 1942, is an outburst of the warlike spirit that could only fail to satisfy the most patriotic by extending its anger into politics in an ambiguous (not really ambiguous!) fashion:

> Meaning that many
> German Fascists will not be going home
> meaning that many
> will die, doomed in their false dream
> We'll mak siccar!
> Against the bashing cudgel
> against the contemptuous triumphs of the big battalions
> mak siccar against the monkish adepts
> of total war against the oppressed oppressors
> mak siccar against the leaching lies
> against the worked out systems of sick perversion
> mak siccar
>   against the executioner
> against the tyrannous myth and the rèal terror
> *mak siccar*

(pp.28-29)

The use of the Scots phrase *mak siccar* (make sure) reminds us that it is a Highland division which is at the centre of the action, but this is also a means of introducing analogies and allusions, as is done elsewhere throughout the book. One desert is in Africa, but tracts of northern and western Scotland are also a desert, where the Clearances have replaced people with sheep, or indeed with nothing at all: 'the treeless machair', 'Burning byres', 'Dark moorland bleeding / for wrong or right'. And what of the Pharaohs of earlier millenniums, did they defeat the desert with their monuments or did the desert defeat them? The very interesting eighth elegy ('Karnak') inclines to the view that the desert 'had its own way at last', almost in collusion with a kind of desert, a death-wish, a 'craved annihilation' in the minds of the Egyptians. The Hyksos, the Greeks, the Arabs, the 'barbarians' of Cavafy, and now 'Rommel before the gates of Alexandria' are all perhaps 'the necessary antithesis', 'the standard-bearers of the superb blasphemy'. If the thesis is the 'stylised timeless effrontery' of the Ancient Egyptian desert culture, and the antithesis is the barbarian at the gate, can the dialectic complete itself?

> Synthesis is implicit
> in Rilke's single column, (die *eine*)
> denying fate, the stone mask of Vollendung.
> (Deaf to tarbushed dragoman
> who deep-throatedly extols it).

(p.40)

Rilke too visited the Egyptian desert, and its imagery appears in his *Duino Elegies*. But whereas Rilke wanted us to interiorize, and change in terms of art, the great monuments of the past, Henderson is more concerned to ask questions on the historical level, and in the dialectic of history (wars, invasions, oppressions, and minglings of culture) he remains impressed by the extraordinary power of a desert civilization to 'deny fate', not only the fate of destruction and dispersal but even the fate of having its ruins extolled by puny successors. There is a useful discussion of the relation between the elegies of Henderson and Rilke by Richard E. Ziegfeld.[2]

The tenth and last elegy ('The Frontier') makes it clear that Henderson sees how his duty as an elegist must include something more than remembrance: there must be something more active, if the dead are to be appeased, more active even than Wilfred Owen's warnings. The dead will hold us in contempt if we fail to change society, reform government, make freedom and justice efficacious.

> Here gutted, or stuck through the throat like Buonconte,
> or charred to grey ash, they are caught in one corral.
> We fly from their scorn, but they close all the passes:
> their sleep's our unrest, we lie bound in their inferno –
> this alliance must be vaunted and affirmed, lest they
>   condemn us!
> Lean seedlings of lament spring like swordsmen around us;
> the coronach scales white arêtes. Bitter keening
> of women goes up by the solitary column.
> Denounce and condemn! Either build for the living
> love, patience and power to absolve these tormented,

or else choke in the folds of their black-edged vendetta!
Run, stumble and fall in our desert of failure,
impaled, unappeased. And inhabit that desert
of canyon and dream – till we carry to the living
blood, fire and red flambeaux of death's proletariat.
Take iron in your arms!

(pp. 44–45)

In passages like that it is not difficult to see a carry-forward into Henderson's later work with ballad and folk-song, his involvement with CND and protest politics, his exegesis of Gramsci. As Raymond J. Ross has written, 'in one sense, Henderson's poetry never leaves the desert. Subsequent work is imbued with that experience as it is with "the clear imperative of action" to (re)build our human house and to defend it when necessary'.[3]

The sequence has an epilogue, a 'Heroic Song for the Runners of Cyrene', which has been rightly praised, though its extreme stoicism and heroic individualism seem at odds with much that had been foregrounded in the tenth elegy. In a final shift of perspective we are taken back to an earlier Cyrenaica, to the territorial rivalry between the Cyreneans and the Carthaginians, and to their agreed method of marking the frontier at the point where two runners sent out from each capital eventually met. The fleet-footed Philaeni brothers from Carthage raced far into previous Cyrenean territory, were held to have cheated by starting too early, and were killed by the Cyreneans. Carthage raised altars to the brothers as national heroes, but Henderson writes from the side of Cyrene, a city which his note to the poem says 'is for me a symbol of civilised humanity, of our "human house"'. The Cyrenean runners, straining to challenge 'the rough bounds of the desert', to 'reclaim the dead land' for their city-stage, run to meet not simply their opponents but 'history the doppelgaenger'. At the moment of meeting, when 'history the other / emerges at last from the heat's trembling mirror', the intersecting figures are locked in a fatal embrace which solves nothing, historically speaking, for the rival cultures. Heroism is not enough, perhaps? The poem, though with a splendid gesture, escapes from saying so:

> Each runs to achieve, without pause or evasion
> his instant of nothing

> they look for an opening
> grip, grapple, jerk, sway
> and fall locking like lovers
>
> down the thunderous cataract of day.
>
> (p.51)

If the desert is more peopled than the sea, the city is more peopled than the desert. The topographical isolation faced by W.S. Graham on the Cornish coast, or the isolating time-warp effect Hamish Henderson had to be prepared for in writing so intently about the North African desert at one moment of its history, would not necessarily be paralleled, though it could be, in the experience of a city-dweller. Certainly James (B.V.) Thomson, author of *The City of Dreadful Night*, and greatly admired by the third of my poets, Tom Leonard, suffered extreme isolation in London and made his fictional nocturnal city 'dreadful' through its being the haunt of lonely, alienated, or rejected figures. But Leonard, a more robust and directly provocative and entertainingly comic writer than Thomson, is well able to give the required modicum of isolation its head without brooding over its destructive potential, and his poetic world, for all that it may be delivered through a speaker of eccentric inscape ('brackets watch him he has a stoop and funny eyes'), is peopled with a rich range of characters.[4] To put the reality of urban life on the map, and to use a specific, unfictionalized place (Glasgow), were aims of Leonard's that came out of various social and linguistic irritations and challenges as well as out of a broader conviction that the non-urban world, non-urban material, had become less and less interesting. This conviction comes across with vigour in a prose piece called 'Honest', where a troubled writer wonders in Glaswegian why he has difficulty finding the right subject:

> So a thinkty ma cell, jist invent sumdy, write a story about a fisherman or sumhm. But thi longer a think, thi mair a realise a canny be *bothird* writn aboot a fisherman. Whut wid a wahnti write about a fisherman fur? N am no gonny go downti thi library, nsay, huvyi enny booksn fishermen, jiss so's a can go nread up about thim, then go n write another wan. Hoo *wahnt-sti* read a story about fishermen anyway, apart fray people that wid read it, so's they could go n write another wan, or fishermen

that read? A suppose right enough, thi trick might be, that yi cin write a story about a fisherman, so long as thi main thing iz, that thi bloke izny a fisherman, but a man that fishes. Or maybe that izny right at all, a widny no. But a do no, that as soon as a lookt up thi map ti see what might be a good name furra fishn village, nthen maybe went a walk ti think up a good name for a fisherman's boat, nthen a sat nworked out what age thi fisherman should be, nhow tall he wuz, nwhat colour his oilskins were, nthen gotim wokn iniz oilskins, doon frae thi village tay iz boat, ad tend ti think, whut duzzy wahnti day that fur? Kinni no day sumhm else wayiz time? Aniffa didny think that ti masell, if a jiss letm go, ach well, it's iz job, away out ti sea, ana big storm in chapter two, ahd tend ti think, either, here, sumdyz wrote that before, or, can a no day sumhm else wi ma time? An in fact, if a came across sumdy sitn readn it eftir a did write it, if a hud, ad tend ti thinkty ma cell, huv *they* got nuthn behtr ti day wi their time? (*Intimate Voices*, p.72)

So no village fishermen; but teachers, schoolgirls, linguists, priests, hardmen, footballers, broadcasters, pub philosophers, electronic freaks, psychiatrists, council officials, bus conductors, and all the people living and working, or not working, in a large city that has no shortage of problems but also has a marked character, a marked language and a marked resilience, immediately attractive to the poet who is above all 'honest' and wants to start off from that point, of his native place. And native place it may be, but 'starts off from' is the important thing, as it was with the sea and desert of Graham and Henderson. As Leonard himself has said, 'just because you speak in Glasgow dialect doesn't mean you can't be interested in Bartók'.[5] Or Sibelius, as the title of his collected poems, *Intimate Voices*, indicates, referring to that composer's string quartet *Voces Intimae* (Friendly Voices, but also Inward or Secret Voices).

It is significant that Leonard expresses these claims and interests in terms of voices and sound. He uses English, or Glaswegian, or sound-poetry, as the need changes, but his book is a book of voices, and the city comes alive through what its characters say, not through their physical description or through description of the look and atmosphere of the city itself. The city poetry of Baudelaire or Thomson or Eliot makes a strong appeal to the eye, and that is true whether the presentation is realistic or hallucinatory, but in Leonard it is the ear which is the master, and any loss of a romantic or expressionist glow is compensated for by accuracy of tone, sharp compression of meaning, and thought-provoking juxtapositions of cultural shibboleths, structures, and weapons. The concentration on sound, on language, seems perfectly natural when one thinks that the main difference between country and town is that one is quiet and the other is noisy; but more to the point is Leonard's underlying and reiterated theme of the relations between language and power. In a review of a light-hearted book on Glasgow's speech habits, Albert Mackie's *Talking Glasgow* (Belfast, 1978), Leonard objected strongly to what he saw as its patronizing tone:

> I've no doubt that Albert Mackie means well, and that he does feel affection for 'they' Glasgow people he's talking about. But if you don't treat language seriously, you don't treat people seriously.... Nowhere will real linguistic aggression or anger show alongside the of-course-always-bowdlerised 'humour'; the natives here are not even allowed the luxury of getting restless. There are very serious linguistic political points to be discussed here in relation to speech registers as a barometer of economic and political power in Britain, but it would be a waste of time discussing them in relation to this book. (*Aquarius*, 12 (1980), p.124)

It is in cities, and I am thinking of course of the Scottish context, that the full complex web of registers, from thick dialect and patois to the various kinds of standard southern English (either imitated by Scots or heard on radio or television), and including characteristic types of 'Scottish English' which are quite different from 'imitated southern standard' and often have different class and political associations, is to be felt, and Leonard's urban poetry constantly seeks to relate his subjects, whatever they may be (education, football, housing, smoking, crime, philosophy, drinking, sex, religion, unemployment, poetry), to the realities of the language situation. Sometimes the language situation is itself the subject, as in the first of a sequence called 'Unrelated Incidents':

> its thi lang–
> wij a thi
> guhtr thaht hi

said its thi
langwij a
thi guhtr

awright fur
funny stuff
ur
Stanley Bax-
ter ur but
luv n science
n thaht naw

thi langwij
a thi
intillect hi
said thi lang-
wij a thi intill-
ects Inglish

then whin thi
doors slid
oapn hi raised
his hat geen
mi a fare-
well nod flung
oot his right

fit boldly n
fell eight
storeys
doon thi
empty
lift-shaft.

(*Intimate Voices*, p.86)

In that poem the urban environment supplies the eight storeys and the empty lift-shaft, and the suggestion of an incident in a knockabout comedy film would also be urban, but the grotesque-ness of the situation, the black humour of the comedy which is making a perfectly serious point, and the irony of the pro-English speaker's Glaswegian voice are all very much a part of Leonard's own approach. Through urban patois, or patter, he edifies as he entertains. Another poem, 'hangup', is a fragment of conversation, possibly in a pub though no background is given, offering at the same time an extreme naturalism totally sensitive to speech habits and the sudden emergence of a philosophy of art; not only is it amusing, and not only is it convincing, but it echoes his own comment on Bartók quoted above: the speaker has in fact heard about minimalism, and does not necessarily reject it, but he sticks to his belief that you 'have to say something':

> aye bit naw
>
> naw bit
> aye bit
>
> away
> away yi go
> whut
>
> mini whut
> minimalism
>
> aw minimalism
> minimalism aye
>
> aye right
> aye right inuff
> aye right inuff definitely
>
> aye bit
> naw bit
>
> a stull think yi huvty say sumhm

(p.138)

A desire to 'say something' has been the ruin of not a few poets in the past. With Leonard, however, although some of his poems are epigrammatically slight, even throwaway, there is the saving grace of an awareness of the importance of popular forms (ballad, riddle, joke, proverb, folk-rhyme, tall story, music-hall song) which can often be recycled in ways that are both funny and minatory. In this short untitled poem, the nursery rhyme is not only reslanted very pointedly at the end, but given, through its

Glaswegian accent, an additional relevance to the English-Scottish power situation; while in a more general way the linguistic trans-mogrification of the rhyme recalls what Joyce did with/to Humpty Dumpty in *Finnegans Wake*:

> humpty dumpty satna waw
> humpty dumpty hudda big faw
>
> aw thi kingz hoarsyz
> inaw thi kingz men
>
> came charjn up
> n trampld im inty thi grunn

(p.107)

The 'voces intimae' of Sibelius are in Leonard both truly friendly and ironically 'friendly' (that is, buttonholingly aggressive), but they may also be inward-directed, psychologically rather than socio-politically concerned. In 'A Priest Came on at Merkland Street', one of his longer poems in English, the voice is unspoken, an interior monologue from a young man travelling opposite a priest on Glasgow's underground. The poem is printed together with a map of the underground, so that the local urban context is clear. Its subtitle tells us that it is 'A very thoughtful poem, being a canonical penance for sufferers of psychosomatic asthma'. Not everyone has asthma, but the basic situation in the poem is like the very common one (at least in cities with under-grounds) described by T.S. Eliot in 'East Coker':

> Or as, when an underground train, in the tube, stops too
>   long between stations
> And the conversation rises and slowly fades into silence
> And you see behind every face the mental emptiness deepen
> Leaving only the growing terror of nothing to think about.

(III. 18)

The young man's guilty conscience, and feelings of inadequacy and uncertainty struggling with self-assertion and acceptance, are set into action by the 'sad but dignified' face of the priest who sits opposite him; there is no conversation, but the young man's mind is itself a conversation of interior voices, his own at different periods of his life, a priest's, God's, that of Ozymandias, and that

of Mahler in his Seventh Symphony. He clings to the positives
of art as in Mahler, but is haunted by fears of madness and death
in which the confession-box and his coffin are merged, not without an 'I-was-here' urban localization:

> I could write to a psychiatrist
> a cry from the heart
> dear sir
> my name is Ozymandias
> king of Leithland Road
> and then there's the box
> yours sincerely

(p.30)

Also 'intimate', but at the same time reaching out into the
general issues that motivate Leonard, is a pair of poems which
start from father-son relationships: one (in Glaswegian) the voice
of a working-class father talking about his would-be radical student son; the other (in English) the voice of an educated working-
class poetry-writing son talking about his uneducated father. The
first poem is 'The Qualification':

> wurk aw yir life
> nuthnty show
> pit oanthi nyuze
> same awl drivl
>
> yoonyin bashn
> wurkir bashn
> lord this
> sir soan soa thaht
>
> shood hearma boay
> sayzwi need guns
> an armd revalooshn
> nuthn else wurks
>
> awright fur him thoa
> uppit thi yooni
> tok aw yi like therr
> thats whit its fur

(p.50)

The other poem is called 'Fathers and Sons':

> I remember being ashamed of my father
> when he whispered the words out loud
> reading the newspaper.
>
> 'Don't you find
> the use of phonetic urban dialect
> rather constrictive?'
> asks a member of the audience.
>
> The poetry reading is over.
> I will go home to my children.

(p.140)

The scepticism of the socialist father in the first poem is balanced and perhaps overthrown by the understanding and amends-making of the son in the second. Continuity mixes with change, and with an ambiguous but possible sense of progress, when we see that the son in the second poem is himself a father, and may pass on the authenticities and indignations which have moved him to act and write.

Notes

1 *Poetry Book Society Bulletin*, 64 (Spring 1970).
2 'The Elegies of Rilke and Henderson: Influence and Variation', *Studies in Scottish Literature* no.16 (1981), pp.217–34.
3 'Hamish Henderson: In the Midst of Things', *Chapman* 3:5 (Winter 1985), p.18.
4 Tom Leonard, *Intimate Voices: Selected Work 1965-1983* (Newcastle upon Tyne, 1984), p.33.
5 *Radio Times*, 12–18 February 1977, p.14.

The Yearbook of English Studies, vol.17, ed. C. J. Rawson (Modern Humanities Research Association, 1987).

Early Finlay

In this article I am taking 'early Finlay' to mean the decade of his work between 1958, when he published his first book, *The Sea-Bed and Other Stories* and 1967, when he closed his magazine, *Poor. Old. Tired. Horse.*, establishing himself at Stonypath, and turned his attention to the evolving concept of a garden which has since become so famous. Any division of an artist's life is artificial, but in some ways the logic of Finlay's subsequent and continuous development during the 1970s and 1980s can be more clearly realized by examining the earliest phase of his work.

If one uses the broad categories of 'literature' and 'art', this is his most literary period, when he is writing short stories, plays, and both traditional and concrete poetry, as well as moving out into poster–poems, poem–prints, poem–cards, and poems as physical objects in glass or other materials. At the same time, it has to be remembered that he started off his career as an artist, and his early books, as if to acknowledge this, are nearly all illustrated, both *The Sea-Bed* and *The Dancers Inherit the Party* (his first book of poems, 1960) having woodcuts by the Yugoslav artist Zeljko Kujundzic, and *Glasgow Beasts, an a Burd Haw, an Inseks, an, aw, a Fush* (1961) having papercuts by John Picking. An even closer marrying of text and illustration came with Picking's artwork for *Concertina* (1962). Nevertheless, in these publications, as also in his plays which although they belong to the early period were published later (1965-1970), the literary component remains extensive and dominant.

The short stories, which have an admirable economy and simplicity of style, are more sure-footed than the plays, but there are many points of contact between the two groups. The play *The Estate Hunters* is simply another version of the story 'Straw'. Similarities between the play *Walking Through Seaweed* and the story 'The Sea-Bed' are not so direct, but are clearly there: the two girls talking together, one ordinary and down-to-earth, the other imaginative and trying to describe the importance of walking barefoot with a friend throughout seaweed to the sea, are paralleled by the two boys in the short story, one interested merely in catching fish, the other unable to indicate his strong but strange feelings about the depth and movement of the sea. In both cases, the imagination has been stirred by something that is more an absence than a presence, something set deep into the non-human world: the girl does not know why she wants to get to the sea, the boy has been shaken by the sight of a huge cod which quickly vanished and which he did not even try to catch.

> He could feel the sea behind him, and he felt his friend at his side. Then, into his mind where the sea had been putting its cold, dark pictures, came pictures of familiar objects he saw every day without really looking at them. He saw his father's pipes (he had several pipes), his mother's knitting needles, the Libby's calendar that hung up above the mantelpiece, and his own white mug filled with brown tea. They were familiar things but now he saw them as if for the first time.

This is a very Wordsworthian kind of imaginative transformation: mysterious and refreshing, but unwitty and non-symbolic (even the cod resists symbolization), and it is different from approaches Finlay was to use later on. Perhaps a closer pointer to his future development is seen in the riddling visual transformations in the story 'The Boy and the Guess', where the ancient (classical, if you like) device of asking someone to identify a riddlingly described object is used to open up a very Finlayesque vein of metaphor. It's a pony, tied up with a rope when not in use, nibbling the grass below a high dyke. It's an old-fashioned caravan with a door in two halves, so that you can lean on one and look out of the other. No, it has no wheels, no wings, It turns out, of course, to be one of Finlay's chief recurring images, a fishing-boat. His pleasure is to see it transformed into other things which he equally wants to recommend to our attention: a munching horse, an old caravan.

This, so far, is in prose, but the early (pre-concrete) verse shows the same interest in transformation, sometimes adding in an element of verbal play that might seem proper to the more intensely organized language of poetry. In an attractive love-poem, 'The Gift', the speaker opens and wonders at what appears to be the strange gift from his lover of 'a dehydrated porcupine'; he strokes it and discovers it is in fact a pine-cone, accompanied by a written message:

'I hope it did not prick you, dearest mine,
I did not mean you to be hurt at all.'

The engaging complicity, one might say, of sender and receiver
is sealed not only with the visual likeness of the two objects but
also by the verbal link of -*pine* and *pine*-. In a more playful poem,
'Catch', the visual similarity of a lobster ('lapster') and a helicop-
ter is neatly exploited when a fisherman catches the one and
thinks it might be a small example of the other. Why not, when
the two words by their sound-link suggest a new transformation,
helicapster: 'There's lots are caught in the sea off Scrabster.'
Although Finlay did not, in his own work, push his new interest
in concrete poetry in the direction of sound-poetry, his early
verse is very much aware of the sound of words, whether in the
spirit of play, as in 'Catch', or humorously dialectical, as in the
booklet of *Glasgow Beasts*, or slyly incantational, as in the 'Poem
on My Poem on Her and the Horse':

A little horse came treading through the snow
At which she said, Poor Horse, poor horse thou art
Poor little horse to have that heavy cart,
To have that cart, to have to make it go.

And then I thought, Oho, I thought, Oho
She's thinking of her own small saddest part.
Poor horse. Poor horse. Poor horse. Poor horse. Poor cart.
And in her eyes the snow, you know, the snow.

Perhaps the traditional, rhyme-and-metre poem which fore-
shadows his later interest most unmistakably is 'Scene', where
the metamorphic imagination, still with the lightest touch, sets
out without any argument the sense of a natural world where
structure and order are inherent, if we have eyes to see:

The fir tree stands quite still and angles
On the hill, for green Triangles.

Stewing in its billy there
The tea is strong, and brown, and Square.

The rain is Slant. Soaked fishers sup
Sad Ellipses from a cup.

'As I am open to it, so it ripples out' was Finlay's note at the end of the altogether delightful *Concertina*, which is still a poem with illustrations and not a concrete poem, but clearly paving the way for *Rapel* in the following year, where the step into concrete had been taken. Being 'open to it' in the work produced before 1963 meant the simplicity of the stories, the atmosphere of the plays, the charm and surprise of the poetry. Associations were themselves more 'open' than defined or directed, as indeed in the *Concertina* note quoted above, which 'explains' (his own inverted commas) the words 'Barley!' and 'Keys!' as they have just been used in noon-day and night-time scenes: 'The sudden halt in a game, hush, the silence of noon-day, moon-day, barley-fields; the dark halt of night-time, a darker silence, stars, locks: keys. . . .' This romanticism may seem to be at a great distance from his more hard-edged and strongly politicized work of the 1975-1985 decade, but it is important to remember that there is a Coleridge, and even a Loki, lurking in Finlay all the way through; he never becomes pure Vitruvius or Panzerman.

Nothing could be more 'open to it' than *Poor. Old. Tired. Horse.*, the magazine which Finlay edited in twenty-five numbers from 1962 to 1967. In both format and contents it was something quite fresh in the Scottish literary scene at that time, and its Scottish provenance was all the more important to Finlay because of the international range of contributors; the country of origin was put in brackets at the end of each contribution, so that for example in the first three numbers writers from Scotland rubbed shoulders with writers from England (the weasel-word Britain was not used), the USA, Russia, France, Italy, Finland, Poland, Hungary, and Japan. The first poem in the first number was a sound-poem, and the last poem in the last number was a one-word poem; yet as soon as you decided this must be an avant-garde or experimentalist magazine you discovered that its policy was also to rescue neglected poets from the past like John Gray and Hamish McLaren. And as soon as you decided that heavily portentous numbers devoted to the art theory (not even the art!) of Ad Reinhardt or Charles Biederman implied an equally unyielding functional or abstract literary commitment, you were presented with a 'teapoth' number rich in unportentous homely fantasy and charm. Some issues were thematic, some general; some illustrated, some not; some hand-drawn, some printed; some with fine artwork and layout, some with – not so fine. Few magazines encouraged such a marked sense of anticipation from number to number. The ability to disconcert inevitably draws some flak, and Finlay, taking a leaf from Hugh MacDiarmid's book, advertised the magazine thus in *The Scotsman*: ' "Utterly vicious and deplorable" – Hugh MacDiarmid.' But *P.O.T.H.* flourished, and its Scottish contributors included, in addition to its editor and the present writer, George Mackay Brown, Robert Garioch, Douglas Young, Tom McGrath, Helen Cruickshank, Crombie Saunders, J.F. Hendry, and D.M. Black. The magazine did publish concrete, semiotic, and sound poetry, and its reputation among those who had not seen it was that it was 'some sort of concrete poetry broadsheet'; this was not true, but perhaps it overlaps on the fact that well-crafted thing-y poetry was preferred to expressionist or confessional 'depth'. Cf. '. . . . the example [of using the experience of the Nazi death-camps] suggests that the whole idea – now in fashion – of 'depth for depth's sake' might well be looked at critically' (letter to Stephen Scobie, 4 August 1967, quoted in *White Pelican*, vol.1, no.2, Edmonton, Canada, Spring 1971). There was no minimalist or even miniaturist gospel, but the magazine's title did tip its hat to Robert Creeley, from whose poem 'Please' (in *A Form of Women*, 1959) it is taken, and Creeley does stand for certain cat-like gestures and anti-large preoccupations.

> This is a poem about a horse that got tired.
> Poor. Old. Tired. Horse.
> I want to go home.
> I want you to go home.
> This is a poem which tells the story,
> which is the story
> I don't know.

Quite unCreeleyan, however, was the magazine's inclusion of poets who dealt with the larger sociopolitical issues: Mayakovsky, József, Neruda, Günter Grass, and writers from Cuba and Brazil. If the result is eclecticism, it is an eclecticism that two decades later seems to belong so much to the spirit of the Sixties as to have gained more unity and harmony than it appeared to possess at the time. It undoubtedly succeeded in its aim of opening Scotland out to new names and new ideas, and all at the astonishingly unélitist price of 9d (4p) which was held throughout the five years of its existence.

Concrete poems made their first appearance in *P.O.T.H.* in

no.6 (March 1963), and both Finlay and his commentators have described the mixture of acknowledgement and uneasiness with which he regarded the international concrete poetry movement. It is clear that it offered many suggestions to him in the areas of syntax, structure, metaphor, and metamorphosis. Also, under its alternative title of 'visual poetry' its possible or actual links with painting, sculpture, and architecture spoke directly to the artist in Finlay. He used it, contributed to it, learned from it, moved on. It is significant that collections of his fairly straight or mainstream concrete poetry, such as *Telegrams from My Windmill* (1964) or *Tea-leaves and Fishes* (1966) are less fully satisfying than books which he has designed wholly round one idea, so that the book virtually becomes the poem. These two collections are (inevitably) uneven in quality, and one tends to pick out the poems one admires and neglect the others, but in the more 'designed' publications one has to grasp a much more original approach, where the poem-book or book-poem has become a halfway-house to the poem-object which he developed, at Stonypath and elsewhere, beyond the period of his work being discussed in this essay. In distrusting the miscellanism of poems-in-a-book (as, with the demise of *P.O.T.H.*, he was tacitly distrusting the miscellanyism of items-in-a-magazine), he had embarked on his more heroic attempt to relate language to the world in a three-dimensional way. The turning pages of a book, the use of blank pages, of transparent pages, of coloured paper, all this was a beginning, an adumbration of the three-dimensional 'world out there'. Eventually the words had to be on objects – carved, sandblasted, or whatever – and placed, like that old wordless jar in Tennessee, somewhere in the environment. As Finlay has himself said, it had been one of his earliest questions, back in the Fifties when he was writing his short stories, 'How can one write TREE and it *mean* TREE?'

In *Canal Stripe 4* (1964) the long horizontal pages, turned over, read 'little fields / long horizons / little fields long / for horizons / horizons long / for little fields'. The words, at the bottom of the page, suggest a boat drifting along a canal and the word-play (the l/f alliteration, the adjective/verb transformation of 'long') suggests in its sound as well as says in its meaning that there is a natural linkage of the near and the far; and in human terms (since it is human language that is being used, not boats and fields) we are being told we must expect to oscillate, perhaps for ever, between the homely and the infinite.

The page-turning in *Ocean Stripe 3* (1965) enacts the biblical story of the Flood, and can do so with the utmost verbal economy because of the near-coincidence in the English language of 'ark' and 'arc'. Four times the ark is still there, on the same spot of each page, but on the fourth page you can glimpse the word 'arc', high up, showing through the paper, and finally, as you turn again and remove the cloud which is hiding the rainbow, the rainbow – overlapping pages of red, yellow, and blue – appears. The accidental sound-identity of 'ark' and 'arc' helps to clinch the *idea* of the divine covenant, but it is the hidden flash of the brightly coloured pages which shows the *joy* of the promise. As in *Rapel*, we have suprematist and fauve elements coming together.

In *Autumn Poem* (1966), perhaps the most attractive of these kinetic poems, the conception of 'turning over' which starts from turning the pages is itself moulded into the body of the poem, where a series of photographs (first a square patch of earth, later a circular patch suggesting the sphere of the whole earth) is covered by transparent pages bearing the words of the poem. 'Turning over the earth' (square patch) is followed by 'the earth turning over' (circular patch), and this in turn modulates back, in the movement of the seasons, to 'Turning over' (circular patch) 'the earth' (square patch). Here, the use of photographs taken by someone else (Audrey Walker) further objectifies the poem, and suggests also that word and world are being, if not brought into one, forced to confront each other. Nevertheless, like the token three-colour rainbow of *Ocean Stripe 3*, the flat globe of *Autumn Poem* is there to remind us that we are still in *mir iskusstva*, the world of art.

A further development of the confrontation, in *Ocean Stripe 5* (1967), is more striking but more problematic. Each page prints the photograph of a different fishing-boat (taken from *Fishing News*) above a quotation on sound-poetry or concrete poetry taken from Kurt Schwitters, Ernst Jandl, or Paul de Vree. There are few obvious connections between boat and text, beyond the fact that boats' registration-letters (indicating port of origin) have been used by Finlay in concrete poems, and that both photographs and texts do have a kind of climax at the end, when rougher seas accompany more far-reaching (but less modernist, indeed anti-modernist) statements – 'Poetic feeling is what the poet counts on' and 'It is impossible to explain the meaning of art; it is infinite'. The romanticism, or fauvism, of this (strongly underlined by the cover photograph of a choppy, boatless sea, swirling under louring cloud and a dash of light) is balanced by a 'postscript' which brings us back the suprematism; a Schwitters poem consisting entirely of short groups of letters, like the letters on fishing-boats. Whether, in the voyage of this book, the good ship modernism has sunk, though not without trace, is an open question. The Aivazovskian cover certainly proclaims that *those* horizons are not longing for little fields. 'Models of order' are not in order. This is a stark ocean, and the only stripe on it is a stark zigzag of light.

This tantalizing, difficult, but important book is a good point at which to close. Its visibly unruly sea should be placed against the neatly distanced message of 'Pond-stone' (in *Stonechats*, from the same year of 1967):

> HIC IACET
> PARVULUM QUODDAM
> EX AQUA LONGIORE
> EXCERPTUM

An inscribed stone in a pond marks the grave of a drop in the ocean. Finlay was to go on, working with others, to make many inscribed stones, but the languageless sea is still there, very big, very challenging, full of life and death and not art.

Alexander Trocchi: a Survey

Most of the critical writing on Alexander Trocchi – and it is not much in any case – has centred on his best-known work, *Cain's Book*. This is understandable, and no doubt that novel will remain his chief claim to fame, but it might be useful in the present essay to place it within a more ranging and comparative survey of his various writings, partly because there is not a greatly diffused sense or knowledge of these, even among the well read (a frequent fate of underground or semi-underground productions), and partly because he himself wanted all his writing to be seen as a continuum of communication, of self-definition, of modes of consciousness, rather than as a sculpture park of 'novels' or 'short stories' or 'poems' or 'essays'.

> It wasn't that writing shouldn't be written, but that a man should annihilate prescriptions of all past form in his own soul, refuse to consider what he wrote in terms of literature, judge it solely in terms of his living.
>
> (*Cain's Book*, p.131)

Such existential beliefs help to account for the formidable amount of energy Trocchi put into editorial and publicistic writing. When he began editing *Merlin* in Paris in 1952, he not only created a magazine which would be a vehicle for talents he thought important – Christopher Logue, Henry Miller, Sartre, Genet, Nazim Hikmet, Ionesco – but also through his own thoughtful, persistent, and unshrill editorials was able to map out a new direction for 'Europe's independent minds', or perhaps more strictly a new non-direction, since so much of his argument was directed against directionism, against absolutisms whether Russian or American, against the Cold War which had piled such a mountain of bitter fruit in the very marketplace of victory. Meanwhile the first Russian sputnik went up in 1957, and the exploration of space and the Russian–American space race began.

Without ever becoming anti-science, Trocchi felt the writer's complementary task was to become a 'cosmonaut of inner space'; the independent minds might well be nonconformist, alienated, iconoclastic, but whatever effect they had or wanted to have on society should have a psychological rather than a political mainspring. As co-editor (with Richard Seaver and Terry Southern) of the anthology *Writers in Revolt* (1963), Trocchi either wrote or underwrote the unsigned introduction, which asserted that both 'language and subject remain threatened by forces whose avowed purpose is to protect those unable to judge or think for themselves' and that what was needed was 'the deliberate avoidance of lip service to assumed values, and adherence instead to deeply personal impulse'. If this seems too inward-looking to justify the 'revolt' of the title, it should be pointed out that the anthology contained most of Allen Ginsberg's *Howl* and an extract from William Burroughs' *The Naked Lunch*, both works with strong contemporary sociopolitical implications, as well as Sade, Genet, Hesse, Baudelaire, Artaud, and the devious Malaparte. These and other names prefigured or were part of Trocchi's 'invisible insurrection' as outlined in his article 'Invisible Insurrection of a Million Minds' (*New Satire*, no.8, June 1963; reprinted in America in *City Lights Journal*, no.2, 1964; published as *sigma* portfolio no.2, London, 1964).

This is Trocchi's most important single essay, and although written with his characteristic clarity and precision it belongs so much to the widespread and endlessly ramifying alternative-society millenarianism of the 1960s that it is hard to clinch a descriptive account of it. Briefly, the aim was nothing if not ambitious: not a Leninist *coup d'état* but a *coup du monde* (his own phrase), a transformation of the mass of society, not from within the mass but through the influence of a 'nucleus of men', something like Plato's Guardians, who are 'capable of imposing a new and seminal idea' and who will work internationally and anti-nationally ('History will not overthrow national governments; it will outflank them'). Artists must have direct access to communities and 'eliminate the brokers', but there is a mild sideswipe at Arnold Wesker's ill-fated Centre 42 and its 'church-bazaar philosophy'. He envisages everything starting with the taking over of a country house 'not too far from the City of London', and the creation within that environment of a 'spontaneous university', a combination of Black Mountain College, Newbattle Abbey, and an Israeli kibbutz; and this repeated from country to country, building up to a worldwide network of cultural and educational rejuvenation. In the sixties, these ideas did find some fertile ground, and the 1968 prospectus of the Antiuniversity of London, with its anticampus in Shoreditch, does indeed include among its antilecturers Alexander Trocchi, who will fortnightly 'describe in immaculate intellectual terms the spiritual attitudes and the new economic scaffolding which must be brought into play as the tactical bases of any possible evolution of man'. The severe deintoxication so many countries have had since these heady days gives such pronouncements the flavour of a document already historical. National governments, far from being overthrown or outflanked, have proliferated and will evidently continue to do so, and to gain or keep real power; psychology, inwardness, ideas of exile and expatriation now seem indulgent in a world which has so many immediate and basic problems and is again in the old Johnsonian phrase bursting with sin and misery; and who would not now be a shade suspicious of wellmeaning phalansteries of potential commissars, even if all their cry was that they would leaven the lumpen millions into light? Nevertheless, the whole antiuniversity movement, and Trocchi's thirty-odd *sigma* portfolios, attracted an impressive body of support, including Joan Littlewood, R.D. Laing, John Arden, Anthony Burgess, Robert Creeley, Kenneth White, Tom McGrath, Norman Mailer, Edward Dorn, Stuart Hall, Barry Flanagan, and Hans Magnus Enzensberger. Perhaps it is in the nature of things that such a dazzlingly loose congeries of idealisms must belong to a certain time and place and cannot be much extended or developed; which is not to say that an element of *exemplum* may not still linger, to tantalize later hard-faced decades.

These literary and paraliterary activities did not bring in much money, and it is usually thought that Trocchi's translations, and his pornographic novels, must have been potboilers. In a sense this is true, but by no means entirely so. The novels he chose to translate have themes that one can see must have appealed to him or offered him an attractive challenge, and they are well translated, in a manner that shows diligence and care. Jan Cremer's *I Jan Cremer* (1965; translated from Dutch with the help of R.E. Wyngaard) is the picaresque portrait of an outsider, a young hipster out of reform school who fights and cons and whores his way across Europe and North Africa, smuggling, selling drugs, painting pictures, bullfighting, even working in a slaughterhouse (a passage uncannily reminiscent of Archie Hind's *The Dear Green Place*), and finally being interrogated by the police for a murder he has seen but did not commit, in a sort of mirror-image of the end of Trocchi's own novel *Young Adam*. One central, self-observing, self-defining character is found in all the novels he translated: in André Pieyre de Mandiargues's *The Girl on the Motorcycle* (1966) the entire book recounts the leather-suited girl's thoughts and memories as she rides out one morning from her husband to her lover (and her death); René de Obaldia's *The Centenarian* (1970) is the sprightly and inventive monologue of an engaging eighty-seven-year-old, recalling his past and looking forward to his century; Valentine Penrose's *The Bloody Countess* (1970) is a fictionalized biography of the terrible sixteenth-century Hungarian countess, Erzsébet Bathory, who bathed in the blood of over six hundred murdered young servant-girls before she was caught, totally unrepentant, and tried; and in Jean Douassot's *La Gana* (1974) we have a blowzy, bizarre, Henry Miller-ish *Bildungsroman* of an unhappy and outrageously treated boy growing up into some sort of damaged teenage semi-maturity, the maturity of a solitary, hiding at the end like an animal in his dead uncle's room.

Whether tragic or comic, these are all studies in isolation, as are Trocchi's own two novels, and there are many incidental similarities. The motorcycle in *The Girl on the Motorcycle* has a function similar to that of the barge in *Young Adam* and the scow in *Cain's Book*, where movement in space sets off a displaced movement in the character's perception of time, so that he/she shudders or rocks or drifts through memories, present impressions, and imagined futures in a disorienting way. Or again, the old man in *The Centenarian* is not merely monologising for our benefit, he is writing his story down on a series of jotters he buys at the beginning, just as Joe Necchi in *Cain's Book* is actually writing *Cain's Book*. Hangings occur or are about to occur at the end of *The Bloody Countess* and *Young Adam*, and in *Cain's Book* the hero mentions his obsession with the image of a hanged man and actually suspends a doll in a noose from the mast of his boat, fearing that he has been living or writing in such a way that 'it can lead me only to the hangman'; to which one should add that Trocchi closes an essay on Orwell in *Evergreen Review* (vol.2, no.6, autumn 1958) by contrasting Orwell's 'vulgar democratic unreflectiveness' and *passé* concern for sociopolitical factors at the expense of all others with the occasional far deeper insight into the individual human soul he showed himself capable of in his 1931 essay 'A Hanging' – and Trocchi quotes the passage where the wretched Indian on his way to execution steps aside to avoid a puddle.

In some of these translated novels there is a marked erotic interest, as there is also in *Young Adam* and *Cain's Book*, in his poems, and in the flamboyant and bitty *The Fifth Volume of Frank Harris's 'My Life and Loves': An Irreverent Treatment* (1958) (which is about 35 per cent Harris and 65 per cent Trocchi). Explicitly erotic writers like Henry Miller, Jean Genet, Allen Ginsberg, and William Burroughs were among the heroes of the 'revolt' with which Trocchi was associated, and there would therefore be nothing very surprising if his potboilers turned out to be porno-graphic potboilers. Without trying to insert a 'so-called' before the 'pornographic', one can still see a great deal more in these books, in the whole context of Trocchi's work, than the panting punter might suspect. In the best of them, *Helen and Desire* (1954, under the pseudonym Frances Lengel), there is again the isolated single central character through whose present consciousness and re-lived memories an existentialist, libertarian, anti-work-ethic philosophy of life is clearly formulated; and again the teller of the tale (a woman from Australia, held captive for sexual purposes by Arabs in Algeria) is herself writing it down, as her own novelist. The book is fairly regularly punctuated by her sexual encounters, both straight and gay ('I moved in the hot-house world of scented boudoirs, and flirted with the husbands whom I cuckolded') so that there is something for everyone, and the erotic descriptions are lush with the sort of metaphors that would have appealed to the later Metaphysical poets ('writhed on soft gimbals', 'the amorphous sludge of my breasts', 'sliding on soft graphite'); but on the other hand the main conduct of the narrative is nicely matter-of-fact in a Moll Flanders mode. As the book's title suggests, she is desire incarnate. Her narrowly religious father (a Scottish immigrant, one suspects!) had precipitated her adolescent reaction of complete amoral promiscuity, and as she travels through Asia and the Middle East she comes to live for immediate, non-lasting encounters. 'What would I do with a man for twenty-four hours in a day?' 'All great lust is impersonal.' 'The western God, the Jewish God, was invented to make the hatred of life logical.' 'I am anxious to record everything, to break through the shameful shell of civilised expression.' At the end, fed for aphrodisiac purposes on honey, almonds, and hashish, and eagerly awaiting the next unknown evening visitor, she feels she is beginning to disintegrate, like Joe at the end of *Young Adam*, and her story ends in mid-sentence. Despite the fact that it has to meet the demands of its underground genre, this is far from being a negligible novel.

Thongs (1969) (and the title says it all) is a more broken-backed and unsatisfactory book from any literary point of view, but it has features that deserve mention. Like *Young Adam* and *Cain's Book* it has a strong Scottish, and specifically Glasgow connection. Like *Helen and Desire*, it has an isolated female figure as its central character. And like *Helen and Desire* and *Cain's Book*, it uses the device of the central character writing the novel which (maybe) the reader is reading. As in *Helen and Desire*, or more to the point perhaps as in Hogg's *Confessions of a Justified Sinner*, an 'editor' is printing the woman's own story as written in her personal notebook. Gertrude Gault (the same surname as that of Ella and Leslie in *Young Adam*) grows up in the Gorbals district of Glasgow and is the daughter of the Razor King. A violent and vicious environment is described, in terms almost parodically reminiscent of McArthur and Long's *No Mean City* except for greater literacy in the style, and the heroine's predisposition to being a victim, a willing one as it turns out, is traced back to a brutal father and a brutish society. At the age of fourteen she watches her father in a squalid sexual assault on his mistress, Hazel; he then thrashes his daughter with his black leather belt, and she discovers her masochism. Hazel, it emerges, is also a masochist, and introduces her to the owners and clients of a west-end mansion devoted not only to sadomasochistic pursuits but to the furtherance of a secret order whose headquarters are in Madrid. There is a Holy Pain Father, there are twelve Pain Cardinals, and a whole descending hierarchy of whippers and whipped. Although more than half of the book is set in Glasgow, the action finally moves to Spain, where Gertrude becomes Carmencita de las Lunas, is advanced high in the order, and dies as a martyr, scourged and crucified, and eventually a cause of pilgrimage. The theme of 'hanging', it will be noted, is here too, as well as the familiar self-isolation from society's norms, so the book readily finds its place within Trocchi's *oeuvre*. But it is virtually two separate stories, neither of them very persuasive, and the melodramatic Glaswegian mythology he falls back on is very different from the moving and beautifully observed Glasgow scenes in *Cain's Book*.

Erotic, but rather more publicly printable, are many of Trocchi's poems, collected in *Man at Leisure* (1972). He is essentially a man of prose and not of verse, but the verse is in some danger of being forgotten altogether, so a brief comment, at least, is in order. These poems, reminding us sometimes of Christopher Logue, sometimes of Alan Jackson, sometimes of Tom Leonard, seem to bear out a statement Trocchi (or the narrator) made in *Cain's Book*: 'I find myself cultivating a certain crudity of expression, judging it to be essential to meaning, in a slick age vital to the efficacy of language' (p.71). Not all the poems have 'crudity of expression', but where it is used it is generally to underline sexual liberation or political satire. For the former:

> The stinking cauldron
> of inhibition soup
> had its lid lifted
> by Attacunt Peep
> the hairy mind-wrestler
> the child with which
> god blessed her
> womb, and the sweet lust
> by which it was irradiated....
>
> ('The Stinking Cauldron')

A characteristic political passage comes indelibly marked with the ampersands, contractions, and lowercase of the Beat era:

> Concerning white geese of dover
>
> now, the minister of aircraft production
> the hon. john dracula
> has just signed a contract fr a
> progressive manufacture 'f
> 1,000 dreadnaught mk fck
> tactical bombers
> their eventual delivery
>   'to procure
>   peace'
>   fr the geese
>   in 1980
>
> &

in commending the governmental decision
brigadier general paralysis
    met with derision...
        ('Lessons for Boys and Girls II')

Probably the best poem is a long five-page piece, in a more straightforward style, called 'A Little Geography Lesson for my Sons and Daughters'. It is about 'the east' and 'the west', and although it is not a dialogue it is rather like a medieval 'dialogue of soul and body', where strengths and shortcomings of two opposed subjects are set out. The wise came from the east, but 'its wisdom is dried up'. The wisdom of the west is a book of rules, 'not quite indispensable / for those who travel by Pullman'. The east is 'a dark uterus' waiting to be truly and fruitfully impregnated by the west, but artificial barriers keep the two apart.

> If there is anything that isn't clear
> I refer you to the chronicles of Zarathustra
> or to the Chieh-hein of the Llama Swingitup. [*sic*]
> if you can't get hold of these,
> *see me*, please.

Trocchi's short stories and novels are the literary centre of his work, and bring together most of the ideas, attitudes, and themes already looked at. The four stories in *New Writers III* (1965) emphasize human isolation. In 'A Being of Distances' a middle-aged son who has been to his uncle's funeral returns by train to London and keeps thinking about his father, a widower now and a lonely man like himself; meeting his father at the funeral, talking to him, but not staying, has left him disturbed and empty, 'a being of distances'. 'The Holy Man' is a more grotesque, Hoffmannes-que story about a dilapidated French residential hotel inhabited by mostly ageing and variously handicapped persons – a hunch-back, two blind men, a dwarf, a dumb man, a one-legged woman, a one-eyed man. Interest centres on the man in the attic who has boarded up his window and never leaves his room; food is brought to him, excrement is removed. No one knows anything about him, but he excites much speculation. Here, the isolated man does not present his own case but is seen only through the eyes of others. In 'Peter Pierce', a man on the run from the police takes refuge in a room below that of an eccentric ragman. Before the narrator goes away at the end of the story, he has built up a tentative but never very illuminating relationship with the ragman who lives almost in a world of his own. The narrator feels he has been in touch with some mystery, 'face to face with the subhuman', and records the strangeness of the experience very much as Wordsworth relates his encounters with solitaries in *The Prelude*. 'A Meeting' is described elsewhere as being 'from a novel in preparation', and its characters appear also in the story 'The Rum and the Pelican' (*Merlin*, vol.2, no.3, 1954). It makes little impact, and hardly stands by itself, but its unprepossessing hero, a thin, round-shouldered bespectacled clerk making desultory conversation with a female colleague in a bar, shares the lost, dislocated, aimless quality of life we observe in the main characters of the stories. The *accidie* that seeps into these tales makes us think of *Dubliners*, and Trocchi's style, low-key but precise, is a cousin of Joyce's 'scrupulous meanness'. A certain obsession with naturalistic detail – making cocoa, looking at a greasy fork, comparing old pen nibs – is strongly reminiscent, in a Scottish context, of James Kelman; in both cases it probably comes from the *nouveau roman*. The short stories are a mixed bag as regards quality, though two of them, 'A Being of Distances' and 'Peter Pierce', are worth anthologizing. But Trocchi seems to have sensed that he needed to propel his figure of the outsider into the more ample space of the novel, give him adventures, give him enough time to allow a fertile interchange between present and past, give him also enough interaction with other characters to define the exact nature of his detachment (the classic pattern: being alone and desperately wanting relationships, having relationships and wanting to be alone; not Sartre's *Huis Clos* but 'L'enfer, c'est les autres / moi-même / les autres / moi-même / les autres, etc., etc.').

The fascination of all this for a Scottish author is not hard to see, and although Trocchi learned from Sartre and more obviously from Camus's *L'Etranger*, we also cannot help noticing links back to Hogg's *Justified Sinner* and forward to Alasdair Gray's *Lanark*: the dislocation of time, the problem of the hero's self-identification, the tension between natural guilt and its abnormal absence, the story within a story, the prominence of father-son relationships, the presence of serious crime, whether real, imagined, or uncertain – all these aspects would be picked up even if a Scottish background had not been given to his novels by Trocchi himself, the actual setting of the Forth and Clyde Canal in *Cain's Book*, the lurid Gorbals of *Thongs*. Whether Trocchi ever fully came to terms with his Scottish upbringing and early environment, in the sense in which Joyce and Beckett did in relation to Ireland, is arguable. Joyce managed it by compulsive memorializing and indeed re-mythologizing of Dublin, Beckett by the occasional Irish setting, the flavour of Irish names and words, the marked un-Englishness of the tone of voice. But Trocchi, desperate to deparochialize, was swept into the new internationalism of the later 1950s and the 1960s, especially on its French-American axis, and it may be that decisions made too quickly at that time caused his difficulties in assimilating and using his own past. Nevertheless, it should be remembered that in his famous public clash with Hugh MacDiarmid during the Writers' Conference at the Edinburgh Festival of 1962 – an international event if ever there was one – Trocchi's claim was not a stateless or cosmopolitan claim: he was there on the panel of Scottish writers, and he claimed (if we strip off the colours of rhetoric) to have contributed more to Scottish literature during recent years than Hugh Mac-Diarmid had done. The argument was not so much a simple nationalism v. internationalism debate as it seemed at the time; it was rather an argument about how, in the early 1960s, a Scottish writer should go about his business, and whether a change of direction was due, whether it was time to take a closer look at what was happening elsewhere, whether openness of spirit rather than hugging of certainties would be good for Scotland. The significance of that moment in the McEwan Hall was that the evidence could not quite be brushed off by the largely Scottish audience, as it might have been if it had been given by one of the foreign speakers like Mailer or Burroughs; it was one of their own who was talking. With some, inevitably, he never passed the scandal barrier, the drugs-and-sex-rootless-drifter reaction, and despite his obvious intelligence, and the controlled style of his prose, it seems likely that his unjust neglect as a writer was not unconnected with various sorts of moral disapproval. In actual fact, *Cain's Book* no more proselytizes for heroin than *Young Adam* does for murder. It is true that Joe Necchi takes drugs, both by himself and in the company of friends whose wild lifestyle is rendered fairly mercilessly; but he is also a writer, who vividly recalls and evokes a past and a present unconnected with drugs. When he was a boy in Glasgow his parents took in lodgers, at whose habits his father is always ready to explode:

My father came in.
'I'm going out,' he said. It sounded like an ultimatum.

'You went out last night, Louis,' my mother said. 'I have nothing to give you.'

'I didn't *ask*, did I?'

'I gave you two shillings last night.'

'I didn't ask you for any bloody money!'

'Don't lose your temper, Louis.'

'I'm not losing my bloody temper! I didn't ask you for any bloody money! We've never got any bloody money because you're too bloody soft on them, the whole bloody lot of them! Pitchimuthu with his bloody fried sardines and that old bloody cripple in the blue room! Kept me out of the bathroom all bloody day with their bloody carry on!'

'Louis, you just stop this! Stop it at once! Go on out if you must, but don't begin that business all over again!'   (p.251)

In his present, working on a scow off New York, he records immediate detail, fixing a flux as it passes:

When I woke up this morning around eight I found I was the last scow in a tow of four moving like a ghost-ship in fog. I say 'a tow of four' because last night there were four of us. Actually I cannot even see the scow ahead of me. I know we are moving because the wrinkled brown water slides like a skin past my catwalk. I threw an empty can overboard. It bobbed in the wake of my stern for a few seconds and then, like something removed by a hand, it was out of sight. I suppose I can see in all directions for about fifteen feet. Beyond that, things become shadowy and at the same time portentous, like the long swift movement of the log which floated by a few minutes ago.   (p.180)

In terms of plot and characters, neither *Cain's Book* nor *Young Adam* comes to an end. *Young Adam*, a thinner and less impressive book than *Cain's Book*, but in some ways a preparation for it and a story that does stick in the mind, leaves its hero, Joe 'Taylor' as he calls himself, listening to a judge condemning a man to death for a murder he did not commit but which Joe did commit (or it may have been an accident, though he accepts responsibility for it). It is as if he is frozen, paralyzed, totally unable to save the innocent man. 'I cannot remember how the court broke up. All I know is that suddenly Mr Justice Parkington was gone and the disintegration was already taking place' (p.162). The novel closes rather powerfully on that unspecified 'disintegration'; more like the end of a film than the end of a novel. *Cain's Book* likewise refuses to 'end', except that its last two paragraphs are almost lapidary in their attentiveness to the problem of making a non-ending satisfactorily close the book. 'This, then, is the beginning, a tentative organisation of a sea of ambiguous experience, a provisional dyke, an opening gambit' (p.251). We may be tempted to think that the man drifting and writing in his scow on the Hudson River is writing a drifting book about his scow on the Hudson River, but the 'organisation', the 'dyke', the 'gambit' all suggest control, forethought, shaping of material. At a second reading, the dramatic function of the 'embedded' scenes from his early life becomes clearer; there is a similar proceeding in Gray's *Lanark* and *1982, Janine*, and in some of the films of Tarkovsky. But was it written as novel or antinovel? Six years before he finished writing it, Trocchi wrote in one of his editorials in *Merlin* (vol.2, no.2, Autumn 1953):

> In a literary climate in which we are exhorted to remember that 'novelists ought to write novels' – where accent, that is, is laid upon plot – we might point out that the imperative is redundant, that novelists, we suppose, and by definition, do, although serious writers, we feel, may not.

Hm. Well. No more is said, but the gauntlet comes down with a distinctly glittery clatter. It is surely time now for critics, admitting the force and range and originality of Trocchi's work, to take it up.

Note

Quotations in the text are from the following editions:
Cain's Book (Calder, 1963) (first published 1960).
Young Adam (Heinemann, 1961) (first published 1954, under pseudonym Frances Lengel).
Man at Leisure (Calder & Boyars, 1972).
Helen and Desire (Olympia Press, London, 1971) (first published 1954, under pseudonym Frances Lengel).
Writers in Revolt, ed. R. Seaver, T. Southern and A. Trocchi (Fell, New York, 1963).
New Writers III (Calder, 1965).

Glasgow Speech in Recent Scottish Literature

The acceptable emergence of Glasgow speech, both as an object of linguistic study and as a medium for serious writing, is recent and still has much headway to make, but one can say today with some confidence that the long-ingrained attitudes – linguistic, social, aesthetic – which hindered that emergence have lost the almost automatic respectability they once enjoyed. In the fifty-page introduction to the first volume of *The Scottish National Dictionary*, virtually nothing is said about the language of Glasgow. After a brief reference to the 'glottal catch', which the editor notes with some irritation ('not by natural development') has spread to other parts of Scotland, the speech of this large conurbation containing half the population of the country is dismissed in one sentence: 'Owing to the influx of Irish and foreign immigrants in the industrial area near Glasgow the dialect has become hopelessly corrupt.' That was written many years ago, and William Grant's refusal to come to grips with the unsavoury and amorphous phenomenon of Glasgow must seem today to be not only improperly moralistic but strangely incurious. But moralizing or sceptical attitudes towards Glasgow dialect evidently take much dislodging. In 1974, in an article quoting favourably from Glaswegian prose by Alan Spence and George Friel, J. Derrick McClure makes the more general point that what must in the end limit such writers is 'the impoverished and bastardised Scots spoken in present-day Glasgow'.[1] Strong words! Yet surely all language is, if one wants to use the term, bastardised (and that word, half French and half Greek, is a good example of the process); and it is the rural dialects of Scotland which are impoverished, not the thriving and inventive urban speech of Glasgow. McClure's underlying argument is, however, one that would need careful consideration, since his case is that naturalistic recorders of local speech like Friel and Spence cannot draw upon literary, traditional, non-local forms of Scots such as allow (say) Fionn Mac Colla in his prose to 'exploit the full expressive potential of the Scots language'. Obviously this is a possible view, yet one cannot help thinking that it is not entirely divorced from those pro-rural, anti-urban feelings which have found it so hard to accept the fact that whatever 'Scotland' or 'Scottish tradition' is, it must *include* Glasgow, it cannot cast it out or refuse to come to terms with it or to see its 'case'. Even if we accept the arguments put forward for a modern generalized literary Scots, as against a naturalistic locally-based Scots, such a Scots ought to include a significant admixture of Glaswegian forms and idioms if it is to be true to the linguistic realities of the country.

Reluctance to confer status on urban Scots has in the past excused itself mainly on the ground that slang rather than dialect is involved. That this belief will not pass muster, despite the fact that Glasgow like every large city uses much slang, was argued persuasively by Alexandra J.L. Agutter and Leslie N. Cowan in their article on 'Changes in the Vocabulary of Lowland Scots Dialects'.[2] But a dislike or fear of slanginess or uncouthness has undoubtedly been an inhibiting factor on writers as well as educators in the first half of the century. J.J. Bell, author of *Wee Macgreegor* and many similar couthy and popular books which sold very widely in the Glasgow area (and elsewhere), wrote in his autobiography, *I Remember* (1932), about the two grand-mothers he recalled from the 1870s:

> Of fair education, not slipshod in her grammar, she used the vernacular uncompromisingly – and that at a period when a great many Glasgow people were coming to regard the ver-nacular as 'not very nice'. At the same time, she was down on slang, such as it was in those days... Perhaps she was faith-ful to the old tongue because she had originally come from Paisley. I can remember that her sister used it, but that none of her nephews and nieces did so. She was the only person who made it really familiar to me. My other grandmother might, in a moment of freedom, have uttered the word 'bairns', but she would surely have swooned at hearing the word 'weans' issue from her own lips. Strangely enough, though listening to it daily, I echoed very little of her Lowland Scots; but, more that twenty years later, when attempting the first of a series of Glasgow sketches, the makings ultimately of a certain little book, I looked into my memory and found the old words and phrases I needed.   (pp.74–5)

Bell, in fact, made little distinction between 'Glaswegian' and 'Lowland Scots'; and his fictional dialogue, while liberally sprinkled with Glaswegian features, is an amalgam owing much to the homely humours of late nineteenth-century Kailyard. In his introduction to the New Library Edition of *Wee Macgreegor* (1933) Bell wrote:

> I am well aware that I have been suspected of eavesdropping on tramway cars and elsewhere, and of furtively lurking in close-mouths, and in sundry other places, in order to gain my knowledge, such as it is, of the Glasgow, or Lowland dialect; but the truth is that, just as I have never deliberately 'studied' a fellow-creature, I had never made any effort to 'learn' the speech of the people of the period. While I was familiar with the older men in my father's factory, who used the vernacular as a matter of course, I feel certain that I acquired little or nothing there. Indeed, I cannot doubt that from the lips of my paternal grandmother, a lady of the old school, who died when I was seven, fell all the quaint words and phrases – many of them embodied in nursery rhymes – into my memory, there to lie quiet till the years should bring a use for them. (p.8)

Ironically, at the same time as J.J. Bell was writing this introduction, Alexander McArthur in Glasgow's Gorbals was putting the finishing touches to his first draft of *No Mean City*, the book eventually published in a collaborative version with the London journalist H. Kingsley Long in 1935, and rich in the bad language which Bell (and Bell's grandmother if she had known about it) would never have countenanced. *No Mean City*, crude and melodramatic though it was, had a certain archetypal power about it, reminiscent of effects in Jack London and Frank Norris, which made it not really surprising that it should have sold millions of copies and should seldom be out of print for long, even today. It was also a landmark in the wide currency it gave to Glasgow dialect, even though its London publishers, with an eye to their English readers, put those always irritating, non-accepting inverted commas round words like 'buroo', 'rammy', 'model', 'single-end', 'flyman', 'hairy', and 'sherricking'.

But any dialect breakthrough, in prose fiction, brings problems, and not only those of comprehension. The case against the use of dialect was put succinctly by Allan Massie, in a review of Iain Crichton Smith's novel *A Field Full of Folk* (*The Scotsman*,

8 May 1982), where he praised the dignity and seriousness the book gained by being resolutely non-regional. 'His characters are not insulted by dialect or by phonetic transcription of their speech'. This is clearly a dig (as we shall see) at other recent Scottish novels; but what of the general point? Are the servants in *Wuthering Heights*, the rustics in Hardy, the miners in Lawrence, the farmers in Lewis Grassic Gibbon, the Cockneys and Irishmen in Kipling, the Southerners in Faulkner, all to be regarded as 'insulted by dialect'? The answer is surely given by Mark Twain in his prefatory note to a great dialectal story, *The Adventures of Huckleberry Finn*: 'In this book a number of dialects are used, to wit: the Missouri negro dialect; the ordinary "Pike-County" dialect; and four modified varieties of this last. The shadings have not been done in a haphazard fashion, or by guess-work; but painstakingly, and with the trustworthy guidance and support of personal familiarity with these several forms of speech.' In other words, a loving particularity, not a putdown or a relegation. Nevertheless, a problem remains. It is hard to envisage a *Wuthering Heights* written *entirely* in Yorkshire dialect. Is this a snobbish or merely a realistic scepticism? It is realistic in the sense that a novel by its nature is interested in social gradations and distinctions, and that these, because of the nature of educational systems, often involve striking differences of speech. A dialect which was used into the highest reaches of education would in fact become a language, and would then itself begin to split into new dialects.

In Glasgow novels and short stories one main difficulty has been how to avoid too offputting a disjunction between realistic Glaswegian dialogue and a heavy authorial English in the narrative. Edward Gaitens' *Dance of the Apprentices* (1948) strikes a good balance but in a sense does acknowledge the existence of the problem, as the young shipyard apprentice, Eddy Macdonnel, grows up a great reader – of Dickens and Keats, Swinburne and Wells, pamphlets on socialism, anarchism, and pacifism – and not only loses much of his local language but is given less and less dialogue as the novel progresses; so that at the end we watch him, in prison as a conscientious objector during the First World War, entirely through the language of the author who purports to describe his thoughts, and beyond an occasional 'ach' or 'och' these thoughts are in pure English:

Thank God the long day was almost over. As he walked he

avoided looking at the door. If he remembered not to look at it he might not dream of it to-night. Would he sleep till morning? Yes. His nerves had been tranquil to-day and he had thought happily for a long time. Perhaps the draught the doctor had given him had steadied him.   (p.274)

Self-education – political awakening – deglaswegianisation – that is a well-known and often-delineated process. As a father in *Dance of the Apprentices* says of his schoolboy son. 'He's goat tae stick tae his English.' The Glasgow (and Glasgow-Irish) dialogue in Gaitens is lively and adequate, but it is not at the centre of the author's interest, and he shows no sense that anything might be lost if education or upward mobility in society should dilute or destroy the native speech.

In a similar sort of *Bildungsroman* (though set at a later time), *The Dear Green Place* (1966), Archie Hind uses the failure of his working-class hero to fulfil his ambitions as a novelist as an opportunity for expressing more directly negative views of Glasgow speech. Mat Craig probes the reasons for his failure:

Was it the language he spoke, the gutter patois into which his tongue fell naturally when he was moved by a strong feeling? This gutter patois which had been cast by a mode of life devoid of all hope or tenderness. This self-protective, fobbing off language which was not made to range, or explore, or express; a language cast for sneers and abuse and aggression; a language cast out of the absence of possibility; a language cast out of a certain set of feelings – from poverties, dust, drunkenness, tenements, endurance, hard physical labour; a reductive, cowardly, timid, snivelling language cast out of jeers and violence and diffidence; a language of vulgar keelie scepticism.   (p.226)

This angry English, if we believe Hind as the author, represents the actual thoughts passing through Mat's mind as he walks about the city – 'collecting his thoughts', 'taking inventory of himself', 'ticking it all off in his mind'. The language is meant not to be authorial, but Mat's own. And this is not at all impossible, given the self-educating process he has undergone. Yet Hind is careful to show the persisting substratum, two pages later, when Mat suddenly and unintentionally verbalises his daydreaming in actual speech, his Glaswegian self addressing his anglified self:

A voice, a shrugging Glesca keelie voice said to him, 'Ye're nut on, laddie. Ye're on tae nothin'.' Mat looked around the empty ferry, but still the voice spoke. 'Ye're nut quoted. A gutless wonder like you, that hasn't got the gumption of a louse.'   (p.228)

These deeply divided feelings about local speech do not prevent Hind from writing a moving and vivid novel, but they do mean that Glaswegian is not positively exploited for its creative potential, and this is where more recent fiction-writers have taken a new course. The seventies was a decade when Glaswegian began to fight back, in fiction, drama, and poetry. The 'gutter patois' of Archie Hind's soured hero became both an area of experiment and a badge of pride. Though certainly not devoid of polemic, this movement has by no means always wanted to show an aggressive face, but it has wanted to claim that if you want to use urban dialect it is first of all necessary to *listen*, and in doing so, to find distinctions and subtleties which the usual (and sometimes mythical) stereotypes writers have drawn on in the past have blunted or overlaid or simply missed. Emphasis on what is actually spoken, rather than on what legend or popular belief or the music-hall may in part have substituted for it, leads to thoughts about spelling, about that 'phonetic transcription of speech' which Allan Massie, in the passage quoted above, congratulated Iain Crichton Smith on having eschewed. The short stories of Alan Spence, James Kelman, and Alex Hamilton have addressed themselves to this controversial issue.

The stories in Spence's *Its Colours They are Fine* (1977) are blessed with very freshly and nicely observed dialogue and an orthography that few would regard as excessive.

He sipped at it, fingering the blackened, brittle toast. He pushed the plate aside and started to retreat.
'Ah canny face the burnt offerin hen.'
'Ye need somethin in yer stomach.'
'Aye, maybe efter. Ah'm no feeling too good.'
'Aye, well hell mend ye, that's aw ah kin say.'
'Noo don't start! Ye gave me enough shirrikin last night. Bloody dog's abuse.'
'And no bloody wonder!' she said. 'God forgive me.' (slipped in like punctuation as she put down a plate so she could cross herself.)

'Ach be reasonable Mary. Ah mean it wis the boay's last night a freedom before e pits is heid 'n the auld noose.' He yanked an imaginary rope above his head and jerked his neck to the side. But that brought back the nausea, so he sat down before going on.

'We hid tae gie um a wee bit send aff, ye know whit ah mean.'

'Ah know whit ye mean awright, an ah know wherr ah'd send the perry yiz! Noo got ootma road. An will ye go an... DO something ABOUT yerself!' ('The Rain Dance', p.115)

In that extract, the new and pleasing accuracy appears in words like *shirrikin*, which indicates the normal pronunciation (not the one given in SND); *kin* (not in SND, either in itself or under *can*, though it is the regular Glasgow pronunciation); *boay* (not in SND, either in itself or under *boy*, though again it is the standard and distinctive Glasgow pronunciation); and *perry yiz* which looks the most outlandish of the lot but is in fact a good transcription of perfectly ordinary usage.

In a second extract, it may be noted that the language is more Glaswegian than it seems, since the ostensibly English words *team*, *mental*, and *brilliant* all have to be translated or decoded into the lyrical-sinister specifics they have in the city's teenage subculture – specifics which the context of the whole story makes reasonably clear.

Through the doorway the crowds were beginning to spill out. Shuggie's eyes were fixed,, watching for the two boys.

'Shouldnae be long noo,' he said.

'This should be good,' said Eddie. 'Didye see that wee guy's face when ah says we wur the Govan Team! Jist about shat is sel. That wis the best laugh. Fuckin tremendous!'

Shuggie laughed and reached into his pocket, feeling the steel comb with the long pointed handle.

'Mental!' he said.

'Brilliant!' said Rab.   ('Brilliant', p.109)

James Kelman's stories are set in London, Manchester, and Jersey, as well as in Glasgow, and most of them are in English, often (as he says) 'with this Glasgow accent'; but two are of special interest on the present occasion as being written wholly in Glaswegian. 'Nice to be Nice' (in his volume of short stories *An Old Pub near the Angel*, 1973) is a first-person narrative by a

Glasgow speaker, a device which usefully solves the problems often raised when local dialogue and English narrative are juxtaposed, though obviously courting the limitations imposed by the articulacy and interestingness of the speaker. In this story the narrator is a humorous, shrewd, good-hearted middle-aged man whose wife left him years ago because of his horse-betting. He describes himself as a better listener than talker, which, by an acceptable paradox, implies that he would also be one who would keep his talking for his writing. He lives in a room and kitchen, but is willing to share:

> Anywey it wis jist young Tony who'd firgoat his key, wi that wee mate a his in a perr a burds. Christ whit dae ye dae? Invite thim in? Well A did – nice tae be nice – in anywey thir aw right they two; sipposed tae be a perr a terraways bit A ey fun Tony aw right in his mate's his mate. The young yins ir aw right if ye lea thim alane. A've eywis maintained that. Gie thim a chance fir fuck sake! So A made thim it hame although it meant me hivvin tae sit oan a widdin cherr kis A selt the couch a couple a months ago kis ay that auld cunt Erchie in his troubles. The four hid perred aff in wir sittin oan the ermcherrs. They hid brung a cerry-oot wae thim so A goat the glesses oot in it turned oot no a bad wee night, jist chattin away aboot politics in the hoarses in that. A quite enjoyed it although mine you A wis listenin merr thin A wis talkin bit that's no unusual. Wan i the birds didny sae much either in A didny blame her kis she knew me although she didny let oan.
>
> See A used tae work beside her man – aye in she's nae chicken, bit – nice tae be nice – she isny a bad lookin lassie in A didny let oan either.   (p.94)

Although one might not always agree with the spelling – *cerry-oot* would be safer as *kerry-oot* even if this disguises the verb – there is a continuous appeal to the ear to recognize the truth of signalled distinctions, as for example in *that wee mate a his, kis ay that auld cunt Eerchie,* and *Wan i the burds,* where *a, ay,* and *i* all represent English 'of', but with correct contextual variations. Some would say that way madness lies; readers must be allowed to make their own mental variants of unstressed words whose spelling is known to be only conventional in any case. Perhaps. But there is clearly a value in calling attention to the realities of a speech that has never yet been fully described.

In Kelman's other story, 'The Hon' (in *Short Tales from the Night Shift*, 1978), he goes a step farther and uses Glasgow dialect for a straight third-person narrative. The language suits the black humour, which unrolls jerkily like an underground cartoon:

> Auld Shug gits oot iv bed. Turns aff the alarm cloak. Gis straight ben the toilit. Sits doon in that oan the lavatri pan. Wee bit iv time gis by. Shug sittin ther, yonin. This Hon. Up it comes oot fri the waste pipe. Stretchis right up. Grabs him by the bolls.
> Jesis Christ shouts the Shug filla.
> The Hon gis slack in a coupla minits. Up jumps Shug. Straight ben the kitchin hodin onti the pyjama troosirs in that jist aboot collapsin inti his cher.
> Fuck it he says Am no gon.   (no page number)

The publisher's blurb to Alex Hamilton's *Gallus, did you say? and other stories* (1982) makes the claim that this collection is 'a landmark in publishing history, representing as it does the first conscious decision to reproduce in extended written prose the sounds of Glasgow English, as faithfully as non-phonetic transcription will allow'. The dubious term 'Glasgow English' makes it hard to know exactly what the claim is, since in fact only two of the stories use Glaswegian throughout, for both narrative and dialogue. The dialogue in all the stories, however, does go nearer than that of other fiction writers to 'faithful non-phonetic transcription'. Its strangeness on the page is immediately reduced if one reads the stories aloud, when the frequent Creole-like *zan* and *zim* and *ziv* and *zoaffice* sort themselves out in the flux. The most interesting technique occurs in 'Moonlighting', a cautionary tale about an unfortunate wealthy couple in Newton Mearns, recounted by a broad-speaking Glaswegian who retails it as he heard it from his presumably equally broad-speaking brother, a handyman working at the detached two-car home. Nice ironies are obtained by reporting the Newton Mearns couple's dialogue as the reporter would himself speak it; high marital comedy with an extra dimension: A car has vanished:

> 'Aw naw!' e ixplodes. 'Whitdji mean, *sno sittin therr eni merr!* A motir hisnae goat leg zan feet a it sain thitit kin jiss get up n tay ka walk tae itsel whinivir it feels lik a wee daunir doon thi toon! Yi lee vit wherr yi lee vit; yi pit oan thi haunbrake; yi

loack thi door – n when yi cum back it's sittin jiss wherr yi
walk taway fae it. UmAh right urumAh no right, ih? UmAh
right urumAh wrang?'   (p.23)

Without drawing extravagant conclusions, one can perhaps
find from such examples how dialect prose fiction is edging its
way into new territory, and at the same time is consolidating its
own ground by giving – what had never been given before – a
truthful account of the spoken tongue. In this, it stands halfway
between drama and poetry. In drama, there is in one sense no
problem, since a play is all voices and no narrator, so that the
most extreme naturalism, however odd it might seem if the play
is printed, will be perfectly acceptable on the stage. In poetry,
there is for an entirely different reason, and again only in one
sense, no problem, in that the 'voice' of the poem, whatever the
poet's own voice or accent or dialect may be, is something in
itself, recreated through form and structure away from whatever
naturalism the poet has started with. Both poet and dramatist,
for opposite reasons, are more free than the writer of prose
fiction. It would appear therefore that 'more can be done with'
local dialect in plays and poems, and especially, because of their
natural complexity, in poems. What would be too easy would
be to assume that no problems are involved – whether problems
of communication or problems of limitations of creative potential.

Since the 1940s, and more particularly since 1970, plays in
Glasgow dialect and usually with a Glasgow setting have regularly appeared, proved popular, and built up a tradition. Because
of the language, the tradition has been mainly realist and working-class, and often political; strong on humour and pathos, on
veracity, on the pleasures of recognition, less strong on imagination, on shock, on analogies and vistas. The succession of plays
that would include Ena Lamont Stewart's *Men Should Weep*
(1947), George Munro's *Gold in his Boots* (1947), Roddy McMillan's *All in Good Faith* (1954) and *The Bevellers* (1973), Bill Bryden's *Willie Rough* (1972), Hector MacMillan's *The Sash* (1974),
Tom McGrath's *The Hard Man* (1977) and John Byrne's trilogy
The Slab Boys (1978), *The Loveliest Night of the Year* (1979; later
re-titled *Cuttin' a Rug*), and *Still Life* (1982), has made a powerful
impact, and has employed a wide range of themes: war, politics,
unemployment, crime, football, religion, work. Linguistically,
of course, there is less to be learned from the printed text of a

play than from that of a poem or novel. A play text is a script for performance, and the language indicated by the playwright is filled out and may indeed be transformed by actors and director. Because of the assumption that authentic accents will be available, playwrights have not been so consciously concerned as their recent fellow-writers in fiction and poetry to sharpen orthography. The language in *All in Good Faith* is just as convincing as that in *The Hard Man*, except for the greater realism in the use of swear-words in the later play, and one or two more indicative spellings like *loat* for lot, *stoap* for *stop*, and *wahnt* for *want*. What most of the plays do particularly well is to modulate between more-Scottish and more-English according to dramatic occasion and emotion, in ways that actors can manage and the silent reader of a novel cannot. In *The Bevellers*, which deals with the initiation of a new apprentice in the bevelling shop of a Glasgow glassworks, there is a well-marked difference between the wildly racy and inventive fury of Rouger, caught in the act with a girl, and speaking as if he had been brought up on centuries of flytings and Gavin Douglas's 'fowth of langage' –

> Ya knee-crept, Jesus-crept, swatchin little fucker, ah'll cut the bliddy scrotum aff ye! Ah'll knacker an' gut ye, ah'll eviscerate ye! Ya hure-spun, bastrified, conscrapulated young prick, ah'll do twenty year fur mincin you. Ye hear me? Ah'll rip ye fae the gullet tae the groin, ah'll incinerate ye!... Another minute, ah wid have scored where he's never scored, an' you shankered it, ya parish-eyed, perishin bastart.   (pp.50–1)

– and the quiet, level reminiscence of Bob as he talks to the apprentice and thereby brings the work theme of the play into clear focus –

> You might think this is a rough trade and rough folk in it. But that's jist because we havenae broke away fae the oul' days – no a'thegither anyway. Ye cannae wipe oot years o' hard men an' hard graft jist because the machinery changes a wee bit. No that it's a' that different, mind you. The wheels are a wee bit different here an' there, like the carborundum stone. That used to be the ould mill wi the hopper feeder and a sand-drip. That's when boys younger than you really grafted. Cairryin pailfuls o saun an' sievin it in the trough beside the mill. They still use them in wan or two places yet,

an' if somethin' had taw go wrong at Peter's end we might
have tae use it yet, but it's no likely. As ah said, there wis a
lot o Irishmen in this game at wan time. The Rouger's oul'
man wis a beveller. You think he's twistit. Ye want tae have
seen his oul' man. They worked on piece work, each man
seein his job through fae start tae finish, an' they had tae shift.
The Rouger's father wis a beaster. He'd collect his ain wages
at the end o the week an' take the Rouger's tae. That wis the
last they'd see o him tae the pubs shut on Setterday night.
They were lucky if he had enough left tae get them pigs' feet
fur the rest o the week.   (p.34)

The Hard Man uses a different kind of contrast, which works
much better in the theatre than the printed text would lead us to
believe. Tom Mcgrath, writing in collaboration with Jimmy
Boyle whose life-story is the basic material of the play, uses a
full, broad Glaswegian for the quick succession of scenes presenting the early years of the hardman and his acquaintances, but
intersperses these with solo passages directly addressed by Johnny
Byrne (= Jimmy Boyle) to the audience; and these speeches,
coming from the older Byrne who has done much reading and
educated himself, are (as printed) virtually in English. The seeming artificiality of the disjunction disappears in the theatre, where
a strong Glasgow voice or accent in the actor transforms the
'English' passages and readily effects continuity.

How far we should be happy with the large gap that may exist
between printed and performed texts is another matter, though
it is difficult to see what can be done about it. When John Byrne's
'Slab Boys' trilogy was produced at the Traverse Theatre in Edinburgh in 1982, Simon Berry gave it an enthusiastic review in the
Times Literary Supplement (23 July 1982) and noted that its 'particular joy' was its 'authentic use of West of Scotland patois'.
Put on at the Royal Court Theatre in London later in the year,
the trilogy drew an equally sympathetic response from the London critics, with comments on the language ranging from 'the
Glaswegian accents are intense' (Victoria Radin) through 'it takes
a little time to tune into the dialect' (Robert Hewison) to 'though
the language is Glaswegian it is never as impenetrable as legend
holds' (Ned Chaillet). However, one could read the printed text
of the three plays (published by Salamander Press, Edinburgh,
1982) and be only very intermittently aware that the characters
are speaking Glaswegian or West of Scotland patois. This seems

a pity, even if the aim is a wider readership. Texts of plays tend to establish themselves, and the result might be with plays of this kind that homogenized and emasculated versions could emerge, as more suited to very English or very American markets. The disgraceful dubbing of the Glasgow voices in the film *Gregory's Girl*, for American export, is a warning.

In the use of Glasgow dialect in fiction or drama, it is difficult to pick out one name as being central to the development; in poetry, such a name does at once offer itself: Tom Leonard. At the beginning of the 1960s, the present writer began using Glasgow speech in a few poems like 'Glasgow Green' and 'Good Friday', but with only a sketchy indication of pronunciation through spelling; the full Glasgow characteristics were meant to be supplied by the reader, preferably reading aloud. The main purpose was to suggest that, as in 'Glasgow Green', the local speech could be employed in poetry in a serious context far removed from the usual music-hall associations. Later, I tried extending this through a range of different Glasgow voices in 'Stobhill' (1971), again with the intention that the poetry, though printed in a book, should also be read aloud, and this time with the spelling brought nearer to pronunciation. Tom Leonard brought out his *Six Glasgow Poems* in 1969, and went on to publish actively and variously during the 1970s. Other poets joined in – Stephen Mulrine, Tom McGrath, Alan Spence, David Neilson – until there was something that in hindsight might be called a movement, although at the time it was ill-defined. The book *Three Glasgow Writers* (1976), which contains prose by Alex Hamilton and James Kelman, and poetry and prose by Tom Leonard, shows the wider links of a 'Glasgow school' which is not confined to poetry.

It is a not unexpected feature of such movements, when a language or dialect is being looked at afresh or given a push in a new direction, that poets will make translations as a test or challenge, to see what the language can do. Alan Spence's versions of haiku by the Japanese poet Issa (1763-1827), included in his book *Glasgow Zen* (1981), are affectionate reworkings from a poet who himself liked 'voice' and dialect:

> wid ye lookit
> the state ae it –
> me in ma new jaicket!

or

> the full moon shinin
> on this buncha heidbangers
> (me included)

Very different are the rude and reductive versions of Catullus by David Neilson (*XII from Catullus*, 1982), where the Latin poet's persona of 'a drunken, impoverished and acid commentator' interested in the 'rather déclassé activities' of his friends (as the translator's prefatory note describes it – though there is more to Catullus than that) finds no barriers in Glasgow demotic. The translations are very free, pared–down, laconic (the *oculos . . . oculis . . . oculis . . . oculi* of No. 82 become a single *contak lensis*), but comparison with the originals generally shows that points survive, if tone does not – and who can be sure what tone a Catullus poem had for his contemporaries? The more satirical modes work better than the lyrical; but the experiment was well worth doing. Here is No. 83, 'To Lesbia's Husband' ('Lesbia mi praesente viro mala plurima dicit'):

> Gaun ye clown
> ye canny see
> through Lesbia furiver
> cursin me
>
> Roar an laff
>
> it's nothin new
> thit you'd be better aff
> if she effed at you.

The remarkable work of Tom Leonard opens up a new range of possibilities. His Glasgow-language poems, though usually quite short, bring together in highly concentrated form a number of separate interests: 'voice' and sound and the transcription of sound; sociolinguistic and political concern; poetic structure, and especially line-structure; and comedy, from the playful to the ferocious. What he does *not* want, the journalistic and vaudeville stereotyping which in the past has made it so hard for seriously intended writing to emerge in Glasgow, was very clearly spelt out in a cobra-like review of Albert Mackie's pawky vade-mecum *Talking Glasgow* (1978):

It's another of those 'warm-hearted' linguistic racist affairs, where all of 'us' good middle-class or ex-working-class folk can sit back and have a good laugh at how 'they' working-class Glaswegians talk.... Not a 'fuck' or a 'cunt' will disturb the pleasant time to be had by the reader.... As is usually the case with this sort of production, not listening accurately is the necessary precondition for perpetuating the various cosy myths.... But if you don't treat language seriously, you don't treat people seriously.... Nowhere will real linguistic aggression or anger show alongside the of-course-always-bowdlerized 'humour'; the natives here are not even allowed the luxury of getting restless. There are very serious linguistic political points to be discussed here in relation to speech registers as a barometer of economic and political power in Britain, but it would be a waste of time discussing them in relation to this book. (*Aquarius*, no.12, 1980, p.124).

'If you don't treat language seriously, you don't treat people seriously.' The consequences, for a writer brought up speaking broad Glaswegian, are formidable. The young apprentice in Roddy McMillan's play, *The Bevellers*, had been good at English at school and had written good essays. 'Might no talk it very good, but ah was a'right when it came tae writin it doon' (p.35). The comedy, or tragedy, depending on how you look at it, is that young Norrie can write but not speak English, and can speak but not write Glaswegian. He will probably never speak English, since he is not bookish or ambitious, and he has been thoroughly brainwashed into believing that it would be wrong to write Glaswegian, so he never will write it. It was not McMillan's concern to develop this point, but if Leonard had written the play it would have become a main theme. In his highly amusing but also very perceptive prose monologue, 'Honest' (in *Three Glasgow Writers*), Leonard presents the classic triple search of a young Glasgow writer for theme, language, and audience. The speaker toys with the idea of writing a story about a fisherman, and decides that with a bit of research and hard thinking he could manage it, but urban scepticism breaks in. The fisherman's life is not really very interesting: 'kinni no day sumhm else wayiz time?'. As for writing about it: 'can *a* no day sumhm else wi ma time?' And reading about it: 'huv *they* got nuthin behtr ti day wi their time?' As for language, is this not shifting sand? –

But ifyi write down 'doon' wan minute, nwrite doon 'down' thi nixt, people say yir beein inconsistent. But ifyi sayti sumdy, 'Whaira yi afti?' nthey say, 'Whut?' nyou say, 'Where are you off to?' they don't say, 'That's no whutyi said thi furst time.' They'll probably say sumhm like, 'Doon thi road!' anif you say, 'What?' they usually say, 'Down the road!' the second time – though no always. Course, they never *really* say, 'Doon this road!' or 'Down the road!' at all. Least, they never say it the way it's spelt. Coz it *izny* spelt, when they say it, is it? (p.47).

But after an abstract discussion on the difficulty of getting others to take your writing seriously, the monologue quickly shifts gear and ends with an anecdote of almost surreal defiance:

'Ahma writur, your only a wurkur,' a said, to thi plumbir.
'Fux sake Joe stick wan on that kunt,' said the apprentice.
'Ball and cocks,' said the plumber, 'Ball an cocks. A firgot ma grammur.'
'Gerrihtuppyi,' a said, to thi apprentice.
'Lissn pal yoor tea'll be up na minit,' said the plumber.
'Couldny fuckin write a bookie's line ya basturdn illiturate,' a said, ti the plumber.
'Right. Ootside,' said the plumber. 'Mawn. Ootside.'
Sorry. That comes later.   (p.49)

Any answer to this agon between the writer and the worker, between the highly literate but regarded-as-illiterate Glaswegian monologist and the illiterate plumber whose language is not rejected but given status by the act of writing, 'comes later'. Leonard's poetry enjoys every kind of dramatic contest and contrast between different voices, accents, registers, social classes, philosophies. One man after assuring him that 'thi langwij a thi guhtr' is all right for funny stuff but no use for emotional or intellectual matters falls down an empty lift-shaft; another speaker argues with him in favour of electronics instead of the parochialities of 'bunnit husslin'; a linguist who regrets she has 'lost her accent' is mocked and asked if she would really 'swear to swerr'; a glib 'liaison co-ordinator' is attacked for having no real experience of unemployment, alcoholism, or 'hoossyz fawnty bits'; a series of characters like figures in a medieval morality-poem try to tell him that his language is 'disgraceful', and the

charge, while not denied, is defied: 'all living language is sacred.'
This emphasis on 'living language', however comedic the means
may be which are used to talk about it, is important to Leonard
because it is related to the realities of power in society, to what
we believe or are persuaded to believe is true, and the defence of
his concern with what people actually say, as opposed to what
they are taught to say, or what they hear others say, or even
what they think they themselves are saying, is that to sweep
speech under the carpet is to academize, and indeed tarmacadamize,
systems of stasis and control that are perpetually in need of re-
examination. Not surprisingly in such a slippery subject, irony
is one of his favourite weapons, and Glaswegian finds one of its
happiest expressions in the transvestite linguistics of 'Unrelated
Incidents – 3', which is also highly thought-provoking about the
matters just discussed:

> this is thi
> six a clock
> news thi
> man said n
> thi reason
> a talk wia
> BBC accent
> is coz yi
> widny wahnt
> mi ti talk
> aboot thi
> trooth wia
> voice lik
> wanna yoo
> scruff. if
> a toktaboot
> thi trooth
> lik wanna yoo
> scruff yi
> widny thingk
> it wuz troo.
> jist wanna yoo
> scruff tokn.
> thirza right
> way ti spell
> ana right way

ti tok it. this
is me tokn yir
right way a
spellin. this
is ma trooth.
yooz doant no
thi trooth
yirsellz cawz
yi canny talk
right. this is
the six a clock
nyooz. belt up.

(*Three Glasgow Writers*, p.36)

Notes

1   'Modern Scots Prose Writing', in *The Scots Language in Education*, Association for Scottish Literary Studies Occasional Papers no.3, p.62.
2   'Changes in the Vocabulary of Lowland Scots Dialects', in *Scottish Literary Journal*, Supplement no.14 (Summer 1981), p.54.

Scotland and the Lowland Tongue, ed. J.D. McClure (Aberdeen University Press, 1983).

Index